# The Natural World of
# NEW ZEALAND

# The Natural World of
# NEW ZEALAND

VIKING

Penguin Books (NZ) Ltd, Cnr Rosedale and Airborne Roads, Albany, Auckland 1310, New Zealand
Penguin Books Ltd, 27 Wrights Lane, London W8 5TZ, England
Penguin USA, 375 Hudson Street, New York, NY 10014, United States
Penguin Books Australia Ltd, 487 Maroondah Highway, Ringwood, Australia 3134
Penguin Books Canada Ltd, 10 Alcorn Avenue, Toronto, Ontario, Canada M4V 3B2

Penguin Books Ltd, Registered Offices:  Harmondsworth, Middlesex, England

First published by Penguin Books (NZ) Ltd, 1998

Printed by Bookbuilders, Hong Kong

Endpapers: white daisy (*Celmisia incana*) • Page 1: Archway Islands, Golden Bay • Pages 2–3: seahorse and black coral, Fiordland • Pages 4–5: Weddell seal under sea ice, Antarctica • Pages 6–7:
wandering albatross over Southern Ocean • Pages 8–9: Lead Hills from Knuckle Hill, Nelson •
Pages 10–11: dusky dolphins, Kaikoura

| | |
|---|---|
| Publisher | Geoff Walker |
| Project editor | Pat Field |
| Editorial | Nicola Strawbridge |
| Research assistant | Kate Mitcalfe |
| Design | Kate Finnie, Dexter Fry, Gerrard Malcolm |
| Page make-up | Marilyn Gravette, Maria Jungowska, Gerrard Malcolm |
| Illustrations | Chris Gaskin, Dave Gunson, Derek Onley (see Contributors, page 399) |
| Illustration production | Bill Paynter |
| Maps | Nikki Perry, Alex Townsend |
| Proofreader | Toni Mason |
| Indexer | Diane Lowther |

# ACKNOWLEDGEMENTS

With a book of this scope, my debts are many. Numerous scientists paved the way with the raw material which forms the basis of the book. Their co-operation in discussing issues and in refereeing copy is much appreciated.

Many helped to nurture the project, with words of encouragement and practical assistance. John Begg was always ready with sound advice on all matters of natural history; Mark Bellingham allowed me to bounce ideas off him about content; without Hamish Campbell the sections on geology, fossils and minerals would have been much the poorer; Ian Close, Forest & Bird Editor, provided valuable leads on many matters; Bill Brander lent a patient ear to numerous natural history anecdotes; Michael and Ann Hutching provided accommodation and support.

Geoff Walker at Penguin Books boldly took up the challenge of producing the book, moulding the basic idea into workable shape. His unflagging support and enthusiasm have been greatly appreciated. Nicola Strawbridge played an invaluable role in tying up the loose ends. Pat Field edited skilfully, with untiring commitment. Designer Dexter Fry, assisted by Gerrard Malcolm, saw the project to completion.

Thanks to those everywhere involved in natural history and conservation, especially fellow conservationists at the Royal Forest and Bird Protection Society. They have all fostered my interest in natural history, and, as importantly, helped instil in me the need to protect it. And finally to my father who shared his love of nature with me and helped inspire my direction in life.

*Gerard Hutching*

*For Adele, Sam and Elinor*

# CONTENTS

# INTRODUCTION

In every New Zealand animal and plant, no matter how humble, there is a story. In fact, often the most insignificant-looking plants or unremarkable animals are the ones which, after a little investigation, turn out to be the most fascinating.

In *The Natural World of New Zealand* readers can learn about some of the intriguing life histories that unfold not only in far-off forests and mountains, but also on their own doorsteps, for nature in all its complexity thrives in suburbia as well as in the wilderness.

This book is divided into two sections:

Part I delves into the past to find out why New Zealand's natural world is so special and different to that of other countries, looks at the impact that humans have had upon the environment and highlights important habitats.

Part II is an A-Z of natural history. Here the 'icons' of the natural world—the black robin, huhu grub, katipo, kiwi, orange roughy, tuatara—have individual entries. Where plants or animals are less well known, they are sometimes grouped under a general heading such as 'hebes' or 'spiders'. Within Part II special sections describe natural processes or features such as earthquakes and rivers. This part of the book concludes with a section of fascinating facts and a map showing New Zealand's important natural elements and conservation areas.

# Part I
# In the beginning

# Unique New Zealand

*'New Zealand is as close as we will get to the opportunity to study life on another planet.'*
Jared Diamond, US ecologist

To ecologists, oceanic islands are fascinating laboratories for studying the evolution of life. Starting off with the same life forms widespread elsewhere on Earth, islands such as New Zealand, Hawaii, New Caledonia and Madagascar have subsequently charted fresh evolutionary courses, throwing up species which exist nowhere else.

But of these oceanic islands, New Zealand stands the most apart. It is by far the largest and most remote, has had dry land for at least 100 million years (much longer than Hawaii), and developed without land mammals.

Around 80 million years ago the lands of Australasia—New Zealand, New Caledonia, New Guinea and Australia—were one, sharing the same soils, plants and animals. But then, through the process of continental drift, the land masses moved apart, each to embark on its own unique evolutionary path.

On the face of it, New Zealand should not be expected to have a more diverse fauna and flora than other countries lying in similar latitudes. In contrast with tropical, less disturbed lands, our temperate climates and turbulent geological histories do not provide ideal conditions in which to breed diversity. New Zealand's geographical isolation would also appear to be an added barrier to the creation of a multiplicity of species.

Nevertheless, 50 percent of penguin species breed in the New Zealand region, as do 54 percent of albatrosses and half the world's petrels, shearwaters and prions. Unusually for an island, often a large number of species evolved from a single ancestor—the moa, for example, radiated into around a dozen species. Such speciation is more often observed on continents.

For its size, New Zealand has the most diverse lizard fauna in the temperate world, and a large percentage of its plants occur nowhere else (93 percent of alpines are endemic).

## Mammal-free zone

In earliest New Zealand no mammals roamed the land, although bats flew (and later also scrabbled around on the ground) and seals—fur, elephant and sea lions—lolled on coastal rocks. When New Zealand 'set sail' into the Pacific away from Australia, it carried with it ancestors of primitive mammals such as platypuses and echidnas; one of the enduring mysteries of New Zealand biogeography is the fate of these. Why should these egg-laying mammals survive in Australia but not New Zealand?

## Is it a bird?

Today, with the moa extinct, few more than 200 takahe (confined to remote Fiordland), and 53 kakapo on three islands, it is difficult to imagine the ecological role these birds once played in the environment.

New Zealand was home to the great 'bird experiment'. Without competition from browsing mammals, birds occupied niches that birds nowhere else did, and some became as large as mammals. Moa became the equivalent of giraffes; millions of takahe grazed like sheep; kiwi filled the niche of northern-hemisphere shrews and New Guinea long-beaked echidnas; and the terrifying Haast's eagle leaped upon the backs of its prey like a tiger. Tiny wrens, their legs short but strong, scurried around the forest floor like mice. Birds which have lived in New Zealand for the longest time, such as the kiwi, kakapo, kokako

*The ancestors of kiwi such as this great spotted kiwi* (Apteryx haasti) *evolved more than 130 million years ago, making the kiwi the most ancient of living New Zealand birds.*

and a host of extinct birds, all became flightless. Threatened by few or no predators, these birds ceased to put effort into flight, instead concentrating on reproduction.

## Frogs—here, there and everywhere

In New Zealand frogs were abundant throughout the country until kiore arrived, and were much more significant ecologically than in other countries. The largest of the six species of frogs were up to 90 mm long. Unfortunately three species (the largest) have become extinct, and the others are reduced to small remnant populations. Unlike frogs elsewhere, the New Zealand species do not need running water in which to breed.

## Lizard life

Compared with other temperate countries, New Zealand has an abundance of lizards. Australia has eight times the number of species, but the country is 29 times larger, and the UK has just three species compared with New Zealand's 60. To give their offspring a head start in life (vital during successive Ice Ages), New Zealand geckos give birth to live young, unlike geckos elsewhere which lay eggs. From studies on islands, it appears that lizards played a significant role in plant pollination on the mainland before predators reduced their numbers.

## Prehistoric plants

Long isolation from other lands has enabled New Zealand's vegetation to develop along its own unique lines, so that more than 80 percent of its flowering plants occur nowhere else. The great

*Like the vast majority of New Zealand alpine plants, the daisy* Celmisia incana *is an endemic species.*

podocarps, whose lineage stretches back almost 200 million years, flourished to a greater extent in New Zealand than anywhere else. A climate that ranges from subtropical to subantarctic, together with a varied geology, encouraged a multiplicity of plants. The stress that a dynamic and changeable environment placed upon plants would have fostered speciation and adaptation.

## Insects and snails

Like the birds, some New Zealand insects also became flightless giants, for example the weta, which trace their origins back 200 million years and have been described as 'insect rodents'.

New Zealand's land snails, sporting spectacular coiled shells, are among the world's oldest. In many other parts of the world such original ancient lineages have died out, replaced by the ubiquitous European garden snail.

*The last of its evolutionary line, the tuatara has remained virtually unchanged over millions of years.*

# *People and the environment*

Sailing south from the tropical climes of the Cook Islands or the Society Islands, the first humans to arrive in New Zealand might have felt rather cold, but would not have gone hungry. Birds, seals and fish were in abundance, and the humans few. The animals, which had never seen people or other land mammals, would have been curious rather than afraid, ripe for the cooking pot or earth oven.

## A land of plenty

A sign of the plenty that greeted those first settlers (later to be described as moa hunters) are the thousands of moa bones that have been uncovered at midden sites, and the amount of moa flesh that remained on the bones—the tastier portions were eaten, the remainder discarded.

Still alive when Maori landed were a host of birds which are now extinct. Within a few hundred years most were gone, the larger ones—for example the swan, pelican, flightless goose and adzebill—presumably hunted for food. Haast's eagle may have been exterminated by Maori in self defence.

The smaller species, such as weta, lizards, frogs, snails and wrens, were overrun by a tide of kiore, the Polynesian rat brought to New Zealand as a food source. Some scientists speculate, on the basis of radiocarbon dating of rat bones, that kiore first arrived around 2000 years ago, possibly with humans who did not survive initial settlement. For the next 1000 years until the first bona fide Maori settlers became established, these rats may have formed vast hordes that swept through and destroyed the country's unique fauna.

The only other animal that survived the journey from the tropics was the Polynesian dog, the kuri, which played a useful role in hunting birds such as moa and the strongly scented kakapo.

## Plundering the land and sea

The weapon which made the greatest impact on the landscape was fire. South Island east coast forests were set on fire to drive out and make moa easier to catch, or to clear land for agriculture. Raging out of control, the fires destroyed vast tracts of forest, reducing forest cover from about 85 percent of the country to 55 percent.

Modern techniques of fishing, with their attendant huge catches, blind us to the fact that Maori were also efficient large-scale fishers. Archaeologists have estimated that northern Maori were taking 1200 tonnes of snapper a year. In 1885 a fishing line approximately 2000 metres

*In humans' inexorable sweep across the planet, New Zealand has been one of the last staging posts.*
Mt Taranaki—War Canoe *by G F Angas.*

*Kereru, made thirsty by eating miro berries, were lured to drinking troughs snared with strategically placed nooses.*

long was used in the Bay of Plenty to haul in 37 000 fish. There is evidence to show that shellfish had also declined in some areas before Europeans arrived.

However, for much of the 19th and 20th centuries scientists maintained that Maori had little impact on the environment, and were not to blame for extermination of the moa and other species—the Maori period of New Zealand history has been described as the 'golden age that never was'.

## Learning to conserve

Nevertheless, it appears that by the time of European arrival, Maori had learned the limits of Aotearoa's resources, and had started to live within them. Strict protocols attended the cutting down of trees, and rahui (bans) were placed upon the taking of a resource until it had recovered. Food was still hunted, but the demise of the moa and seal colonies ushered in a more settled agricultural lifestyle.

How anti-environmental were Maori? Undoubtedly they had an adverse impact on the environment, but their record has to be seen in the context of their knowledge of ecological processes. Today we know about species loss and how it occurs; if we proceed with actions that might cause further extinctions, we can rightly be accused of moral evil, but in preliterate societies such events are better seen as tragedies.

## The fruits of the earth

Since the 1980s there has been a growing clamour by some Maori for the right to harvest species—not only plants for weaving and whalebone for carving but also birds for eating. Is cultural harvest, as the term implies, a sustainable use of native species for traditional purposes? In the case of weaving plants such as pingao, kiekie and flax,

there is little practical difficulty in supplying material, provided sufficient is planted. However, managing birds, some of which are in low numbers, for sustainable harvest is a more complex undertaking. Of wild native species, only muttonbirds are harvested, and the muttonbird population of around 20 million might be robust enough to sustain a regular take. In the North Island the species killed most often is the kereru, which is at risk of extinction in some areas. Some Maori have also argued for a cultural kill of seals, a traditional food.

Proponents of cultural harvest point to 'traditional environmental knowledge' (TEK) which Maori have accumulated over the centuries, and which they argue is 'scientific' in its own right. But whether TEK practices are sufficiently rigorous today is questionable. Guns have replaced spears, human population is greater, introduced pests are a plague and conservation problems have become global. The royal albatross is a species likely to be near the top of a harvester's wish-list, but can harvesting of such a slow-breeding and long-lived species be justified when it already faces a major threat to its existence from longline fisheries which have been responsible for the deaths of thousands of birds?

*Evidence is growing that the deaths of albatrosses and other seabirds on tuna longlines are pushing the populations of some species into serious decline.*

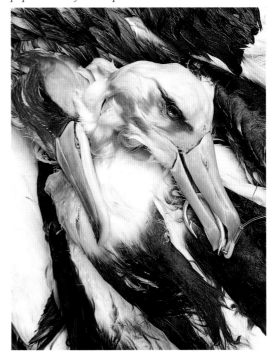

## Modern colonisation

Armed not only with muskets and ploughs, but also with a different ethos about their relationship to the natural world, the second wave of colonists to New Zealand had a far greater impact on the environment than the Maori.

## From forest to farm

James Cook and subsequent explorers sized up the country for its suitability for settlement, as well as a source of resources for the Empire. When botanist Joseph Banks and Cook drifted up the Waihou River in 1769, they came away impressed by the size of the trees lining the river, Banks remarking that the swamps 'might doubtless easily be drained'. His observation proved accurate; just over 100 years later the dairying boom resulted in the huge sweep of forest on the Hauraki Plains being cleared and drained.

Elsewhere forested plains, recognised as the most fertile sites, were earmarked for development. These lowland ecosystems, known as nga uruota (groves of life) had been kept essentially intact because of their immense value to everyday life: as sources of food or plant materials for clothes and dwellings—all things which sustained the Maori culture. The Hutt Valley, where in 1840 settlers 'couldn't move for forest', was virtually cleared over the following 30 years.

## Offshore pillage

But before agriculture reshaped the landscape, sealers and whalers began their bloody work in 1792 at Dusky Sound. Operating mainly around Fiordland, Stewart Island, the islands of Foveaux Strait and the subantarctic islands, the sealers killed their prey for its valuable fur.

As brief as it was brutal, the sealing period ended in 1845, by which time the only seals left were on inaccessible islands. No accurate tally was ever taken of the slaughter but it amounted to hundreds of thousands of animals. Whalers—British, Australian and American—sought sperm, southern right and humpback whales in the waters off New Zealand, but by the 1840s the industry was in decline.

## Enter the aliens

Besides the toll exacted on the animals they hunted, sealers and whalers inadvertently damaged fragile island environments by releasing sheep, goats, cattle and other domestic animals, which they hoped might avert starvation if sailors were marooned. Rats, unwelcome hitch-hikers on sailing ships, had come ashore in the 18th century with Cook and their invasion continued with the sealers and whalers.

During the 19th century European settlers introduced animals which had a disastrous effect on the environment: possums, rabbits, goats, deer, tahr, chamois. Attempts to right these wrongs—for example, bringing in ferrets, stoats and weasels to get rid of the rabbit plague—backfired. Today millions of dollars are spent each year in controlling these pests, which continue to make inroads into native species.

Significant too in their impact on biodiversity have been exotic plants. Some, such as radiata pine, have proved useful to the economy; others, such as gorse, have been a drain on it.

## A riot of burning

The first large-scale farming began in the wide open spaces of the South Island's tussock grasslands, transforming the Canterbury Plains and other areas into vast sheep runs. Maori had burned the tussocklands centuries before; now the runholders used the practice to promote plant growth. Lady Barker wrote of the 'exceeding joy of burning: it is a very exciting amusement ... and the effect is beautiful, especially as it grows dusk and the fires are racing up the hills all around us'. For the early runholders' purposes,

*(Below) The forested plain depicted by Charles Heaphy in 1840, with Somes-Matiu Island in Wellington Harbour beyond, has been transformed into today's Lower Hutt cityscape (right).*

*'Logs, at the door, by the fence; logs, broadcast over the paddock; sprawling in motionless thousands away, down the green of the gully.' B E Baughan's 1908 poem described scenes that were repeated throughout New Zealand. (Above) Bushland cleared for farming near Auckland, 1910. (Facing page) In kauri forests such as this one near Taupaki, logging was carried out on a grand scale.*

the burning worked. In 1878 Central Otago sheep numbers reached 11.3 million; by 1950 the same land could support only 10 percent of that figure.

The great podocarp forests of Northland and the central North Island were prized for their timber, first used as spars and masts on ships, then for housing. The wastage was appalling, as often the forests were viewed as an obstacle to farming and were ruthlessly torched rather than harvested for timber.

## The silence of the birds

As a result of such wholesale destruction of the landscape, the decline of species has continued. More than half of the bird species that greeted Maori on their arrival have disappeared, and many others are dwindling. Australian scientist Tim Flannery, recalling Joseph Banks's astonish-

ment at New Zealand's 'deafening' bird chorus, writes: 'It was a glorious riot of sound with its own special meaning, for it was a confirmation of the health of a wondrous and unique ecosystem. To my great regret, I arrived in New Zealand in the late twentieth century only to find most of the orchestra seats empty. Walking through the ancient forest, whose still-living trees were once browsed by moa, I heard nothing but the whisper of leaves blowing in the wind. It was like the rustle of the last curtain fall on an orchestra that will be no more.'

## Repairing the ravages

Perhaps because so much has been lost, New Zealanders have become strong environmental advocates. The Department of Conservation (DOC) is a world leader in exterminating pests such as

rats, cats, possums, goats and pigs from islands. It has pioneered the introduction and transfer of threatened species and shown the world how offshore islands can be used as refuges for species that would be doomed on the mainland.

New Zealanders have become expert at restoring battered habitats. Islands such as Tiritiri Matangi near Auckland or Mana near Wellington, where virtually all the forest was destroyed, are being replanted and restocked with animals in imaginative projects involving professionals and the public. On the mainland, birds such as the kiwi, kaka, kokako and weka have a tenuous hold in their present habitats, but DOC has ushered in an intensive style of management to increase their populations.

Alliances have been forged with industry and pledges made that native forest will no longer be cut. The conservation ethic has been embraced wholeheartedly by New Zealanders, with initiatives consistently and passionately supported by widely diverse sections of society.

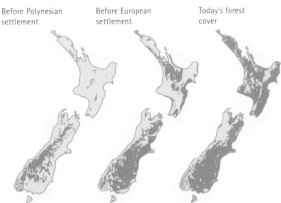

Before Polynesian settlement  Before European settlement  Today's forest cover

## NEW ZEALAND NATIVE FOREST COVER

*Before humans arrived in New Zealand, forest covered about 85 percent of the land area, falling to 55 percent by 1800 following fires deliberately or accidentally lit by Maori. European settlers accelerated that loss, although the present period is witnessing significant regeneration in some areas.* The State of New Zealand's Environment, 1997.

# The evolution of New Zealand

About 600 million years ago an unparalleled explosion of life occurred on Earth as the first multicelled animals proliferated in the oceans. Until then, conditions on the planet had been inhospitable to anything other than single-celled micro-organisms. New Zealand at this time, and for hundreds of millions of years to come, was part of the supercontinent called Gondwanaland, which included present-day South America, Africa, Arabia, India, Malagasy, Antarctica, Australia, New Guinea and New Caledonia. All these regions share many plants

**190**
million years ago
*Ancestors of moa, tuatara and kiwi appear. First podocarp trees*

**225**
million years ago
*Reign of dinosaurs begins. First mammals appear*

**275**
million years ago
*Ammonoids flourish. Land animals and plants increase in diversity*

**120**
million years ago
*Gondwanaland begins to break up. Tasman Sea forms. First flowering plants appear*

**350**
million years ago
*Amphibians invade the land. Early plants form the basis of a major coal-forming period*

**400**
million years ago
*Vertebrate fishes increase. First insects appear*

**500**
million years ago
*Early marine vertebrates evolve*

and animals. Around 120 million years ago the Tasman Sea made its first appearance and Gondwanaland began to be dismembered. This, together with the oceanic gap opened up between New Zealand and Antarctica, meant that new plants and animals found it more difficult to reach New Zealand. As New Zealand became steadily more distant from these lands over the next 100 million years or more, its distinctive character emerged. Many life forms, for example the dinosaurs or the seed ferns called *Dicroidium*, have come and gone; others such as the podocarps, kiwi, wren, wattlebirds, and weta, remain as reminders—albeit often fragile ones—of our unique evolutionary past.

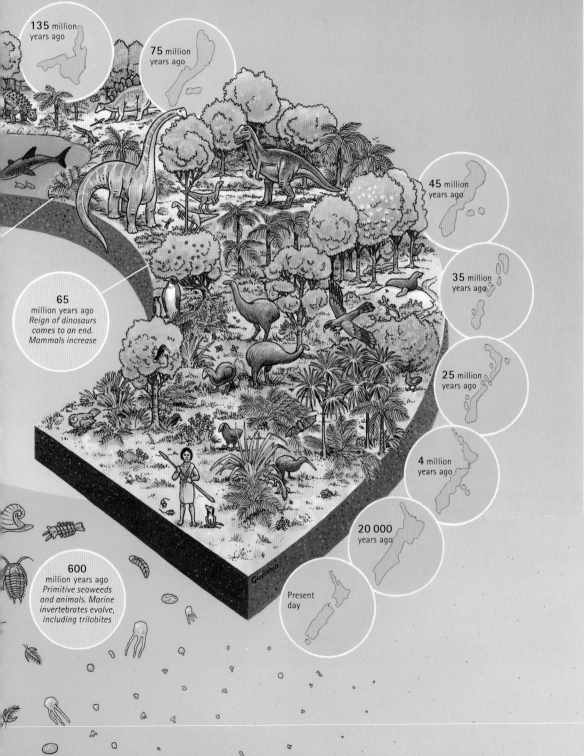

**135** million years ago

**75** million years ago

**45** million years ago

**35** million years ago

**65** million years ago
*Reign of dinosaurs comes to an end. Mammals increase*

**25** million years ago

**4** million years ago

**20 000** years ago

Present day

**600** million years ago
*Primitive seaweeds and animals. Marine invertebrates evolve, including trilobites*

## Reign of the dinosaurs

Between 235 and 65 million years ago, during the Mesozoic era, reptiles reigned supreme, evolving into myriad groups and species. Until recently it was believed that the largest reptiles—dinosaurs—had bypassed New Zealand, but fossil bones hidden in rocks have started to reveal long-hidden secrets of the country's ancient past. Many of the plant types from this drier, warmer era would be unrecognisable today, but others such as the ancestors of the kauri, rimu, and kahikatea had a strong family resemblance to present-day specimens.

This scene, set in the late Cretaceous period (95–65 million years ago), shows a lone megalosaur—a 4-metre-long carnivore—sizing up a group of short-armed, vegetarian hypsilophodonts, while in the background a band of giant, four-legged sauropods browse on trees. Approximately 65 million years ago a great global cataclysm or environmental change brought an end to the dinosaurs and ushered in the era of mammals—except in New Zealand, where birds became dominant.

# Habitats of plants and animals

## Alpine

At first glance the subalpine zone, where intense cold, heat, dryness and wind can occur in a single day, does not appear to be a hospitable location for life. Yet here plants persevere, softening mountainsides with green and decorating them with bright flowers. Animals too find niches to adapt to, even if they have to spend long periods in semi- or total hibernation.

Gorging itself on nutrient-rich snowberries, the world's only alpine parrot, the kea ❷, builds up fat stores for the cold winter ahead. A good supply of food is important to feed kea chicks, which are often hatched in the depths of winter. The kea does the snowberry a favour, spreading its seeds far and wide.

Even more of an alpine bird is the rock wren ❸, whose diet is dominated by beetles, spiders, flies and other insects. Whereas the kea moves down to the treeline in bad weather, in the coldest temperatures the rock wren remains a permanent resident of the frozen mountains, sheltering in rocks and insulated by a blanket of snow.

Gaining maximum warmth from the sun, the black mountain ringlet ❾ basks on a rock, its dark, heat-absorbing wings spread flat. Only when it has heated to about 32°C—10 to 15 degrees above the air temperature—does the ringlet become active.

Flies are important plant pollinators as well as scavengers. Like the black mountain ringlet, the bat-winged cannibal fly ❶ warms itself in the sun before setting out to hunt, seizing insects on the wing and sucking them dry.

Plants have evolved a variety of mechanisms to cope with the alpine climate, leaf-eating insects and browsers. The branches of the outlandish-looking vegetable sheep ❽ hug the ground, sending up tightly packed leaf shoots which grow no higher than their neighbours. Cold, drought, rain and grazers are all rebuffed by this world-famous cushion plant. To ensure pollination during the all-too-brief summer months, some plants such as forsteras ❿, the showy great mountain buttercup ❹ or the mountain daisy ❺ climb above the competition so that they will be noticed by alpine flies, moths ❻ and beetles ❼.

# Forest

New Zealand's forests, encouraged by a mild, wet climate, resemble tropical rainforests more than their temperate counterparts in the northern hemisphere. A typical North Island conifer broadleaf forest has five layers: emergent, canopy and subcanopy trees, shrubs and ground plants. In comparison, a European forest has only three layers. Because of a lack of cold winters or dry spells, most New Zealand plants are evergreen. Ferns, climbers and perching plants abound in these dripping southern rainforests.

In terms of biological diversity, New Zealand's forests lie part-way between tropical jungles and North American forests. New Zealand has 2200 flowering plant species compared with Great Britain's 1750, and Papua New Guinea has 9000, underlining the productivity of the wet tropics.

Balanced on a kahikatea branch 50 metres above the forest floor, the rare North Island kokako ❷ feasts on the tree's berries. In a good year one tree can produce 800 kg of the lush purple and orange fruit.

In the next layer down a kaka ❸ enjoys the nectar-laden flowers of a northern rata. The nectar is also appreciated by possums, and a centuries-old tree can be destroyed in a few years of intensive possum browsing. A tree-climbing ship rat ❶ has made its nest in the middle of an epiphyte perched on a large limb of the rata.

Kereru ❺, the only bird capable of swallowing large seeds whole and distributing them throughout the forest, relishes the big oval drupes of tawa ❹ , one of the dominant subcanopy hardwoods.

The forest gecko ❻ clambers about the twiggy branches of a coprosma to reach its succulent fruits. Shrub fruit comprises a significant proportion of the diet of the gecko.

In northern forests and shrublands the brown kiwi ❼ is at its most plentiful, the warmer climate encouraging a proliferation of worms and insects that the flightless bird takes with its long, probing beak.

Among the ferns and mosses of the forest floor, earthworms, land snails ❽ and the peripatus ❾—a half worm, half insect—are just a few of the animals that consume the forest litter, making available minerals that are then taken up by the trees in a continuous cycle of regeneration.

# Freshwater stream

Although freshwater rivers contain only 1 percent of the world's water, they nevertheless harbour a great diversity of life. Oxygen, carbon dioxide and nutrients—the staples of existence—are constantly replenished by running water. In the turbulent waters where a river begins there is little in the way of food, but plankton and detritus provide the foundation for a more complex web of life in the downstream reaches. Drenched with copious rainfall, New Zealand has abundant waterways providing niches for a variety of plants and animals.

Crowding close on the banks of a fast-flowing North Island river, beech trees continuously shed their small leaves, providing nutrients for the insects and other invertebrates living in the waters below. During a mast (heavy seeding) year, 6000 seeds per square metre cover the trees; in other years, hardly any.

On the downstream side of rocks, a blue duck parent forages for caddisfly larvae ❷ while remaining on guard against predators attracted by its newborn ducklings. Dragonflies ❶ and damselflies patrol the river in search of prey which they capture on the wing. In turn they fall victim to darting fantails, which are very manoeuvrable, using their large fanned tails to stop in mid-air and change direction.

Beneath the surface, dragonfly nymphs ❹ are voracious feeders, using a hinged lower lip with pincers attached, which flicks out to capture insects, tadpoles and even small fish. Lurking in the shadows are native freshwater fish: koaro ❼ and short-jawed kokopu ❺, which favour rivers in unmodified native forest. The juveniles of both species are the delicacy known as whitebait. Highly territorial, the introduced brown trout ❸ rises to the water's surface to take the hatching adults of mayflies, caddisflies and other insects. Trout also prey on koaro and kokopu.

The scavenging koura ❻, the freshwater crayfish, recycles insects and leaves and stirs up fine sediments, ensuring the river ecosystem remains in a healthy state for other animal life. To avoid predators, it generally feeds at night rather than during the day.

# Wetland

Wetlands, whether they be shallow lakes, peatlands, marshes or subalpine bogs, form at the indistinct and ever-changing boundary between water and land. Some of New Zealand's important wetlands are Northland's Kaimaumau Swamp, Whangamarino Swamp and Kopuatai Peat Dome in the Hauraki Plains, Lake Wairarapa, and Waituna Wetlands in Southland. Wetlands are among the most threatened habitats in the world; in New Zealand 90 percent have been destroyed since the arrival of European settlers. Vital for wildlife, they are easily damaged by pollution, drainage or reclamation.

Moving noiselessly among the jointed rushes and raupo, a solitary bittern ❸ poises to jab at a small fish, while a newly hatched stonefly ❹ on a brown raupo seedhead prepares to search for a mate. Harakeke, the lowland or swamp flax, is the species preferred for fibre. Cabbage trees, victims of 'sudden decline' disease in pasture and suburban gardens, thrive in the healthy environment of a wetland.

The amphibious green tree frog ❶ leaps 10 times its length to capture a caddisfly ❷. The number of New Zealand caddisfly, mayfly and stonefly species amounts to more than 400, with many yet to be described. Such a diversity of invertebrates creates the ideal conditions for frogs to breed and develop.

Beneath the surface, a common bully ❼ constantly guards its nest of eggs which have been laid on a milfoil ❻, an abundant underwater plant. An eel ❽, having reached maturity, will soon start its long journey to the sea and ultimately to a destination near the equator to spawn.

In shallow water the mallard ❺ dabbles for plant matter; out deeper, New Zealand's only diving duck, the scaup ⓫, probes the wetland floor for freshwater snails ⓬ in a dive which may last over a minute. A black shag ❾, as at home in the freshwater environment as in the marine, dives to capture a sharp-spined perch ❿. Less popular with anglers than trout, the introduced perch has an appetite for a variety of food, including insect larvae, zooplankton and small fish.

❶

# Estuary

Estuaries are as productive as rainforests, and four times more fertile than pasture. The driving force behind an estuary's productivity is the immense quantity of enriched organic material—the debris from vegetation—that is washed through it daily by the ebb and flow of the tide. Attracted by this muddy larder are animals that have to contend with huge daily changes in salinity, from totally salt water to completely fresh water. Ecologists define three distinct estuarine zones: the subtidal (areas of permanent water), the intertidal (the area where the high tide reaches) and the high-tidal (the area just above the mean high-water mark, flooded only during high spring tides).

Forming a buffer between land and sea, salt-marsh plants such as the reddish-brown glasswort ❸, the white-flowered remuremu ❹ and the common yellow bachelor button ❺ trap sediments carried down by rivers and protect the shore from erosion. A banded dotterel ❷ forages among the vegetation for insects while a kingfisher ❶ flies overhead in search of larger prey such as mice.

At the intertidal zone, mud crabs ❾, mud snails ❻ and whelks ❼ feed on sea lettuce ❽ and the sediment of fine detritus. Too minute to be seen except with a microscope, animals such as the copepod—something between bacteria and shellfish—feed on the rich coating of bacteria found on debris.

Some New Zealand estuaries are extraordinarily fertile. Pauatahanui Inlet near Wellington shows a density of 263 000 copepods per square metre, among the highest recorded in the world.

Among green swards of eel grass, juvenile fish such as red cod ❿ and flounder ⓫ thrive. Except when it is very young, the flounder usually spends its life in the estuary, stirring up mud for its invertebrate food, but the cod is a less permanent resident. Eel grass beds are prime nurseries for numerous fish species. Unlike seaweeds, eel grass has a branched root system which helps to stabilise muddy banks.

Just below the surface, cockles ⓬ filter plankton from the soup of the water above. A mantis shrimp ⓮ and worm ⓭ burrow down into the mud, coming to the surface only to feed.

# Sandy shore

An exposed sandy shore is one of the most exacting and extreme habitats, supporting a group of highly specialised plants and animals. These have to withstand drying by unchecked onshore winds, and cope with burning salt spray, high temperatures and low nutrients. Plants are continually threatened with burial or being undermined. Big seas, caused by storms or high tides, can spell doom for birds nesting on the sand.

Among *Muehlenbeckia* plants ❺, a female coper butterfly ❹ lays its eggs. It does not have much time to ensure the continuation of its species—at most these butterflies live 10 days.

The native sand-binding plants pingao ❷ and spinifex grow upwards to avoid being buried by the sand which gradually accumulates around them to create a dune. Introduced to control erosion, marram grass has outcompeted these native plants and wherever it grows, has replaced them.

Among the dunes live specialised insects such as the sand-dune hopper ❼ , which flees predators by burrowing into the sand with its peculiar sand-digging leg paddles. The wingless shore earwig ❻ , largest insect of the sandy shore, is commonly found beneath driftwood. Droning at dusk across the dunes is the heavy, shiny-winged sand scarab beetle ❽ .

Oystercatchers ❶ take their chances breeding on sandy areas just above the high-tide mark, and the New Zealand pipit ❸, its tail continuously flicking up and down, probes the high-tide flotsam for sandhoppers.

Just beyond low water live bivalves such as the morning star ⑪, the tuatua ⑫, the pipi ⑬ and the large ostrich-foot ⑭. At low tide or after storms they lie exposed on the sand; a black-backed gull ❾ scavenging along the shore attempts to break one open by dropping it from a height.

Scourge of swimmers, the aggressive paddle crab ⑩ likes to insert its razor-sharp pincers between the two halves of a tuatua or pipi, forcing the shell finally to open and yield the flesh inside.

# Rocky shore

The ebbing and flowing tide influences an amazing variety of plants and animals compressed into just a few metres of rocky shoreline. In that narrow space species have evolved to cope with an array of environmental conditions, from dry most of the time to wet all the time. Ecologists have likened the changes that occur in the 3 metres from high tide to low tide to those that occur from the top to the bottom of a 3000-metre mountain.

Perched on cliffs above the sea, the gregarious white-fronted tern ❷ nests among the pink ice plant *Disphyma australe* ❸. High in the splash zone, which the ocean wets only during spring tides or storms, the hardy periwinkle ❺, a type of snail, grazes on algae and lichens.

Warm-water splash barnacles ❹ and the red anemone ❼ share the high-tide zone with the radiate limpet ❽ and the eight-jointed chiton ❻.

At the mid-tide zone, the bladders of Venus' necklace ❿ are filled with water to prevent the plant from drying out. Also conserving moisture, small black mussels ❾ clump together. Mussels are a favourite food of the reef starfish ⓫, which uses its arms to force the mussel shell apart in order to devour the succulent flesh inside.

Vital elements in the food chain, seaweeds such as the kelps *Ecklonia* and *Lessonia* ⓬ form dense underwater forests which are grazed by kina ⓭ and paua ⓱. Hidden in crevices below the kelp line lives the spiny crayfish ⓯. Bull kelp protects the coastline from being eroded by the relentless buffeting of the ocean.

Ungainly on land but a superb acrobat in the water, the New Zealand fur seal ❶ swims among swirling bull kelp fronds near its breeding colony. Common fishes of the area include the leatherjacket ⓮, which nibbles constantly at seaweed, and the voracious blue cod ⓰.

One way to avoid drying out is to live in rock pools left by the departing tide, but even these are not perfect havens: rock pools can become warm in hot weather and lose salinity when it rains heavily.

# Part II
# Our natural heritage

# Albatrosses

Soaring over the chill waters of the Southern Ocean in search of food, albatrosses are among the most majestic of birds, their streamlined bodies and long slender wings enabling them to fly for weeks at a time without landing.

Of the 14 species of albatross currently described, seven breed in New Zealand waters, the most in any country in the world. However, in 1997 albatross classifications were revised using DNA techniques, expanding the total number of species and suggesting that 13 of 24 species will be recognised as breeding in the New Zealand region. Some of these graceful birds are described as mollymawks, but they all belong to the same family. Mollymawk was the name given to small albatrosses by sailors; the word comes from the Dutch *mallemuck* (foolish gnat), referring to the way the birds throng around fishing boats like gnats, to steal food.

Southern-hemisphere albatrosses rarely cross the equator or venture south past the region of drifting Antarctic ice. Taking advantage of the strong westerly winds that sweep the Southern Ocean, the birds continually soar above the sea, landing on the water only to sleep or to feed.

Over the centuries the albatross, often an awesome presence for sailors isolated for months at sea, has been associated with many myths. It was commonly believed that is was bad luck to kill an albatross. This belief may have arisen from Coleridge's poem *Rime of the Ancient Mariner*,

*Resting after the rigours of a fishing trip, a Campbell Island black-browed mollymawk in pensive mood.*

### New Zealand's Albatross Breeding Species

Royal (*Diomedea epomophora*)
Wandering (*D. exulans*)
Shy mollymawk (*D. cauta*)
Black-browed mollymawk (*D. melanophrys*)
Grey-headed mollymawk (*D. chrysostoma*)
Buller's mollymawk (*D. bulleri*)
Light-mantled sooty albatross
　　(*Phoebetria palpebrata*)

where the albatross is compared to Jesus. In fact some sailors were only too ready to kill albatrosses, as this diary entry from emigrant Elizabeth Yeoman, en route to New Zealand from Britain in 1864, testifies: 'A lovely day, Mr Laurie & a steerage passenger each caught an albatross, such beautiful creatures, they measured 10 ft 9 from wing to wing, all the ladies were begging the feathers, which will look lovely in hats & are very valuable.'

## Breeding

Albatrosses invest much effort in breeding and raising chicks, so much so that some breed only every 2 years. The wandering and royal albatrosses are, along with the kiwi, record beaters for the amount of time spent incubating eggs: up to 83 days. Once the chick is hatched the adults feed it regurgitated fish and squid gathered during lengthy, long-distance fishing expeditions.

These two albatrosses hold two other bird records: for the slowest birds to begin flying and the slowest to breeding maturity. In order to prepare itself for the years it will spend at sea before returning to its birthplace to breed (6–15 years), the fledgling requires great quantities of food. Between 216 and 303 days after hatching, the chick is finally ready to fly.

The royal and the wandering albatrosses are not unique in the heavy investment they put into breeding. The light-mantled sooty albatross and grey-headed mollymawk are both known to be biennial breeders, and all albatrosses lay just one egg. Much is made of the fact that albatrosses are monogamous (as are 90 percent of all birds); monogamy makes good sense because eggs have to be continuously incubated, and the chicks fed for a long time—jobs which need to be shared if breeding is to be successful. Where albatrosses differ from other monogamous birds is in the fact that they develop a genuine pair bond over their

*(Above) In spring newly mature northern royal albatrosses at the Chathams gather to perform their courtship dances and pair off for breeding. (Right) This white-capped mollymawk chick will not fly until it is 10 months old.*

long lives, whereas many bird species are faithful more to a nesting location and by returning to the same site each year are likely to meet their partner of previous seasons.

A vital ingredient of the breeding cycle is the courtship ritual. In the case of albatrosses it is very intricate, with much bill snapping and groaning. Allopreening (the preening of plumage) is an important element; not only does it serve to get rid of lice and fleas, but also cements the social bond between birds.

## Decline in numbers
Over the past 20 years some species of albatross have declined at a significant rate, unwitting casualties of the bluefin tuna fishing industry. Australian scientist Dr Nigel Brothers estimated in 1991 that at least 44 000 albatrosses and petrels

## *Aerial exploits*

Its stomach full, the wandering albatross takes off to begin the return journey back to the nest and the hungry chick it is responsible for. Gliding with regular upward swoops, the huge bird flies almost effortlessly with the wind behind or at an angle to it. Not for a week and another 6500 km will it see land.

Our knowledge of the flying feats of albatrosses has been expanded enormously since 1992 when French and British, followed by New Zealand and Australian, scientists began placing transmitters on the birds and tracking them by satellite. One bird travelled 13 000 km in a fortnight on a fishing trip.

Albatrosses are able to perform these flying feats for three reasons: they have streamlined bodies, long slender wings, and they use the technique of dynamic soaring. It has been estimated that a 9-kg wandering albatross uses only 1 per-cent of its bodyweight to fuel a 100-km flight.

*Albatrosses are dynamic soarers, building up speed as they dive downwind, turning into the wind when they near the water to give them lift, then gliding upwards until they begin to slow, when they dive once again.*

*New Zealand scientists have been satellite-tracking albatrosses for some years now; the map shows the flight path of Hinemoa, a wandering albatross which flew on a 5601-km return feeding journey from the Auckland Islands to the Tasman Sea in 2 weeks.*

were being killed each year in the Japanese fishery which covers huge areas of the Southern Ocean.

Like driftnetting, the scale of longline fishing is staggering. Each boat casts a thick line up to 130 km long with a series of branch lines off this, each about 35 metres. The longline carries up to 3000 hooks enticingly baited with squid and fish and takes 5–6 hours to set. More than 100 million hooks have been set each year in the southern oceans. As the longlines are fed out, the birds dive for the free lunch and are caught on a hook.

While the fishing industry investigates ways of stopping the deaths, numbers of some albatross species continue to drop. Even if the deaths stopped immediately it could take decades before numbers rebuilt. Whether too great a toll has been exacted for some varieties of this magnificent ocean nomad is too soon to tell.

## Royal albatross

The only mainland albatross breeding colony in the world is found at Taiaroa Head on the Otago Peninsula. There a small population of around 27 pairs of the royal albatross (*Diomedea epomophora*) or toroa has set up home since 1920. The total population, including juveniles and immature birds, is around 100.

By far the greatest numbers of toroa (7000 pairs) nest at Motuhara (the Forty Fours) and the Sisters in the Chatham Islands. The southern race

*About 25 million years ago the volcanic Auckland Islands rose from the ocean; today they provide large seabirds such as the white-capped molly-mawk with a safe breeding haven.*

*Seabirds such as the northern Buller's mollymawk have to rid their blood of the excess salt they ingest. They excrete a concentrated salt solution through the long tubular nostrils at the top of their bills.*

of the species, calculated at 8600 pairs, lives on the subantarctic Auckland and Campbell islands. Each October the royal albatrosses return from their winter fishing grounds off southern South America, the male arriving first to prepare the nest (see page 232) for his mate's egg—a mate to whom he is bonded for life. During the courtship ritual of newly mature toroa, the birds pirouette and open their huge wings wide, uttering a hoarse scream before finally pairing off.

By October the next year the last of the fledglings leave the colony, not returning to Taiaroa Head for 3–6 years.

Life on the Otago Peninsula is not easy for the albatrosses. As well as coping with the everyday difficulties of storms, a possible loss of a parent or an erratic food supply, these mainland toroa face predators such as ferrets, stoats and cats. They can also be affected by fly strike—blowflies lay eggs on young chicks which risk being eaten

alive when the maggots hatch. Between 1984 and 1994, 15 chicks were killed by fly strike and nine by predators. A new hazard is that visitors might disturb the albatrosses. Between 1980 and 1996, the numbers of people viewing the birds jumped from 3000 a year to 33 000. The available undisturbed nesting area in the reserve has been reduced by 50 percent and, reluctant to conduct their courtship display in public view, some pairs are nesting in unsuitable sites.

The world's oldest recorded seabird was Grandma, a breeding royal albatross first banded by Dunedin ornithologist Dr Lance Richdale in the 1937–38 season at Taiaroa Head. In November 1988 she hatched Button, and disappeared for good the following year. Her age then was estimated at more than 62 years (assuming she was 9 years of age when banded). She raised 10 chicks of her own and fostered three others with one of her four mates, Green White Green.

## Wandering albatross

The wandering and royal albatrosses have the greatest average wingspan of any seabird. Of the specimens that have been accurately measured, the largest range from 3.3 to 3.63 metres. New Zealand's subantarctic islands are the stronghold for the wanderer, which also breeds at the Crozet, Prince Edward, Heard and Kerguelen islands in the south Indian Ocean, and on South Georgia and Gough islands in the south Atlantic. Sometimes this albatross can be seen flying alone off the mainland coast, attracted by a fishing boat.

# Anemones

Sea anemones are beautiful coastal creatures armed with stinging tentacles to capture passing prey. The latest studies of New Zealand anemones have revealed a surprising number of species, many more than had been thought to exist.

At least 110 species of anemones have been described, but a further 50 could be added to the list, giving New Zealand one of the richest anemone fauna in the world. Spanish specialist Dr Oscar Ocana Vicente, who made the discoveries in 1996, suggests that such a high diversity is caused by New Zealand's wide latitude range and large variety of habitats—from mangroves, rock pools, reefs and boulder beaches to black coral trees. The number of anemone species recorded in New Zealand is double or more that in other regions such as the Mediterranean, the north-eastern Atlantic, the Caribbean, Japan and the northwestern Pacific.

Most anemones remain in one place, consuming whatever comes their way, but others, such as the wandering anemone (*Phlyctenactis tuberculosa*), move about by walking on their tentacles.

*Tentacles swaying with the current, an anemone waits for passing victims to stray into its path. The tentacles are covered with stinging, paralysing barbs which are fatal to small crustaceans such as shrimps, but provide some immune fish with refuge from predators.*

# Ants

New Zealand has a relatively insignificant collection of native ant species—only 10, compared with Australia's 5000. However, the number of introduced species is climbing by the decade: in 1960 there were 14, by 1991 this had jumped to 28 although some of these may not have survived. In the 19th century several species arrived in soil used for ballast in sailing ships, which was then dumped in port. Australian hardwood poles and railway sleepers provided a number of Australian species with a free ride across the Tasman, and fire ants have come in from Asia and Africa on aircraft, though fortunately are not known to be established yet.

Some of these introduced species, such as the Asian white-footed house ant (*Technomyrmex albipes*), have given ants a bad name, harassing householders in warmer parts of the country as the insects search for jam or honey. By contrast the 10 native species, which largely occur in soil, leaf litter or rotten logs in forests, play a valuable role akin to that of worms in mixing and aerating the soil. They are also useful scavengers, cleaning up and recycling animal and vegetable material.

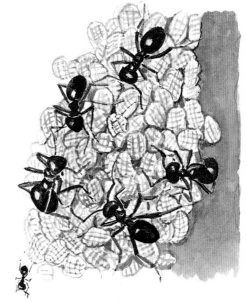

The most common native ant is the southern ant (*Chelaner antarcticus*) which occurs in a variety of habitats, from wet to dry, and at both high and low altitudes.

Ant colonies are superorganisms: each ant is programmed to perform certain tasks according to its size and age. There are three 'castes' in a colony: males which usually have wings; reproductive females (queens) whose wings are cast off after fertilisation; and workers or sterile females. These worker ants are the most numerous members of the colony; it is their job to carry out the foraging and nursing duties.

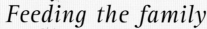

## *Feeding the family*

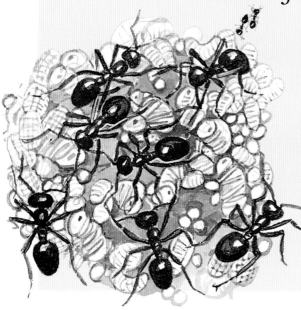

Some native ants 'tend' aphids, scale insects and other plant-sucking bugs in their nests so that during winter they can feed off the sweet secretions of these insects (see page 156). In other cases the ants are saved the trouble of carting insects underground: some mealy bugs live on roots and the ants carefully excavate around the roots in order to help themselves to the bugs' honeydew. Usually ants climb trees to reach the insects. The native striated ant (*Huberia striata*), abundant in the South Island, carries a small land mollusc back to its nest where the flesh is devoured.

*In the wild, ants satisfy their hunger for sweets by feeding on insect honeydew—under and above ground.*

*Scrabbling around on the forest floor, the short-tailed bat seizes on a dragonfly. Although it also catches prey on the wing, it is the world's only bat to hunt on the ground, aided by stronger hind legs than most species and specially evolved folded wings which act as front limbs.*

# Bats

New Zealand has only two native land mammals—the long-tailed bat (*Chalinolobus tuberculatus*) and lesser short-tailed bat (*Mystacina tuberculata*)—each with a body the size of a person's thumb and a wingspan of 300 mm. Until 1967 there was a third species, the greater short-tailed bat (*Mystacina robusta*), but after rats invaded its island home of Big South Cape near Stewart Island it became extinct.

Maori, who did not distinguish between the species, called bats pekapeka. According to ethnologist Elsdon Best it was common practice to smoke bats out of the hollow trees they lived in by a fire lit inside the lower part of the tree. Stupefied by smoke, the animals fell to the ground and were gathered for eating, although

Sir Peter Buck wrote that bats were 'unimportant as a source of food'. One of the most famous New Zealand war sites is at Ruapekapeka, literally 'bat's nest'.

Of the two species, the short-tailed bat is the more endangered; it is scattered throughout the North Island in isolated populations at Taranaki, National Park, Waikaremoana, Omahuta and Warawara forests in Northland, and Little Barrier Island. In the south the bat survives only in isolated outposts, with colonies on Codfish Island, in northwest Nelson and in Fiordland. However, fresh discoveries of populations are being made all the time as new technology enables scientists to track them down. On 12 February 1997 a colony of short-tailed bats was discovered in the Eglinton Valley, Fiordland. The last time they had been seen in Fiordland was in 1871 at Milford Sound where some were found in the

*Using echolocation to pinpoint
its prey, a short-tailed bat
homes in on a puriri moth
while another bat hunts on the
forest floor.*

furled sails of the ship HMS *Clio*.
Other recent finds include populations in Whirinaki Forest, the southern Kaimanawas and the Waitotara
Conservation Area. Scientists believe
the ancestors of this bat probably
arrived from South America by way
of a forested Antarctica more than
35 million years ago and possibly
up to 70–80 million years ago.

Like many of New Zealand's ancient animals, the short-tailed bat is a
zoological oddity, the only one of the
world's more than 990 species that forages
for food on the forest floor. It has several adaptations to assist this behaviour: robust hind legs
with small claws and a way of neatly furling the
delicate outer wing membrane under thicker sections of membrane so the wings can serve as
front limbs. Its unusual hunting habit has also led
to its decline, making it an easy target for predators such as cats and rats. But the often earthbound bat is also an adept flier, sometimes
travelling 30–40 km in a single night, and is capable of travelling at 60 km/h.

The Codfish Island and Little Barrier Island
short-tailed bat is, like the kakapo, a 'lek' species,
a term describing the way in which males congregate in sites in order to lure females for mating.
Males choose small holes in trees from which to
'sing' for up to 10 hours a night for 10–12 weeks.
The high-pitched pulsating warble can be heard
for a distance of over 50 metres.

More common than its short-tailed cousin is
the long-tailed bat, presumed to have blown over
from Australia about 1 million years ago. Today it

is distributed widely in native forests throughout the North and South islands, although few large roosts exist now compared to 100 years ago. Extensive searches in Nelson, the West Coast, Canterbury and Stewart Island have revealed few sightings, and they are rare or absent at several South Island sites where they were widespread in the 1960s. Scientists are now wondering whether their optimism about the bat's numbers may have been misplaced.

Like the short-tailed species, long-tailed bats prefer to roost in old, hollow trees rather than caves. Fluttering fantail-like in search of insects along forest margins, rivers and over lakes, they are often mistaken for birds or puriri moths. Recent research in Fiordland's Eglinton Valley has revealed that long-tailed bats keep nursery colonies. Because the bats shift to different roosts each night, their babies must be carried by the mothers—an impressive feat of strength. One baby weighing 7.5 grams was recorded being carried under the wing of a 13.5-gram mother.

It is believed both New Zealand bat species give birth to just one offspring a year, in December or January, but little else is known of their life histories. The role of bats in plant pollination has recently been highlighted with the discovery that the endangered wood rose (*Dactylanthus taylorii*) has co-evolved with the short-tailed bat and is often pollinated by it (see page 369).

Like dolphins, bats rely on echolocation to detect prey and to navigate their way through forests in the dark. Recent advances in technology that exploit the bat's 'sonar' system have helped New Zealand scientists learn much about bat behaviour. Bats emit high-frequency sounds, usually through their mouths, in rapid pulses at frequencies too high for the human ear to pick up, but ultrasonic detectors convert the pulses to audible 'clicks' through the detector's speaker. Tiny radio transmitters weighing only a fraction of the bat's weight can also be glued to the fur on the animal's back to enable researchers to track its activities.

## *Did you know?*

During winter (and sometimes during cool periods in summer) New Zealand bats go into hibernation, believed to be more profound than that of the archetypal hibernator, the bear. Bats' temperatures drop to a much greater extent than those of bears, usually to just above the ambient air temperature. In one overseas experiment a bat kept in a fridge for 350 days emerged none the worse for wear.

Department of Conservation scientists have toyed with the idea of taking advantage of bat hibernation to protect the short-tailed bat on Codfish Island during the proposed kiore poisoning programme. They thought of capturing the bats and placing them in cool storage for the time it would take to safeguard them, but rejected the idea because of the size of the fridges that would be required, opting to keep the bats in large cages instead. To test whether the bats could survive refrigeration, the scientists put 20 in a fridge at 4°C for various periods; 16 survived after five stints in the fridge.

## New Zealand's Bats

*The map shows the areas of confirmed bat sightings 1980–92.*

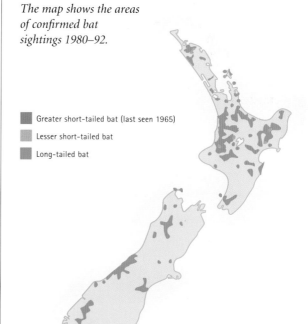

Greater short-tailed bat (last seen 1965)

Lesser short-tailed bat

Long-tailed bat

*The hardiest of the beech species, mountain beech grows to the treeline and is often covered by snow. On the eastern side of the Main Divide, it is usually the only tree at high altitudes.*

# Beeches

The concept of continental drift, accepted as a scientific fact today, had its share of doubters when it was first popularised in the 1960s. One of the pieces of evidence produced in its favour was that of the worldwide distribution of southern beech (*Nothofagus* species).

Beech seed does not survive in the ocean, wind does not carry it far, nor is it spread by birds or other animals. So how is one to account for the presence today of beech trees in regions as far apart as New Zealand, southern South America, Tasmania, southeast Australia, New Caledonia and New Guinea? Evidence has even been uncovered of beech once growing in Antarctica.

Not only do beech trees in the various countries look similar, they also share the same parasitic fungi, mosses and flightless sucking bugs inhabiting their bark. At first botanists raised the possibility of land bridges connecting the lands now forested with beech, but the scenario commonly accepted now is that until 80 million years ago these countries were all joined together in one supercontinent, Gondwanaland.

Today beech forest makes up almost half the total area of native forest in New Zealand. Pure beech forest accounts for 2.8 million ha of native forest, while beech combines with podocarps and broadleaf in another 1.3 million ha.

Although beech has existed for more than 100 million years, it has not always been as dominant a species as it is today. The fortunes of beech have been linked to factors such as geological and climatic change. For example, in the warm period between 7000 and 9000 years ago there was just one pocket of beech-dominant forest, in inland Taranaki. Elsewhere, podocarp species such as rimu held sway.

As the earth began to cool 7000 years ago, beech started to eclipse other forest species, until around 2500 years ago the transformation of the landscape was largely complete. The process of change continues today, evidenced in the 'beech gap' on the West Coast. Here no beech grows between the Taramakau Valley near Hokitika and the Mahitahi Valley in south Westland. The most likely explanation is that glaciers destroyed the forest. Podocarp and broadleaf trees, whose seeds are spread far by birds, have recolonised the gap. Beech, which advances naturally only metres a

## BEECH-DOMINANT FOREST
*The absence of beech-dominated forest in Taranaki is most likely explained by volcanic eruption, and in central Westland is a result of the last Ice Age when glaciers marched out to the coast, destroying the forest in their path.*

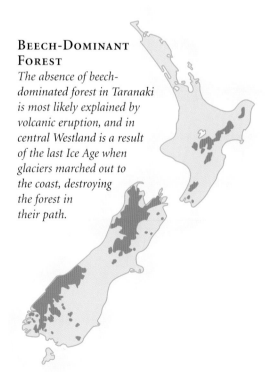

year, is inexorably moving to close the gap and may one day do so, providing climate and other conditions are suitable.

Modern New Zealand has four species of beech—red, hard, black and silver. Sometimes a fifth species is referred to, the mountain beech, which is a form of the black beech. A feature of beech tree ecology is beech 'mast' years when the trees seed prolifically.

Over a 56-year period in central and southern New Zealand, beech flowered 19 times, each time following high temperatures. It never flowers in consecutive years, needing at least 2 years to build up the necessary nutrients.

*Three beech species clothe the slopes above one of the arms of Lake Te Anau. In the foreground mountain beech meets snow grass; across the lake, red and silver beech crowd the water's edge, gradually replaced by mountain beech at higher altitudes.*

### NEW ZEALAND'S BEECHES

- Red beech/tawhairaunui (*Nothofagus fusca*), the tallest of the beeches, grows from Te Aroha to Fiordland, favouring low-altitude, fertile sites.
- Silver beech/tawhai (*N. menziesii*), a cold-tolerant tree found in all but the most infertile soils. Of all the species, silver beech is the one most widespread in Fiordland. Intriguingly, it is the only beech found in the Catlins forest of southeast Otago.
- Hard beech/tawhairaunui (*N. truncata*) grows from Greymouth north except for small anomalous patches in south Westland. Hard beech is often confused with red beech (Maori considered the two the same species).
- Black beech (*N. solandri*), along with mountain beech, is the honeydew tree of the northern South Island.
- Mountain beech (*N. solandri* var. *cliffortioides*) is a hardy tree which tolerates infertile soils. It grows up to the treeline along the Southern Alps, but also down to sea level in the deep south.

## The changing fortunes of beech

As a timber tree, beech has never been the first choice of millers, although wood-turners can use it to produce quality furniture. Contorted, disease-infested trees play havoc with saw blades and drying the timber is notoriously difficult. In the 19th century beech was a popular building material, but milling companies have recently viewed it as good for little but chipping for export to Japan where it is converted into paper.

Since the 1970s the South Island beech forests of north Westland and Southland have been the subject of major conservation arguments. The now-defunct Forest Service proposed a 173 000-ha beech-to-pines conversion of north Westland forests, an idea New Zealanders found so alarming that 341 160 people signed the 1977 Maruia Declaration, stopping the scheme in its tracks. Most of the forests became reserve land as a result of the 1986 West Coast Accord.

During the 1980s about 1400 ha of privately owned native forest, mainly beech, was chipped each year. Areas were completely stripped of vegetation; sometimes they were subsequently planted in pines but often they were left to revert to gorse and scrub. The Forests Amendment Act of 1996 put an end to such large-scale clearance.

Future arguments over beech will centre on north Westland where 98 500 ha has been set aside for production, and the western Southland forests of Rowallan and Longwood where cutting rights to 12 000 ha have recently been vested in a timber company.

*Native bees, unlike honey bees, are generally solitary. Useful pollinators, bees of the* Leioproctus *genus are skilful navigators, able to find their nests among hundreds of others with unerring accuracy, even when the entrance holes to their sand tunnels have become covered up while they are away.*

# Bees

The honey bee (*Apis mellifera*) is the best-known bee species—with good reason, for it provides us with one of nature's most health-giving foods. The first honey bees arrived in New Zealand in 1839 when they were imported from England by a Miss Bumby, sister of a missionary who lived in the Hokianga.

Bumble bees (*Bombus* species) were introduced in 1873, but did not successfully establish until 1885. Until they arrived, plants such as red clover and lucerne could not set seed.

New Zealand also has 32 species of native bees, similar in many respects to the honey bee except that they do not make honey and are generally solitary. They gather nectar and pollen as food for their developing larvae and also pollinate the flowers they visit. Trees that native bees especially favour are manuka, rata and pohutukawa. Over millions of years of evolution native bees and plants have developed a relationship which is mutually beneficial.

New Zealand's bees belong to the two most primitive bee families: Colletidae and Halictidae. The largest is about the size of a honey bee, the smallest looks like a tiny fly. Colletidae can be divided into two quite different subfamilies: the Colletinae comprising 19 species of robust, black, hairy, ground-nesting bees, and the Hylaeinae consisting of eight species of yellow-faced, mainly black, tube-nesting bees. The halictid bees are sparsely hairy, black or greenish. An unaggressive group of bees, the native species all have a sting, but a weak one.

The behaviour of one species, the sand-nesting *Leioproctus metallicus*, has been closely studied. This bee often has to tunnel through sand in order to leave its burrow; after gathering food it first circles overhead to find its bearings, then returns with pinpoint accuracy to its nest.

*The chafers comprise an enormous group with about 90 species including beneficial insects such as dung beetles, but also a great number of pests.*

# Beetles

More than half New Zealand's insects are beetles, some of them adapted to extreme habitats: thermal pools, mountain tops, soaking West Coast forests, dry Otago regions.

Like many island animals, New Zealand beetles are largely flightless, a condition attributed partly to the country's strong winds. Presumably the insects were encouraged to lose their wings to keep them in one place! Because of the lack of small mammals such as mice in prehuman New Zealand, beetles also tend to gigantism.

A number of beetles are endangered including the Coromandel stag beetle (*Dorcus* species) and the Marlborough ground beetle (*Megadromus* species). Habitat loss, disease and the introduction of predators have all played their part in changing living conditions for native beetles—changes which for the most part have not been of benefit to these insects.

# Bellbird

'This wild melody was infinitely superior to any that we had ever heard of the same kind; it seemed to be like small bells most exquisitely tuned …' wrote James Cook on first hearing a bellbird. One of New Zealand's three honeyeaters (the others being the tui and the stitchbird), the bellbird (*Anthornis melanura*) or korimako is an outstanding songbird.

Today the bellbird is relatively abundant, but in the 19th century, bird authority Sir Walter Buller considered it was heading for extinction because of rat depredation. In fact around the 1860s the bellbird did disappear from much of the country; it recovered in most areas, but not from the Waikato northwards (excluding the Coromandel). To this day its temporary disappearance is a mystery, although it is suspected that a disease imported by mynas and sparrows was responsible.

Although described as a honeyeater, the bellbird has a varied diet, eating berries when there is no nectar, and insects. As a nectar-eater it plays an important role in the forest, pollinating many plants and spreading seeds. While it is more common in native forest, it also occurs in exotic forests, orchards and gardens.

Maintaining the same territory from year to year, the bellbird breeds from September to January, the female laying three or four eggs and incubating them for 14 days. Just 14 days after hatching, the juveniles are fledged.

Most bellbirds are coloured olive-green-yellow, but some vary in their coloration. A striking trio spotted in a Nelson forest in 1984 closely resembled canaries in their colouring.

From a distance males and females appear similar, but near to hand they show important distinctions. The male, which is slightly larger, has less drab feathers and a purple gloss on its head, while the female has a narrow white stripe below the eye. Males have red eyes and females brown. Males tend to feed more on nectar and drive the females away from nectar-bearing plants, so the females resort to eating more insects and berries.

North of Auckland, during winter males fly from offshore islands, such as the Poor Knights, Hen and Chickens and Little Barrier, to the mainland to feed. Females do not, hence the bellbird has not re-established in Northland. Since 1988 bellbirds have been released at various points north of Auckland and on Waiheke Island in attempts to relocate the species. The Waiheke experiment appears to have been successful.

There are three surviving subspecies of bellbird: the mainland, Three Kings Islands (*A. obscura*), and Poor Knights Islands (*A. oneho*) varieties. A fourth from the Chatham Islands (*A. melanocephala*) became extinct in 1906.

*Furnished with a slender, curved bill and brush-tipped tongue, the bellbird feasts on the nectar of one of its favourite plants, the tree fuchsia.*

# Birds–endangered

Conservation agencies throughout the world use as a guide for their work the International Union for the Conservation of Nature classifications of species. There are three main categories: 'endangered' for the most at-risk species, followed by 'threatened', then 'rare'. The Department of Conservation (DOC) has refined the classification process by assessing which species have the highest priority for conservation action. It is not just a numbers game, as some species given a high priority may have large populations, such as the North Island brown kiwi. DOC assesses:
• Taxonomic distinctiveness (is the species unique?)
• Status of the species (how many individuals are there, how wide is the geographic distribution, what is the population decline rate?)
• Threats (is the habitat protected, is there a predator problem?)
• Vulnerability (is the species dependent on a specific habitat or diet, can the animal be successfully bred in captivity?)

*The Chatham Island oystercatcher* (Haematopus chathamensis) *has the dubious distinction of being the rarest oystercatcher in the world. A strictly accurate count is difficult to obtain, but the best guess puts numbers at around the 100 mark.*

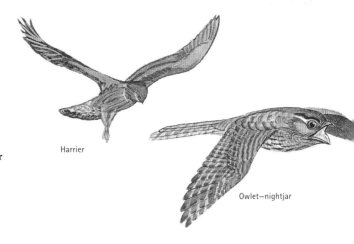

Harrier

Owlet–nightjar

• Human value (what importance has the species in human eyes?)

As a group, birds are the main focus of conservation work in New Zealand, a fact which is occasionally criticised by those who believe threatened plants, lizards or insects justify more funds being spent on them. However, birds do have a special place in New Zealand: 75 percent of species occur nowhere else and 59 percent of these are threatened, with many of them in extremely low numbers.

The Department of Conservation operates a Threatened Species Trust which channels funds from business for endangered birds. Besides benefiting individual species such as kakapo, kokako, black stilt and takahe, such high-profile support raises awareness among the community about the need for conservation generally.

# Birds–extinct

Only in Hawaii have as many birds become extinct in recent times as in New Zealand. These island groups, both remote from continents, evolved a variety of birds remarkable for their giant size, flightlessness and absence of fear of predators—often because there were none. From fossil bones, scientists have estimated that at least 35 species of birds became extinct from the time

Maori arrived in New Zealand until Captain Cook's first voyage here. Until the 1960s it was believed that these birds were on the verge of extinction when Maori arrived, but this was not the case: having survived the last Ice Age 10 000 years ago, the birds were thriving in the warmer climatic conditions.

The unlikelihood of so many birds that had lived for millions of years in New Zealand disappearing all at once has been confirmed by irrefutable evidence in the hundreds of archaeological sites around the country. Radiocarbon dating shows that the goose, duck, swan, pelican and many other unusual birds were present in abundance when the first Maori stepped ashore.

Since European settlement a further seven species have become extinct and a significant number of birds are on the brink of disappearing for good.

Among the species that have become extinct in New Zealand are: the moa (see page 218), New Zealand pelican, flightless goose, New Zealand swan, Finsch's duck, New Zealand hawk, Haast's eagle (see page 151), New Zealand quail, snipe-rail, New Zealand giant coot, Chatham Island rail, Hodgen's waterhen, Dieffenbach's rail, adze-bill, Chatham Island snipe, giant owlet-nightjar, New Zealand raven, Stephens Island wren (see page 370), two stout-legged wrens, piopio, huia (see page 158), laughing owl and the bush wren.

Notable among the species that lived in pre-European New Zealand were:
• A huge sea eagle (*Haliaeetus australis*) which lived around the Chatham Islands coasts and possibly the mainland, swooping down to feed on fish, carrion, penguins and other seabirds
• The large, slow-moving, flightless goose (*Cnemiornis*) which would have fallen easy victim to Maori and their dogs
• A bird unrelated to any other called the adzebill (*Aptornis*) which weighed up to 10 kg and stood 800 mm high.

Sea eagle

# –*Species lost to time*–

S ome of the most unusual birds to have flown over—or in most of these cases, walked on— the earth are depicted in this feathered gallery. When Maori arrived in New Zealand most of these species were flourishing in good numbers, but by the time of European arrival, nearly all had disappeared.

Piopio

Huia

Flightless swan

Flightless goose

Flightless pelican

Adzebill

Hodgen's waterhen

New Zealand quail

Dieffenbach's rail

New Zealand giant coot

Chatham Island snipe

Chatham Island rail

Stephens Island wren

Birds which have become extinct in the past two centuries include:

• Piopio or New Zealand thrush (*Turnagra capensis*), an unwary, inquisitive forest bird and a beautiful songster

• The attractively coloured New Zealand quail (*Coturnix novaezelandiae*), a casualty of hunting, habitat burning and disease

• The laughing owl (*Sceloglaux albifacies*), known principally for its call, described by one listener as 'a peculiar laughing cry, uttered with a descending scale of notes'.

The last official sighting of the laughing owl was in south Canterbury in 1914 when a dead specimen was discovered. One of prehistoric New Zealand's few night-time hunters, the large laughing owl ate insects, small birds and bats. To the present day people report hearing the peculiar cries of the owl, but until a positive sighting is made it is presumed extinct.

Following habitat destruction and the introduction of predators, the final nails in the coffin for New Zealand's birds were often the enthusiastic but misguided bird collectors of the 19th century. No one better summed up the paradoxical outlook of the times than Sir Walter Buller, who used to lament the passing into extinction of some birds at the same time as he shot them.

*The short, forward-curving black plume above the head of the California quail (*Callipepla californica*) makes it the easiest gamebird to identify. Introduced in the 1860s, this quail is well established in semi-open country and along riverbeds.*

# Birds—introduced

Of the more than 130 species of birds known to have been released in New Zealand since European settlement, 41 have successfully established themselves.

From the 1860s acclimatisation societies were formed in most of the major centres with the purpose of introducing animals, usually from Europe. Sometimes this was done for a sentimental reason, such as wanting to see familiar birds from 'home'; sometimes it was for sport (game animals such as ducks and pheasants); and on occasion the grounds were ecological.

Just as rats, mice and other new species arrived with the settlers, so did smaller animals: insect pests such as the codlin moth, cricket, various beetles, ticks, lice, all made a home here. James Drummond of the Department of Agriculture, writing in 1907, recalled 'vast hordes' of insects during the mid-19th century, and reported one startling incident:

'In the Rangitikei district, an army of caterpillars hundreds of thousands strong was overtaken by a train as the insects were crossing the rails to reach a field of oats. Thousands were crushed under the wheels of the engine, and the train suddenly stopped. It was found that the wheels had become so greasy that they revolved without advancing, as they could not grasp the rails. The guard and engine driver placed sand on the rails, and a start was made,' wrote Drummond.

The settlers reasoned that one way to control the insects was to bring in birds. Soon people were collecting birds in England to bring them across the equator and through the chill latitudes of the Southern Ocean. Failures were plenty but some species did not require many individuals to found an antipodean population.

Like many species introduced into a new environment where they have the field largely to themselves, the numbers of some of these birds swelled to pest levels. Sparrows (*Passer domesticus*), skylarks (*Alauda arrensis*) and thrushes (*Turdus philomenus*) were accused

*The array of thorns surrounding this blackbird nest will deter the most determined raider.*

of ruining crops, and sometimes 'sparrow clubs' were formed which paid children to bring in sparrow eggs and birds.

While most introduced birds are accepted today as valued elements of the environment—after all, in many settled areas they are virtually the only birds—a few are still not welcome. Magpies and mynas, introduced in the 1860s, are becoming notorious for their damaging impact on many native bird populations. The Australian magpie (*Acridotheres tristis*) and the Asian myna (*Gymnorhina philomelos*) are most obvious in urban and rural areas that have pockets of native bush, and on forest margins. They attack native birds during the nesting season, often forcing the natives to abandon nests.

Canada geese (*Branta canadensis*) are another introduced problem. The 40 000-strong South Island population damages pea and grain crops, eats grass and fouls pastures in Canterbury. As a result, the Fish and Game Council has carried out an annual cull, but protests from animal rights

*Some scientists believe that of all the introduced birds, mynas may be the most threatening to native bird populations. Mynas are guilty of vigorously attacking other birds and destroying their eggs and chicks.*

*Song thrushes (above) are well-known inhabitants of suburban gardens where they hunt for worms and snails. They are especially adept at breaking open snail shells against rocks in order to get at the flesh inside.*

campaigners have made it doubtful that these culls will continue.

Few native birds have adapted to the change in the New Zealand landscape from forest to pasture; in the new niches which the agricultural/urban landscape has provided, the introduced species have prevailed. Other than the paradise shelduck (see page 104), no endemic birds have increased since human settlement. The native birds which have done well, such as the kingfisher (see page 184) and silvereye (see page 314), are no different from their Australian counterparts and are relatively recent arrivals.

The changing nature of the New Zealand environment has seen an increasing 'Australianisation' of bird species during the 20th century. Other recent additions from across the Tasman include the welcome swallow (see page 330), hoary-headed grebe and the spur-winged plover (see page 273).

The latest newcomer is the nankeen night heron (*Nycticorax caledonicus*) which was confirmed breeding at Jerusalem on the Whanganui River in 1995. Whether this attractive-looking bird, which has a reputation for destroying other birds' nests, will be permanently welcome is too early to say. Officially it has been granted protection as a New Zealand native because it is a self-introduced bird. It occurs throughout the western Pacific, the Philippines and Indonesia.

# Birds—migratory and wading

Around March and April, some birds migrate from New Zealand to faraway destinations such as the Arctic, or closer ports of call such as Australia. Migration also occurs within New Zealand as birds such as the wrybill (see page 371) or kotuku (see page 195) leave their South Island breeding areas for northern wintering-over grounds, or sometimes in bad weather birds move from mountain to lowland areas. However, compared with birds from large, less isolated land masses, New Zealand birds are generally not prominent migrators.

The reason why birds migrate is obvious to us today, but Aristotle saw it another way: he thought the purpose of their migration was to

avoid excessive heat and cold. In fact the key to migration is food; Arctic migrants, for example, can exploit the rich feeding areas in the northern hemisphere when their chicks are born, then escape the freezing winter and scarcity of food for fertile estuarine New Zealand larders.

Some birds are 'loop' migrators, travelling in huge arcs before returning to their breeding grounds. From New Zealand the muttonbird or sooty shearwater flies to Japan before heading across to the North American west coast and back to the Snares and islands surrounding Stewart Island. Many birds migrate by night—there are no predators at this time, the air is less turbulent and they have been able to feed during

*For many birds such as the lesser knot the seasonal urge to migrate is so powerful that it outweighs the danger and discomfort involved in travelling thousands of kilometres.*

### FREQUENT FLIERS
*Migratory birds usually follow well-defined routes called flyways, where they can stop off during the journey to refuel. The red-necked stint (see box page 64) takes the East Asian flyway, with stopovers in Japan, the Philippines, Papua New Guinea and Australia, before arriving in New Zealand.*

the day to prepare themselves for their journey. Larger birds such as herons, birds of prey, and pelicans are diurnal fliers, able to hitch rides on thermals (rising currents of warm air).

Birds are motivated to move by both an internal clock and stimuli in the external environment. Experiments with birds kept in rooms with 24-hour light have shown they roost at the same time every day. However, even though migrators are prompted to depart by this internal clock, they are also governed by the weather, how well fed they are for the long journey ahead, and whether other birds are showing signs of wanting to leave.

Birds use an array of navigational devices: eyesight, a magnetic sense, and smell and hearing. They have their own compass that allows them to line up their course against the reference points of the sun and stars. Scientists believe that birds have a magnetic sense, by which they respond to the Earth's magnetic field through nerves in the head. Even when the sun is obscured, birds know where it is by sensing the pattern of polarised light—which humans cannot perceive—and use this as a navigational aid. Studies on

*Dressing to impress, like many migrants, the curlew sandpiper's* (Calidris ferruginea) *rich chestnut-coloured breeding plumage is in striking contrast to its normal drab grey-brown attire.*

homing pigeons have shown they may be able to hear very low-frequency sounds, known as infrasound. Typical examples of infrasound are the rush of air through a canyon or waves crashing on a shore. Such low-frequency sounds travel remarkable distances, and it has been postulated that birds use these sounds to guide them on their route.

How do juvenile birds such as petrels manage to find their way to traditional migrating areas, when their parents leave well before them? It appears they are somehow programmed to fly to a preordained destination.

Occasionally, birds make navigating mistakes, or are blown off course. Usually these problems of direction are temporary and the errant traveller corrects itself before continuing too far. However, one southern-hemisphere black-browed mollymawk somehow crossed the equator (normally impossible for an albatross to soar across because at the doldrums there is no wind) and now spends its life among gannets nesting on the Shetland island of Unst. There it builds a nest every year in the forlorn hope of finding a mate.

Champions among migrators are Arctic terns which are occasionally seen on the New Zealand mainland on their way to and from the poles. During their lifetime, which can last 30 years, some of these birds may travel 1 million km.

(See also entries under individual bird names.)

## Did you know?

At just 30 grams the tiny red-necked stint (*Calidris ruficollis*) is as light as a sparrow, yet each summer manages the incredible feat of flying from the Arctic to New Zealand—a distance of 10 000 km.

## THE DESTINATIONS OF SOME OF
## NEW ZEALAND'S MIGRATORY BIRDS

ALASKA
Broad-billed sandpiper
Eastern bar-tailed godwit
Pacific golden plover
Red-necked stint
Turnstone

AUSTRALIA
Little tern
Terek sandpiper
White-fronted tern

CANADA
Turnstone

CHINA
Little tern
Pacific golden plover
Terek sandpiper
White-winged tern

CIS (FORMER USSR)
Asiatic whimbrel
Broad-billed sandpiper
Curlew sandpiper
Eastern bar-tailed godwit
Knot
Long-billed curlew
Red-necked stint
Siberian sandpiper
Turnstone

JAPAN
Little tern

# Bittern

Different species of the solitary, swamp-dwelling Australasian bittern (*Botaurus poiciloptilus*) or matuku are found in both the northern and southern hemispheres; as well as occurring in Australia and New Zealand the local species extends to New Caledonia. Described as a rare protected native in New Zealand, its population

is estimated at only about 1000, although it may well be higher because the bird is hard to find.

Bitterns are distributed throughout the North, South and Stewart islands, their strongholds being swampy areas of Northland, Waikato, Bay of Plenty, Manawatu, southern Wairarapa and on the West Coast. Although they have disappeared from the Chathams, there are still some bitterns on Great Barrier Island.

In contrast to other herons which all live in open habitat such as paddocks or shorelines, the bittern relies on camouflage to deceive predators. It shuns the limelight, by night stealthily stalking its prey of eels, frogs, freshwater crayfish and insects among dense wetland vegetation. If it is disturbed during the day, it stretches its well-camouflaged neck skywards, imitating a reed; if the wind is blowing it sways back and forth in rhythm with the vegetation. This 'surveillance posture' enables the bird to get a clearer view of its surroundings and fix an approaching predator with both eyes.

Males especially are very aggressive towards one another. The strong bill, so useful in capturing prey, is also used to jab at or spear other bitterns. The birds do not form pairs; a male mates with several females in his territory and he does not help at the nest.

Although secretive by day, at night during the mating season, which can last from June to February, the male bittern announces its presence to nearby females with loud booming, a sound that Maori associated with melancholy.

The bittern's northern-hemisphere cousin, the Eurasian bittern, has one of the most far-carrying songs of any bird, audible for up to 5 km, and the New Zealand bittern produces a similarly resonant sound.

Bitterns are not known for their flying feats, which makes the appearance of a little bittern (*Ixobrychus minutus*) from Australia quite extraordinary. Presumed to have been blown across the Tasman on a favourable wind, this individual was spotted in February 1987 walking past a Westport supermarket. The exhausted and starving bird was restored to health and later released into Birchfield Swamp, north of Westport.

*The bittern in its 'surveillance posture', enabling it to focus both eyes on a potential threat. Among reeds, the bittern becomes almost invisible, so well do its markings blend in with the surroundings.*

*Tomtits proved to be ideal foster parents to black robins, caring for them from egg stage to independence.*

# Black robin

'New Zealand holds her breath in hope', wrote naturalist David Bellamy in the 1980s, referring to the seemingly insurmountable odds against the survival of the Chatham Island black robin (*Petroica traversi*). At that time the population was reduced to just five birds, with only one effective breeding pair, Old Blue and her mate Old Yellow. The Wildlife Service decided to put into action a daring and desperate programme of cross-fostering. Fifteen years later the species had been saved, with more than 200 black robins flourishing. It was a rescue mission that captured the imagination of bird lovers, children, politicians, and concerned and caring people throughout New Zealand and beyond.

The modern story of the black robin begins in 1871 when the naturalist H H Travers discovered the species living on Mangere Island, 130 ha in

> ## Did you know?
>
> In a desperate move to increase the black robin's population, black robin eggs were placed in Chatham Island tits' nests. This was very successful but a difficulty arose: some robin chicks learned tomtit behavioural traits—these became 'imprinted' upon the foster-species and they were reluctant to breed with other robins. In one interesting case the malimprinting came through to the next generation, affecting a robin whose parents had been raised by tomtits.
>
> To overcome the problem, robins raised by tits were returned to robin nests just before they fledged, and so reached maturity knowing what species they were.

# Old Blue and Don Merton

Two individuals are inextricably linked in the black robin story: Old Blue, the matriarch of the species, and Don Merton, the Wildlife Officer whose innovative techniques helped save the species from extinction.

When Old Blue died, at the advanced age of 13, in late 1983 or early 1984 (the exact date is unknown), the cabinet minister in charge of the Wildlife Service announced her death and the news was carried around the world. As the last breeding female, Old Blue in effect saved her species.

A number of factors make the black robin story all the more remarkable:
• Although the average lifespan of a black robin is only 5–6 years, Old Blue did not start breeding successfully until about 9 years of age.
• Most black robins breed with the same mate for life. Old Blue switched mates in 1978—a fortunate choice, for her new partner was

Old Yellow, with whom she raised 11 chicks.
• All black robins today are descended from Old Blue and Old Yellow, the only bird species living in the wild where the parentage of every individual is known and can be traced to a common ancestor.
• A plaque has been erected in the Chatham Islands in honour of Old Blue.

In memory of the famous female robin, every year the Royal Forest and Bird Protection Society grants 'Old Blue' awards to people who have made outstanding contributions to conservation.

As a boy, Don Merton experimented in cross-fostering goldfinch nestlings to his grandmother's canary; 35 years later this experience became the basis of the successful black robin-tomtit cross-fostering project.

Don Merton is widely praised for his work with endangered birds and has been awarded a Queen's Service Medal and an honorary doctorate. Working initially for the Wildlife Service, and since 1987 for the Department of Conservation, he has been involved in ground-breaking conservation management both in New Zealand and overseas where his skills are much appreciated.

*(Above) Old Blue was a great-grandmother by the time she died at the unusually old age of 13 years. (Top right) Don Merton, known as the 'godfather' of the black robin, holds Bridget.*

*For about 100 years the Chatham Island black robin was confined to tiny Little Mangere Island, akin to being on 'an aircraft carrier moored in the Roaring Forties', according to wildlife officer Don Merton.*

size, and on a tiny (7-ha) rock stack nearby called Little Mangere Island. Once widespread on other islands in the Chathams, the robin had been driven to these last outposts by cats, rats and forest clearance. Late last century when cats became established on Mangere Island, it disappeared from there.

In 1938 three daring ornithologists climbed the near-vertical cliffs of bleak, windswept Little Mangere to discover a thriving robin population. However, in the late 1960s muttonbird poachers cleared bush for a helicopter landing pad, the island's vegetation on which the birds depended for their survival quickly degenerated, and the robin fell into a decline.

By 1976 the population was down to seven. Don Merton and other Wildlife Service officers decided to shift the remaining birds to Mangere Island which had been planted with 120 000 trees and from where the cats had now died out. It was a bold plan. The birds had to be netted, carried down a sheer, 60-metre cliff face, ferried on a small boat then landed on a treacherous, slippery boulder beach. By a miracle all seven birds arrived safely at their new home and survived.

Unfortunately the robin was not yet out of the woods. It has a very slow reproductive rate and while new chicks were born over the next few years, some older birds died. By September 1980 only five remained. What to do?

Again, Don Merton hatched a scheme: eggs were taken from the robins and placed in the nests of Chatham Island warblers and tomtits which he hoped would raise the robin chicks as their own. The loss of their eggs would also encourage the robins to lay again, providing more chances of chicks hatching.

Unfortunately the warbler proved to be an unsuitable substitute parent, but the following season (1981) eggs were fostered to tomtits on neighbouring South-East Island. The tomtits incubated, hatched and raised the first robin foster-chick to independence.

However, there were still some complications. Because the tomtit lived on South-East Island, eggs had to be transferred in a hazardous operation, and robin juveniles then had to make the return trip to Mangere Island. This problem was overcome when permission was granted to start a robin population on South-East Island in 1983.

*Black stilt numbers are gradually being built up through raising chicks in captivity and placing fertile eggs into the nests of wild birds.*

# Black stilt

Beset by predators, suffering the loss of its habitat to hydroelectric schemes and under threat of interbreeding with its cousin the pied stilt, the black stilt (*Himantopus novaezelandiae*) leads a precarious existence in the South Island's Mackenzie Basin. Considered the world's rarest wader, the black stilt numbers around 80 in the wild, although this varies season by season.

Superbly well adapted to the braided-river environment of the South Island's high country which is its stronghold, the black stilt or kaki (the Maori name suggests its yapping cry) has coped less well with the changes that have followed human settlement.

Thousands of years ago when the stilt arrived from Australia it possibly resembled the present-day pied stilt (*Himantopus himantopus*) with its black and white markings, but it has evolved to become a quite different bird. Just why it is coloured black is a mystery, although one theory maintains that having settled close to cool, mountainous areas, it changed its plumage to prevent losing heat. The black stilt is also larger,

## River restoration

In 1990 the Department of Conservation (DOC) and the Electricity Corporation of New Zealand (ECNZ) launched Project River Recovery in an attempt to repair some of the damage done to the black stilt's habitat. As part of a compensatory agreement for not allowing water to be returned to the Pukaki River, ECNZ agreed to spend $3.2 million over 7 years on repairing and enhancing habitats.

DOC have used this funding to remove lupins and willows from riverbeds, and to recreate wetlands. Diggers excavated a number of ponds into which barley straw was placed to attract aquatic invertebrates—vital for feeding the stilts. Large wetlands of several hectares each have been constructed or are being planned.

In a little more than a decade the population of wild black stilts has trebled to 120—around 80 birds in the wild and the remainder in captivity.

*Picturesque though they are, the colourful Russell lupins that grow in the braided rivers of the Mackenzie Country are a menace to black stilts, infesting and taking over areas where the birds might breed.*

with shorter legs, than its pied relative. The differences do not end there: in its behaviour the black stilt is quite distinctive from the pied. It is more aggressive and hardier, most birds choosing to winter over in the sometimes frozen landscape of the Mackenzie Basin rather than head to warmer northern harbours and estuaries.

However, although these differences have equipped it to deal with a braided-river habitat and cool temperatures, the black stilt has a lesser ability than the pied to avoid predators such as cats, rats and mustelids—an ability the pied stilt learned over thousands of years in Australia where there were more natural predators.

When a predator threatens a pied or black stilt's nest, the stilt parent feigns vulnerability, pretending to have a broken wing, and lures the predator away, but the black stilt performs this trick less well. Ensuring safety by numbers, colonies of well-camouflaged pied stilts generally nest on mounds surrounded by water. By contrast, black stilts are accustomed to be on their guard against enemies from the air—harriers and falcons. Nesting from early spring in dry areas, they are ready prey for hungry cats and ferrets.

The black stilt has lost many of the island sanctuaries which naturally occur in beds of braided rivers. Canals have replaced rivers as water has been diverted for hydroelectric power generation or irrigation. To add to the problem, introduced plants such as the colourful Russell lupin, broom and willow have invaded the few suitable breeding areas that remain.

Furthermore, the few surviving black stilts are threatened with hybridisation from pied stilts. If a mate of the same species is unavailable, the black stilt will choose the darkest-coloured hybrid stilt.

Since the late 1970s conservationists have been attempting to save the black stilt, at first by breeding them at the National Wildlife Centre at Mount Bruce. Three aviaries have now been built at Twizel where 80 eggs a season can be hatched and 30–35 birds hand-raised. Another strategy is to return eggs to wild foster-parents just before they hatch.

However, predators remain an ever-present problem. Against this threat various measures from electric fencing to intensive trapping have been tried, but stilts continue to be killed. Recently video cameras have been used to pinpoint exactly which predators are to blame.

# Blue duck

In the fast-running waters of New Zealand's mountain and bush rivers, where swirling torrents would sweep away animals that were less well adapted, the blue duck (*Hymenolaimus malacorhynchos*) happily spends its entire life.

Superbly suited to its wild river habitat, the blue duck has strong webbed feet to propel it across rushing water. Newborn chicks, blessed with large feet to cope with the strong current of a stream swollen with spring snow melt or a flood, appear to run across the top of the water.

When feeding, blue ducks forage mainly for caddis-fly larvae among the stones in riffles and in the lee of large boulders. Scientists speculate that the fleshy flaps on the upper bill protect it from being worn down by rocks.

The blue duck is a year-round river specialist, a distinction it shares with only three other duck species: the South American torrent duck, the African black duck and Salvadori's duck of Papua New Guinea. Named whio by Maori after the distinctive whistling call of the male, the blue duck is one of New Zealand's ancient bird species

*Virtually from the moment they are hatched, blue duck chicks can cope with fast-running rivers. Such torrent ducks are a rare breed; there are only four species in the world.*

*The blue duck and the torrentfish have comparable diets and feeding conditions. As a consequence, the two very different animals have evolved similar feeding and mouth structures. The upper jaw in each has a thick, semicircular, fleshy 'lip' and the lower jaw recedes so that when the beak or mouth is closed, the lower jaw tucks inside the upper, allowing the top jaw to move evenly and closely across rocks as the animal feeds.*

whose numbers have been drastically reduced by predation and habitat destruction. It has been difficult to gain an accurate count of the ducks; the best estimate puts the population at between 2000 and 4000, with slightly more in the North Island than in the South.

Not only do blue ducks mate for life, but once they mark out a territory, a pair will remain there always. Males are renowned for their aggression while guarding their territory, fending off marauding males which attempt to steal their females. Fights also break out if birds cross into each other's boundaries, as the 19th-century explorer Charlie Douglas discovered when he once walked some way up a creek, driving every blue duck ahead of him. 'On reaching the flats there was 13 pairs of ducks with their numerous offspring engaged in a sort of Donnybrook. They fight with their wings, trying to hit with a spur on the tip, but with all their fighting they don't appear to hurt each other much. On going up the same creek next day I

found … every pair was back to their own ground and with all their young with them.'

At the end of each breeding season, once juveniles have gained full adult plumage they disperse up-river. Around July they search for a vacant territory of about 1 km in length, sometimes squeezing in between the territories of other ducks. Until recently it was thought that the blue duck was not a good flier but a sedentary bird— that is, it remained in the same river system. However, some ducks have been discovered to cross from one side of the Southern Alps to the other. One juvenile travelled from the Otira Valley (west of the Main Divide near Arthur's Pass) to the Mingha Valley in the east—6 km in a straight line or 25 km flying distance following the river.

This is good news for the species' long-term survival as there have been concerns over inbreeding, and the wider the species is distributed, the greater the genetic diversity. Nevertheless, it appears that inbreeding is a natural part of the blue duck's makeup. For example, a study on the Manganuiateao River near Mount Ruapehu uncovered brother-sister and even grandmother-grandson pairings.

On the other hand, the fact that blue ducks are better fliers than believed has complicated matters for those trying to conserve them. An attempt to relocate two pairs of adult ducks from Ohakune to Mount Taranaki was foiled when the pair returned more than 100 km to their home territory in a few days.

## Did you know?

The river habitat of the blue duck is so harsh that the plastic leg bands attached to them wear through in a year and identification numbers stamped into the thick stainless steel bands, also placed around their legs, soon become illegible. Tonnes of sediment transported down the swift-flowing rivers play a part in the wear and tear.

# Brown teal

The brown teal is an endemic duck which has not adapted well to changes in its environment. One of the four rarest waterfowl in the world, on mainland New Zealand it favours swamplands and kahikatea forest where there are slow, meandering creeks and overhanging, secretive banks.

There are three subspecies of brown teal, known to Maori as pateke: about 2300 occur on the mainland and offshore islands such as Great Barrier (*Anas chloritis*); more than 2000 on the islands surrounding Auckland Island (*A. aucklandica*); and a maximum of 100 on tiny Dent Island near Campbell Island (*A. nesiotis*).

The subantarctic teals are the least 'duck-like' of New Zealand ducks. Instead of flocking together prior to breeding, they remain in pairs and guard territories all year round. Both species are flightless, but just why has not been established. One theory is that it is an advantage not to be able to fly among the powerful winds of the Furious Fifties, which might carry the birds to South America! Flightless birds normally increase in size, but the subantarctic teals are actually

*Washed-ashore kelp beds provide rich pickings for the Auckland Island teal which feasts on dense concentrations of kelp flies and amphipods. The greatest numbers of teal pairs are found near the largest kelp beds.*

significantly smaller than other ducks. Once the mainland brown teal occurred from Northland to Stewart Island and the Chathams, but following land clearance during the 1880s its numbers began to shrink. In the South Island it is now reported only in Fiordland; the largest population (1500) is at Okiwi on Great Barrier Island. Ducks Unlimited and the Department of Conservation have raised birds in captivity for release in the wild, but on the mainland these have largely been killed by predators.

Intensive management is the key to brown teal survival on the mainland. At Mimiwhangata, north of Whangarei, flocks showed a decline from 1988 when counts were first made. In 1996 the count was down to 16, but following a year of trapping feral cats and mustelids, the count rose to 51. Nearby Teal Bay, where no predator control was carried out, showed a much smaller increase. Scientists are now attempting to assess how much predator control is needed for the greatest gain.

# Butterflies and moths

New Zealand has few butterfly species—only 24, whereas Australia has around 360, North America 700 and tropical South America 6000. More abundant food and warmer temperatures produce greater numbers of butterflies.

On the other hand there are more than 1700 moth species here, although it is easy to mistake moths for butterflies as some of the former are seen flying during the day. Both belong to the family Lepidoptera, meaning scale-winged—it is the scales on the wings which give them their form and pattern.

Butterflies and moths can be told apart in three main ways: butterfly antennae are long and tipped with knobs, while those of moths are hair-like or feathery without knobs; at rest, butterflies

*Red admirals prefer to use the native ongaonga as a food plant for their larvae, but in gardens the introduced stinging nettle is an effective substitute. When ichneumon wasps were introduced in 1932 to control the white butterfly, they also attacked red admirals, and as a result this beautiful native butterfly species has declined.*

*Described as one of
the copper species,
the wings of the boulder
copper male butterfly
are tinged purple.*

*The sun-loving common copper butterfly is
widespread throughout New Zealand, usually
laying its eggs on* Muehlenbeckia *plants.*

close their wings above their bodies so only the
undersides are visible whereas moths usually
spread their wings flat; and butterflies are active
during the day while moths generally fly at night.

## Butterflies

Of the 24 species of butterflies, 11 are found only
in New Zealand. Another five species live both in
New Zealand and elsewhere, and a further eight
periodically arrive, with the help of favourable
westerly winds, from Australia. Some of these,
such as the common blue, have become established; others, such as the painted lady, regularly
cross the Tasman but do not survive the New
Zealand winter.

Undoubtedly the monarch, an occasional visitor to people's gardens, is the best-known butterfly. A relatively recent arrival, this handsome
North American species is thought to have
island-hopped across the Pacific during the mid-
19th century, reaching New Zealand by 1873 (it
could have been earlier but reports are conflict-
ing). This incredible feat of migration is possible,
considering that in North America monarchs
have flown 2200 km in a year.

In New Zealand the monarch is totally dependent for its food on the swan plant or milkwood
which does not occur naturally but is planted in
gardens. The monarch does not like the cold;

after a particularly chilly winter the population in
centres from Wellington south can take several
years to return.

Occasionally found also in gardens, the red
admiral as a caterpillar feeds on the native nettle or
ongaonga, unaffected by the plant's poison which
can kill large animals (see page 236). The name
of this butterfly is a corruption of the name
'Admirable', applied to its European relative and
carried over to the New Zealand species.

Of all the exotic butterflies that have become
established, the cabbage white has had the most
devastating impact. Following its arrival in
Napier in 1929 it moved at remarkable speed
around the country, decimating plants belonging

### Did you know?

The striking colours of some caterpillars and
butterflies, such as the monarch, might seem
to make the insects more easily noticed and
therefore eaten by birds or lizards. However,
it is believed that such a display is a warning
to predators to keep away. Monarchs and
some other butterflies eat foods which
contain toxins, giving them an objectionable
taste or smell. A Canadian scientist who
tested the theory by eating monarchs
reported they did not taste at all, while
another ate caterpillars with no ill effects.
Obviously, though, the warning display works
because few brightly coloured butterflies or
caterpillars are eaten by enemies.

to the cabbage family. The introduction of small ichneumon wasps which eat the caterpillars or chrysalis of the cabbage white has succeeded in keeping the pest's numbers in check.

## Moths

Most people think of moths as drab, colourless flying insects which are attracted into their houses at night by lights. In reality many moths are active during the day and are as gorgeous as butterflies, with colours which can range from gold and orange to blue and brown. However, two-thirds of New Zealand's species live in mountainous areas, mainly in the South Island, where their vivid displays generally go unnoticed.

These alpine moths are not only important plant pollinators; they also provide clues about the origins of the Southern Alps. Most New Zealand moths are old species—only 2.4 percent of moths have been blown in from overseas—so by studying their distribution patterns scientists hope to piece together the puzzle of how the mountains were formed.

Perhaps a third of moths fly by day. Some, such as the brightly coloured magpie moth (*Nyctemera annulata*), are often confused with butterflies. Just as monarch butterflies warn off enemies, so do magpie moths and their caterpillars let predators know they are unpleasant to eat. However, the shining cuckoo is not deterred by

## Disguise artist

Cabbage trees, especially in gardens, are often 'moth-eaten'. The caterpillars of the cabbage tree moth (*Epiphryne verriculata*) remain near the stem of the tree by day, then at night move out to eat the green leaves.

The moth itself is a master of camouflage, not only resembling the colour of the dead leaf on which it rests, but also sitting in such a way that its wings and body match the veins of the leaf.

*By making itself appear similar in appearance to a decaying cabbage tree leaf, the cabbage tree moth artfully deceives predators who might otherwise find it a tasty morsel.*

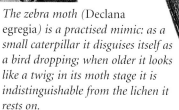

*New Zealand's largest moth is the puriri moth, sometimes mistaken for a bat when it flies at dusk.*

*The zebra moth (Declana egregia) is a practised mimic: as a small caterpillar it disguises itself as a bird dropping; when older it looks like a twig; in its moth stage it is indistinguishable from the lichen it rests on.*

*The European cinnabar moth, introduced in 1929 to control ragwort, has only partially established, being found mainly in the lower North Island. It is often mistaken for a butterfly.*

the taste or the hairy spines of the caterpillar because it has a way of rendering them harmless (see page 92).

New Zealand's largest and best-known moth is the puriri (*Aenetus virescens*) which is found only in the North Island. The wings are a bright apple-green, although a yellow and a red form have been reported, and the larger female has a wingspan of 150 mm. Between September and January the adults fly, but their lives are short. Males survive for only a day, while females carry on for 2 days. During this brief period the adults mate, then the female lays eggs at random as she flies through the forest. When the eggs hatch the caterpillars bore into the trunks of trees such as maire, beech, wineberry and the puriri which gives the moth its name.

Maori were familiar with the convolvulus hawk moth or sphinx moth (*Agrius convolvuli*) whose caterpillars used to plague kumara plots.

One method of controlling the pest was to tether hungry seagulls in the kumara plantations.

A recent immigrant attempting to become an unwelcome permanent resident is the white-spotted tussock moth (*Orgyia thyellina*), a native of Japan, Korea, Taiwan, China and the Russian Far East. Little is known about the moth, but it is regarded as a huge threat to New Zealand native and exotic trees. In 1996–97 a multimillion-dollar aerial spraying programme was carried out in Auckland's eastern suburbs. However, subsequent findings of caterpillars put the success of the programme in doubt.

Most night-flying moths navigate by using the ultraviolet light given out by stars. A bright house light or street lamp is capable of 'bending' them off course so they fly in ever-decreasing circles around the light. This seldom happens on moonlit nights. Moths also rely on odours and sounds to find their way.

*One of the largest cabbage trees in New Zealand is this 3-metre-diameter* Cordyline australis *specimen on Moir-Lea farm, Pakawau, Golden Bay. Farmer Bruce MacHardy is dwarfed by the tree.*

# Cabbage trees

Prized by Maori for their varied uses and admired by landscape architects for their bold, tropical form, cabbage trees are quintessential New Zealand plants.

The cabbage tree belongs to the genus *Cordyline*, of which there are 14 species found naturally in warm to temperate regions from Malaysia (one species) through Queensland (seven), Norfolk Island (one) and New Zealand (five). The species growing in India, Africa and South America are almost certainly introduced. Around the world the cabbage tree has a number of distinctive relatives: the Joshua tree in California, the aloe in South Africa and the grass tree in Australia. Often claimed to be the world's largest lily, the cabbage tree is no longer strictly a lily, taxonomically speaking, although it belongs to the lily family group.

About 15 million years ago the cabbage tree arrived in New Zealand from Asia, to which the country was then linked through archipelagos and islands. Today New Zealand's five species are unique to this country, with *C. australis* the most common, occurring throughout the North and South islands. Once here, the trees evolved to cope with a temperate, as opposed to tropical, climate and developed features to help them survive in the harsher conditions. The leaves became thinner and stringier in response to the wind. Water and food was stored in the club-like roots, enabling the plant to withstand long dry periods.

Maori used to call the cabbage tree ti kouka and found myriad uses for it in daily life: from the roots, stems and leaf buds came food, drink, or chewing-gum; from the leaves were made kete, ropes, sandals, rain capes, bird snares and thatching for houses; it was also a source of medicine for colic, dysentery and diarrhoea. The unmistakable tree marked tracks through swamps, burial grounds, river crossings, and 'signposted' offshore fishing grounds. After the birth of a baby, Maori bury the placenta under special cabbage trees called te whenua.

The cabbage tree's hardiness and indestructibility is reflected in the Maori lament for a deceased loved one: Waiho kia tangi ahau ki taku tupapaku, kapa he uru ti e pihi ake (let me mourn for my dead one; it is not as if he would spring up again as the cabbage tree does).

Seemingly dead cabbage trees are able to 'come back to life'. A Northland gumdigger made a chimney for his hut fireplace out of hollow cabbage tree trunks placed side by side and nailed together. A fire was kept alight continuously for some months until the stems were burned through and only parts of the outside bark left. A short time after the man left the place, a mass of green shoots grew out of the cambium (the single-celled growth layer of the trunk) in the ground below the blackened chimney.

In another case, cabbage trees lay on a beach for 8 months, periodically soaked by salt water before being planted again and successfully growing. The cabbage tree possesses such remarkable regenerative powers because on its rhizome there are thousands of buds capable of sprouting into a new tree.

Cooked cabbage tree shoots, said to be similar in taste to artichokes, were enjoyed by Maori as a vegetable, especially to accompany fatty foods such as titi (muttonbird) or pork. However, early Europeans preferred the taste of the nikau palm, which at that time, like other palms throughout the world, was called a 'cabbage tree' because of its tender, edible green 'heart'. The palm-like *Cordyline* was also referred to as a cabbage tree, and the name stuck to that species.

A sixth species of cabbage tree, *C. fruticosa*, which is common in the tropical Pacific, is believed to have been brought to New Zealand

*Some cabbage trees were deliberately planted by Maori to serve as 'footprints' or direction markers. These stand near the mouth of the Clarence River.*

*The broad-leaved mountain cabbage tree, tropical in appearance, grows best in cool high-altitude areas.*

by Maori. Known as ti pore, it was grown in plantations in Northland (the only area warm enough) and the rhizome steamed in large earth ovens. Recent research has shown that *C. fruticosa* is sweeter than cane sugar (fructose is another name for sucrose). This species died out at the end of the 19th century once sugar and sweets arrived with Europeans. Because the plant could not seed in New Zealand it disappeared once the plantations were abandoned.

Scientists believe that many of the cabbage trees growing on farmland are survivors from land clearance in the 19th century, and may be a dying breed unless they are fenced off from domestic animal grazing. The Department of Conservation has instigated a recovery programme, hoping to protect key stands of trees through fencing them, and encouraging the retention of recreation of wetlands—the tree's favoured environment. It also recognises that cabbage trees are under stress because they grow alone, without any of their traditional associated wetland vegetation.

## Mystery killer

Since the early 1980s the cabbage tree has been the victim of a syndrome called 'sudden decline'. From Northland to Nelson the skeletons of thousands of dead cabbage trees bear stark testimony to the presence of some destructive agent, probably a bacterium.

It is believed that environmental changes may have led to the disease. The most widely held theory is that an insect—possibly the Australian passion-vine hopper—is spreading infection from tree to tree; this would explain why sudden decline affects trees in open country more than in native forest or natural wetlands because the passion-vine hopper inhabits open farmland and cities. Now definitely retreating, sudden decline remains a mystery.

*Two cabbage trees, victims of sudden decline, stand as stark memorials to the destructive effect of the mysterious disease that has carved a swathe through the trees from Northland to Nelson.*

### New Zealand's Cabbage Trees

- *C. australis*, the most common cabbage tree, grows to 600 metres above sea level. Widely planted in suburban gardens and in paddocks, it is found naturally in swamps and forest margins. Maori used to eat both the rhizome and stem.
- *C. indivisa*, a large-leaved species, is also known as toi or the mountain cabbage tree. It prefers high altitudes, growing abundantly in the rainforests of Mount Taranaki and Tongariro National Parks.
- *C. banksii*, named after botanist Joseph Banks, occurs on forest margins from North Cape to Banks Peninsula and Westland, and is less common than *C. australis*.
- *C. kaspar* grows naturally only on the Three Kings and Poor Knights islands but is popular in gardens. Regarded as a form of *C. australis* until 1956, it has broader, shorter leaves and a generally clumped habit.
- *C. pumilio*, a dwarf cabbage tree growing naturally in forests as far south as Kawhia in the west and East Cape in the east, is easily mistaken for a grass plant.

# Castle Hill buttercup

In 1989 taxonomists dropped a botanical bombshell: the Castle Hill buttercup, one of the few plants in the country that had a special reserve to protect it, was declared no longer to be a species. Several famous names in New Zealand botany had been instrumental in protecting the plant when it appeared that it might become extinct. At the time they believed that the buttercup, christened *Ranunculus paucifolius* in 1899 by pioneering botanist Thomas Kirk, was the only one of its kind.

*R. paucifolius* occurred in a 6-ha area of limestone debris in a gently sloping basin surrounded by cliffs, west of Castle Hill Station. Former curator of the Otari Plant Museum, Walter Brockie, fenced off a small area of the high-country sheep station in the 1940s and transplanted some buttercups into it. Compared to those open to sheep grazing, the plants inside the fence thrived. Later, soil scientist and conservationist Lance McCaskill persuaded the government to designate the area a nature reserve. Ringed by barbed wire, the 400 or so plants located among the limestone tors of

*If not for the splash of yellow from its flowers, the Castle Hill buttercup would be difficult to distinguish from its limestone scree background.*

the lower Waimakiriri Basin in Canterbury are among the most difficult to gain access to—at least on the mainland. By creating this reserve, McCaskill also protected a suite of nationally threatened plants: the limestone forget-me-not (*Myosotis colensoi*), a swarding sedge (*Carex inopinata*) and a recently discovered primitive grass, the limestone wheatgrass (*Australopyrum calcis*) as well as other elements of a fascinating intermontane limestone flora.

In 1965 buttercup specialist F J Fisher downgraded the status of the plant to a subspecies of a buttercup that is widely distributed throughout the South Island mountains. Its new name was *Ranunculus crithmifolius* ssp. *paucifolius*.

The final blow to the plant's botanical standing occurred in 1989 with the decision by the authors of the authoritative *Flora of New Zealand* (Vol. 4) to remove even the subspecies title. Now the Castle Hill plants are considered just one of the more variable populations of *R. crithmifolius*. Or are they? In fact, most of the buttercups found on the eastern side of the Southern Alps prefer to grow on fine greywacke scree, whereas the Castle Hill buttercup is unique in growing on limestone scree at a relatively low altitude and so continues to enjoy a high level of protection.

# Cat

From the moment cats arrived in New Zealand they proved to be a menace to native wildlife, as ornithologist George Forster noted during James Cook's second voyage in 1773, while the *Resolution* was moored in Dusky Sound: a cat 'regularly took a walk in the woods every morning and made great havoc among the little birds, that were not aware of such an insidious enemy'.

By the 1830s feral cats were well established on the mainland and were contributing to the loss of birds and lizards. Their greatest impact, however, has been on islands, the most celebrated case of bird extinction occurring on Stephens Island (see Wrens, page 370). Cats have been introduced to at least 30 islands, including Raoul, Auckland, Campbell and the main Chatham Islands.

But they have also been eradicated from biologically important islands such as Cuvier, Little Barrier, Kapiti, and Stephens. On Little Barrier an epic eradication programme from 1978 to 1980 saw 27 000 poison baits laid. Only 151 cats were known to have been killed, although others must have died without being found. Once the cats had gone, the stitchbird population on the island leapt from 500 to almost 5000 in just a few years.

The 'rediscovered' Stewart Island kakapo population had to be shifted during the 1980s to Codfish and Little Barrier Islands after it was discovered they were being killed by cats. On the mainland the black stilt, kiwi and lizards are some of the rare and vulnerable species that fall victim to cats.

On the plus side, cats have helped to keep rabbit, rat and mice numbers down, and where these animals are the most plentiful they form the greatest percentage of the cat's diet.

*A cat's diet varies depending on where it lives. A 25-year study in the Orongorongo Valley near Wellington showed rats, rabbits and possums made up most of the diet of feral cats. However, while birds do not figure prominently in cats' diets, vulnerable species such as the little blue penguin, already down to small numbers, can be seriously affected by cat predation.*

# Caves

Limestone caves are the most common type of cave in New Zealand and the world. Other types which exist in New Zealand are marble, sea, lava, sandstone and igneous rock caves.

At one time much of New Zealand was limestone, but most of it has been eroded away. In areas where it remains, some of the most beautiful and bizarre landforms exist—the so-called karst limestone regions, named after a limestone district in the former Yugoslavia.

New Zealand's limestone rocks were laid down during the Oligocene geological period that lasted from 38 to 26 million years ago. Enormous numbers of shells and skeletons of marine organisms combined into a thick strata of sediment that, over time, cemented together to become rock beds. The great majority of New Zealand's limestone landscapes originated during this era: Takaka Valley, Aorere, Patarau, Buller, Oparara, Heaphy, Punakaiki. Here, as well as in the

*Beneath the unremarkable-looking Waitomo landscape lies a spectacular hidden world of caves, sinkholes and complex shafts. In the Ruakuri system, one of three systems known collectively as the Waitomo Caves, slowly seeping water creates the limestone caves. As rainwater leaches through the soil it takes on enough carbon dioxide to form a mild solution of carbonic acid, which penetrates cracks and fissures in the limestone. When the water level eventually drops, vast air-filled caverns remain. Water continues to drip, creating stalactites and other cave formations. Eventually the water running through the caves exits into the Waitomo Stream.*

*All the elements that make up a unique karst landscape are found in the Paparoa Range, north Westland. These dramatic shapes are reflected in the glassy surface of the Fox River.*

Waitomo area in the North Island, are the country's great cave systems.

Many caves are complex systems of passageways several kilometres long, which penetrate to a depth of hundreds of metres beneath the surface. Nettlebed Cave on Mount Arthur is the deepest cave in the southern hemisphere.

### New Zealand's Deepest Caves

| Cave | Area | Depth (m) | Length (km) |
|---|---|---|---|
| Nettlebed Cave | Mt Arthur | 889 | 24.2 |
| Ellis Basin Systems | Mt Arthur | 781 | 28 |
| Bulmer Cavern | Mt Owen | 749 | 38.8 |
| Bohemia Cave | Mt Owen | 662 | 7.3 |
| HH Cave | Mt Arthur | 623 | – |
| Incognito/ Falcon System | Mt Arthur | 540 | – |
| Greenlink/ Middle Earth | Takaka Hill | 394 | – |
| Windrift | Mt Arthur | 362 | 4.4 |
| Harwoods Hole | Takaka Hill | 357 | – |
| Gorgoroth | Mt Arthur | 346 | – |

Caves are nature's vaults, containing irreplaceable records of biological, climatic, cultural and landscape history. The limestone caves of the South Island have revealed much information about New Zealand's ancient birds. Honeycomb Hill, near Karamea, is a treasure trove of extinct moa, goose, duck and eagle bones.

# Cicadas

The cicada spends most of its life underground before emerging briefly during summer as an adult to face the hazards of mating and egg laying. Some of New Zealand's 40 species are known to stay at least 5 years as larvae buried in the soil where there is plenty of food. No one has satisfactorily answered the riddle of how the males and females of each species manage to time it correctly so that they become adults simultaneously and can reproduce. An American cicada species holds the record for the length of time spent underground—17 years. A Japanese scientist has advanced the theory that cicadas' behaviour was adopted as a survival strategy during the Ice Age of 2.5 million years ago. When the climate cooled it may have led to the extinction of most cicada

*The controlling muscles that cicadas use to work their timbals, or musical organs, can operate at up to several hundred times per second.*

species and the few survivors would have had to adapt genetically to ensure their short mating periods coincided.

The noisiest cicadas are males, as the Greek poet Xenarchus observed more than 2000 years ago: 'Happy are cicadas' lives, for they have voiceless wives.' He was not strictly accurate, as the females do produce a subdued mating call. But the fact remains that the male cicada is the rowdiest insect of them all. Its song is made by the rapid movement of a timbal which oscillates up to 600 times a second. Behind the timbals most of the abdomen is hollow, creating a resonating chamber that amplifies the sound.

Sometimes the noise produced by cicadas can be literally deafening. United States scientists measured the noise produced by thousands of cicadas in a single tree and found it to be 80–100 decibels at a distance of 18 metres, whereas the sound of a pneumatic drill at a similar distance was 70–90 decibels.

Little is known about many of the New Zealand cicadas. The only protected species and the one with the most restricted distribution is Myer's cicada (*Maoricicada myersi*), found along the Orongorongo riverbed near Wellington. Cicadas camouflage themselves according to habitat: yellow species in tussocklands, green in forests, black or grey species in rocky and alpine areas.

When English settlers first arrived in New Zealand, Maori described their speech as te reo kihikihi, 'cicada language', because of its harshness compared with the more melodious Maori.

# Coprosmas

For years plants of the *Coprosma* family have been the unwitting fall guys of New Zealand botany. So numerous and difficult to identify are many of the small-leaved, twiggy shrubs that botanists have often given up the struggle with the catchphrase, 'Call it a coprosma'.

Of the more than 50 coprosmas (not all have been named yet), around 30 are the small-leaved, divaricating variety, branching at a wide angle to produce a tangled form. The fact that there are so many divaricating shrubs gave rise to a lively debate during the 1970s, after two scientists suggested the shrubs grew in such a way as a defence against moa browsing. The counter-argument said that small-leaved, tangle-branched shrubs protect growing points and leaves from wind, drought and frost.

Coprosmas not only have a variety of leaf forms, they also exist in a wide range of habitats. *C. arborea* grows in northern North Island forests and is a small tree; *C. repens* or taupata is one of the hardiest coastal shrubs (also known as the mirror plant in the USA and Australia because of its glossy green leaves); *C. tenuicaulis* favours swamps; *C. perpusilla* is a prostrate plant of high tussock areas.

*(Above) The bark of* Coprosma rhamnoides *is used by spinners to make an orange dye.*
*(Right) Kanono (*C. australis*) has glossy red berries.*

*Coprosma berries come in a number of different colours, including the purple of this prostrate* Coprosma acerosa *var.* brunnea.

*Taupata (*Coprosma repens*) is one of the hardiest coastal shrubs, found from Westport north. Although* repens *means creeping, in sheltered conditions it will grow 8 metres high.*

One of the least appealing coprosmas is the aptly named stinkwood (*C. foetidissima*) which gives off an offensive smell when bruised. Wrote botanist Sir Joseph Hooker after the plant had been in his cabin for half an hour: '... the smell was horrible and pervaded ... the lower deck.'

The coprosma is related to the coffee plant and brews have been concocted from taupata seeds, but the resulting drink does not compare to the real thing. Maori ate the juicy coprosma berries, but they are generally regarded as insipid, and in some species bitter.

# Corals

Until 1981 virtually nothing was known about New Zealand's most notable coral, the black coral (*Antipathes fiordensis*) of Fiordland and Stewart Island. In fact it was not even named scientifically until 1990.

While corals are normally associated with the tropics, several types never form reefs and live in colder waters. Black coral is one of the less familiar varieties, and the Fiordland species is among the most unusual in the world. In particular, this black coral occurs closer to the surface than black corals elsewhere in the world—including the Poor Knights Islands. It is unusual to spot black corals shallower than 40 metres from the surface, but in the unique underwater ecosystem in Fiordland they are attached to rock walls as close as 6 metres from the surface, although they have been recorded below 100 metres on those same walls.

The top 40 metres of water in the fiords is a fragile band of life (see page 118). It exists through a combination of high rainfall and nutrient runoff from the surrounding forests. As warm westerly winds approach the southern coast they meet cool alpine air, condensing to rain—about 7 metres falls on the fiords annually.

As the rainwater spills down thousands of rivers it picks up tannic acid from decaying vegetation. This freshwater layer, the colour of weak tea or beer, lies 3–4 metres above the seawater and does not mix with it because there are no waves in the protected fiords. Only a weak yellow-green light filters through to the marine realm below, reducing photosynthesis. This means that seaweed, which needs brighter light, does not occur in the great forests typical of the outer coasts; instead, species normally restricted to caves and deep water flourish on the steep rock faces of the fiords.

More than 7 million colonies of the protected black coral live in the fiords, the largest and shallowest population of the world's black corals. The colonies secrete a substance called chitin which forms a fragile, tree-like skeleton. When living, black coral appears white because the small white polyps obscure the dense black skeleton beneath. Scientists estimate black coral grows at only about 24 mm a year, suggesting some trees could be older than 300 years. The Fiordland black coral exists in an unusual co-operative relationship with the long-armed snake brittlestar, which

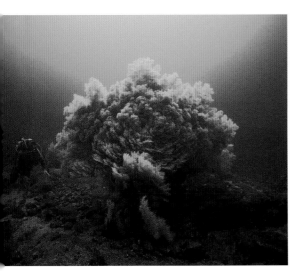

*Resembling a giant cauliflower, a black coral tree grows on a ledge 10 metres below the fiord surface.*

wraps itself around the coral's branches. At first it was thought that the brittlestar fed on the coral animals or polyps, but during a period of relative drought the fascinating reality of their relationship was revealed.

With little rain, light levels rose, leading to a rise in plant plankton production which smothered the coral colonies. Many colonies died, but those with brittlestars survived because the brittlestars cleaned the coral as they fed on the mucus given off by the polyps.

In 1995 a $3.5-million underwater observatory was opened at Milford Sound to allow the public to view the fiords' unique underwater world.

New Zealand has only two intertidal corals, the cup coral (*Flabellum rubrum*) and *Culicea rubeola*, although there are 105 deeper-water species. The only reef-forming corals—similar to tropical corals—are found in the warm waters off

*A long-armed snake brittlestar (*Astrobrachion constrictum*) rests tightly coiled around the branches of a black coral. Distant relatives of starfish, some brittlestars stay on the same perch year after year. A small but fearless scarlet wrasse, a species well known for biting divers' lips, swims by.*

## The secret sculptors

Mention coral and people think of a white, stony substance. But in fact coral animals, or polyps, are what create the intricately sculptured hard material or 'rock' that we know as coral reefs, or the free-standing black coral 'trees' found in Fiordland. Related to the jellyfish, polyps live inside protective limestone cups, feeding by sweeping the water with their tentacles and stunning microscopic prey. Most corals are white, although some prized varieties are black or red.

*The polyps of this cup coral (Flabellum rubrum) are animals. Being a temperate species, it will not harden to create a reef.*

the Kermadec Islands, an isolated group of islands halfway between New Zealand and Tonga. At a maximum of 2 metres in diameter the Kermadec colonies are miniature in comparison with tropical reefs.

# Crabs

Crabs are one of the important scavengers of the coastline, cleaning up organic scraps and in turn providing animals such as fish and birds with an important source of protein.

In New Zealand more than 80 crab species have been identified, although only 30 are common. Like all crustaceans, crabs are joint legged (10 legs in the case of crabs), have two pairs of an-

tennae and moult their shells as they grow larger. Crabs protect themselves in a number of ways. Their shell-like cover or carapace acts like a suit of armour, and they can give a potential predator a painful nip with their powerful claws—swimmers know only too readily when they have met up with a swimmer crab (*Ovalipes catharus*). Other crabs use more cunning ploys to escape detection. Some can change colour to match rocks or sand nearby, while the decorator crab (*Notomithrax* species) adorns itself with seaweed. Hermit crabs (*Pagurus* species) take refuge in empty sea-snail shells and have stinging anemones standing guard to ward off enemies. When they have to move 'house' because the old shell is too small, they coax the anemones to shift with them to the new shell.

New Zealand's largest crab is the subantarctic giant crab (*Jacquinotia edwardsii*), measuring 200 mm across the carapace and 1 metre from the end of one leg to the other. Large though this crab is, it has little meat and is therefore not a species sought by commercial fishers.

# Crayfish

Popularly known as a crayfish, this tasty crustacean is marketed as a 'rock lobster' although scientists prefer the term spiny lobster.

Although the crayfish's hard shell is good armour against predators, its replacement when the animal is growing can cause problems. About 2–3 months before it sheds its shell, the crayfish starts to build a new, soft shell beneath the present one. Closer to the moult, it becomes sluggish and stops feeding. Once it moults out of the old shell, it takes some days for the replacement to harden and during this time the crayfish is very vulnerable to predators such as grouper, blue cod, dogfish and octopus.

New Zealand has two species of coastal rock crayfish, the red rock crayfish (*Jasus edwardsii*) and the packhorse or green rock crayfish (*J. verreauxi*). There is also a deepwater species of the genus *Projasus*, but little is known of it.

The most common of the two coastal species is the red rock crayfish which occurs from the Three Kings Islands in the north to the Auckland Islands in the south and across to the Chathams. It is also common around the coasts of southern Australia.

The larger green rock crayfish, found mainly north of Bay of Plenty, breeds mostly around Cape Reinga. In October females move about 20 km out to sea into waters at least 100 metres deep where they hatch eggs. Here they take advantage of the high water movement and upwelling near Cape Reinga which helps larvae to disperse rapidly. Crayfish larvae float in waters 10 to hundreds of kilometres offshore before being transported near shore where they change into a crayfish-looking puerulus. The metamorphosis into a fully mature crayfish takes between 3 and 8 years, depending on their location.

Biologically the two species of crayfish are similar, with five pairs of legs and a pair of antennae or 'feelers' which are used for defence and for touch. Crayfish have traditionally been described

*In spite of its impressive size, the subantarctic giant crab has little flesh.*

*A startled hermit crab finds itself momentarily outside its refuge. As these crabs grow, they have to move into bigger accommodation.*

*Crayfish can live as long as 30 years. Around the Gisborne area female crayfish often reach sexual maturity at 3 years although they do not grow to the minimum legal size until 9 years. Stewart Island crayfish reach the legal minimum size at 6 years, but take another 2 years to become sexually mature.*

as scavengers, but this is not strictly accurate. Usually night-feeders, they target small shellfish and are capable of opening oysters or eating paua.

When captured, crayfish are dark red or green according to the species; however, when placed in hot water to cook they turn bright red. Pigments in the crayfish undergo a chemical change in the presence of heat, forming a compound that colours the animal red.

Crayfish have been one of the mainstays of the fishing industry. Overfishing saw catches plummet until the 1990s, but better management of the fishery has led to an increase in stocks. The heyday of the industry was the mid-1950s when around 6500 tonnes were taken annually. Today that has dropped to nearer 3000 tonnes. Exports are worth $100 million a year.

*Did you know?*

Crayfish are capable of migrating astonishing distances. A juvenile packhorse crayfish has been recorded travelling 1070 km. Every spring, some juvenile red rock crayfish in the South Island migrate against the coastal current to breeding areas. They travel south along the east coast, west through Foveaux Strait and north along Fiordland. Red rock crayfish can move as far as 460 km, with rates of 6.8 km a day recorded. Scientists believe such migrations compensate for the drift of larvae.

# Cuckoos

In the northern hemisphere the first sighting of the cuckoo each year is regarded as an indication that spring has arrived, for it is then that the bird migrates from warmer climates to breed. New Zealand's two species of cuckoo arrive around the beginning of October, the forests ringing with their unmistakable calls, especially that of the long-tailed cuckoo, which is a harsh shriek.

The long-tailed cuckoo (*Eudynamys taitensis*) spends the New Zealand winter in a wide range of Pacific islands, from the Bismarck Archipelago in the west to French Polynesia in the east. In early October it returns to the same site it occu-

pied the year before, the female laying an egg in a host nest then taking no further part in raising the young.

A relatively heavy bird at 125 grams (especially compared to one of its hosts, the brown creeper, which weighs in at only 12 grams), the long-tailed cuckoo will attack nests and eat chicks and eggs. Generally, though, its diet consists of wetas, stick insects, cicadas and other bugs.

No population count of the long-tailed cuckoo has been carried out, but the bird appears to be relatively common. However, even though it is fully protected in New Zealand, in the Pacific its habitat is being whittled away through logging. The shining cuckoo (*Chrysococcyx lucidus*) has a similar problem. In March it migrates to the

## Cuckoo express

In comparison with the long-tailed cuckoo, the glossy green shining cuckoo is diminutive at 25 grams, about the same size as a sparrow. The world's smallest cuckoo, it is nevertheless a remarkable flier. Assuming it flies to the Solomons direct, with Lord Howe and Norfolk islands the only possible stop-off points, the return journey of 6000 km is regarded by Auckland Museum cuckoo expert Dr Brian Gill as 'the most spectacular transoceanic migration by any landbird'.

Some shining cuckoos take a more leisurely route to their wintering grounds, flying via Australia, which extends the return trip to 12 000 km but gives more opportunity for 'rest and recreation'.

*Possible migration routes of the shining cuckoo. Some birds fly as far as western Indonesia.*

western Pacific countries of western Indonesia, New Guinea and the Solomon Islands, where logging has decimated tropical rainforests in some areas. Happily its host in New Zealand, the grey warbler, has adapted well to human settlement and therefore the shining cuckoo is well distributed throughout the country.

Shining cuckoos prefer caterpillars and beetles such as ladybirds to most other foods, even though their prey have defences aimed at warding off predators. For example, ladybirds discharge a toxic fluid and caterpillars of the magpie moth have a dense covering of barbed spines. In order to avoid being damaged by the spines, the cuckoo casts off mucous membrane from its stomach wall and regurgitates it, rendering the prickly mouthfuls harmless.

## Did you know?

Cuckoos are the parasites of the bird world, saving themselves the trouble of building a nest by laying their eggs in another bird's nest, then letting that bird do the hard work of feeding the cuckoo chick. The shining cuckoo takes advantage of the grey warbler in this way, while the long-tailed cuckoo uses the whitehead in the North Island and the yellowhead and brown creeper in the South Island.

When the cuckoo quickly lays an egg in the borrowed nest—making sure the warbler or yellowhead is not looking—it often removes one of the host's eggs so the same number remain, thus fooling the host bird into thinking nothing has changed. Cuckoo eggs always hatch before warbler, yellowhead, whitehead or creeper eggs. Once the cuckoo chick is a few days old, it pushes the other eggs or chicks out of the nest so that it receives the parent host's undivided attention.

*Seemingly oblivious to the identity of the interloper in its nest, the whitehead is an attentive parent to the long-tailed cuckoo chick.*

*Daisies come in all shapes and sizes and occupy a variety of habitats. The green cushion daisy (Celmisia bellidioides; left) is found on rocks in the South Island up to 1600 metres, while the subalpine rough-leaved tree daisy (Olearia lacunosa; below) can grow as tall as 7 metres.*

# Daisies

To most of us a daisy is a relatively insignificant introduced flower we grow in the garden, but in fact it is the largest of New Zealand's plant families. New Zealand daisies can be small trees or shrubs, or strange mountain plants such as the world-famous vegetable sheep.

Most New Zealand daisies are alpine plants (see page 262): mountain daisies (*Celmisia*), vegetable sheep and relatives (*Raoulia*), edelweiss (*Leucogenes*), and the cotulas (now described as *Leptinella*). Celmisias alone account for more than 60 species. Other daisies are less obviously 'daisy-like' than the celmisias. From sea level to subalpine slopes grow a number of tree daisies of the *Olearia* genus. One known well to trampers is the serrated-leaved leatherwood (*O. colensoi*), which occurs just above the treeline.

Also belonging to the daisy family is rangiora (*Brachyglottis repanda*), the bushman's friend, whose large leaves prove useful when campers and trampers run out of toilet paper. Maori sometimes chewed the gum of this plant or used it as a cure for bad breath. It was reputed to be poisonous if swallowed.

# Deer

Few environmental issues in New Zealand have raised temperatures quite so high as the arguments over the impact of deer. Disputes continue to this day.

On one side, conservationists argue that deer are one of the most damaging pests to native vegetation; on the other, hunters downplay deer's influence and believe that if any control is needed, they should carry it out. Some contend deer are simply taking over the role that moa used to play and others continue to release deer illegally into forests in order to ensure a good supply of game.

The first deer to arrive in New Zealand were a red deer (*Cervus elaphus scoticus*) stag and hind sent from England in 1851. Introductions of other species followed soon after: fallow deer (*Dama dama dama*) in 1864, sambar (*C. unicolor unicolor*) in 1875, sika (*C. nippon*) in 1885 and white-tailed (*Odocoileus virgineanus*) in 1909. United States President and outdoors enthusiast Theodore Roosevelt arranged for a shipment of wapiti (*C. elaphus nelsoni*), the largest member of the deer family, to be swapped for some native birds and tuatara in 1905.

As early as 1893 warnings were being sounded about the impact of deer on vegetation. Not only native forest was at stake: by the 1920s the State Forest Service reported that exotic plantations

*Prized as a trophy animal by hunters, who consider it to be more difficult to shoot than the red deer, the Asian sika was restricted to the central North Island until the early 1980s when it was illegally released in lower North Island forests.*

# Deer on the move

W ild deer are continuing to spread through-out the country, as this 1996 map shows. Many of the new populations are the result of farm escapes. Between 1985 and 1995 the value of farmed red and fallow deer dropped, and farmers became less concerned about maintaining boundary fences. At the same time, deer were illegally released by hunters.

Note that the map does not show the distribution of red deer, which are present in most native forests including Northland, the Coromandel, Taranaki and Banks Peninsula—areas from which they had been absent until the 1990s.

| | ESTABLISHED RANGE | NEW POPULATION |
|---|---|---|
| Sika | | |
| Fallow | | |
| Sambar | | |
| Rusa | | |
| White-tailed | | |
| Wapiti | | |

had also suffered from deer browsing. Public pressure saw a change of policy towards deer so that protection was lifted in 1930 and the New Zealand Government began to pay hunters to shoot animals. By the mid-1950s the government was employing a hunting force of 100–125 men who were shooting 50 000–65 000 deer a year.

Helicopter hunting and deer farming put a new slant on deer control from the 1970s. Suddenly live deer became extremely valuable as farmers started to build up herds by capturing wild stock. Deer numbers fell and wily deer avoided the more open, subalpine areas to take cover in forests.

During the 1990s the Department of Con-servation has largely ignored deer control, opting to rely on commercial and recreational hunting and 1080 poison to keep deer numbers in check. A 3-year Landcare Research study of the impacts of deer in North Island forests, published in 1996, showed that even though deer ate only 1.1 per-cent of the foliage produced each year in a forest, this was enough to have a long-term effect on the health of the forest. Deer eat seedlings, favouring lancewood and broadleaf species, thus are more damaging than possums, which prefer to eat the

## Did you know?

In the 1930s when deer numbers were at their peak a tramper saw 1200 deer during a 3-hour walk up the Dart Valley, western Otago. During the same decade in the D'Urville Valley (part of Nelson Lakes National Park) a stockman shot 148 deer from horseback in a day.

fresh leaves of mature trees. Deer effectively wipe out future generations of their favourite foods.

Many of the new populations of deer, especially in Northland, result from farm escapes, but more than 30 percent have occurred because of illegal releases. Only 6 percent of the new populations are from natural dispersal. Some hunters bought animals to release in neighbourhood forests, while others went so far as to helicopter sika deer deep into the Tararua Ranges where they have thrived. The chances of eradicating these new populations are slim; in 44 areas where action has been taken, no more than eight populations have been exterminated.

Apart from destroying forest, deer also carry bovine tuberculosis. Hunters who translocate deer are often responsible for the spread of tuberculosis to areas free of the disease, and are thus culpable of endangering New Zealand's valuable pastoral industry.

*At the forest edge a red deer stag raises its head and roars its readiness to fight any rival for control of a harem of females. In fact stags rarely come to blows; the winner is usually the one that bellows loudest.*

# Dinosaurs

Until dinosaur enthusiast Joan Wiffen told a 1980 Royal Society symposium in Wellington that she had uncovered evidence of land-based dinosaurs, it had been widely believed none had roamed prehistoric New Zealand.

On the other hand there were plenty of fossils of marine reptiles, large, predatory swimming beasts that dominated the seas between 235 and 65 million years ago.

Wiffen and other amateur fossil hunters found the clues to New Zealand's dinosaur past in the remote Te Hoe Valley, 40 km north of Napier and bordering the Urewera National Park. Here, where millions of years ago sea water lapped against what is now inland forest, dinosaur bones have been preserved.

Following years of painstaking work cutting rocks, lifting them out of the bush, extracting and preserving the precious bones, Wiffen and her colleagues revealed that at least five types of dinosaurs had ranged the New Zealand landscape:
- the carnivorous theropod, standing about 2 metres tall and weighing 400 kg
- the vegetarian hypsilophodont
- the fearsome-looking *Ankylosaurus*, a monster wearing armour plate and weighing 500 kg
- the flying pterosaur
- a sauropod called *Diplodocus*, a smaller relative of the plant-eating *Brachiosaurus*, largest dinosaur of them all.

*The meat-eating, armour-plated* Ankylosaurus *weighed about 500 kg.*

*Diplodocus is the largest land dinosaur to have lived in New Zealand. Related to the huge* Brachiosaurus *which weighed 100 tonnes,* Diplodocus, *also a plant-eating sauropod, grew to a modest 10 metres.*

# Dolphins

Of the world's 60 dolphin species, nine occur in New Zealand waters. Some, like the common dolphin, are found in quite large numbers, but others such as Hector's are some of the rarest dolphins in the world.

Dolphins have long been held in high regard in this part of the Pacific; Maori believed that after one reached a high level in this life, one became a dolphin, and many families had a dolphin which was their aumakua or protective ancestor in the sea.

Dolphins belong to the Delphinidae family and are distinguished from porpoises by their long beaks and numerous pointed teeth. Porpoises have no beak and their teeth are spade shaped. Just one porpoise, the spectacled (*Australophocoena dioptrica*), has been recorded in New Zealand waters.

Of the New Zealand dolphins, three are common, and Hector's dolphin, although rare, is frequently seen around the coast. The striped, spotted, hourglass, southern right and Risso's dolphins are all scarce in the seas around New Zealand. One Risso's, however, occupies a permanent place in New Zealanders' affections: the famous Pelorus Jack (see box page 100).

## Hector's dolphin

Numbering between 3000 and 4000, Hector's dolphin (*Cephalorhynchus hectori*) is not only one of the world's rarest dolphins, but also one of the smallest, growing to a maximum length of only 1.4 metres. As it is the only dolphin found exclusively in New Zealand waters it has earned the title of the 'downunder' dolphin. Maori knew it as either tutumairekurai (special ocean dweller) or tupoupou (to rise vertically). Hector's dolphin is more of a South Islander than a North Islander.

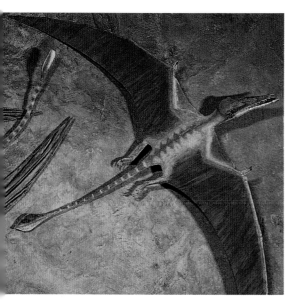

*Pterosaurs took to the air 150 million years before birds and bats. They were the largest animal ever to fly (some had wingspans of 15 metres), although the New Zealand pterosaur was comparatively small with a wingspan of 3 to 4 metres. (Reconstruction Auckland Museum.)*

*A fearsome predator, the mosasaur was a marine lizard which terrorised the seas between 205 and 135 million years ago. Armed with large, sharp teeth, mosasaurs could dive as deep as 500 metres in search of prey. In this reconstruction at the Canterbury Museum, a mosasaur attacks a long-necked plesiosaur, another marine reptile.*

> ### Did you know?
>
> In harmony with their world, dolphins are streamlined to move through the water with ease. Unlike sharks, which move their tails side-to-side, dolphins propel themselves with up-and-down movements of their tail flukes.

*In New Zealand, common dolphins are seen in sometimes large numbers in northern waters which they prefer to the cooler oceans further south.*

*Hector's dolphin is easily recognised by its rounded dorsal fin. To stop these dolphins from being caught in gill nets, scientists have been experimenting with acoustic 'pingers', alerting dolphins not using their own sonar to turn it on so they can detect the nets. Early results have been promising.*

Most live around Banks Peninsula, Te Waewae Bay in Southland or on the West Coast between Karamea and Okarito. They rarely move away from their home patch and are usually seen no more than a few hundred metres offshore, in pairs or groups of up to 12.

Between 1984 and 1988 some 230 Hector's dolphins were recorded killed in set nets along the Canterbury coastline. As a result the New Zealand Government, in the face of strenuous opposition, introduced a ban on set nets in the region. Tour operators now conduct popular Hector's dolphin tours of Akaroa Harbour.

## Common dolphin

As indicated by their name, common dolphins (*Delphinus delphis*) are one of the most widely occurring of the world's dolphins. In New Zealand waters this streamlined species can be seen in coastal waters in schools of several thousand.

The common dolphin is recognisable by its colouring—dark grey to black with a purplish sheen on the back coming down to a point on each side below the dorsal fin. The belly is white and the underbody grey at the back, changing to creamy-brown at the front. Around the eye it sports a distinctive patch. When moving at speed, the common dolphin makes long, smoothly arcing leaps. Gregarious by nature, it is especially playful, going out of its way to ride on the bow wave of a boat.

## Dusky dolphin

Duskies (*Lagenorhynchus obscurus*) prefer the colder waters of New Zealand, south of Cook Strait. Around Kaikoura, where they are the most common dolphin, they have become a popular tourist attraction. Their appeal lies not only in their friendliness to humans, but also their acrobatic abilities. The dusky is a relatively small

### NEW ZEALAND'S DOLPHINS

Common dolphin (*Delphinus delphis*)
Bottlenose dolphin (*Tursiops truncatus*)
Striped dolphin (*Stenella caeruleoalba*)
Spotted dolphin (*S. attenuata*)
Dusky dolphin (*Lagenorhynchus obscurus*)
Hourglass dolphin (*L. cruciger*)
Southern right whale dolphin (*Lissodelphis peronii*)
Risso's dolphin (*Grampus griseus*)
Hector's dolphin (*Cephalorhynchus hectori*)

## A dolphin's best friend

New Zealand appears to have been especially blessed by the number of dolphins that have enjoyed interacting with humans, including the Risso's dolphin Pelorus Jack (1888–1912), Opo (1955–56), Horace (1978–79) and Maui (1992–94). For 24 years Pelorus Jack guided ships between Nelson and Wellington, cavorting around their bows or riding their pressure waves just below the surface.

Opo, named after the Northland town of Opononi where the dolphin appeared in 1955, established a special relationship with some children, allowing them to touch her and ride on her back. All that summer, visitors flocked to Opononi to watch the dolphin at play. The following year Opo was found dead, possibly from stranding or the victim of an accidental gelignite explosion.

The most recent high-profile relationship of a dolphin with humans has been that of a female bottlenose named Maui, who from 1992 exuberantly enjoyed the company of divers and boaties around Kaikoura and then later in the Marlborough Sounds.

2 metres in length and has no beak. It travels in groups of 20–50 and is a fast swimmer, easily reaching speeds of up to 20 knots.

### Bottlenose dolphin

The broad 'grin' of the bottlenose (*Tursiops truncatus*) endears this dolphin to humans. Opo was a bottlenose, like TV's Flipper and the famous dolphins of Monkey Mia in Western Australia. At nearly 4 metres in length, and reaching weights of 275 kg, the bottlenose is one of the largest dolphins in the Australasian region. One pod of about 60 lives permanently in Doubtful Sound, unusually far south for this species. Here it is close to the limits of its ecological tolerance.

# Dotterels

Few New Zealand birds have as precarious an existence as the New Zealand dotterel—a large claim to make in a country of so many endangered birds. This small sandy-shore bird has the odds stacked against it, and the population figures tell the story.

Records from the mid-19th century show that dotterels were widespread throughout the country, even breeding on the braided rivers of the South Island. Since this time the situation has changed dramatically: there are now two populations, one in the North Island (*Charadrius aquilonius*) from Northland to an area South of East Cape, which numbers around 1350, and the other on Stewart Island (*C. obscurus*) with a total of about 100. Other than a few wintering-over birds near Bluff (see map page 102), the New Zealand dotterel has completely disappeared from the South Island.

Until recently the North Island and Stewart Island dotterels were regarded as the same species but they are now described as subspecies. There are obvious physical differences between the two: because it lives in a colder climate, the Stewart Island subspecies is larger, heavier and darker than its northern cousin.

In the north the New Zealand dotterel mostly lives and breeds along sandy beaches where in spring its well-camouflaged eggs lie in the merest scrape of a nest. Prime areas of dotterel real estate, the beaches provide all-round visibility and

*New Zealand dotterel nests, no more than shallow indentations in the sand, are often hard to see. People jeopardise breeding when they disturb the birds because when the parent has to leave the nest, the eggs are exposed to the elements.*

proximity to good feeding grounds. If the location is suitable, the dotterels are not too fussy about who their neighbours are—they have been observed breeding in harbour dredgings, oil refinery grounds and beside airport runways.

Under natural conditions the dotterel often risks losing its nest, for example in high tides during cyclones. But two further factors have combined to threaten the northern New Zealand dotterel's future: human disturbance and predation. As sandy beaches have been developed for housing and ports, or planted in pine trees, the dotterel's habitat has been squeezed out. In areas where it continues to breed, humans disturb it when taking themselves or the dog for a walk.

Once disturbed, dotterels typically leave the nest and try to lure the invader away. In doing so, however, they run the risk of allowing the eggs to cool off or overheat (if the sun is out) while they are absent.

Marauding animals such as cats, rats and hedgehogs eat dotterel eggs and chicks. At Tawharanui just north of Auckland, regional park staff have killed 400 hedgehogs in 4 years, yet eggs continue to be lost to hedgehogs. Since the mid-

**Did you know?**

Adult dotterels pretend to be injured, trailing an apparently broken wing along the ground, to lure a predator away from the nest. Before starting the display, the dotterel moves furtively away from the nest so as not to alert its enemy to the nest's location. Once the predator has been enticed sufficiently far, the bird flies off to safety.

1980s groups such as the Royal Forest and Bird Protection Society have attempted to rescue New Zealand's remaining dotterels by fencing off nesting areas and appointing voluntary wardens during the breeding season. It is too soon to judge whether these efforts are succeeding.

# Dotterel territory

New Zealand dotterels live in two widely separated areas. Interestingly, since 1990, North Island dotterels have nested south of the previously noted limit at East Cape.

Stewart Island's dotterels gather in three flocks. One flock winters on the South Island near Bluff, a second commutes between Mason Bay and The Neck, and the third is at Cooks Arm in the south of the island. The three main breeding areas are at Mount Anglem, Mount Rakeahua and Table Hill.

Ninety Mile Beach

East Cape

STEWART ISLAND

Mt Anglem

Bluff

Mason Bay

Mt Rakeahua

The Neck

Table Hill

Cooks Arm

*Larger and darker than the northern New Zealand dotterel, its southern cousin nests on the top of Stewart Island mountains. Since conservationists started cat trapping in the mid-1990s, the Stewart Island population has increased from a critical low of 60 to near 100.*

*A mere scrape in the sand, the nest of the New Zealand dotterel offers little security from the myriad dangers facing this vulnerable species.*

Further south, the Stewart Island population is menaced by cats rather than humans, for the areas where the dotterel lives and breeds are little affected directly by people. In 1955 there were around 218 birds but by 1992–93 the number had fallen to 60. The Stewart Island dotterel chooses the inhospitably cold summits of Mount Anglem, Mount Rakeahua and Table Hill to nest. Just why cats have become a problem for nesting birds in the last decade is not clear as cats have been on the island for 150 years. However, the good news is that following intensive cat trapping, the dotterel population has bounced back to the 100 mark. The longevity of the New Zealand dotterel is possibly a factor in why it has hung on. The oldest bird recorded lived longer than 31 years; there is a disputed age of 42 for another.

Two other species of dotterel which breed in New Zealand—the banded dotterel (*C. bicinctus*) and the black-fronted dotterel (*C. melanops*)—are in a less perilous situation. About 50 000 banded dotterel live mainly in the South Island, 30 000 of which migrate to Australia in March. The black-fronted dotterel expanded out from Australia to begin breeding here in the 1950s. Today its population is 1700 and growing, concentrated around Hawke's Bay, the lower North Island, and the South Island's east coast.

# Dragonflies

Like many other insects, dragonflies have large compound eyes, composed of separate units, to help them catch prey on the wing. Certain moths and dragonflies have as many as 28 000 units in each eye, each unit complete with lens and light-sensitive retina. Flexible necks also give dragonflies excellent all-round vision.

In summer dragonflies patrol lakes and rivers on the lookout for suitable insects to eat. Once something is spotted they seize the prey with their legs then swiftly devour it with their powerful mandibles.

Dragonflies and their relatives the damselflies have teeth (hence their family name Odonata, from the Greek for tooth). New Zealand has 11 species of dragonflies and six of damselflies. Dragonflies are larger and spread their wings when they are resting, whereas damselflies fold their wings loosely over their body.

The two insects have a similar life-cycle. Instead of becoming pupae, the eggs hatch into larvae or nymphs which live in fresh water and have a unique adaptation—a 'mask' or hinged lower lip with pincers attached. When the nymph spots a potential victim, the lower lip unfolds,

*Dragonflies and damselflies (such as this common redcoat damselfly) have prominent compound eyes made up of thousands of individual eyes that give the insect all-round vision and enable it to spot the smallest movement of prey.*

## *— Dragonfly sex —*

**D**ragonflies and damselflies are unique in the way they mate. The male must first deposit sperm in a genital pocket under his abdomen, then grasp the female behind her head so the two can curl their bodies around, forming a wheel. Dragonflies can often be seen flying in tandem, copulating, while the female deposits eggs on the water or in the tissues of aquatic plants.

flicking out to hook the prey with the pincers. Nymphs are voracious feeders, eating insects, tadpoles and even small fish; in their turn they are the target of predators such as frogs, birds and trout. Finally emerging from the water, the nymph splits its skin to reveal the adult insect. When its wings have dried and hardened, the dragonfly is ready to skim away.

The best-known native dragonfly is the giant black and bright yellow 'devil's darning needle' (*Uropetala carovei*), so named because in olden days a troublemaker was threatened with having his ears sewn up by the insect. Large though this insect may be, with a wingspan of 130 mm, 275 million years ago a species of dragonfly boasted a massive 700-mm wingspan.

Two species of native damselfly, the red and blue (*Xanthocenemis zealandica* and *Austrolestes colensonis*), are often seen during summer flashing vivid scarlet and electric blue over the surface of water as they search for prey.

Dragonflies are the fastest of all insects, capable of cruising at 40 km/h and increasing their speed in bursts to 58 km/h. They can also hover and make quick turns up, down or sideways—no other insects match their agility.

# Ducks

The term 'duck' covers nine species in New Zealand, though not every one of them is called a duck. Shelducks, teals, shovelers and scaups are all part of the duck family, along with the more common species such as mallard and grey ducks.

Around South Island high-country rivers and lakes, and North Island pastureland, paradise shelducks give themselves away by their characteristic calls: a deep 'zonk zonk' from the male and a shrill 'zeek zeek' from the female. In comparison with other endemic ducks, the paradise shelduck (more commonly known as the paradise duck) has gained from forest clearance. It declined during the 19th century, mostly because hunters declared open season on it, but stricter hunting controls have enabled paradise duck numbers to climb. A 1981 census recorded 70 000 in the North Island and 50 000 in the South Island, and their numbers have continued to increase.

Unusually among ducks, the female paradise duck is more eye-catching than the male, her pure white head contrasting with her rich orange-chestnut body. The male's head is almost black, his body dark grey.

The endemic scaup is best noted for its ability to dive. Smaller than other ducks, with what one commentator has described as a 'rounded toy-rubber-duckie profile', the scaup inhabits deep South Island lakes and North Island hydro and dune lakes. It numbers around 20 000.

An introduced species, the mallard has swiftly become New Zealand's most common duck with a population of around 3 million, although that

*Diving birds such as the scaup have special soft lenses in their eyes which allow them to focus below the surface.*

*Paradise duck pairs stay together for life, even if it is a brief one—life expectancy is just 2.3 years. Female paradise ducks have an unmistakable white head and chestnut-coloured body.*

figure has dropped from the high of 5 million recorded in the mid-1980s.

The mallard's success has been at the expense of the native grey duck which has declined dramatically. Although wetland drainage and the loss of other wild places has taken its toll on grey ducks, the bigger, more adaptable mallard has prevented grey ducks colonising farm dams and city parks. Mallards have simply outcompeted greys for the new habitat.

Mallards and grey ducks interbreed. At present about 40 percent of the combined mallard-grey duck population are birds of hybrid origin.

(See also Blue duck, page 71 and Brown teal, page 73.)

## NEW ZEALAND'S DUCKS

**Endemic**
Paradise shelduck (*Tadorna variegata*)
Blue duck (*Hymenolaimus malacorhynchus*)
Brown teal (*Anas* species)
New Zealand scaup (*Aythya novaeseelandiae*)

**Native**
Grey duck (*Anas superciliosa*)
Grey teal (*A. gracilis*)
Australasian shoveler (*A. rhynchotis*)
Chestnut-breasted shelduck (*Tadorna tadornoides*)

**Introduced**
Mallard (*A. platyrhynchos*)

# Earthquakes

New Zealand is not known as 'the shaky isles' for nothing. Every year thousands of earthquakes, most not felt, occur as the massive Pacific plate and the Indo–Australian plate jostle against each other. Stressed to breaking point, rocks within the plates eventually give way with a jolt, relieving the stress but making the earth shake, with occasionally catastrophic effects.

New Zealand earthquakes are caused in a more complex fashion than in many other parts of the world. There are two processes at work: one of the plates sinking under the other (subduction); and the plates sliding sideways past each other. The Alpine Fault results from the latter process. (See page 134.) In New Zealand's main seismic region (from the Kermadecs to the upper third of the South Island), the Indo-Australian plate rides over the Pacific plate, but from Fiordland south the reverse happens.

As a result of these massive geological pressures, the central volcanic region is stretching at 7–8 mm a year. If an event occurred every 200 years on the scale of the 1987 Edgecumbe earthquake, when the two sides of the main fault moved apart by 1.5 metres, in 1 million years the Rangitaiki Plains would be 8 km wider at the coast.

A shock of Richter magnitude 6 or above occurs on average once a year in New Zealand, magnitude 7 once in a decade, and magnitude 8 only about once a century. Nevertheless, New Zealand's earthquakes are not as severe or continuous as in many other countries. Most earthquakes here are shallow, originating within the Earth's crust, which has an average thickness of 35 km, and most occur within the Axial Tectonic belt running through central New Zealand. Large earthquakes are 10 times more likely to occur in this belt than outside it. (See also page 377.)

*The most damaging earthquake in New Zealand's recent history hit an unsuspecting Napier at 10.47am, 3 February 1931, resulting in the loss of 256 lives.*
*(Inset) Buckled railway lines and a toppled locomotive were powerful testimony to the force of the 'quake that shook Edgecumbe in 1987.*

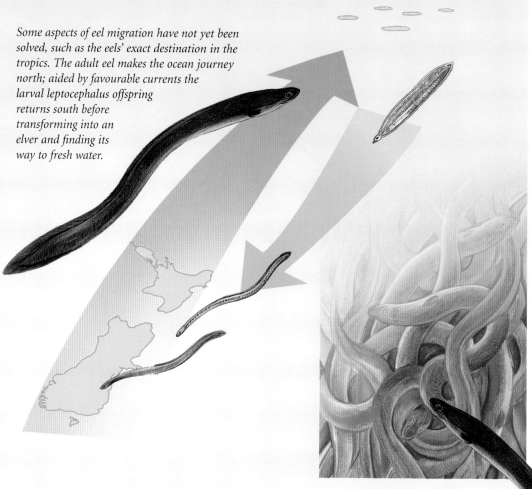

Some aspects of eel migration have not yet been solved, such as the eels' exact destination in the tropics. The adult eel makes the ocean journey north; aided by favourable currents the larval leptocephalus offspring returns south before transforming into an elver and finding its way to fresh water.

## The epic journey of eels ...

For decades a New Zealand eel will remain in a river, lake or wetland before beginning one of the most intriguing animal migrations, travelling to the tropical Pacific to spawn and die. Just what triggers their urge to do so is unknown. The average age at which a long-finned male migrates is 23 years, a female 34. Short-finned males begin the journey at 14 years and females at 22.

Before they start their 5000-km journey, both species change shape, becoming more streamlined. Their eyes enlarge, probably in order to see better in the dim light of the ocean depths. Sex organs grow and fat reserves diminish. It is believed that they do not feed during their arduous trip.

Some scientists believe that the short-finned eel spawns northeast of Samoa and the long-finned east of Tonga. Writer Tony Ayling has imagined the spawning process: '. . . a great press in the lightless depth almost 4000 metres down. Their bodies are thin after the foodless swim from New Zealand but their bellies are swollen with ripe roe that may make up a quarter of their

# Eels

Only in the last few decades have many of the secrets of freshwater eels been uncovered, and aspects of their life-cycle remain a mystery. Scientists are still working on the great puzzle of exactly where New Zealand eels migrate to in order to spawn.

In New Zealand there are three species, the long-finned (*Anguilla dieffenbachii*) which is found only here, the short-finned (*A. australis*) which also occurs in Australia and throughout the South Pacific, and the mottled long-finned eel (*A. reinhardtii*). This Australian immigrant seems to have arrived only recently in rivers from Taranaki to Northland, but looks set to become a permanent resident. Little is known about its behaviour in New Zealand.

Different not only in size, colour and shape, the long-finned and short-finned also occupy distinct habitats, the former preferring streams and rivers sometimes quite a distance inland, while the latter is mainly restricted to lowland rivers, lakes and wetlands.

The long-finned is so named because its dorsal (top) fin is longer than its anal (bottom) fin, whereas the short-finned species has fins almost the same length. Long-fins are brown or grey-black, whereas short-fins are an olive-green on the back and white on the belly. The long-finned eel is the larger. Reliable reports describe females measuring 1.75 metres and weighing 24 kg, while

*These eels were being prepared for drying at Lake Forsyth (Wairewa) near Christchurch, 1948. Eels were preserved by smoking over slow-burning fires then hung out to dry in the sun and wind.*

more doubtful accounts have claimed weights of as much as 50 kg for females.

However, commercial fishing means the days of such giant eels are past, at least for the meantime. Few eels are heavier than 10 kg today.

Eels are prodigious climbers. Elvers (young eels) making their way up-river have been recorded climbing the 43-metre Arapuni dam on

## ... *10 000 km through ocean and river*

entire bodyweight. The spawning eels probably intertwine to help squeeze out their eggs and sperm, maybe hundreds of eels in a single spawning mass, each shedding thousands of eggs and millions of sperm into the water to mingle and fertilise. Finally, with their sexual products spent, their bodies battered and exhausted of energy, the eels die.'

Once fertilised, the eggs hatch into a larval stage called a leptocephalus, a leaf-like larva only 60 mm in length which floats on ocean currents and possibly swims for as long as

15 months before reaching New Zealand. Near the coast, the leptocephalus transforms into a 'glass' eel, a slender transparent form of the fish that makes its way inland up rivers. It is believed that the scent of fresh water may provide the catalyst for this transformation.

After a few days in fresh water the glass eels begin to take on a darker colouring and to develop a stomach and intestines. They are now elvers, the stage before becoming an adult eel, and begin to migrate up rivers to their penultimate destination.

*Long-finned eels live the longest of the three species in New Zealand. Some individuals are cannibals; a 2-kg eel caught in Lake Brunner had a 0.5-kg eel in its stomach.*

the Waikato River. Waterfalls of 20 metres have not deterred them—as long as they can find a damp surface and they are not heavier than 5 grams, elvers will find a way up.

Considered by Maori to be the progeny of supernatural beings, eels were a diet staple, particularly south of Banks Peninsula where kumara was hard to grow. In late summer and autumn, during the annual migration from lakes such as Forsyth (Wairewa) or Ellesmere (Waihora) near Christchurch, Maori would dig channels in which they captured thousands of eels which could be preserved for months by smoking and drying in the sun.

---

> ### Did you know?
>
> Eels may be among the longest-living animals; a 10-kg eel could be as old as 60–70 years. Scientist Don Jellyman of the National Institute of Water and Atmospheric Research has found eels in Lake Rotoiti with an estimated age of more than 100 years.

At present about 1300 tonnes of eels are harvested commercially every year. Scientists are attempting to spawn eels in captivity as stock for farming and for releasing into rivers and lakes. So far they have managed to spawn them, but have failed to rear larvae beyond a few days. If the work succeeds, hundreds of thousands of elvers will be released into hydro lakes.

# Falcon

A jet-fighter among birds of prey, the falcon (*Falco novaeseelandiae*) usually downs its prey on the wing, employing aerial manoeuvres which demand precise aerobatic skills.

One of two New Zealand raptors, the falcon waits on a perch until it sights its quarry, then becomes a sleek, narrow projectile, diving in what is called a stoop to capture prey with its sharp talons. A stooping falcon can attain speeds of 180 km/h, killing victims before they know what has hit them. In contrast to the falcon's hunting method, the Australasian harrier (see page 152), the other New Zealand raptor, soars above the ground before attacking prey.

*So honed are its hunting skills that the 500-gram falcon is capable of killing a 3-kg takahe.*

In tussock country falcons prey mostly on sky-larks, pipits, yellowhammers, finches, thrushes, blackbirds and starlings. In forest they catch mice, rats, silvereyes and warblers. Unlike harriers they do not have a taste for carrion. While the female guards the chicks, the male catches the food, taking it to a 'plucking post' 50–200 metres out of sight of the nest. He then gives the food to the female who alone feeds the two or three chicks.

In North Island forests falcons use mature forest to roost in, and hunt around forest edges. Tall rimu, kahikatea and rata are favoured as places to hide food and from which to launch attacks. Unlike falcons elsewhere, the New Zealand falcon nests in the same place year after year. Generally these birds do not roost in areas where they might be disturbed, but there have been two recent sightings of them near a house and a road.

A fierce demeanour is no guarantee of survival. Of the three forms of falcon, only the eastern (found in the South Island high country) is in any secure numbers, with 3000 pairs. There are no more than 800 pairs of North Island bush falcons and around 200 pairs of southern falcons, a form confined to Fiordland, Stewart Island and the Auckland Islands.

Greatest threats to falcons include the logging of the tall trees they use for nesting, and being shot at by pigeon fanciers who resent their prize racing pigeons falling victims to the swift birds of prey. With the decline of native bird species, falcons are more likely to hunt introduced birds, which brings them into closer contact with people—not often the best recipe for survival for wild birds.

Being a predator at the top of the food chain, the falcon risks a build-up of organochlorine residues in its system from pesticides such as the now-banned DDT. When birds of prey are contaminated, their eggshells become thin and breeding suffers. Studies of the Auckland Islands falcon have shown that it carries high levels of heavy metals, but the source of these is uncertain.

# Fantail

For a small bird the fantail or piwakawaka is a prolific breeder, hatching up to 16 chicks during the breeding season between August and January. The chicks do not all come at once, but the productive birds are capable of raising four broods,

*Did you know?*

Why don't perching birds such as fantails fall off a branch when they are asleep? The secret is in the toes: perching birds have four toes, three pointing forward and one, stronger than the others, pointing to the rear. As the bird sits on the branch, its rear or hind toe closes around the branch from below while tendons automatically pull all the toes tight.

each usually of four young. Capturing enough insects to feed the demanding young is a time-consuming business, but the fantail is equal to the task. An expert flier, its spread tail allows it to stop in mid-flight and switch direction, giving insects on the wing little chance of escape.

Fantails employ three feeding methods: hawking, flushing and feeding associations. A hawking fantail flies from a perch to capture prey it has spied; where the vegetation is open and patchy and the bird can see for long distances—along streams or forest margins—the fantail will fly through swarms of insects, snapping at several at a time. When flushing, a fantail works in denser vegetation, catching prey by disturbing it. The fantail's third method of feeding is to follow another bird or animal (humans walking through the forest are often accompanied by fantails) and take insects which their movement disturbs. On islands where they occur, saddlebacks are frequently followed by fantails because the saddlebacks are especially vigorous feeders, provoking insects to fly into the air where they can be caught by the fantail.

The fantail has been one of the few native birds to increase its population and expand its range since large-scale forest clearance as it prefers to live on the edge of a forest or in revegetating areas. There are three subspecies: the North Island (*Rhipidura placabilis*), the South Island (*R. fuliginosa*) and the Chatham Island (*R. penitus*). Totally black fantails are rare in the North Island but 12–25 percent of the South Island variety are black.

An unusual fantail spotted and photographed by Department of Conservation staffer Peter Bourke near the headwaters of the Orautaha Stream, north of Raetihi, in 1989, had a yellow beak, black eyes and entirely white plumage.

Fantails often move down to lowland areas during winter to escape the cold. In 1970 a farmer at Pigeon Bay, Banks Peninsula, found seven fantails in a shed sheltering from a storm, roosting together on a wire loop.

Maori mythology attributed to the fantail (and the rail) responsibility for bringing death into the world. The fantail's part in this occurred when Maui, thinking he could overcome death, tried to enter the sleeping body of Hine-nui-te-po (great woman of the night) through the pathway of birth. The fantail, watching, thought he looked so ridiculous that it burst out laughing and danced for joy. Woken by the noise, Hine-nui-te-po killed Maui.

# Ferns

For a temperate country New Zealand is endowed with an unusually large diversity of ferns. Most of the world's more than 10 000 species grow in the warm, moist tropics; about 200 species—from tree forms up to 20 metres high down to tiny, filmy ferns 20 mm long—are found in New Zealand and in a wide variety of habitats.

Most ferns occur in rainforest where they need constant dampness and humidity to survive. However, some have carved out niches for themselves in seemingly inhospitable areas, from dry, rocky cliffs exposed to the searing sun, to coastal sites where they are inundated with salt spray. Others grow in the freezing environment of high alpine areas.

Although we tend to think of ferns as lacy, feathery plants, they come in a surprising array of leaf forms. Climbing ferns such as mangemange (*Lygodium articulatum*) can resemble vines, the fronds of the leather-leaf fern (*Pyrrosia eleagnifolia*) are thick and tongue-like, while the hound's tongue fern (*Phymatosorus diversifolius*) is large and leafy.

New Zealand ferns can be categorised according to their growth forms: tufted, creeping, climbing, perching and tree ferns.

Tufted ferns are also known as crepe ferns. The scientific name of the best known, the Prince of Wales fern (*Leptopteris superba* or magnificent thin fern), indicates how highly it is regarded in the botanical world. In Fiordland and on the

*Tawa is just one of the many host trees on which the high-climbing fern* Blechnum filiforme *grows. Scientists have discovered that the fern's rhizomes contain ß-sitosterol, the major component of a drug used to lower blood cholesterol levels.*

# *Fern babies*

On most ferns the undersides of the leaves are covered with dark spots called sori which are sacs containing many spores. When the spores are mature, the sacs burst open and scatter their dust-like granules to the wind. Landing in favourable places, the spores germinate into near-microscopic heart-shaped plants with tiny root hairs called prothalli. These short-lived plants then produce sperms and eggs which unite to create a new fern.

Some ferns multiply by other means. The hen and chickens fern, *Asplenium bulbiferum* (right), produces small bulblets, miniature reproductions of itself, which take root when the mature fronds on which they sit droop to the ground.

*Named for the shape of its fronds, the see-through kidney fern belongs to the group of filmy ferns.*

West Coast the trunk of this striking fern grows a metre high and each frond can be more than a metre long, whereas in drier parts of the country the fern is much smaller.

Creeping ferns such as the New Zealand maidenhair (*Adiantum aethiopicum*) have small, delicate fronds and slender rhizomes running through the soil or on rocks or trees.

Bracken or rarahu (*Pteridium esculentum*) is another creeping fern, growing in open and revegetating areas. A staple of the Maori diet, bracken was described by Joseph Banks as a kind of 'bread'. The roots, called aruhe, were gathered in spring or early summer and left to dry. Later they were cooked over an open fire, then beaten to remove the hard outer skin before the mealy inner was eaten.

One of the most common perching ferns is the hanging spleenwort (*Asplenium flaccidum*) which grows on a wide variety of trees and in a number of different forms.

Best known of the 10 species of tree ferns is the silver fern or ponga (*Cyathea dealbata*) which has been widely adopted as a national symbol, and the mamaku (*C. medullaris*). The silver fern, which grows as far as 45 degrees south, takes its name from the light underside of the fronds which can be used as a signpost for travellers in the bush, with the tips pointing the way. Growing

up to 15 metres in height, the mamaku is New Zealand's tallest tree fern and occurs throughout the country. Several parts were eaten by Maori: the pith, the bases of the frond stems and the uncurled part of the new shoots.

Filmy ferns are a group of about 30 species found in a variety of habitats. Some are perching plants, others remain earthbound. The unusual kidney fern, raurenga (*Trichomanes reniforme*), grows only in New Zealand, forming large mats on the forest floor. During a drought its fronds shrivel up but as soon as the rain comes it unfolds luxuriantly.

*Dicksonia squarrosa* or wheki bears distinctive long brown fronds hanging from under the crown and trailing down the trunk like a skirt.

Two normally unassuming ferns gained a relatively high profile at the end of the 1980s because of an argument as to whether a gondola should be built above Christchurch's Port Hills. Both rare ferns, *Pleurosorus rutifolius* and an undescribed species of *Pellaea* grow in an improbably hostile situation in vertical crevices or on the ledges of rocky outcrops, where they are rarely touched by rain. Conservationists were concerned that these 'hot rock' ferns would be adversely affected by a gondola built on the Mount Cavendish Scenic Reserve. However, the ferns continue to thrive.

*(Top) The striking Prince of Wales fern grows best in damp conditions. (Above) Signifying new growth, the koru shape of the fern has become the central motif in many New Zealand logo designs.*

# Fernbird

So secretive is the North and South Island fernbird (*Bowdleria punctata*) that very little is known of it. Living in swamps, scrub and pine plantations, it is rarely seen but occasionally heard uttering its 'u-tick' call. Often the 'u' sound is made by one sex and its mate answers immediately with a 'tick'.

The fernbird is a perching bird belonging to a large family called the old world warblers. Elsewhere the birds are known for their musical songs, but not the New Zealand species. Unlike other old world warblers, the fernbird cannot fly for more than 100 metres.

Less threatened by predators, the Snares Island subspecies (*Bowdleria caudata*) is easier to study than its mainland relatives. A healthy population of 1500 live in *Olearia* and *Senecio* forests on the islands, coming out to feed among the sea elephants, sea lions, seals and penguins, where insects abound.

Stewart Island and neighbouring Codfish Island are also home to two different subspecies of fernbird. The chances of the small Codfish Island population surviving are greater now that possums and weka have been removed; if kiore are also eradicated, the most serious predators will have vanished.

*Fernbirds are more likely to be heard than seen in their favoured scrub and wetland habitat. There are five subspecies: North Island, South Island, Stewart, Codfish and Snares Island.*

*In October and November ferrets give birth to between four and eight kittens. After 3 months the young are ready to leave the area where they were born to seek out their own territory.*

# Ferret

Just how dangerous are ferrets (*Mustela furo*) to native wildlife? According to the *Handbook of New Zealand Mammals*, 'the impact of feral ferrets on the New Zealand environment is difficult to assess'. The author noted that some birds such as the black stilt and the royal albatross were killed by ferrets, but 'elsewhere the ferret apparently presents little threat to … wildlife'.

However, recent research has shown that ferrets are a significant factor in the decline of kiwi, and may well be lowering the populations of other species. Little is known about the effects of ferrets on other species because few have been as well studied as the kiwi.

Until the late 1980s there were no ferrets in Northland, the stronghold of the brown kiwi. However, following the collapse of the fitch fur-farming industry (fitch is the term for a farmed ferret), many farmers went bankrupt and simply released their animals into the wild. From that time there was a dramatic decrease in kiwi in Northland. Not only can ferrets kill kiwi chicks, they are also one of the few predators—besides dogs—which are capable of killing adult birds.

Today New Zealand supports the largest population of wild ferrets of any country in the world. Originally introduced in the Conway River valley

*The world's highest sea cliff and centrepiece of Fiordland National Park, Mitre Peak plunges 1692 metres to the waters of Milford Sound. To the left, Mount Phillips stands guard over the entrance to Sinbad Gully.*

in 1879 to control rabbits, they soon turned to eating native birds. By the time it was recognised they were a pest it was too late, and in 1903 the legal protection they enjoyed was removed.

Scientists mapping their distribution have noted that ferrets have not been recorded in regions where rainfall is above 1500 mm a year and where there are few rabbits. However, it appears they are now colonising such areas—escapees from a failed fitch farm were spotted in the mid-1990s at Haast, south Westland, and the ferret population is becoming widespread throughout the two main islands.

# Fiords

The fiords of New Zealand's southwest corner are a tribute to the sculpting power of ice. During the last glaciation which ended 10 000 years ago, gravels and boulders trapped in ice attacked the tough Fiordland parent rock, carving out some of the most impressive U-shaped valleys in the world.

That original Fiordland rock is among the oldest in New Zealand, dating back more than 500 million years. Subjected to enormous heat and

## FIORDLAND'S UNDERWATER WORLD

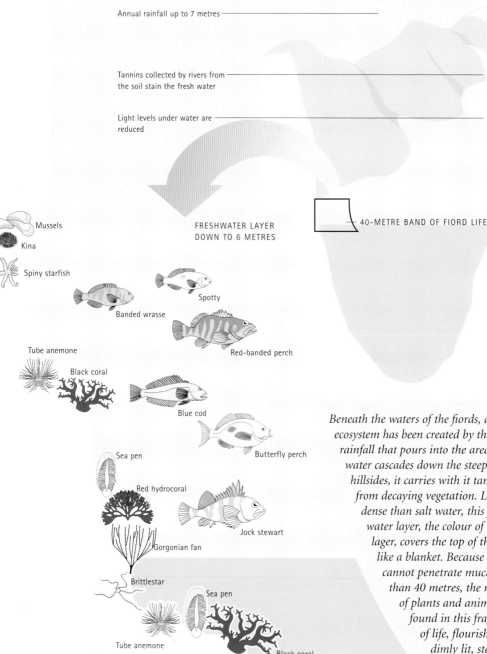

Annual rainfall up to 7 metres

Tannins collected by rivers from the soil stain the fresh water

Light levels under water are reduced

Mussels

Kina

Spiny starfish

FRESHWATER LAYER
DOWN TO 6 METRES

40-METRE BAND OF FIORD LIFE

100m

200m

Banded wrasse

Spotty

300m

Red-banded perch

400m

Tube anemone

Black coral

Blue cod

Butterfly perch

Sea pen

Red hydrocoral

Jock stewart

Gorgonian fan

Brittlestar

Sea pen

Tube anemone

Black coral

*Beneath the waters of the fiords, a unique ecosystem has been created by the massive rainfall that pours into the area. As the water cascades down the steep, granite hillsides, it carries with it tannins from decaying vegetation. Less dense than salt water, this fresh-water layer, the colour of tea or lager, covers the top of the fiord like a blanket. Because light cannot penetrate much deeper than 40 metres, the majority of plants and animals are found in this fragile band of life, flourishing on dimly lit, steep rock faces.*

pressures deep in the Earth's crust, this rock—which is a combination of diorite, granite and gneiss—is the most durable in the country.

When the glaciers retreated, seawater flooded into the troughs that had been gouged out, creating fiords or steep-sided inlets. Along with Norway and Chile, New Zealand has some of the most spectacular of the world's fiords.

Rising 1692 metres sheer above the waters of Milford Sound, Mitre Peak is the world's highest sea cliff. It is one of 14 fiords, or sounds as they were mistakenly named by James Cook—a sound is a drowned valley, whereas a fiord is a valley carved out by glaciers.

The southern fiords are longer than the northern, broader at the point where they meet the sea, and dotted with a multitude of hummocky islands. The coastline of the fiords is about 1000 km. Deepest of the fiords is Doubtful Sound at 421 metres, while the longest is Dusky Sound which stretches 40 km inland. The underwater world is famous for its black coral (see page 86).

The fiords abound with important natural and historic features. Breaksea Island at the entrance to Breaksea Sound is one of the largest islands ever to have been cleared of rats; Dusky Sound is the site of the first European building; and at the entrance to Milford Sound, Maori used to seek tangiwai, a fine greenstone.

# Fish—freshwater

Eels, whitebait, trout and salmon are well known freshwater fish, but most people would struggle to name many more. New Zealand's native fish tend to be small, secretive, nocturnal, well camouflaged, not sought after as food, and sometimes confined to remote areas—attributes which have given them a low profile.

Of the 53 species in New Zealand, six are essentially marine fish which regularly enter rivers; 27 of the true freshwater fish are native and 20 have been introduced.

New Zealand has few native fish species compared with countries such as Japan (127) and Australia (190). Habitat clearance and the introduction of predators such as trout have reduced their numbers here considerably.

*The young of koaro (below) are the second most common whitebait catch (see page 366). Galaxiids (inset) get their name from their spots, supposed to resemble the Milky Way galaxy.*

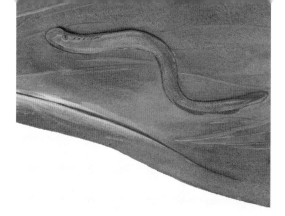

## — *Free lunch for* — *the lamprey*

**S**uperficially eel-like, the lamprey (*Geotria australis*) is a primitive freshwater fish which is best known for its habit of clamping itself to marine fish and sometimes whales, living off their body fluids and tissues. The lamprey's mouth is surrounded by a circular sucking disc which contains a host of small, horny teeth.

Little is known of the lamprey's marine life. When the fish has reached maturity after several years at sea, it makes its way to the coast and migrates up-river.

For the 14–16 months lampreys live in fresh water before spawning (after which they die), they do not eat. The males become grotesque, developing a sagging, wrinkled pouch near the mouth, while the egg-crammed abdomens of the females resemble tightly filled sausages. At spawning, the females' ovaries make up 36.2 percent of their bodyweight.

*Common bully males are diligent fathers, guarding their primitive nest sites until the eggs have hatched. The species is widely found.*

The common torrentfish (*Cheimarrichthys fosteri*) also lives in swiftly flowing rivers, the habitat of the blue duck. Over the aeons the two very different animals have evolved similar feeding structures: both have a fleshy lip on the upper jaw, while the lower jaw tucks well inside the upper, allowing the upper jaw to move evenly and closely across rock surfaces when the duck and fish are grazing (see page 72).

Other native freshwater fish include two smelts, six bullies, a grayling, a flounder and a sand perch.

Between 1987 and 1991, researchers sampled numbers of fish in large rivers. The most common species were eels, torrentfish, all bullies except Cran's bully, and the common river galaxias. Lamprey, koaro, common smelt, dwarf galaxias, black flounder and shortjaw kokopu were all much less common.

(See also entries under individual fish names.)

Galaxiids are the largest family of freshwater fish with 13 species, among them mudfish (see page 226) and kokopu. The delicacy we know as whitebait is the juvenile form of galaxiids. Some, such as the alpine galaxias, live in inaccessible areas or, like the dwarf inanga, are so rare that they are seldom encountered.

The three kokopu species are the giant (*Galaxias argenteus*), the banded (*G. fasciatus*) and short-jawed (*G. postvectis*). The giant and the short-jawed are rare, but the banded, also known as the native trout, still occurs in good numbers. Another galaxiid, the koaro (*G. brevipinnis*), is found in fast-flowing rivers and is acclaimed for its climbing abilities.

# Fish—marine

More than 1000 species of fish live in the waters surrounding New Zealand. Some are wide-ranging fish which occur throughout the world, others derive from the Indian and Pacific Oceans, some are shared with Australia or Antarctica, and a few occur only in New Zealand.

*On the exposed western side of the subantarctic Bounty Islands, a black cod swims among* Durvillaea *kelp and anemones. The black cod is one of a group of cold-water fish that are not in fact related to the true cod family. Its dark striped head, resembling a Maori moko, has also given rise to its popular name, Maori chief.*

The formidable task of describing much of the marine life around New Zealand has yet to be carried out. The world's most oceanic country of significant size, New Zealand has the fourth largest Exclusive Economic Zone (14 times the land area), ranging through 30 degrees of latitude from the Kermadecs to the subantarctics. Its long geographical isolation has generated a fauna and flora frequently different from those in other parts of the world.

Because fish are generally mobile, the number of endemic species is small, mainly fish that live in rock pools, such as cockabullies. The most celebrated endemic is the inquisitive blue cod which

is not a true cod but belongs to a group of tropical species, the weevers.

Marine fish in New Zealand can generally be divided into warm- and cool-water species, but this does not always give an indication of where they occur. For example, southern fish may occur in the north, but in deeper, cooler water. Distribution can depend on suitable living conditions, such as the availability of food.

On the east coast the subtropical convergence (the region where warm subtropical waters meet cool subantarctic currents) plays an important role in fish distribution. The convergence sweeps north from Stewart Island to Banks Peninsula and across to the Chatham Islands and is a meeting point for many warm- and cool-water species. The west coast has no such convergence and water temperatures tend to be more uniform.

Fish are best classified according to their habitats. In New Zealand there are seven:

**Estuaries**: Flounder, sole, spotties and stingrays are permanent residents of estuaries while other fish such as rig, school sharks and snapper use them as breeding grounds.

**Sandy shores**: Less productive habitats than estuaries, sandy shores are home for sand-burying species such as flounder, sole and red gurnard. Kahawai, snapper and trevally regularly pass through these areas.

**Rocky coastlines**: From rock pools to kelp forests, a variety of rich habitats support numerous species such as blennies, kelpfish, butterfish, wrasse, red moki and tarakihi.

**Offshore reefs** (up to 150 metres deep): These are gathering-places for species which are dependent on a fixed area, and more wide-ranging (pelagic)

fish. Conger and moray eels, rock cod, sea perch and red moki are territorial, moving hardly more than a few metres. Blue maomao, the leatherjacket, demoiselles, hapuku and bass grouper are less bound to the reef but still dependent on it for food. Finally, the abundance of fish attracts sharks, barracouta, kingfish and jack mackerels.

**Continental shelf** (up to 200 metres deep): This is less species-rich than other habitats, but contains more fish of each species. Examples of these bottom-dwelling species are snapper, john dory, red cod, lemon sole, school shark and tarakihi— the sort of fish that end up on the dinner table.

**The shelf edge and slope** (200–1000 metres deep): An idea of the productivity of this zone can be gained from the fact that the annual hoki catch has been higher than 200 000 tonnes. Besides hoki, species which inhabit these depths include hake, gemfish, silver and white warehou, and silver and orange roughies. Migrant pelagic fish such as tuna pass through these waters.

**Ocean waters** (up to several km deep): Bug-eyed and sometimes armed with fearsome teeth, deepwater fish such as the viperfish and black dragonfish are regarded as rarities, mostly because they are not often seen. Migrants like marlin and sharks roam over these depths.

(See also entries under individual fish names.)

*(Left) Few fish can match the snapper for tooth power: mussels, paua and limpets are levered off rocks with their strong, canine-like teeth and crushed with double rows of smooth grinding teeth. (Below) Golden snapper swim with a dazzling striped yellow and brown mado.*

# Flaxes

No fibre plant was more important to Maori than flax; only the cabbage tree came close to rivalling it in its multiplicity of uses.

There are two species of flax: New Zealand flax or harakeke (*Phormium tenax*); and mountain flax or wharariki (*P. cookianum*). However, Maori recognised and named many selections of harakeke on the basis of leaf and fibre characters. Special forms were cultivated and given individual names.

Leaves and the extracted fibre were used to make clothing, sandals, mats, baskets, ropes, fishing lines and nets. Floats or rafts were constructed out of bundles of flower stalks (korari). To sweeten a fern-root meal, flax nectar was added. The plant was also highly valued for its medicinal qualities.

The word flax is a misnomer; the New Zealand plant bears little resemblance to the European flax after which it is named, although both were used for rope making. Until the arrival of synthetic ropes, few fibres could rival flax for strength. Samuel Marsden took some flax to Sydney in 1815 to be made into rope. When the English Navy tested the flax rope it supported almost 6 tonnes, whereas the best English hemp rope bore less than 5 tonnes before breaking.

Along with seals and timber, flax was a resource sought after keenly by Europeans during the 19th century. In fact, so valuable was it that even into the 20th century, in some regions such as Horowhenua the price of land in flax approximated that in dairy cattle.

During the early days of flax processing, Maori women were given the arduous task of separating the fibre from the leaves. In 1867 a machine was invented to do the job, and soon flax-mills became established all over the country, although the machines were never able to achieve the quality of hand-dressed fibre. By the 1930s exports based on flax were in decline, but products such as binder twine, underfelt, carpets, plasterboard, lagging and upholstery materials continued to be made for the domestic market until the 1980s.

---

*Did you know?*

Flax does not flower consistently every year. Scientist Dr Bob Brockie investigated why some years flaxes flowered in great profusion and some years hardly at all, and concluded that a good flowering year depended on the temperature during the April, May and June before flowering. If the combined maximum daily temperatures of these months was a minimum of 54°C, then it signalled a good year. Over a 10-year span he found flowering was exceptional in 2 years, good in 2, average in 3 and hardly evident in 3 years.

Obviously birds cannot rely on flax as a source of nectar, but when it does flower, nectar-lovers such as bellbirds and tui (pictured) feed enthusiastically in spring.

# Flies

New Zealand has no shortage of two-winged flies (order Diptera), including blowflies, house flies and glow-worms (see page 141). The adaptable common house fly (*Musca domestica*) was introduced with European settlement. There are several species of native blowfly, including the greenbottles and the golden-haired.

The aptly named coffin fly is a small native about the size of a sandfly which breeds underground for many generations in corpses.

Once considered to be the rarest fly in the world, the bat-winged cannibal fly (*Exul singularis*) of Fiordland, first recorded in 1901, had seldom been seen until the 1990s when a population was discovered in west Otago. The carnivorous fly rests on rocks, spreading its large, butterfly-size wings to gain warmth in the cold alpine air. Once it is heated up sufficiently to fly, it goes hunting for flying insects. It can change its form of flight from that of a fly to that of a butterfly, allowing it to enter the territories of small alpine butterflies and seize them.

A variety of aquatic flies 'drive' the freshwater river ecosystem. Caddisflies, mayflies, stoneflies and sandflies are major sources of food for animals higher up the chain, such as fish. Each of these species adopts a similar lifestyle: the larvae spend months, or sometimes more than a year, in the river before transforming into adults for a brief time to disperse, mate and lay eggs.

*Cultivated easily, flax is arguably the most useful native plant. Its broad green leaves also hold wide aesthetic appeal.*

Since the 1980s there has been a revival of interest in flax weaving with a consequent demand for the superior cultivars that were nurtured by Maori for centuries. Fortunately, some growers had maintained their special flaxes over the years. Rene Orchiston of Gisborne, anticipating such a resurgence, began collecting traditional weaving cultivars in the 1950s until she held more than 60. Her collection forms the basis of a national flax collection held by Manaaki Whenua/ Landcare Research, at Havelock North and Lincoln, who distribute plants to weaving groups and marae throughout the country.

Examples of weavers' flaxes include taeore which provides long strands of silky white fibre for cloak making; awahou, good for strong kete; and ngaro, easily stripped into suitable lengths for piupiu.

Some insects attack flax bushes, making them worthless for fibre extraction. The caterpillar of the flax notcher moth eats U- or V-shaped notches from the edges of the plant, while that of the flax looper moth eats strips from the lower-leaf surface, creating 'windows' of decayed fibre.

*A robber fly sucks body fluids from a recently caught striped dung fly.*

## A special relationship

The rare bat fly (*Mystacinobia zelandica*) survives only through its relationship with the short-tailed bat. Wingless and blind, the bat fly depends totally on the yeasty droppings (guano) of the bat. Not only does it feed on them, it also lays its eggs in the guano which is at a constant 30°C—just the right warmth for the fly's eggs to develop.

Male bat flies form guard groups to deter the bats from eating them. These males make a high-pitched sound 'like a dentist's drill', according to scientist Mike Meads who has studied them.

The bat fly faces an uncertain future as its host is a rare species. In the 1960s the bat fly that lived on the greater short-tailed bat became extinct along with its host when rats invaded their home on the island of Big South Cape.

*Without the short-tailed bat, the bat fly would not exist.*

# Fossils

Without fossils, our lifestyle would be very different. Most of the energy we use for transport is derived from fossils (fossil fuels). The Taranaki oil and gas reserves are derived from deeply buried coal that formed from forests and swamps existing 80–65 million years ago. Limestone, a rock formed from the accumulation of shells and plankton, is the key ingredient of concrete.

A fossil is any trace or remains of a plant or animal that lived in the prehistoric past—ancient seashells, bones and teeth of now-extinct animals, insects entombed in amber, petrified wood. Even the footprint of an animal is considered a fossil (a trace fossil).

Some rocks are more likely to contain fossils than others. Of the three main types of rock —igneous, sedimentary and metamorphic— sedimentary offers the best chance of finding fossils. Sedimentary rocks are created by layers of mud, sand and gravel in which animal and plant remains are trapped.

Fossils can be found from sea level to the highest mountain tops. Only in the last few million years have the Southern Alps been pushed up to their present height. The rocks that form them

*Minute one-celled animals called foraminifera, the building blocks of limestone and other rocks, are preserved as microfossils.*

were originally deposited as sediment in the sea; fossils left in these rocks help us to determine the history of mountain development.

Without fossil evidence, we would never have been aware that dinosaurs once roamed New Zealand. Dinosaur fossil remains unearthed by Joan Wiffen and others have proved that the New Zealand region was home not only to marine reptiles, but also ones that walked on land (see page 96).

These dinosaurs are of special interest because so few examples of southern temperate dinosaurs are known. By examining fossils, scientists have been able to track the important changes of the

# The fossil connection

The study of fossils, called palaeontology, has enabled scientists to establish the history of life on the planet and a record of time. Each period in the past is dominated by distinctive life forms, for example, the Mesozoic era of the dinosaurs from 200 to 65 million years ago. Geologists have devised a system of dividing up the past which relates to the sequence of life forms, from the Palaeozoic (ancient life), Mesozoic (middle life) to Cenozoic (recent life). Rocks can be dated in relation to the age of fossils found in them.

Fossils provide clues to the composition of past vegetation and how it has changed through time; in turn this helps scientists to determine how the climate has changed. The most common terrestrial fossils are spores and pollen from plants. Dating back long before the dinosaur era are plant fossil remains such as that of the round-leaved seed fern *Dicroidium* (see photo above) which grew around 240 million years ago. The rock it was found in came from the upper Rangitata Valley.

The best-preserved fossils of New Zealand's reptile giants are the skulls of a long-necked elasmosaur and a mosasaur (see photos below). While fossil bone fragments of such reptiles are relatively common, whole skulls are extremely rare. These were discovered by Joan Wiffen and colleagues in the Mangahouanga Stream, northern Hawke's Bay. Both fearsome marine predators lived over 80 million years ago.

*These skulls belonged to a long-necked elasmosaur (*Tuarangisaurus keyesi; *left) and a mosasaur (*Moanasaurus mangahouangae; *right), New Zealand marine reptiles from 85–82 million years ago.*

*(Left) Traces of burrowing shellfish are sometimes preserved in rocks. (Right) This fossil, possibly a flounder, was taken from a cutting on the Napier-Taupo road and dates back 4 million years.*

last 80 million years, the beginning of the time when New Zealand became a 'land apart', separated from the supercontinent Gondwanaland. The history of plants, and the evidence that New Zealand was a land of strange, giant birds, has all been discovered through fossils.

New Zealand's oldest fossils, trilobites from Trilobite Rock in the Cobb Valley, northwest Nelson, have been dated at 530 million years. Trilobites were sea-lice that lived on the bottom of shallow seas, unable to swim far but carried around by ocean currents. Some fossil algae and bacteria found elsewhere in the world are about 3000 million years old.

When they die, marine plankton single-celled animals called foraminifera drift to the bottom of the sea, their shells joining with other bottom-dwelling species to be preserved as microfossils.

In large numbers these microscopic creatures produce limestone and calcareous rocks such as marl and calcareous limestone. Other common fossil-forming components of plankton include nanofossils, tiny single-celled plants that are calcareous like foraminifera, but smaller, and create chalk. Radiolaria are also single-celled animals with a siliceous structure which produce chert and flint when in great abundance.

New Zealand has some interesting 'living fossils' such as brachiopods which live within the intertidal zone. Brachiopods are bivalved shells (but not molluscs) which dominated the world's seas before the advent of mussels and oysters. Most groups of brachiopods are now extinct. In New Zealand they are particularly important in Devonian, Permian and Triassic rocks (from 410 to 190 million years ago).

*Geologist Hamish Campbell sizes up the third largest ammonite fossil in the world, and New Zealand's largest. This 1.42-metre monster was found near Taharoa in the King Country. The creature that inhabited the shell lived in the Jurassic period, about 145 million years ago.*

Did you know?

New Zealand's frogs do not go through a tadpole stage like other frogs; instead, adults lay eggs and the young metamorphose inside the egg sac—their own personal ponds. After hatching, still with remnant tails, they climb onto their father's back and spend the final weeks of development there.

*Masquerading as moss, two Hochstetter's frogs lie on the forest floor. The common belief that Maori did not know of the existence of frogs is perhaps explained by such artful camouflage.*

# Frogs

Like the tuatara (see page 341) and the peripatus (see page 254), New Zealand's native frog species are old-timers, survivors of frogs that evolved several hundred million years ago. They are virtually unchanged from frogs of around 135 million years ago.

Once they boarded the prehistoric 'ark' of New Zealand and drifted away from Australia, New Zealand's frogs failed to keep pace with modern developments such as a tadpole stage, webbing between the toes and a croak. Only the North American frog genus *Ascaphus* shares some of the primitive features of the New Zealand frogs.

At present scientists have described three species of native frogs, all of them endangered. A fourth, found on Maud Island, used to be known as Hamilton's frog, but is now considered a separate species from that on Stephens Island. The four are:

• Archey's frog (*Leiopelma archeyi*), which occurs at Mount Moehau and other forested areas of the Coromandel Peninsula. In 1991 a new population, called the Whareorino frog, was discovered near Te Kuiti. In total these frogs are believed to number thousands.

• Hochstetter's frog (*L. hochstetteri*) is the most widespread of the three species. Found from Pureora Forest and the East Cape northwards through the Coromandel, Hunua, Waitakere and Warkworth ranges to Great Barrier Island and the Whangarei district, this frog also numbers in the thousands.

• Hamilton's frog (*L. hamiltoni*) is confined to a 600-square-metre patch of scree, called the Frog Bank, on Stephens Island in Cook Strait. It is the rarest of the frog species, numbering around 200.

• The yet-to-be-named Maud Island frog, formerly Hamilton's, has a population of at least 19 000.

The discovery of Hochstetter's frog by Coromandel gold diggers in 1852 was a surprise to local Maori who did not have a name for the animal, although the frogs occupied a similar habitat to koura which they ate. Arthur Sanders Thomson wrote about the frog's discovery: 'All present were much struck by its appearance and they said it must be the atua, the spirit or god of the gold, which had appeared on earth; many of them shrunk back from it in horror, and some were inclined to draw particular omens from its discovery at that time.'

These most primitive of the world's frogs live in forests under rocks and stones. They require moisture but not swamps or ponds as other frogs do. Archey's frog, which lives at altitudes of at least 400 metres on the Coromandel Peninsula, can withstand periods of dehydration.

All four frog species are earless and croak-less—at best they squeak and pipe softly. Another primitive feature they have retained is tail-wagging muscles, even though they have no tail. For such small creatures they are relatively long lived, in the case of Hamilton's frog more than 23 years. But perhaps the most fascinating aspect of New Zealand's frogs is the life history of the young (see box page 128).

The survival of the Stephens Island frog, which was 'rediscovered' in 1950, was fortuitous. In 1894 a lighthouse was installed on the island and subsequently much of the vegetation was cleared. Scientists believe the frogs survived among rocks on the island because of the microenvironment that exists there, akin to forest. Hungry tuatara

*This frog, formerly called Hamilton's frog, is now considered a species in its own right. In 1997, 300 of these frogs were transferred from Maud Island to Motuara Island in outer Queen Charlotte Sound, providing a back-up population. Motuara, which became kiore-free in 1993, is also home to saddlebacks.*

regularly encounter the frog but by remaining still it avoids being noticed. This ability to 'freeze'—at least initially—when exposed under rocks or logs by day, has been observed in all four species. After a few seconds of immobility the frog leaps for the nearest cover.

Besides their protective colouring and freezing tactics, the native frogs may possess a third line of defence against predators—their unpalatability, derived from glandular secretions. This is shared with some other frogs: a banded kokopu twice rejected a Hochstetter's frog; on Maud Island a robin momentarily held a frog before releasing it and wiping its bill; and a captive tuatara was offered a live (but sick) Archey's frog but refused to eat it after a few investigatory licks, preferring some live skinks.

Since the arrival of Maori in New Zealand, three species of native frogs have become extinct, the most likely culprit being the kiore.

Four introduced frogs have established, all from Australia: two species of the golden tree frog (sometimes known as the golden bell frog), the brown tree frog and the large green tree frog. Recently a golden tree frog was seen eating a Whareorino frog, the first time predation by an introduced species had been observed.

In Australia the two bell frog species are endangered, and a worldwide decline of frogs has been blamed on an increase in ultraviolet radiation. However, there is no evidence that New Zealand's native frogs have dropped in number from this cause—perhaps because here they are generally nocturnal.

# Fungi

*The elegant* Podoscypha petallopes *forms colonies on tree trunks. It has a tough, leathery texture.*

Think of fungi and usually mushrooms come to mind, yet these are only some of the more visible kinds of fungi. Without microscopic yeasts bread would not rise, nor would wine ferment. Tasty cheeses such as Roquefort or Camembert owe their distinctive flavours to *Penicillium* moulds, while another *Penicillium* species is the source of the drug penicillin.

Most plant diseases and many animal and human diseases are caused by fungi. On the other hand, fungi help many plants to absorb nutrients, and also control the recycling of nutrients. Fungi are in a group of their own, and differ significantly from plants in their lack of the green pigment chlorophyll. Unlike plants which produce their nourishment from water and carbon dioxide (using chlorophyll and sunlight), fungi are unable to produce their own food, depending instead on living or dead organic matter for their nutrition.

In New Zealand there are an estimated 20 000 species of fungi. Of these only about 25 percent are currently recognised and named. Many of these undescribed fungi are microscopic, but there are also several species with comparatively large fruiting bodies.

*Coral fungi such as this* Clavicorona *species differ from other fungi in producing spores all over their bodies, rather than on gills beneath a cap.*

Some fungi, such as the bootlace mushroom (*Armillaria novaezelandiae*), the poplar toadstool and the beech strawberry, are edible and formed a small part of the traditional Maori diet. Another fungus species was also used as tinder for fire lighting.

The bootlace mushroom grows mainly on dead podocarp and beech trees, and also causes an important disease of radiata pine trees and kiwifruit vines. The fungus produces black, resistant, bootlace-like strands (rhizomorphs) under bark and in the soil, which enable the fungus to spread from root to root. Fresh *Armillaria*-decayed wood is bioluminescent and can be seen glowing along bush tracks on dark nights.

*Gannets make sure their nests are just beyond pecking distance of their neighbours. Any bird that overshoots its nest when landing runs a merciless gauntlet of jabbing beaks as it tries to reach its own site.*

# Gannets

The Australasian gannet (*Morus serrator*), known as takapu by Maori, provides one of the most dramatic sights around the New Zealand coast as it plunges into the ocean at high speed for fish.

With three easily accessible mainland colonies, New Zealand is considered one of the best locations in the world to view gannets. Since the first census of gannets in 1946–47, numbers of pairs doubled to 46 000 in 1980–81 and together with non-breeding birds the population at present is at least 90 000 adults.

Scientists speculate that the striking increase may have occurred because there is more of the fish that is the birds' staple diet—pilchards, anchovies, saury, jack mackerel and squid. They argue that commercial fishing has reduced the numbers of barracouta, kahawai, albacore tuna and other fish which prey on the gannets' preferred food.

Compared to other regions in the world where gannets occur (there is a North Atlantic gannet centred on Britain and a cape gannet from South Africa), New Zealand offers a relatively secure haven which would also have led to the population increase.

While there are at least 20 gannetries around New Zealand, including the appropriately named Gannet Island west of Kawhia (where more than 8000 pairs nest), the best known is at Cape Kidnappers in Hawke's Bay where gannets were first recorded by local naturalist Henry Hill in 1870. At that time there were only 50 gannets in the Saddle Colony but today there are around 6500 pairs in the Black Reef, Plateau and Saddle Colonies. In Maori legend Cape Kidnappers was the hook with which the demigod Maui pulled the North Island from the sea. It was named Cape Kidnappers in 1769 by explorer Captain James Cook after local Maori tried to kidnap a young Tahitian from the *Endeavour*.

Another area of mainland real estate that gannets have claimed is at Muriwai just west of Auckland. Here the birds have expanded out from Oaia Island where they have been nesting since the turn of the century, and have colonised a coastal outcrop.

The third mainland breeding site at Farewell Spit differs from the usual rock stack that gannets prefer. Here on three sandy shellbanks more than 900 pairs nest.

An imaginative project on Mana Island, just north of Wellington, might see gannets return to this island they once inhabited. Conservationists have created concrete model gannets and placed them in areas considered suitable for the birds to nest. It is hoped that young gannets returning from Australia will be attracted to the island by the concrete lookalikes. The nearest breeding site, Farewell Spit, is not far from Mana and the chances are that gannets heading for there will find Mana to their liking.

Each August gannets return to the same breeding site—and usually the same mate—to build a nest of seaweed and earth cemented with guano. In October the female produces a single egg; in February/March the grey-coloured juveniles migrate to Australia. Not all the birds manage the trip successfully. Each summer hundreds of young gannets are found beach-wrecked on Northland coasts. As if drawn by a magnet, 2 or more years later the goose-like juveniles, transformed into sleek adults, return to their home colonies.

*When a gannet makes its 30-metre plunge into the ocean for fish it can be travelling at up to 145 km/h. To avoid injuring itself as it enters the water the gannet sweeps back its wings at the last moment so that its sturdy head takes the full force of the considerable impact. Inflatable sacs beneath the skin on the lower neck and breast cushion the shock of entry, while internal nostrils prevent water entering the lungs as the bird dives as deep as 8 metres. Like a number of other birds, the gannet can bring its eyes together and facing forward in order to focus on prey. This ability is vital if it is to catch fish when it dives at high speed into the ocean.*

*Did you know?*

Long narrow wings like those of gannets are built for gliding and soaring on the air currents created around cliff faces. The Australasian gannet is distinguished from the northern-hemisphere gannet by its predominantly black tail and secondary feathers.

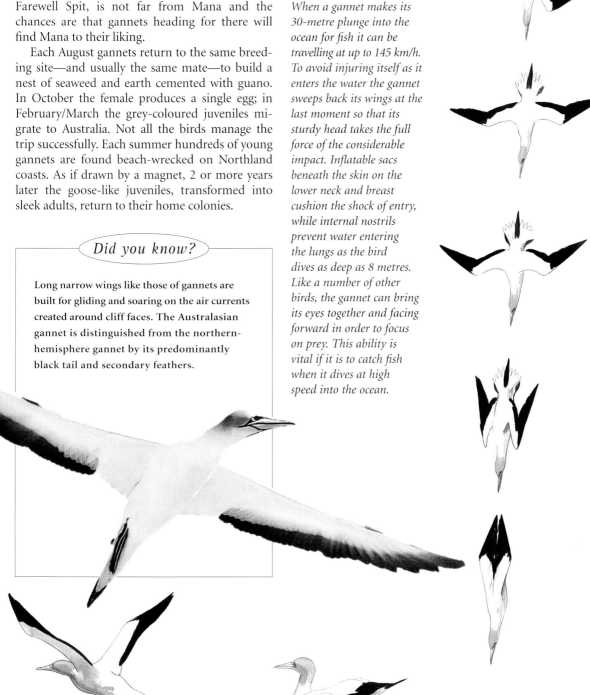

Tonga–Kermadec
Ridge and Trench

Macquarie Ridge
and Trench

Alpine Fault

Chatham I.

Campbell Plateau

Oceanic crust

Continental crust

INDO–AUSTRALIAN
PLATE

PACIFIC PLATE

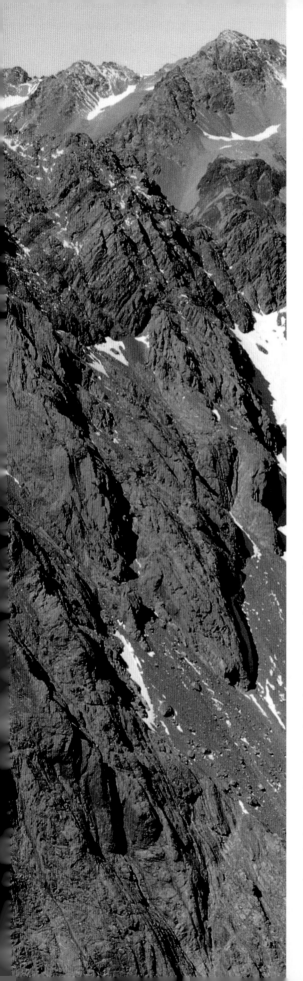

# Geology

New Zealand's geological story began about 600 million years ago, as eroded sediments and volcanic debris from the huge supercontinent Gondwanaland were swept to its coastal fringe, where the land now called New Zealand took shape. The oldest rocks (680 million years) are found near Charleston on the West Coast, in Fiordland and northwest Nelson. Geologically speaking, this does not make New Zealand an extremely old land, since in some parts of the world rocks have been dated at about 4000 million years.

New Zealand has a young, restless landscape. During hundreds of millions of years titanic forces have been at play beneath the crust, as the Pacific plate and the Indo–Australian plate crashed into one another. Mudstones and sandstones have been pressure-cooked to create rocks, then tilted, folded and buckled to produce mountains. Volcanoes have spewed out magma and gas and earthquakes have stretched apart the land or uplifted it from the sea. But land has not only been created; it has also been washed away by erosion, and covered by the sea.

If the Kaikoura Orogeny (mountain-building phase) has been the major rock and mountain-creating force of the last few million years, recent Ice Ages have been the main influences shaping those rocks and mountains. Glaciers have carved out valleys, transporting soil down to the plains and lowlands where today it is productive land. The shape of New Zealand continues to change. As recently as 18 000 years ago the North and South islands were joined with extensive lowlands.

*Formed millions of years ago deep in the Earth's crust, these greywacke rocks of the Malte Brun Range near Mount Cook have been folded and raised at least 20 km, at the same time eroded by wind, rain and ice.*
*(Inset) For the last 20–25 million years, New Zealand has found itself astride the boundary between two of the world's 15 plates. In the north the Pacific plate disappears under the Indo–Australian plate, while to the south from Fiordland the opposite occurs, the Pacific plate riding over the top of the other. In the Southern Alps the two plates slide past one another, creating the Alpine Fault.*

# Geysers

Of all geothermal activity, geysers are the most dramatic, shooting scalding steam metres into the air. These spectacular thermal explosions occur when groundwater reacts with hot volcanic rocks at varying depths within the Earth and is discharged through vents at the surface.

Few, if any, countries in the world have geysers surrounded by city suburbs, as in Rotorua. Geyser systems occur in just seven countries worldwide and are easily accessible only here and in Iceland and the USA. Today New Zealand has a dozen geysers, eight of them at Whakarewarewa in Rotorua where the Pohutu geyser—the 'jewel in the crown' of the field—regularly lets off steam among the other thermal fountains in the area known as 'Geyser Flat'.

It may take hundreds, if not thousands, of years for rainwater to percolate down to the depths where geysers originate. By measuring the amount of tritium in Rotorua boreholes, scientists have been able to show that the water ejected by the geysers is at least 100 years, and possibly thousands of years, old.

Over a century ago 130 geysers were regularly active in five major fields in the Rotorua-Taupo area. Since then the 1886 Tarawera eruption, a dam at Orakeikorako and geothermal electricity projects at Wairakei and Spa have drastically reduced geyser numbers to around a dozen. In an attempt to preserve the remaining Whakarewarewa geysers, the New Zealand Government launched the 'Bore War' in 1987, closing down a number of private bores in the face of large-scale protest by Rotorua citizens.

The draw-off from the wells in Rotorua amounted to 30 000–35 000 tonnes each day of geothermal fluid, compared with a natural discharge of only about 8000 tonnes daily from Whakarewarewa. By 1990 fewer than 150 wells were still operating, down from a high of 430. Between 1967 and 1985 the drop in natural heat flow amounted to 30 percent.

*As water collects in a geyser's tube it becomes superheated above the normal boiling point. The steam created seeks an escape route, sending out powerful jets through a vent. Once the geyser dies down, more water seeps into the tube to create the conditions for another eruption.*

200°C

250°C

300°C

COOL WATER
REPLACES
UPWARD-MOVING
WATER

MAGMA CHAMBER

The Waimangu (Maori for black water) geyser, though short-lived, used to erupt regularly up to 460 metres into the air, much higher than the world's current tallest geyser, the Steamboat in Yellowstone National Park, USA, which achieves a maximum height of 115 metres. From its explosive beginning in 1900 to its lethal end in 1917 when it killed four onlookers, this lofty geyser near Mount Tarawera led a short but turbulent existence. Today its legacy is the Frying Pan Lake from which sporadic eruptions still occur.

*Violent plumes of steam, geysers occur where water is heated by the hot earth below. The Pohutu geyser in the Whakarewarewa field at Rotorua is New Zealand's highest.*

# Glaciers

New Zealand has 3153 glaciers, a relatively large number for such a small country, from Mount Ruapehu in the North Island (with the permanent snowline at an altitude of 2440 metres) down to Caroline Peak (snowline at 1400 metres) in southern Fiordland. Some of these glaciers are small (to qualify in the world's inventory a glacier must be at least 1 ha in area and last two decades without melting), but others such as the Tasman Glacier rank among the largest temperate glaciers in the world.

During the Pleistocene Ice Ages starting 2 million years ago, glaciers were in full cry. On the West Coast they spread right down to the sea, and today glacial moraines lie beneath the ocean.

If New Zealand were again in the grip of an Ice Age, its glaciers would coalesce into one or two giant ice masses. On the other hand, if the climate were warmer many of the small glaciers would disappear. The present climate is considered to offer the optimum conditions to spawn the maximum number of individual glaciers in the Southern Alps.

From north to south, climate and terrain have combined to create a number of different types of glaciers. In the North Island there are just 18 glaciers, all on Mount Ruapehu. Not only are these under threat from climate warming; the geothermal heat from the active volcano underneath also melts their ice. Following Mount Ruapehu's dramatic bursts of activity in 1995 and 1996, the glaciers are probably retreating even more. If the glaciers are covered with a thin layer of ash—as they were in 1995–96—they will melt more quickly than usual; on the other hand, a thick layer of ash deposited by an enormous explosion will insulate the ice and slow its melting.

In the South Island most glaciers occur in the heart of the Southern Alps, between Arthur's Pass and the Darran Mountains of Fiordland. Even so, there are numerous glaciers to the north, often hidden on cold, south-facing slopes. For example, glaciers are tucked away in the Spenser Mountains in Marlborough where Mount Una, the highest peak, is a relatively low 2301 metres.

To the east of the Spensers in one of the country's driest regions, the Inland Kaikouras— topped off by the 2885-metre-tall Mount Tapuaenuku—have eight rock glaciers, New

Zealand's rarest type of glacier. Because there is so little precipitation here, rock debris mixes with ice and creates a wrinkled surface on the glacier like scum on the top of jam.

But one must go to the West Coast to see the most spectacular of New Zealand glaciers, the Franz Josef and the Fox. All the icy drama that elsewhere unfolds over a leisurely several hundred years happens in just a few decades in this rugged landscape where the ice and snow in the basins feeding the two glaciers are as thick as 300 metres.

Only here do glaciers from the Main Divide penetrate rainforest, a phenomenon which occurs in few other countries. This happens because of the huge amount of snow and ice in the Franz Josef and Fox névé, fed by an annual precipitation of up to 15 metres. The only routes for this to escape are the narrow valleys below.

Are New Zealand glaciers advancing or retreating? Photographic evidence of the size of glaciers 100 years ago, along with research into the fluctuations of glaciers, shows that since the end of the 'Little Ice Age' in the mid-19th century, glaciers around the world have receded at a dramatic rate.

Over the last century, the mean reduction in length for all New Zealand glaciers is 1.3 km. Those that have suffered the largest losses are the smaller cirque and alpine glaciers which are half the size they were at the period of the Little Ice Age; large glaciers such as the 29-km Tasman Glacier, New Zealand's longest, are about 25 percent shorter.

With some, the rate of retreat has been spectacular: the Godley Glacier has been recorded as shrinking 66 metres a year. However, some such as the Franz Josef and Fox have shown considerable advances since the late 1980s because of enormous snowfalls in their high basins over several years.

The 'tongues' of the glaciers (see page 139) respond relatively swiftly to increases or decreases in snow at their head, and are therefore valuable indicators of climate change. Scientist Trevor Chinn has calculated that, based on the amount the glaciers have retreated over the past century, the temperature has warmed by 0.6°C.

It appears certain that the warming trend of recent years will continue; already the extent of glacier ice is lower than at any time in the past 5000 years.

*At present the Franz Josef (below) and some other South Island glaciers are advancing, but this forward march is not expected to last long.*

---

### Did you know?

In April 1966 the Franz Josef Glacier in Westland was recorded as moving at the phenomenal rate of 7 metres a day. By comparison the Tasman Glacier flows at 650 mm a day at its peak, while the Meserve Glacier in Antarctica creeps along at a mere 8 mm a day.

There are three reasons why the Franz Josef, which has an average velocity of 2–3 metres a day at its fastest point, slides so rapidly: it is relatively thick, it falls steeply, and it has ample meltwater which acts like a lubricant, hastening its movement. At the time the Franz Josef was recorded moving at its fastest speed, rainfall in the area was especially high.

NÉVÉ

EQUILIBRIUM LINE

ABLATION ZONE
(CONTINUES TO
BOTTOM OF GLACIER)

CREVASSES

AREA OF ABRASION

TERMINAL
MORAINE

The snow and ice that gathers at the head of a glacier is called
a névé. In the case of the Franz Josef and Fox glaciers, ice from
the névé enters a 'throat' where the valley narrows, and the area
from there to the end of the glacier is called the 'tongue'.
Moving over uneven ground and at different speeds across its width, a
glacier is broken up by cracks or crevasses in the ice. At a point called the
equilibrium line the glacier starts to lose more ice than it gains; the area from
this point down to the bottom of the glacier is referred to as the ablation or melt
zone. As a glacier retreats it deposits areas of rocks and debris called moraines which
become the hosts of future plant and animal life.

## *God's great plough*

Not only do glaciers lock up around 75 percent of the Earth's fresh water, preventing potentially devastating rises in sea level which would inundate low-lying cities, but they also help create new soil.

The father of modern glaciology, Swiss scientist Louis Agassiz, last century described a glacier as 'God's great plough', referring to the immense power of the rivers of ice to sculpture the landscape. Until his breakthrough research in the 1840s, it was believed that the biblical Flood had transported rock and debris around the planet. Agassiz's work highlighted the enormous importance of the role of glaciers, mining rock

from mountains and dumping it far from its source. They also grind up limestone and other rocks so that 'the elements of the soil are mingled in fair proportions', as he put it. These elements, when blown out to the lowlands as dust, are described as loess, from the German word for loose or light. In a gusty norwester along the South Island's east coast, great dust clouds of loess can be seen coming off the glacial-fed rivers, finally settling down on the plains to create rich soil.

*Rasping ice has sculptured these rocks in the Waiho Valley below the Franz Josef Glacier.*

*A sticky ambush, glow-worm threads hang beneath a forest bank. The glow-worm larva produces the 'fishing lines' in a continuous process, moving along its nest, gradually increasing the length of each line and repairing those that are damaged.*

# Glow-worm

Caves, river banks and other shady crevices provide a home for New Zealand's most famous fly—the glow-worm (*Arachnocampa luminosa*). From larva to fully fledged fly the glow-worm's life-cycle is about a year, and during all this time it casts the luminous glow for which it is named.

During its early larval stages the eerie blue-green light is at its brightest, gleaming full when the fly is hungriest. From its cradle high in a cave the larva suspends 'fishing lines' of sticky beads which entrap prey such as midges attracted to the light above. Once the victim is trapped, the glow-worm pulls in the line and consumes its catch.

As it transforms from pupa to adult fly, the glow-worm glows erratically. Emerging into brief adulthood, the female continues to emit a light which attracts the male to mate.

In 1995, ecology student Adam Broadley used a time-lapse video recorder to study glow-worm behaviour at Waitomo without disturbing the insects. He captured footage of a female pupa as she emerged from her pupal case, her light shining intensely in order to attract a male. Once the male arrived, the pair copulated for 26 hours—which is almost the whole of a glow-worm's adult life—whereupon a large harvestman spider arrived on the scene and ate both adults before the female had a chance to lay her eggs.

The two species of harvestman spiders which prey on glow-worms are finely tuned to see blue-green wavelengths of light.

# Goat

Captain Cook liberated a pair of goats in the Marlborough Sounds in 1773 and another pair in 1777. Maori are believed to have claimed these early liberations for the cooking pot, although some consider the first South Island goats descended from the second pair.

If the goats died prematurely, it was only a temporary setback to permanent establishment in New Zealand of one of the world's major pests. Sealers and settlers brought more in, releasing many on islands with the aim of providing food for castaways. Being relatively easy targets, goats have been eradicated from 15 of the 20 islands they formerly occupied.

*This male white-coated feral goat sports the 'prisca' type of horn, which grows outwards in an open spiral.*

On the mainland their fate has been linked to their agricultural worth. During the 1980s farmers predicted a bonanza in cashmere and mohair fibre but this has largely failed to materialise.

Goats have a well-deserved reputation for voraciousness, happily devouring most plants including ngaio and tutu, which are poisonous to other animals. Some plants even they find unpalatable however, such as pepperwood and some tree ferns.

Goats' success owes much to their ability to eat a smorgasbord of plants, and to reach areas inaccessible to other animals. As a forest-floor pest, goats rival deer. On subtropical Macauley Island they took just 50 years to transform the indigenous scrubland into eroding grassland. Although the goats were exterminated in 1966, no forest birds were left on the island.

The widely distributed goat populations in the North and South islands are hunted using the 'Judas' technique by which a goat is released into an area with a bell or radio tracking device attached. The naturally gregarious animal seeks out the company of other goats, leading hunters to their quarry.

# Godwits

The most common Arctic wader to visit New Zealand is the bar-tailed godwit (*Limosa lapponica*) which migrates each year in spring after breeding in the northern hemisphere. Between 85 000 and 105 000 stay at mudflats, estuaries and harbours throughout the country; around 70 percent end up in the North Island, the rest fly south. Kaipara and Manukau harbours, Farewell Spit and the Firth of Thames are popular summer feeding grounds.

Leaving their Siberian breeding grounds, the godwits travel via the 'East Asia-Australasian flyway' with usual stopover points in Japan, the Philippines, Thailand, Malaysia and Bangladesh.

Just why the godwit chooses to come as far south as New Zealand is a puzzle, as there are plenty of seemingly suitable habitats further north. However, one theory is that increases in human population have squeezed the migrants out of more northern areas. In their desire to go south, some godwits fly as far as the chilly subantarctic islands.

Godwits undergo a spectacular transformation in plumage from January onwards as they prepare to breed and to make the long journey back to the Arctic. Males especially switch from a dull white and brown to a rich brick-red colouring.

In preparation for their journeys the godwits have to double their normal bodyweight. They then fly for 5000 km (accompanied by juveniles of only a few months old) at altitudes of between 3000 and 5000 metres before stopping off for up to 3 weeks to refuel. Again they have to double their weight for the next 5000-km leg.

*As the male godwit prepares to breed, its plumage changes from dull brown and white to rich brick-red.*

# Gorse

In the early days of European settlement gorse (*Ulex europaeus*) was introduced as a 'civilising' hedge plant; soon it became a noxious pest and, so widespread had it become, by the 1990s it featured as a vegetation type in its own right.

Around Wellington, Marlborough and Nelson about 20 000 ha of steep, low-fertility land is dominated by gorse, while a further 234 000 ha of land in farming use in Southland, coastal Otago, Canterbury, Westland, Nelson and Wellington have large pockets of gorse in gullies, hill slopes and valley bottoms.

Also known as furze in the United Kingdom, gorse in its natural habitat is kept in check by a cooler climate and a number of insects which attack the plant or the seed. In New Zealand, however, the prickly plant flowers in autumn as well as spring and when it was first introduced had no predators.

Something about the New Zealand climate contributes to gorse's prolific growth. In Europe the furthest a gorse pod can eject a seed is 1.2 metres, but in New Zealand a seed can soar 4.8 metres. The small, hard seeds also remain viable for 30–40 years, in that time building up in the soil to as many as 14 million per ha.

The annual cost of gorse has been estimated at $150 million, based on the loss of productive land and the money spent on control, mainly through spraying. Longer-term solutions such as biological control have been attempted, some more successful than others. In 1931 the gorse seed weevil (*Apion ulicis*) was introduced and has become one of New Zealand's most common insects. While it effectively destroys seeds in spring, it is inactive in autumn and thus has barely checked gorse spread.

Since the 1970s scientists have been investigating the suitability of a number of other biological controls. Six have recently been released: two hard shoot moths, the soft shoot moth, the gorse spider mite, the gorse thrips and the gorse pod moth. All are specific to gorse but it is too early to predict their success at control. The only certainty is that biological controls will never completely eradicate the plant.

Gorse does have its uses. It makes good hedges, holds up eroding hillsides, is used for stock feed, provides an important source of early

*Gorse hugs the hills around Wellington, performing valuable service as a nursery crop and paving the way for regenerating native plants.*

spring pollen for bees and can be made into gorse-flower wine. Perhaps it has most value as a nursery plant for native bush. Being a legume, gorse fixes its own supply of nitrogen and is highly productive, providing an ideal ecosystem for native plants to grow in. After some years the gorse, which becomes weak and spindly with age, is overtopped and killed by the native plants.

# Grasshoppers

There are two types of grasshoppers in New Zealand: long-horned and short-horned. Of the four long-horned species, three range throughout the country and also occur in Australia. The short-horned grasshoppers, sometimes described as 'true' New Zealand grasshoppers, are altogether more intriguing; none are widespread and some are quite rare.

The 'true' grasshoppers are related to Tasmanian and Chilean grasshoppers, suggesting a common ancestry going back many millions of years to the time when these countries formed part of the continent of Gondwanaland.

Like their Tasmanian and Chilean counterparts, virtually all New Zealand grasshopper species are subalpine. Of the 15 species of native short-horned grasshoppers, most (12 species) occur in mountainous areas. One of the exceptions is *Phaulacridium marginale*, the only flying native grasshopper, which occurs in lowland areas throughout the country.

*(Above) The slate-grey robust grasshopper is the rarest of New Zealand's grasshoppers.*
*(Right) The short-horned grasshopper (*Paprides dugdali*) is a tussock species restricted to eastern Otago and Stewart Island.*

Some grasshoppers are very rare. The robust grasshopper (*Brachaspis robustus*) occurs in the central and upper Mackenzie Basin and numbers several hundreds. Its decline has been put down to predation from birds and introduced mammals. When rabbit numbers in the grasshopper's habitat climb, stoats, weasels, ferrets and cats prey on the rabbits but then switch to feeding on the grasshoppers.

Only one alpine species, *Sigaus piliferus*, occurs in the North Island where it is common above 1000 metres. In order to conserve energy in their severe mountain environment, New Zealand's alpine grasshoppers spend up to 90 percent of their day resting, making them among the least active of the world's species. In relation to their lifespan and bodyweight, their food requirements are extraordinarily low; by conserving energy the grasshoppers conserve their own habitat. The introduced locust, a type of short-horned grasshopper, fortunately does not devastate crops in New Zealand as it does in many countries.

The katydid (*Caedicia simplex*) and three other species are New Zealand's long-horned grasshoppers. Although lowland species, both fly into alpine areas during the summer.

## Did you know?

The muscles in a grasshopper's back legs are 1000 times more powerful than an equal weight of human muscle.

Not only do grasshoppers have long back legs with mighty muscles, they also have a spring mechanism in their knees between the second and third joints which is triggered when the back legs are flexed. Some grasshoppers have been known to break their legs when they jump, so much force do they exert. On snowy slopes the Southern Alps hairy grasshopper uses its strong back legs like ski poles.

# Grebes

At first glance the completely aquatic grebe might be thought to belong to the same family as swans, geese and ducks. In fact grebes are of an older family more closely related to penguins and petrels, having diverged early on from the lineage that gave rise to these birds.

New Zealand is home to four species of grebe, one of which, the dabchick, occurs only here. The other three—the Australasian crested grebe, the hoary-headed grebe (*Poliocephalus poliocephalus*) and the little grebe (*Tachybaptus novaehollandiae*)—are also found in Australia, and a grebe which closely resembles the crested grebe is common in Europe.

Apart from the dabchick, which numbers 1700–1800, grebes are rare in New Zealand. The hoary-headed grebe was first reported breeding in 1975–76, but apparently has failed to establish, while there are just 50 Australasian little grebes in Northland. Both of these species are recent arrivals from Australia.

The Australasian crested grebe (*Podiceps cristatus*), population 250, is a more permanent resident whose behaviour in New Zealand is markedly different to that of the same bird in Australia, indicating that it has probably lived here for some time. Maori knew it as puteketeke. This grebe's main habitat is the mountain lakes of Canterbury, although it is also found in Otago, on the West Coast, and in Fiordland. In Australia and Europe the grebe migrates in winter from inland waters to the coast, but in New Zealand it remains in its harsh environment all year round.

A shrill whistle gives away the shy dabchick (*Poliocephalus rufopectus*), and explains its Maori name, weweia. The dabchick is now found only in the North Island, though once it was seen throughout the country. Dabchicks live in freshwater lakes and lagoons. They have also been observed to favour sewage ponds, possibly because of the constant water depth and the slightly higher water temperature.

Grebes everywhere are noted for the habit of ferrying their young on their backs, with the New Zealand species no exception. On land grebes are clumsy; they build low-lying nests so that they can virtually swim onto them, but this convenience is sometimes offset when the nests are swamped by waves.

*The crested grebe is one of New Zealand's rarest waterfowl. Because its legs are set so far back on its body it can neither stand nor walk, so spends its life in the water except when nesting.*

# Greenstone

Greenstone (or more correctly, New Zealand jade) is the country's most treasured precious stone. Known to Maori as pounamu, it was a vital element in Maori culture and economy, and continues to be sought after today, mostly for jewellery. So central was its place in Maori life that the South Island was known as Te Wai Pounamu—the land of greenstone.

Most New Zealand jade is found in a belt of rocks in the Southern Alps situated between the Taramakau and Whitcombe rivers on the West Coast. There, rare and unusual ultramafic (rich in iron and magnesium) rocks have been pressure-cooked at temperatures higher than 500°C, at depths greater than 20 km. The jade-rich rocks, later uplifted as the mountains were created, are at least 200 million years old.

Tributaries of the fabled Arahura River carry most West Coast jade, although occasional large rocks are carried down by the river to the coast. For prehistoric Maori, Okahu, Wakatipu and the

Cascade areas were other prime collecting places for the precious pounamu.

Jade is divided into several different varieties, according to colour. Inanga is highly esteemed, its grey-green colour resembling that of whitebait. Kahurangi is a lighter, rarer stone and kawakawa is dark green, like the tree it is named after. The colours are determined by the varying trace amounts of chromium and nickel in the rocks.

Prized by some is another type of jade, called tangiwai, meaning tear drops. Maori used to take the arduous Te Anau-Milford Sound trail to look for tangiwai at Anita Bay, near the entrance to Milford Sound. Because of its softness, this stone was used for carved ornaments.

From the 14th century, Maori blazed greenstone trails across the rugged Southern Alps—Browning Pass and the Greenstone Valley, for example—to transport the precious stone to distant markets. Sometimes slaves were made to carry large boulders from the mountains to the coast for working.

On the West Coast the stone was originally worked into slab adzes or finished ornaments, weapons and tools by flaking and hammering it into shape. Later, a more laborious but less wasteful technique using sandstone and water was used. Carving was a painstaking business. Early explorer Charles Heaphy remarked on how it could take months to work an ornament or tool. He noted that when travelling, carvers would take a piece of stone with them, 'and at every halt a rub will be taken at it'.

Jade weapons and ornaments, passed down from generation to generation, were believed to absorb the mana of their owners. The mere or stout club used to despatch enemies was a warrior's prized possession, while chiefs displayed their rank by the ownership of ceremonial greenstone adzes with beautifully carved handles. Sometimes thin, translucent slices of jade belonging to chiefs were used to carve the first chip in canoe-building ceremonies. To the South Island Maori, jade was vital as currency, traded for kumara which would not grow in the colder south.

In recognition of the pivotal role that pounamu played in the culture of the Ngai Tahu, in 1997 the South Island tribe was granted exclusive rights to its ownership. Today helicopters save humans the task of carrying heavy boulders, and diamond saws and drills do in hours what would have taken months for ancient Maori.

*(Above) The Arahura River, flowing in a swift, tumbling journey from the Main Divide to the Tasman Sea, is the prime source of greenstone. (Lower left) A hei tiki made in the traditional way, and an adze (right) from the Te Tipunga era, 13th–15th centuries.*

# Grouper

Halfway between New Zealand and Tonga lie the Kermadec Islands, the emergent peaks of a chain of volcanic mountains. For half the year the sea is temperate; then between December and June warm, tropical currents create a unique ecosystem where temperate and tropical marine species live together.

One of the most fascinating creatures in Kermadec waters is the spotted black grouper (*Epinephelus daemelii*). At up to 1.5 metres in length and more than 45 kg in weight, the grouper is one of the largest fish in the world.

The Kermadec populations are the last remaining in their natural state after the species was largely wiped out in eastern Australia, Lord Howe Island, Norfolk Island and Elizabeth and Middleton reefs.

Slow moving and trusting (divers can rub them under the chin, sending them into a hypnotic trance), the grouper makes an easy target for spearfishers. It is a territorial fish, guarding an area on its small patch of reef for years. During mock battles, twisting and turning around each other, groupers change colour from plain black to pale blotchy silver. The large fish may live as long as 100 years.

Because the grouper changes sex from female to male halfway through life, the large fish are predominantly males. Taking these ponderous monsters would therefore upset the sex ratio of the species. In 1990 a marine reserve was created at the Kermadecs to protect the grouper and other marine life.

*Long-lived reef inhabitant of the Kermadec Islands and northern New Zealand waters, the lugubrious-looking spotted black grouper is able to ward off the most formidable of natural enemies such as sharks.*

*Although red-billed gulls obtain a lot of food from human sources, they are in their greatest numbers where natural foods abound. The chief item in their diet is plankton, so the largest gull populations are at areas such as Kaikoura and the Three Kings Islands, within close reach of plankton-rich waters.*

# Gulls

The one seabird that people have no difficulty in identifying is the seagull. Since European settlement, many of the natural habitats of the three New Zealand species have been destroyed, yet the adaptable, camp-following seagulls have thrived, exploiting seemingly unlikely niches opened up by human activity.

The handsome black-backed gull (*Larus dominicanus*) has a distribution ranging throughout mainland New Zealand, the Chathams and subantarctic islands, South America, South Africa, and even as far south as the Antarctic coast. It is one of the few birds that has emigrated from New Zealand to Australia to start a population. Birds were first noted on the New South Wales coast in 1938 and started breeding in 1958.

The largest and the most common of the three New Zealand gulls, the black-back can be found in a broad range of habitats, from the coast to farmland to mountain tops. Colonies frequently number several thousand. Gulls make themselves at home in cities, ever ready to explore and exploit the human environment. Tame gulls have been used to get rid of snails in suburban gardens. One bird used to turn up each morning in a Wellington garden, attracted by children's piano practice, and squawk along with the music.

So contrasting is the juvenile gull's plumage to that of the adult that some people take the juvenile for a different species. In its first year the young gull is a dull brown; by the second year it begins to whiten, but it is not until its fourth year, when it has become an adult, that it adopts its distinctive white front and black back.

From a distance the other two gull species can be easily confused because they are a similar size. However, at close quarters the different colours of the adults' bills and feet clearly indicate which species is which.

The raucous red-billed gull (*L. novaehollandiae*) lives in New Zealand (and most offshore islands except the Antipodes), Australia and New Caledonia. One of the world's longest-running studies on a bird population has been carried out on Kaikoura's red-billed gulls (from the late 1960s to the present day), providing fascinating insights into the bonding and breeding behaviour of the birds. For example, 6 percent of the females bond in pairs and raise chicks after one of

*Five weeks after being hatched, this black-billed gull chick will be able to fly. Until then both parents take turns to feed it.*

the females has either solicited a male to mate with her or is forcefully inseminated. The female-female pairings are less successful than male-female, with a third of eggs hatched.

Females have a better survival rate than males, leading to a skewed sex ratio. As a result, some females put off breeding until they are 16 years old, breed once every 3.2 years (instead of every 2.6 years for males), or form same-sex pairs.

Red-billed gulls are generally monogamous. On average, 39 percent of females and 30 percent of males have only one breeding partner throughout their lives. Most gulls breed with birds close to their own age, although when males change partners they tend to team up with an older female.

The study also shows that the continuation of the species relies on a minority of the gulls. Just 15 percent of the females produce 52 percent of all fledglings, while 20 percent of the males produce 58 percent. A large proportion of females (39 percent) and males (36 percent) never breed.

The black-billed gull (*L. bulleri*) is the only gull that occurs exclusively in New Zealand. Less strident than the red-billed, this gull breeds mainly on South Island riverbeds and lake margins. In lesser numbers it occurs in the southern North Island and around Lake Rotorua. Occasionally it strays to Stewart Island and the Snares, but essentially it is a mainland bird. Black-billed gulls are frequent fliers, travelling to where the most plentiful food sources are. At inland sites they frequently search for insects and worms in freshly tilled soil, and along rivers even catch insects on the wing. In winter they head for the coast to join red-billed gulls, eating mainly small fish and shellfish.

A study that measured the fluoride levels in 127 species of New Zealand birds revealed that the gull family showed the widest range of fluoride levels between species. This disparity reflects the different food each species eats. Being generally a coastal breeder which feeds mainly on krill, the red-billed gull had the highest fluoride levels. The seasonally coastal black-billed gull recorded moderate levels, while the omnivorous black-backed gull relies less on food sources containing fluoride. While too much or too little fluoride can affect mammals adversely, it appears seabirds reach a 'fluoride equilibrium', after which excess amounts are excreted. There is no evidence of significant reductions in bird numbers as a result of high fluoride levels.

The black- and red-billed colonies around Lake Rotorua feature in Maori history. In 1823 a group of Arawa people of the Rotorua region were living on Mokoia Island, which lies in Lake Rotorua. On a raid from north Auckland, the Ngapuhi tribe attempted to take them by surprise but the Arawa were alerted in time by the calls of the gulls. Afterwards the Arawa believed that the souls of kinsmen who were killed in the battle entered the gulls, which from then on were protected by a tapu.

## —— *The gourmet delights of greedy gulls* ——

**A** supreme scavenger, the black-backed gull has prospered in the world of humans: appetising morsels from rubbish dumps, fishing boats and sewage outlets are all relished by the black-back. In some areas, however, the gull's success has been to the detriment of threatened native birds such as the New Zealand dotterel, white-fronted tern, little blue penguin and a number of petrels. The predatory gulls have harassed nesting parents, destroyed eggs and killed chicks. In 1995 on Matakana Island near Tauranga, when 3000 black-backs were poisoned as part of a conservation programme, a record number of dotterels fledged.

Black-backs also eat a wide range of other foods: they dig for toheroa, eat rimu seed in a similar manner to kereru and accompany feeding orcas, southern right whales and leopard seals in the hope of picking up choice leftovers. Ornithologist W R B Oliver described how a black-back waited outside a tuatara burrow until an unfortunate victim came out, then seized it and repeatedly dropped it from a height to kill it.

*Black-backed gulls often prey aggressively on other birds. This female is showing a juvenile the art of swallowing a white-fronted tern chick. Note the difference in plumage between the adult and juvenile.*

# Haast's eagle

Often referred to by its Latin name of *Harpagornis* (*moorei*), the now extinct Haast's eagle was the largest bird of prey ever to have lived.

The scientific name *Harpagornis* is derived from the monster of Greek mythology, the harpy, a rapacious creature with a woman's head and trunk and a bird's wings and claws.

Just when it became extinct is unknown, although it is believed to be as recently as 300 years ago, about the same time as the disappearance of the moa and the flightless goose *Cnemiornis*, two birds which figured prominently in the eagle's diet. Once its food sources died out, the eagle would have perished.

The evidence that Maori knew of Haast's eagle is compelling. On the roof of a rock shelter at Craigmore near Timaru a Maori hunter drew a picture of a huge eagle, while two legends speak of giant birds. South Island Maori told of Pouakai, an enormous bird which used to carry off people to its eyrie on Mount Torlesse, and another tale described the Hokioi, a very powerful bird which was a rival of the harrier.

Certainly Maori were justified in being terrified of *Harpagornis*. With a wingspan approaching 3 metres and a weight of 13 kg, it boasted enormous talons and a flesh-tearing beak. To judge by the feats of the largest eagle living today, the South American harpy, which swoops down on monkeys and devours them, *Harpagornis* would have been capable of killing a human. Scientists estimate it was able to down a moa weighing 250 kg.

*Harpagornis* would not have soared over open ground searching for prey as harriers do; its hunting technique was to observe prey from a high perch before diving on the victim, like the harpy, at a speed of 60–80 km/h. Eagle researcher Neville Guthrie writes that an attack by the eagle could best be described as 'similar to getting hit by a case of apples thrown from the top of an eight-storey building'.

*Descending swiftly from a nearby perch, Haast's eagle strikes a moa with deadly effect.*

*Compared with raptors in other parts of the world, harriers in New Zealand are common, most likely because of the wealth of prey, such as the hare this bird has caught, introduced with European settlement.*

# Harrier

Commonly but mistakenly described as a hawk, the Australasian harrier (*Circus approximans*) is one of just two daytime birds of prey (raptors) that breed in New Zealand. The other is the falcon (see page 110). Two hundred years ago there were fewer harriers than today; forest clearance and the introduction of animals such as mice and rabbits favoured the bird and its numbers greatly increased. Of the 23 species of Australian raptors, no others have made their own way here and established, as the harrier is presumed to have done,

although the nankeen kestrel is a frequent visitor. One pair of kestrels was seen around Te Mata Peak from the late 1980s for about 5 years.

Harriers not only capture prey live but also rely on carrion—dead animals—as a source of food. Frequently they can be seen on roads feasting on a dead possum or rabbit before lumbering off into the air at the approach of a car.

On the hunt, harriers soar between 50 and 200 metres above open country looking for the slightest movement from frogs, mice, fish or small birds before diving to seize the prey in their strong talons.

In the past harriers have been unpopular with farmers who claimed—falsely—that the birds killed sheep. During the 1930s and 40s, acclimatisation societies paid bounties for harriers' feet; despite this the bird remained abundant but it declined when rabbits, a favourite food, were killed in large numbers during the 1950s and 60s. In 1985 the harrier became fully protected.

In the air harriers are thrilling acrobats, especially during the July–October courtship period when males and females chase each other across the sky. Sometimes the male dives on the female from a height, forcing her to roll over and present her claws. Later in the season, when the female is incubating the eggs, the male calls the female off the nest with a special 'food call' and the two repeat the dramatic aerobatics. The female flies up to the male and rolls onto her back with legs outstretched to receive the food in her claws as it is dropped by the male. Juvenile harriers hone their flying talents by chasing the adults until they drop prey which the fledglings catch in mid-air.

Food plays an important role during courtship. The male builds a special 'cock nest' in swampland a small distance away from where the female will build a nest, and there offers its mate food, thus creating a bond between them.

It pays to be among the first-born harrier chicks. Not only do the parents give them more food, but older chicks will either eat younger offspring or drive them off the nest. A female parent will also stop brooding a few days after the first egg is hatched, leaving remaining eggs unhatched. This ensures the first-born the best start in life as there is less competition for food.

Today harriers occur throughout the two main islands as well as Stewart, the Chathams and many offshore islands. They occasionally make flying forays to southern islands such as the Snares, Aucklands and Campbell.

# Hebes

With about 100 species, the *Hebe* genus is the largest of any New Zealand plant grouping. Two hebes also grow in South America and one on Rapa Island in French Polynesia; like the kowhai they are believed to have been swept across the ocean on favourable currents.

The symmetrically shaped flowering shrubs come in a variety of forms, from 6 metres in height to tiny shrubs. Generally, the taller the shrub, the closer to sea level it occurs. The North Island is home to more than 20 hebes, but the South Island boasts the lion's share, most of them alpine species. Of the 60 or so commoner species of alpine shrubs, 40 percent are hebes. Many of these have obvious physical affinities to lowland

Hebe odora *grows in subalpine areas of the North, South and Stewart islands from Mount Hikurangi southwards.*

Hebe speciosa, *one of the most widely grown hebes in gardens, is a coastal species now relatively rare in the wild, being found mostly on the northern Taranaki coast.*

*A whipcord hebe,* Hebe cupressoides *is a relatively rare species which grows naturally east of the Main Divide from Marlborough to Otago. Its name reflects its resemblance to a cypress tree.*

*The large-flowered* Hebe macrantha *prefers wetter areas of South Island mountains, blooming spectacularly at altitudes up to 1500 metres.*

hebes with their well-proportioned profiles, but another group collectively described as 'whipcord' hebes bear strong similarities to the scale-leaved conifers.

Both in New Zealand and overseas, hebes are the most popular New Zealand native garden plants. In the wild a number of hebes are rare, including the spectacular-flowering *H. speciosa*; *H. acutiflora*, found adjacent to kauri forests; *H. armstrongii* from the Castle Hill reserve; and *H. ramosissima* from high in the dry Inland and Seaward Kaikoura ranges. Another rarity, *H. cupressoides*, was initially considered a conifer when botanists first came across it last century, so much did it look and smell like one.

The lowland shrub koromiko (*H. salicifolia* and *H. stricta*) has been proven to be an effective remedy for dysentery. During World War II, medicinal hebe leaves were sent to New Zealand troops at the North African front.

Some plants formerly considered hebes are now described under the genus *Heliohebe*, because their flower head is branched rather than ending on a spike. One such is the lavender-flowered *Heliohebe hulkeana* which grows in the wild in Marlborough but is also widely cultivated.

The origin of alpine hebes is unclear: one school of thought says they derived from lowland plants which migrated upwards into alpine areas; another believes they have ancestral ties to northern-hemisphere plants.

# Herons

Herons are one of the most widespread types of birds in the world, although only four species breed in New Zealand: the white-faced heron, the nankeen night heron, the reef heron and the white heron (see page 195).

Before finally starting to breed in 1941 at Shag Point in Otago, the white-faced heron (*Ardea novaehollandiae*) had been reported crossing the Tasman since the 1860s. Taking advantage of forest clearance—this heron enjoys open spaces near swamps, lakes, riverbeds and estuaries—it has swiftly overtaken the reef heron as the most common species. The nankeen night heron (*Nycticorax caledonicus*), a more recent Australian immigrant, was confirmed to be breeding near the Whanganui River in 1995. Less graceful and shyer than the white-faced, the reef heron

*Relative newcomer to New Zealand, the white-faced heron is unusually versatile for a heron in its choice of prey, from fish to frogs to mice.*

(*Egretta sacra*) is found all round New Zealand coasts, only occasionally venturing inland. Like the white-faced, the reef heron occurs in Asia, Australia and some Pacific countries.

With their long legs, herons are efficient foragers in shallow water. The white-faced heron eats fish, frogs, insects and worms. Sometimes its prey is reluctant to submit—one bird was observed to take 9 minutes and 425 prods to subdue an assertive eel!

Like aeroplanes, herons have to manage landing without stalling. They do this through use of the alula wing, a small group of feathers which

*Long legs and patience help the reef heron to stalk its prey. It will stand motionless for a long period or wade slowly and stealthily forwards to avoid alerting potential victims.*

act like the slot on an aeroplane wing. To gain maximum lift on landing, when they almost hover to touch down on their spindly legs, herons have a very large alula.

Heron nests are messy affairs of sticks in trees, which have been haphazardly created over the years. Some become so heavy that they eventually snap the supporting branches.

# Honeydew

Buried in the bark of South Island beech trees lies a tiny scale insect (*Ultracoelostoma assimile*) which plays a key role in the ecology of the forests and is critical to the survival of birds such as the threatened kaka.

Each insect slowly feeds off the sap flowing through the sugar vessels (phloem cells) of the tree. From its hard capsule the insect sends out a long, silvery thread at the tip of which lies a drop of sweet honeydew. This thread is in fact an extension of the insect's intestines, through which it gets rid of any unused sap to the outside.

Since the mid-1980s, when scientists began to intensively study kaka in Nelson forests, the interplay between honeydew and the ecology of the forests has gradually been unravelled. To nectar-eating birds such as the kaka, tui and bellbird, the honeydew provides an energy-rich fuel which is a stimulus for breeding. Insect-eating birds and lizards not only use the honeydew as a food, but find more insects on honeydew trees because of the fertile ecosystem in honeydew forests.

Honey bees feed on honeydew to create a unique, strongly flavoured honey which is exported at a premium price to Europe.

The honeydew dripping on the ground nourishes the soil bacteria, and these in turn fix nitrogen from the air. In an efficient recycling system, the nitrogen is then absorbed by the tree for its own growth.

Unfortunately, wasps have now invaded the beech forests and in a short time have become the greatest harvesters of honeydew, robbing the birds of this rich nourishment. The poor breeding performance of kaka in the Nelson area has been squarely blamed on the effect of wasp competition for honeydew. (See Kaka, page 167, and Wasps, page 351.) By stealing the honeydew, wasps have also reduced honey production—bees stay home to conserve energy and protect their hives.

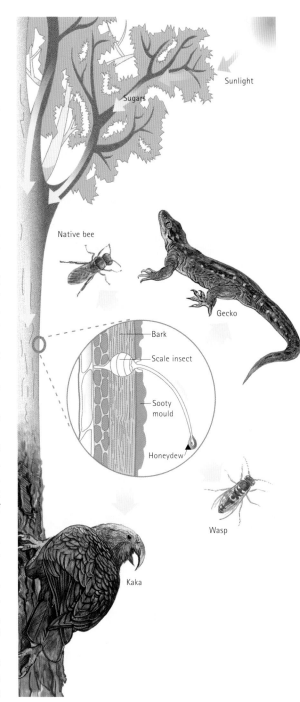

*In South Island beech forests, honeydew created by scale insects is a crucial link in a complex web of life. Insects, lizards and birds all benefit from lapping up the honeydew, and the trees themselves gain nitrogen in the process. Wasps have interrupted the cycle, posing a threat to native animals such as the kaka.*

# Horse

What place do introduced wild animals have in the New Zealand environment? No issue in recent years has focused attention on this question as much as the fate of the Kaimanawa horses.

The more than 1000-strong Kaimanawa herd roams across 65 000 ha of central North Island tussock country, the last surviving remnant of a landscape which once covered 660 000 ha. Since European settlement most of the tussock area has been ploughed under for farming or planted in pine trees.

Descendants of domestic stock released in the 19th century, the horses have been protected under the Wildlife Act since 1981—the only introduced animal privileged with this status. Fifteen years ago they numbered just 174 but are increasing at 20 percent a year, their heavy

*Symbols of untamed freedom or scrawny despoilers of native grasslands? The Kaimanawa horses controversy has raised questions about the place of introduced animals in the environment.*

grazing threatening not only an impressive tussock landscape but also a host of rare plant species. Some of these rare plants are a bidibidi (*Acaena rorida*), *Myosotis pygmaea* var. *glauca*, *Carex berggrenii* and *Ranunculus recens* (var.).

At issue is not only the welfare of the rare plants that are being threatened by the herd's grazing: the harsh subalpine environment is not kind to the horses and many are surviving poorly, in an emaciated condition.

In 1996 the Department of Conservation (DOC) planned to reduce the herd to a manageable 800 by shooting them on site, but emotional pleas by horse-lovers convinced Prime Minister Jim Bolger to grant them a temporary reprieve. Finally in autumn 1997 a large proportion of the horses were mustered into yards from where they were auctioned to the public or in some cases sent to the abattoir.

The furore rekindled the debate over the place of introduced animals in New Zealand. DOC has also been criticised for eradicating a rabbit species from subantarctic Enderby Island and cattle from neighbouring Auckland Islands. Some considered that these animals were valuable from a genetic point of view, having survived in such a harsh environment for so long—a claim made also for the Kaimanawa wild horses, but rejected by geneticists.

*Red tussock eaten out by horses exemplifies the dramatic loss of native tussock in grazing areas.*

*This adult huhu beetle will live only a short while, just enough time to lay the eggs that will become huhu grubs.*

# Huhu grub

According to some accounts, the huhu grub tastes similar to peanut butter; fried quickly and sprinkled with salt it is regarded as a delicacy. The huhu has entered folklore as the insect Maori enjoy eating.

In its adult incarnation it is known as the huhu beetle (*Prionoplus reticularis*), a species of longhorn beetle that burrows into mainly dead trees in order to plant its eggs. Kauri, kahikatea and rimu are all used, but it prefers introduced pines. Attracted by light, the noisy beetle can often be found flying inside houses.

Maori were careful not to eat the huhu larva while it was still feeding, but waited until it had finished and the gut was empty. At that stage it was transformed into the tasty titbit known as tataka. The grub was also used as fish bait.

# Huia

'While we were looking at and admiring this little picture of bird-life, a pair of Huias, without uttering a sound, appeared in a tree overhead, and as they were caressing each other with their beautiful bills, a charge of No. 6 brought both to the ground together. The incident was rather touching, and I felt almost glad that the shot was not mine, although by no means loth to appropriate the two fine specimens.' It is sentiments such as these, expressed by New Zealand's best-known ornithologist, Sir Walter Buller, which sum up the ambiguous attitude of 19th-century naturalists. The view at the time was that birds like the huia were heading for extinction, and while collectors might mourn the bird's passing, they were determined to hoard as many specimens as possible. In 1888, a haul of 646 huia skins was taken within a single month from a population in forest between the Manawatu Gorge and Akitio on the Wairarapa Coast.

Maori always considered the huia (*Heteralocha acutirostris*) of special significance. Traditionally only chiefs were allowed to wear the feathers, and the finest carved boxes—called waka huia—were reserved for housing huia feathers. In the European era such traditions became corrupted so that more and more people claimed the right to wear the feathers.

Prior to European settlement the huia's range had already contracted, because of hunting, habitat destruction and the effects of kiore, to the lower half of the North Island. A wave of new predators, more habitat destruction and collecting for museums or wealthy people's drawing rooms were factors that spelled doom for the trusting bird. The beginning of the end was when a Maori guide placed a feather in the Duke of York's hatband during his visit in 1901 to indicate he was a great chief. Unfortunately the significance of the gesture escaped people and the feathers became a fashion accessory.

The last authenticated sighting of the huia was in 1907 but reports persisted into the 1920s of birds resembling huia being spotted behind York Bay, Wellington.

## The right tools for the job

*The female huia's long curved beak is markedly different from the male's perfectly straight beak.*

One of the huia's main claims to fame—that it was the only bird in which the male and female had beaks of different types—is not true. The bills of males and females of other birds such as the African green woodhoopoe, Hawaiian honeycreeper, and the trembler from the Lesser Antilles are differently sized. However, the huia was remarkable in the extent of the difference in bill size, with the female's fully one-third longer than the male's.

Modern commentators also believe that observations on male and female co-operation in the search for food have been misinterpreted. Writing in 1888, Buller said males and females 'assisted each other in their search for food', noting that the male worked on rotting wood like a woodpecker while the female used her long, slender bill to reach in and take a grub. 'I noticed, however, that the female always appropriated to her own use the morsels thus obtained,' wrote Buller.

# Islands

From the subtropical Kermadecs to subantarctic Campbell Island, New Zealand's islands are biological and botanical treasurehouses which offer the best hope for the survival of many endangered plants and animals. Some examples: Three Kings (the climber *Tecomanthe speciosa*); Little Barrier (wetapunga and stitchbird); Kapiti (little spotted kiwi); Stephens (tuatara); Codfish (kakapo); South-East (shore plover, black robin); Snares (Snares crested penguin).

Different climates also shape the character of the islands. Climatically, there are four distinct regions: northern islands (from the Bay of Plenty north to the Kermadecs); central islands (most in this region are centred on Cook Strait); Chatham Islands; and the wind-swept southern islands of the subantarctics.

## Offshore islands

New Zealand's islands are divided into two groups: offshore or continental shelf islands and outlying or oceanic islands. Offshore islands, of which 634 are greater than 1 ha in area, lie within about 50 km of the coast and were once connected to the mainland during glacial periods when sea levels were lower. Included among these are the islands of the Hauraki Gulf, the Coromandel, Cook Strait and Fiordland.

## Outlying islands

Mostly volcanic in origin, the 34 outlying islands are situated more than 50 km from the mainland, and were never joined to it. A further point of difference is the fact that humans permanently settled only one outlying island group, the Chathams, whereas most offshore islands have supported long-established settlements.

*Kapiti Island, 5 km from the mainland, rises to 521 metres. Rare species on the island include little spotted kiwi, kokako, saddleback, stitchbird and takahe. (Inset) Nearby Long Island in the Marlborough Sounds is home to a small number of little spotted kiwi, established to guard against a catastrophe occurring to the main Kapiti Island population.*

Specks of land in a vast expanse of ocean, the subantarctic islands lie near the limits of the Antarctic Ocean yet are influenced by warmer subtropical currents. Here the nutrient-rich waters support enormous numbers of seabirds and marine mammals.

So important are these five groups of islands—the Snares, Aucklands, Campbell, Bounties and Antipodes—that the New Zealand Government has nominated them as a World Heritage site. To qualify in this category a site must be an outstanding example representing major stages of the Earth's evolutionary history; demonstrate significant ongoing ecological processes; be an area of exceptional beauty; and contain natural habitats harbouring threatened species. On all counts the subantarctics qualify.

Southwest from Invercargill by 200 km lie the minuscule Snares Islands, haven for as many seabirds as are found on the entire United Kingdom coast; due south by another 300 km are the Auckland Islands, 62 000 ha in extent, making them the largest land mass in the Pacific subantarctic. Seventy species of birds have been recorded on the Aucklands, and the wild 'gardens' packed with megaherbs on pristine Adams and Disappointment islands (two Auckland Island satellites) are unrivalled in the region. Furthest south of the islands is Campbell, the finest of all albatross islands, home to five species. The Antipodes, a group of volcanic islands that rose from the sea 1 million years ago, soar in places to 400 metres above the turbulent ocean. East of Stewart Island, the Bounties are a group of rock stacks covered in sparse lichen, algae and thousands of animals.

*Final landed outpost before the frozen wastes of Antarctica, Campbell Island's climate reflects its proximity to the ice-bound continent. It averages just 635 hours of sunshine annually, rain falls on 325 days and the mean annual temperature is a chilly 6°C. Strong winds sweeping unimpeded across the Southern Ocean provide ideal conditions for the southern royal albatross to become airborne. (Inset) The Snares are a small group of islands with a huge population of seabirds and three landbirds unique to the islands: the Snares black tit, fernbird and snipe.*

# Jellyfish

The jellyfish New Zealanders are most likely to encounter is the common jellyfish (*Aurelia aurita*) which is harmless to humans, even though it has stinging cells to capture plankton and other small animals.

Measuring around 250 mm in diameter, the common jellyfish is washed up in the thousands around the coast. Virtually transparent, its reproductive organs show up as a light blue. Some marine animals, including turtles, whales and sunfish, eat large quantities of jellyfish.

Jellyfish are well adapted to a floating existence. Like an umbrella, their rounded bell contracts, forcing out jets of water downwards and propelling the jellyfish forwards. After pumping out a jet of water, the muscles of the bell relax. A layer of jelly-like material called the mesoglea restores the jellyfish's original shape, sucking in water for the next jet. The bodies of jellyfish are 96 percent water (after they are washed ashore they shrivel to a fraction of their former size).

*(Right) Some small fish appear to be impervious to the stinging cells of jellyfish-related animals such as this* Cyanea *species. Trevally outgrow their jellyfish hosts and attach themselves to sharks and manta rays for protection.*
*(Below) A jellyfish 3 metres long floats over a* Macrocystis *forest.*

Related to the jellyfish are animals such as the Portuguese man-of-war (*Physalia physalia*), so called because it resembles a tiny blue galleon, and the by-the-wind-sailor (*Velella velella*) whose curious name is derived from the raised part of its body which acts like a sail.

Unlike jellyfish, these animals cannot swim but just drift around the ocean. They are more accurately described as floating colonies of individual animals, all of which have a different job to do: some act as stinging cells which kill fish and other animals; others are tentacles which transport the food to the mouth; still others keep the apparatus afloat. People can suffer severe reactions when they touch the cells, especially if they are allergic to them.

The by-the-wind-sailor has its own method of obtaining nourishment: algae which find a place in the sun on the drifting creature provide it with extra food.

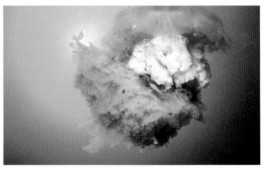

## Harvesting on high

To Maori, fruiting kahikatea were known as mapua because of the huge amount of fruit that could be obtained from the trees. It is not unusual to find trees with 800 kg of fruit. Kereru, bellbird, tui and parakeet flock into the forests and disperse the seeds widely in their droppings.

In death-defying feats of skill, Maori used to climb more than 30 metres of straight trunk, carrying baskets, before reaching the first branch, then venturing out among the thin branches of the canopy where the fruit or koroi were most abundant. The filled baskets were lowered to the ground by a cord.

Other uses were also made of the tree: soot from the burnt resinous hardwood produced a fine pigment used for tattooing, and spears were fashioned from the strong heartwood known as mapara.

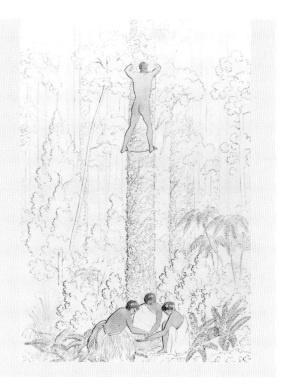

# Kahikatea

New Zealand's tallest native tree, the magnificent kahikatea (*Dacrycarpus dacrydioides*), can reach a height of more than 60 metres and lives for five or more centuries.

Like rimu and most of our other big timber trees, the kahikatea is a member of the ancient Podocarp family (characterised by seed suspended on a fleshy foot; see page 290). Of the New Zealand representatives of this family, the kahikatea is the most senior, with traces of pollen found in Jurassic rocks some 160–180 million years old. Sometimes kahikatea forests are referred to as 'dinosaur' forests because they existed at the same time as the dinosaurs.

Before human arrival, kahikatea spread across most fertile lowlands from North Cape to Bluff. In some regions such as Taranaki, where soil was rich and rain plentiful, it occurred as a component of forest on easier hill country. However, the best-developed stands were found on flood plains and in swampy lowlands.

Great walls of kahikatea lined river banks. Dense kahikatea swamp forests spread across the poorly drained plains away from the rivers. A

mighty kahikatea forest standing between the Thames and Piako rivers was reputed to be the largest in the country.

Long-lived kahikatea support whole ecosystems on their trunks and branches. In a recent study in south Westland, scientists counted 28 different seed plants and ferns, together with many lichens, mosses and liverworts among the plants smothering one kahikatea—a possible world record for the diversity of climbing and perching plants on a single tree.

Sometimes the large epiphytes, colloquially known as 'widow makers', tumble to the ground during storms, endangering the lives of people walking underneath.

In 1947 the New Zealand Forest Service succinctly summed up the prevailing attitude towards kahikatea forest: 'The problem is a simple one. It is merely dairy farming versus white pine forestry: and there can be little doubt about the decision. Dairy farming demands such land (and timber) in the national interest and kahikatea forests are therefore impossible.'

The death knell for large tracts of kahikatea had already sounded long before. As soon as the dairy industry discovered that odourless, resin-free, soft kahikatea made ideal butter and cheese

*This photograph dramatically shows the life and death of a kahikatea forest at Cook River Flats, south Westland. Changing its course from the right to left side of its flood plain in 1967, the Cook River destroyed a large area of kahikatea forest. On the fertile silt that remains, kahikatea will gradually reassert itself.*

boxes, the trees were cut down in the thousands and most had disappeared by the 1930s.

When Europeans initially sighted kahikatea, they held loftier ambitions for use of the timber. 'The finest timber my eyes ever beheld' was James Cook's appraisal—he and others felt the straight-as-arrows trunks would make ideal spars for British Navy ships.

However, trees from swampy areas were prone to rot; the first exporters of kahikatea for spars were disappointed in the timber's performance and word spread about 'inferior' kahikatea. But as colonists discovered, timber of a more yellow tinge from drier sites was the equal of any other, and was often used for construction.

Today mature kahikatea forest exists in extensive stands only in south Westland; elsewhere, such as the famed 40-km stretch from Piako to Thames once covered by forest, only scattered remnants dot the dairy-dominated landscape.

From Westland National Park south to Haast there is a total of 9850 ha of kahikatea forest in areas such as Ohinetamatea, Hunt's Beach, Ohinemaka, Mataketake, and Tawharekiri forests. This area is now totally protected as part of the Southwest World Heritage site, which was gazetted in 1991.

*Nest epiphytes—microhabitats sustaining hosts of insects and birds—adorn this stately kahikatea.*

# Kaka

The kaka (*Nestor meridionalis*), along with the kea, the kakapo and the two species of parakeets, is an endemic New Zealand parrot. Related to the alpine kea, the sometimes raucous kaka is a forest bird. There is a North Island and a South Island subspecies; the latter has a brighter plumage but otherwise they are difficult to tell apart.

When Europeans arrived in New Zealand they remarked on the abundance of kaka, despite the thousands that were regularly hunted by Maori for food and for the red feathers under their wings. Today numbers have fallen drastically to around 10 000, and fears are held that because many of these birds are old, in a few years insufficient kaka of breeding age will be left to successfully continue the species.

In the North Island they are most common in Pureora and Whirinaki forests, or on islands such as Little and Great Barrier, the Hen and Chickens, and Kapiti. They are in sparse numbers in forested South Island areas; the largest South Island population is on Codfish Island.

Kaka have been the victims of forest destruction. In 13 comparisons between logged and unlogged forest, kaka had disappeared from 10 sites after logging, and in the remaining three had declined markedly. Possums have a liking for the same food as kaka, such as mistletoe, and the birds are vulnerable to predators such as stoats.

*Compared to that of the North Island kaka, the plumage of the South Island subspecies is a richer red, and the crown is almost white. After the pigeon, the kaka was traditionally the most common bird eaten by Maori, although with its powerful beak it could sometimes make short work of snares designed to catch it.*

Five females monitored around Nelson Lakes National Park have all been killed by stoats, leaving a shortage of breeding females.

Researchers who have intensively studied the Nelson Lakes kaka have discovered that two important food sources for the birds are honeydew (see page 156) and the kanuka long-horn beetle. So prized is the beetle that kaka will spend up to 2 hours digging for the grub. One study showed the kaka uses up more energy hunting for the beetle than it gains from eating it, but the assumption is that this food provides important nutrients for growth and reproduction.

In order to gain sufficient energy to dig for the beetle, kaka sip the sweet honeydew found on beech trees, but since the 1970s wasps have largely deprived them of this (see page 352). Researchers have found that in forests where there is no honeydew, such as in south Westland, kaka dig into rata trunks to drink the sap. This food is also under threat as possums move south, destroying the rata (see page 284).

At Nelson Lakes, kaka have been fed a supplementary diet in an attempt to improve their breeding performance. Predator-proof nesting boxes and wasp-proof feeding stations have also been provided. In 1997 Sir David Attenborough launched a 'mainland island' programme near Saint Arnaud, in which 700 ha of forest will be intensively trapped against possums, rats and stoats, to protect the kaka.

*Using its delicate, brush-tipped tongue, a North Island kaka dines out on pohutukawa nectar, Little Barrier Island.*

*Only in the most inaccessible areas such as rock overhangs, where deer and goats cannot get a toehold, does the kakabeak survive.*

# Kakabeak

Modern-day gardeners are not the only ones to have appreciated the showy kakabeak: Maori also planted it in their gardens, making it likely that the wild plants near Kaipara Harbour result from centuries-old cultivations. Aside from Kaipara, the only region where kakabeak still grow in the wild is the East Coast and Urewera National Park, the probable source of the Kaipara plants.

Though widely grown in gardens, kakabeak or kowhai ngutukaka (*Clianthus puniceus*) is one of New Zealand's rarest plants in the wild, numbering somewhere between 200 and 500 specimens— botanists cannot be accurate about the tally as helicopter searches disclose new plants every year. Most garden kakabeak are descended from just a few plants; few of the wild types are represented in the cultivated population.

Similar to tutu, kakabeak is a light-demanding coloniser of slip sites. It is prone to attack from a range of insects and fungi and is browsed by deer, goats, sheep and cattle. Like other members of the pea family, the kakabeak is especially sought after by introduced slugs and brown snails. Although kakabeak come in a wide variety of shapes and forms because of the different habitats they occupy, there is only one species. On exposed sites, plants are relatively low growing, while specimens such as 'kaka king', which was washed away from a stream bank north of Tolaga Bay during Cyclone Bola in 1988, are tree-like. Flower colours range from red to pink and there is even a variety with a white stripe.

The main flowering period is from September to December, but flowering can occur in two periods, or sometimes all year round.

# Kakapo

Flightless, nocturnal and the heavyweight of the parrot world at a maximum 3.6 kg, the kakapo (*Strigops habroptilus*) is one of the most endangered birds in the world. In 1997, after the successful hatching of three chicks, the population stood at just 54.

Unique among New Zealand birds, the kakapo is a 'lek' species. Each breeding season males congregate nightly in an area and call to the females to mate. The male fashions out a bowl high up on a ridge, usually with some natural reflecting surface, such as a rock, behind it. He then develops an air sac which can be puffed out like a balloon, and starts 'booming' (see page 171). The kakapo's boom carries the furthest of any bird—up to a record distance of 7 km.

The kakapo is not closely related to other parrots and is the only representative of a unique subfamily whose scientific name means 'owl-faced soft feathers'. A vegetarian, it naturally lives on roots, leaves and fruit. Even though it cannot fly, the kakapo is an adept tree climber and a free ranger—during the breeding season females travel kilometres to find food for their hungry chicks. A further distinguishing feature is the kakapo's solitary behaviour, although this has been exaggerated by the fact that there are now so few birds. Outside the mating season, male and female paths seldom cross.

Prior to human arrival the kakapo was widespread throughout New Zealand. By feeding at night it avoided being attacked by Haast's eagle (see page 151) and if it hid in trees by day it was well camouflaged. Since then humans, dogs, cats, stoats and rats have preyed on it, and deer and possums have eaten its favoured foods. Being a ground nester it proved easy prey for such predators. Even until the late 19th century kakapo were still in central North Island forests but swiftly they retreated to Fiordland, Stewart Island and forests west of the Southern Alps.

Explorer Charlie Douglas wrote of the ease with which they were captured: '. . . they could be caught in the moonlight, when on the low scrub, by simply shaking the tree or bush until they tumbled on the ground, something like shaking down apples. I have seen as many as half a dozen kakapos shaken off one tutu bush this way.'

*Facially the kakapo resembles an owl, hence the tag 'the owl parrot' given it by early Europeans. In Maori its name means night parrot.*

*A male kakapo does a courtship 'dance' in the Transit Valley, Fiordland. Dominant males rule the roost when it comes to breeding, mating with several females, while subordinate males can go for years without mating. One such unfortunate is Snark, born in 1981, who by 1997 had not yet started to breed, although he had been booming at a subservient bowl since the early 1990s.*

Between 1895 and 1908, Richard Henry, an early champion of native birds, attempted to relocate more than 400 kakapo to Resolution Island and other islands in Dusky Sound, but after the arrival of stoats in 1900 they were all killed. Three kakapo were released onto Kapiti Island in 1912; incredibly one survived until 1936 even though it was menaced by wild cats, dogs and rats.

Until 1977 it was thought that kakapo survived only in remote Fiordland valleys, but that year more than 100 were discovered in southern Stewart Island. During the 1980s, as it became clear the island was no haven against marauding cats, the kakapo were relocated to Little Barrier, Maud and Codfish islands.

Since 1990 aluminium giant Comalco has helped sponsor the kakapo in one of the most intensive and expensive bird recovery programmes ever attempted. At least $3 million (more than $1 million from Comalco) has been spent on breeding research, miniature 'spy cameras' and night-vision equipment so that nests can be monitored. At times up to 10 people are employed solely on kakapo-related work.

Successful kakapo breeding appears to be closely related to heavy fruiting by the dominant trees in the locality. On Codfish Island, for example, during a 'mast' (heavy fruiting) year, rimu trees produce copious quantities of seed, vital food for the kakapo chicks which increase their weight to around 2 kg in 4 months. Rimu fruit takes 18 months to mature; by feeding on the immature fruit the kakapo receive either a hormonal or visual trigger to breed, and later the chicks feed on the mature seed. Scientists are investigating the hormonal and nutrient content of rimu. In the

## Did you know?

The kakapo appears at first sight to be the most gentle of birds. However, last century some male kakapo were observed to fight to the death if they met on tracks, and if males and females were caged together, the females would invariably be killed by the males.

# *Kakapo courtship*

The courtship ritual of the male kakapo is complex and lengthy. Around their track and bowl systems, kakapo are meticulous gardeners (bottom left), clearing any vegetation in their path. Satisfied that the bowl it has chosen will amplify its boom far and wide, the male inflates its air sacs and begins a marathon booming performance (centre), sometimes for 6–8 hours a night, for as long as 3 months.

Having finally enticed a female to its lek to mate, it then displays elaborately with its wings outstretched.

future they may try incorporating simulated rimu fruit in the birds' diet, or injecting the trees themselves with gibberellins (the hormones plants use to trigger fruiting). Genistine, a phytoestrogen, is in very high concentrations in green rimu fruit. This may well be a stimulus to breed, priming the endocrine system. Radical interventions such as artificial insemination of the birds may also be trialled.

Mast rimu fruiting years usually occur every 3–5 years. However, on Codfish Island the last mast year was 1981; since then the rimu crop has appeared to be heading for a mast year on four occasions, including 1996–97, but has failed each time. Kakapo are given supplementary foods such as nuts, apples and sunflower seeds to help them into breeding condition as well as provide the mothers with a food source for the chicks.

Between 1982 and 1996 only three chicks survived to independence. Dobbie and Stumpie were hatched in 1991 on Little Barrier Island. Hoki was hand raised after being discovered starving, and is now on Maud Island. However, without human intervention during the 1980s, the kakapo would be much closer to perishing. Since being transferred to islands, the kakapo adult mortality has decreased to around 2 percent annually. In the race to head off extinction, scientists (and the kakapo) have time on their side. The oldest known bird in the wild is at least 20 years old and some probably live up to 50 years.

*The most successful kakapo breeding year since 1981 occurred in 1997, when three chicks were raised. One of the females which successfully bred in 1981, Alice, was still thriving in 1997.*

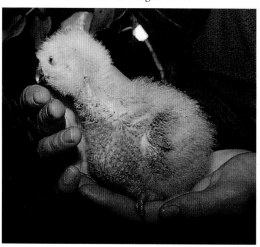

# Kamahi

For a tree that is probably the most common in our forests, the kamahi (*Weinmannia racemosa*) keeps a low profile compared to other species. It is found from Thames south, growing at sea level on the West Coast but up to 900 metres elsewhere; in the kauri forests of the north its relative, towai (*W. silvicola*), carries out a similar canopy-dominating role.

Kamahi and towai seedlings often begin life as epiphytes on tree ferns, their tentacle-like roots hastening the demise of the host. At high altitudes, moss-festooned kamahi, stunted and contorted by high winds and cold temperatures, are aptly described as 'goblin' forests.

Among native trees, kamahi bark is the richest source of tannin and has been used extensively by leather tanneries.

*Twin candle-like spikes of creamy kamahi flowers brighten up the forest in November and December.*

# Karaka

The karaka (*Corynocarpus laevigatus*) was so important to Maori that tradition claimed it had been introduced with the first canoes from the Pacific. Maori may well have carried karaka seed from the islands with them—similar trees occur in the Pacific and Queensland, Australia—but the plant is also native to New Zealand and the Chatham Islands.

Its significance can be gauged by the fact that it was one of the few trees Maori deliberately cultivated. Groves of karaka trees are a pointer to the existence of prehistoric settlements, or commemorate events such as a victorious battle. On the Chatham Islands, groves of karaka (locally called kopi) adorned with Moriori tree carvings are protected in the Hapupu National Reserve.

A handsome coastal tree, the karaka was mostly prized for its yellow berries which became an important element of the Maori diet. However, they had to be treated with care as they were poisonous. Modern-day science has identified a number of nitrocompounds, rare as natural products, in the berries. These compounds— karakin, caronarian and cibarian—are toxic to grass grub larvae and could possibly be developed commercially for use as a control.

The kernels were the important part of the fruit. Ripe berries which had fallen from the tree were collected in baskets and trodden with bare feet in water to take away the fleshy outer pulp. The kernels were then cooked in an earth oven for 24 hours and placed in still water—which acted like a storehouse—until they were eaten. Alternatively the berries were cooked in hot pools and then rinsed. The treatment removed a highly toxic glycoside which can cause convulsions or even death. A 1976 study by Dr L Gluckman showed that, after leprosy and infestation with

*Light snow-like coatings on dark foliage, kanuka flowers are at their best at the height of summer. The kanuka longhorn beetle, which bores into the plant, is an important food for kaka.*

# Kanuka

Together with manuka, kanuka (*Kunzea ericoides*) is one of the key regenerating forest trees, providing a nursery for a diversity of forest types to grow. Taller than manuka, to which it is related (both are members of the myrtle family), kanuka is sometimes regarded dismissively as 'scrub', yet one magnificent specimen in the Auckland Domain is over 17 metres tall.

Unlike manuka, kanuka flowers in clusters of white, fragrant blooms. The leaves of kanuka are soft, not prickly.

Chemical tests have established that kanuka contains the insecticide leptospermone which provides an effective remedy against intestinal worms. Maori used to treat open wounds with a poultice of pounded capsules.

As a timber, kanuka's hardness and durability have been valued for wharf piles and fences. Sadly, its most common modern-day use is for burning in home fires.

Compared with mature forest trees, scrubby plants like kanuka and manuka are much more productive. Kanuka/manuka forest in the Marlborough Sounds produces almost 8 tonnes of leaf litter per hectare annually, close to the litter output of tropical rainforest. Generally, the closer to the wet tropics, the greater the leaf fall. By comparison, centuries-old trees such as rata and rimu conserve their nutrients, producing only 3.2 tonnes of leaf litter per hectare each year.

---

*Did you know?*

If a person became poisoned through eating karaka berries, Maori custom was to bury them up to the neck in sand—presumably the most effective method of stopping the convulsions that followed poisoning!

*The pungent odour of ripe karaka berries around New Zealand coasts is a reminder that summer is drawing to a close.*

tapeworm, the most common complaint Maori suffered in pre-European times was karaka or tutu poisoning. A natural antidote used to combat the convulsions brought on by eating unprepared karaka kernels was a preparation of the coastal kohekohe plant, containing properties similar to quinine. The kohekohe cure may not have stopped the patient dying, but apparently it helped straighten the unfortunate victim's limbs before death.

Karaka trees grow naturally only as far south as Banks Peninsula and south Westland, some specimens attaining heights of 20 metres. Their berries are a favourite food of kereru.

# Katipo

The katipo is New Zealand's most poisonous native spider, yet most New Zealanders have never seen one, let alone been bitten by one.

As the only native spider known to have killed people, the katipo has acquired a fearsome reputation. Two deaths from katipo have been recorded, both in the 19th century, but the development of an antivenom effectively means that humans are no longer at risk. Only the female katipo is able to penetrate human skin to deliver its venom.

Possessing a poison many times more potent than the venom of a rattlesnake (but in much smaller quantities), the katipo renders its prey paralysed though still alive, so that it has a fresh meal at its disposal.

There are two endemic species. *Latrodectus katipo* is found on most North Island sandy beaches but only part-way down the South Island's West Coast and as far south as Dunedin on the east coast. It is distinguished by a red stripe on top of the abdomen. A second spider, only recently recognised as a species in its own right, is *L. atritus*. It has a wholly black abdomen and occurs on Taranaki, Hawke's Bay and Bay of Plenty beaches.

Katipo prey on beetles and make their webs close to the ground at the base of grasses, in dry cracks or crevices or under driftwood. Young spiders, called spiderlings, eat each other.

A trans-Tasman relative, the more aggressive red-back, is now well established and because it is more adaptable, with a wider habitat including homes and gardens, will pose more of a threat in the future. Another cousin is the feared American black widow spider.

Ironically the katipo itself is a threatened species. A South African immigrant, the false katipo (*Steatoda capensis*), is now widespread around New Zealand coasts and appears to be displacing the native species.

*Only the mature female katipo, recognised by the red stripe down her back, is poisonous to humans. Katipo (night stinger) weave a small tangled nest in driftwood and grasses above the high-tide mark.*

*Shedding bark at regular intervals, the kauri trunk grows straight and clean, unencumbered by epiphytes which proliferate in the crown. For hundreds of years its timber has been prized for building.*

# Kauri

North of a line between Kawhia and Te Puke grows the New Zealand kauri (*Agathis australis*), unrivalled among New Zealand trees for its size and grandeur.

The kauri is a tree with an ancient lineage. Its ancestors were contemporaries of the dinosaurs more than 130 million years ago. Today, kauri species exist around the western Pacific—in the Philippines, Borneo, Malaysia, New Guinea, Vanuatu, Australia, New Caledonia and Fiji.

About 2 million years ago, before a cooler climate forced warmth-loving plants to retreat northwards, kauri trees used to grow naturally as far south as Southland.

In the forest the kauri plays host to a wide range of plant and animal life. High up in its crown grow epiphytes, perching plants which are

Tane Mahuta and Te Matua Ngahere, New Zealand's largest living kauri trees, have been aged at between 1200 and 1500 years. Kairaru, which was destroyed by fire in 1886, was estimated to be at least 4000 years old.

Lord of the forest Tane Mahuta (below) is the largest living kauri. Huge as it is, with a girth of 13.77 metres, it would have been dwarfed by the largest recorded kauri, Kairaru, which was 20.12 metres in girth.

extremely important food sources for birds such as the kokako. From the heights of the kauri, the kokako sings in order to mark out its territory. Other important birds and animals found in kauri forest include the red-crowned and yellow-crowned parakeets, brown kiwi, pied tit, kaka, and Hochstetter's and Archey's frogs.

Even in death the kauri can play an important role. In 1973 when the huge Kopi from Omahuta Sanctuary was blown down during a cyclone, a colony of rare short-tailed bats was found in its trunk. The bats continued to live in the hollow trunk as it lay on the ground.

The term 'kauri forest' may give an impression of forest totally dominated by kauri; in fact, within a forest a mature grove may occupy only a few hectares, the remainder being a mix of plants including taraire, towai and kohekohe.

Kauri trees normally grow some distance apart, with the spaces in between occupied by kauri grass and the giant, sharp-leaved ghania, the white rata vine, Kirk's tree daisy, hangehange and mingimingi.

To Maori, the kauri was ranked second only to totara. Its timber was used for boat building, carving and housing. Kauri gum was used for fire starting and heating, and as a chewing-gum once it had been soaked in water and mixed with the milk of puha. It was no casual event to fell a tree, and such an important occasion was always accompanied by ritual.

The first European contact with kauri was an unhappy one. In 1772 the French expedition led by Marion du Fresne put into the Bay of Islands

## KAURI RANK

| Ranking | Name | Locality | Girth (m) | Trunk height (m) | Total height (m) | Trunk volume (m³) |
|---|---|---|---|---|---|---|
| 1 | Tane Mahuta | Waipoua | 13.77 | 17.68 | 51.5 | 244.5 |
| 2 | Te Matua Ngahere | Waipoua | 16.41 | 10.21 | 29.9 | 208.1 |
| 3 | McGregor Kauri | Waipoua | 13.69 | 12.25 | 40.8 | 170.6 |
| 4 | Te Tangi o te Tui | Puketi | 12.38 | 13.10 | 50.9 | 155.1 |
| 5 | Moetangi (no. 1) | Warawara | 11.06 | 20.03 | 49.0 | 149.0 |
| 6 | Tanenui | Manaia | 10.08 | 18.29 | 47.2 | 135.7 |
| 7 | Yakas | Waipoua | 12.29 | 12.04 | 43.9 | 134.2 |
| 8 | Hokianga | Omahuta | 9.58 | 20.73 | 53.3 | 131.1 |
| 9 | Tairua (no.1) | Coromandel | 9.78 | 22.86 | 49.7 | 128.3 |
| 10 | Moetangi (no. 2) | Warawara | 10.62 | 11.44 | – | 118.5 |

*Long after kauri forest has disappeared, translucent fossilised gum can be found buried in the ground where ancient trees once stood.*

for shelter and there felled two kauri, intending to use them for ships' masts. However du Fresne and 25 of his men were slain by a group of Maori and the half-made spars were abandoned.

This was a temporary setback to European exploitation of kauri. Initially it was sought after for ships' spars, but with Pakeha settlement it began to be logged for housing and for the export trade. Kauri forests once covered at least 1.2 million ha; today they have been reduced to 80 000 ha.

In the fight to preserve the remaining kauri forests, several names stand out. Professor Barney McGregor, a feisty Auckland University botanist, was largely responsible for the creation in 1952 of the Waipoua Sanctuary, home to the 'top three' giant kauri. To convince politicians of the need for the sanctuary, he organised a petition which attracted so many signatures that it was trundled into Parliament on a wheelbarrow. At the time, the Forest Service, imbued with the philosophy that forests needed to be tended to be kept 'healthy', complained Waipoua would become a 'museum for kauris to rot in'.

Latterly, taking up the 1907 call by botanist Leonard Cockayne to create a kauri national park, Royal Forest and Bird Protection Society president Gordon Ell has expanded the vision to encompass all the substantial scattered remnants of kauri forest for a national park. This would include forests such as Puketi, Omahuta, Herekino, Warawara and Trounson.

# Kea

Usually described as a mountain parrot, the kea (*Nestor notabilis*) actually prefers to live at the timberline rather than in the true alpine zone. Nevertheless, it has the distinction of being the only parrot apart from some Andean species to be familiar with snow.

Today the kea occurs only in the Southern Alps of the South Island and the mountain ranges of Otago, Westland, Nelson and Marlborough. However, it once ranged over areas of the North Island, evidenced by the find of kea bones in a Waitomo cave in 1962.

A highly intelligent bird, the kea's antics are a continuing source of entertainment to trampers and other high-country visitors. Its pranks are not always appreciated, however, especially by people whose property it damages or destroys.

Like most parrots, kea are relatively long lived, with the oldest recorded in the wild living for more than 20 years. Between July and January females lay up to four eggs either in a hole in the ground or under logs. Females do all the incubating and feeding.

While the 'nuclear family' of parents and chicks is the basic kea group, the parrot is also a highly social animal. Young males in particular enjoy congregating in 'gangs' to raid skifields and

*Some biologists believe a sense of playfulness in animals is one of the signs of a superior intelligence. Using that criterion, the kea must rank high among the bird brains of the world.*

tramping huts for food. In the past, there were plenty of natural foods available full of fats, but high-country tussocklands have been extensively grazed and burned, reducing food sources. Rubbish bins are fascinating to keas and the birds are often seen making a beeline for yoghurt and cottage cheese containers, as well as sausage scraps and butter paper. Sour cream with or without baked potatoes is another favourite.

Kea and farmers have not got along since sheep were first introduced into remote parts of the South Island last century. 'Rogue' keas were accused of driving mobs of sheep over cliffs and feasting on the spoils.

In response, a bounty system was established, which lasted from 1890 to 1971, with a reward for each kea beak handed in, allowing the numbers of kea killed during that time to be accurately gauged—at least 150 000. Some people were able to earn a reasonable living from the bounty. During the 1930s Depression a kea beak was worth 10 shillings, a small fortune in those financially straitened times. Since 1986 the kea has been fully protected.

Kea defenders have always played down the rapacity of the birds and have generally been reluctant to admit that they might have a taste for

*Whether in the form of cheese or a Hutton's shearwater chick from the Seaward Kaikouras, fat is a vital part of the kea's diet.*

> ## Did you know?
>
> Kea have been described as the bossiest birds in the world. Captive kea at the Konrad Lorenz Institute in Austria were provided with a wooden see-saw with a perch at one end that lifted the lid of a feeding box at the other. The percher could not reach the food itself, and as soon as it left the perch, the lid closed. Dominant birds always fed at the box while subservient birds did the perching. If they neglected their duties the underlings were chased back, and dominant birds never fed the subordinates.

sheep. However, documentary film-maker Rod Morris recently captured evidence that keas do attack sheep, sometimes riding on their backs in order to feast on the woolly animals' kidneys.

Fortunately attitudes have changed and no longer is there a call for a bounty to be placed on the kea. Most people, including farmers, now recognise that sheep have invaded kea territory. Sheep can be vaccinated against blood poisoning caused by kea attack. Furthermore, not all keas share the same liking for sheeps' kidneys; 'rogue' keas can be removed from an area if they are causing a problem.

Morris has a theory on why keas attack sheep: he believes they are after fat to 'charge their batteries' for winter. Many nest at that time of the year and need to be in top condition. On the trail of the fat theory, he has also documented keas eating muttonbird chicks, homing in on the stomach oil and peeling back the skin to get at the subcutaneous fat.

Speculating, Morris wonders whether keas used to ride the extinct moa in search of tasty kidneys. In doing the same to sheep, are they acting out some ancient memory? This speculation is partially borne out by the work of palaeoecologists Richard Holdaway and Trevor Worthy who have studied moa bones in North Canterbury's Pyramid Swamp. Besides discovering compelling evidence that the giant Haast's eagle attacked moa trapped in the swamp, they also found signs of damage in the moa's pelvic region by a smaller beaked bird—presumably the kea. The flightless moa became extinct between 300 and 500 years ago (see page 218).

# Kelps

The great brown seaweeds of New Zealand's coasts are called kelps, their sinuous leathery shapes providing food for a variety of sea life and acting as a protective buffer between the ocean and the shore.

Bull kelp is the largest seaweed. The two New Zealand species are the common bull kelp (*Durvillaea antarctica*) and another known only by its scientific name, *D. willana*. The large-fronded bull kelps are more common and grow to greater size in the south.

Maori used the broad stipes of bull kelp to ingeniously fashion tough, waterproof bags in which they stored muttonbirds. Bull kelp provides nourishment for cattle in areas where pasture is limited; farmers on Stewart Island feed their herds with kelp, and for the feral cattle on subantarctic Enderby Island the plentiful seaweed was a diet staple.

*(Above) Bladder kelp and blue moki dance in a current off the Otago Peninsula.*
*(Below) Honeycombed on the inside, the common bull kelp is able to float on the surface, thus maximising its ability to photosynthesise.*

The palm-shaped paddle weed (*Lessonia variegata*) grows in more exposed waters than its relative, the bladder kelp. The smallest of New Zealand kelps, *Ecklonia radiata*, has a branched holdfast, narrow stalk and trails shiny ribbons. Intolerant of strong light, it reaches its maximum height of 3 metres in subtidal kelp forests.

Like all seaweeds, the bladder kelp's growth is limited by temperature. Scientists suggest that, because sea surface temperatures are not always available and can vary over short distances, the bladder kelp is a useful temperature indicator. Since bladder kelp and salmon prefer similar temperatures (below 16–17°C) prospective salmon farmers would do well to observe the distribution of bladder kelp when they site their farms.

## Did you know?

The bladder kelp (*Macrocystis pyrifera*), common around New Zealand coasts from Cook Strait south, is the fastest-growing plant in the world. It can grow half a metre a day, reaching its full length of 35 metres in only 3 months.

# Kereru

Known to Maori of the north as kukupa but in the remainder of the country as kereru, and to Chatham Island Maori as parea, there are two subspecies of native pigeon: the North, South and Stewart Island subspecies (*Hemiphaga novaeseelandiae*); and the Chatham Island subspecies (*H. chathamensis*). While they are still widespread throughout New Zealand (most common in Northland, the King Country, Nelson and the West Coast), in certain areas they are in serious decline, mainly because of hunting. The parea numbers only about 150, but is increasing.

Fully protected since 1921, the handsome kereru had hunting restrictions placed on it as early as 1864. Today it is a potent symbol of the conflict that can arise between Pakeha and Maori conservationists, who want to preserve the bird, and Maori traditionalists who claim their rights to harvest the pigeon as of old.

Tracing Northland bird populations in six forests between 1979 and 1993, Department of Conservation (DOC) scientists estimated kereru numbers had been reduced by 50 percent. A study near Whangarei showed that pigeons today live an average of only 3 years in this area, compared with 6 years elsewhere. In most cases a kereru will die before it can replace itself.

The difficulties facing the pigeon are compounded by the relatively recent arrival of possums in Northland. Not only are they competing for food, they are also destroying pigeon nests.

Unlike gamebirds such as quail, pheasants and ducks, all of which lay clutches of 8–16 eggs, the pigeon is more sparing, laying only one per clutch. A Marlborough study has shown that only 15–20 percent of pigeons breed successfully each year.

Between September and February, mainland pigeons lay their eggs in a makeshift tangle of a nest. The birds fetch twigs of manuka, kanuka, totara or other podocarps; finally, after 30–60 twigs have been gathered they build the nest, frequently interrupting the exercise to indulge in courtship flights and head bobbing. Around egg-laying time both birds, but more particularly the male, demonstrate their flying abilities with a series of stalls, swoops and dashes. The Chatham Island subspecies delights in 'hang-gliding' in the strong up-current along the south coast.

*Offshore islands such as Little Barrier may offer the best opportunity for kereru survival, at least in the north where hunting pressure could see the handsome pigeon become locally extinct.*

When fruit is in short supply in spring, kereru can be seen in suburban gardens feasting on fresh willow, poplar and elm leaves, and the flowers of kowhai, tree lucerne and broom.

In Northland the staple fruits of the kereru are puriri during the summer and autumn, miro through autumn and winter and taraire in winter and spring.

Kereru are most likely derived from an ancestral fruit pigeon from Australian or New Caledonian forests. It is believed they have existed in New Zealand for some millions of years, sufficient time for them to have evolved into a species quite distinct from other fruit pigeons. For example, it is the only pigeon with 12 tail feathers (the others have more) and it performs an elaborate territorial display flight.

## Parea

The Chatham Island pigeon, a quarter again as large as its mainland cousin, is inching its way out of the endangered category. By 1990 it was reduced to only 40 birds, but by 1997 there were 150. Much of the credit for this jump in numbers goes to Bruce and Liz Tuanui and Bruce's parents, who have set aside 1200 ha of their farm to protect the pigeon. DOC staff, joining forces with local landowners in the bid to rescue the bird, have fenced off areas against stock and carried out predator control, leading to improved breeding.

The chief reason for the parea's decline was the fact that possums were robbing the birds of their food. A key ingredient in the parea's breeding success is the availability of the succulent hoho fruit (*Pseudopanax chathamica*), a type of lancewood. Other trees that provide most food for parea are kopi (karaka), karamu, matipo and mahoe. Most of the natural habitat remaining on the Chatham Islands is *Dracophyllum* forest and shrubland, unsuitable as food.

Once the forests were fenced off against stock, and possums were trapped intensively, regeneration was rapid. Islanders, unused to the sight of the large, handsome birds, are amazed to see them ranging widely.

The parea has a purple tinge on the neck and breast, slightly greyer plumage and a more colourful bill than the mainland pigeon.

## A large appetite for large seeds

With the extinction of the moa and other giant ground-dwelling birds, the native pigeon, kereru, remains the only bird capable of swallowing and spreading large seeds throughout native forests.

Kereru eat the fruits of at least 70 species of plants and have an average feeding territory (in Northland at least) of 25 square kilometres, making them the most important seed-dispersing birds in New Zealand forests.

It is the only bird that can wrap its bill around and swallow the large berries of karaka, taraire, tawa, puriri, miro and several other trees. The kereru has become a pivotal species for the continued health of the forest, making its preservation of far-reaching importance.

*In contrast with the rock pigeon common in city parks and gardens, which is naturally a grain eater, the forest-dwelling kereru feeds exclusively on fruits, leaves and flowers.*

*The tropical affinities of the climbing plant kiekie are revealed in its large and distinctive fruit, which bear a close resemblance to others in the* Pandanus *family to which kiekie belongs.*

# Kiekie

'December', wrote the West Coast explorer Thomas Brunner, 'was a glorious month of dietary amongst the natives of the coast . . . the fruit of the ekiakia (kiekie) is then ripe, called by the native tawara, and is very luscious, more like a conserve than a fruit.'

Another early settler, Rod McDonald, observing Maori in the Horowhenua, said Maori treated the kiekie plants in the forest as their 'orchards'. 'The tawhara was a toothsome sweet in a land where sweets were few . . . where the kiekie grew high on the trees the ripening tawhara was watched carefully. As the time drew near when it would be at its most luscious stage, a flag was hung out in a conspicuous place . . . a warning that for the time being that bush was tapu and no one might enter to pick tawhara until the prohibition was removed.'

Kiekie (*Freycinetia baueriana* ssp. *banksii*), an endemic plant of a genus of climbing or scrambling shrubs also found in Australia, Malaysia and the Pacific, was important to Maori both for its fruit and in weaving. The flowering season lasted only a fortnight and the fruit was regarded as the finest of the forest. In weaving, the plant's fibre was used in several ways, including making rain capes and fish traps; the leaves were used for mats, baskets and tukutuku panels. Today, with the resurgence of interest in the art of weaving, kiekie is much in demand but in short supply. Rats and possums eat the fabled fruit and the plants are not found in large numbers.

# Kina

Armed with a formidable spiky exterior, the kina or common sea urchin (*Evechinus chloroticus*) is plentiful in shallow water along the length of New Zealand's coast.

It does not move fast; in fact it does not have to move at all as it can wait for food to attach itself to its spines. However, where there is abundant seaweed, masses of kina devour large forests. Eager eaters, kina numbers build up to as many as 50 per square metre.

Some kina may be as old as 15 years, and grow as heavy as 1 kg. For Maori kina are a delicacy, to be eaten—they used to say—when the kowhai is in bloom. It is then that the gonads or roe of the kina become bright and swollen.

*Two kina climb an* Ecklonia *kelp to reach the tender fronds at the top.*

Kina spawn in a similar fashion to corals. In spring, eggs and sperm are produced by the gonads of sexually mature kina (3–4 years old), then a few days before the full moon they are released. The eggs and sperm fuse to create minute larvae that float away in the plankton until they settle 2–3 months later.

Because they are triggered to release their sperm and eggs by the phase of the moon, the males and females of each species can closely synchronise their sexual activity.

# Kingfisher

Kingfisher is something of a misnomer for kotare, the New Zealand kingfisher (*Halcyon sancta*), which differs from other kingfishers in having an appetite for mice, small birds, cicadas, lizards and worms, as well as fish. It likes to capture live prey, and can sometimes be seen feeding young with a tasty morsel such as a mouse.

Although it occupies a variety of habitats, the kingfisher tends to keep to the coast, where it takes advantage of a rich food supply. Mud crabs, shrimps and fish are all taken by this skilful flier.

Because it has a varied diet, the New Zealand kingfisher is not as prone to high juvenile mortality as other kingfishers. Truer to its name, the British species is totally reliant on fish. While adult birds are generally successful when diving for prey, juveniles succeed in only one dive in 10. However, driven by hunger, they will dive repeatedly until their feathers become waterlogged and they drown.

The kingfisher is one of the native birds that has benefited from forest clearance and the creation of open farmland. A relatively recent Australian immigrant, it is found throughout the country and on most offshore islands, but not the Chathams or subantarctics. The further south and further inland, the less common is the kingfisher, and in winter upland breeders move to lower altitudes or the coast.

Its nest is usually in a knothole, a roadside cutting or coastal cliffs. The eggs hatch about 20 days after they are laid in spring and the juveniles become independent at 26 days old.

Another Australian member of the kingfisher family is the kookaburra (*Dacelo novaeguineae*), which has a tenuous hold in New Zealand. Introduced to Kawau Island in the early 1860s by Governor George Grey, its population now numbers around 500, mainly from Auckland north to Whangarei. The distinctive characteristic of the kookaburra is its boisterous 'laugh'.

*Fish form only a small part of the diet of the New Zealand kingfisher which is skilled at capturing a variety of prey.*

# Kiore

Kiore (*Rattus exulans*), the Pacific rat, is the world's third most widely distributed rat, occurring in mainland Southeast Asia, Indonesia, the Philippines and many islands of the Pacific as well as New Zealand.

Brought to New Zealand by the Maori because of its value as a food, kiore remained an important source of protein for humans until the 19th century. However, it also had an adverse impact on the environment, eating birds' eggs, a number of animals, and plants.

It has been implicated in the local or total extinction of species of flightless beetles, giant weta, land snails, frogs, lizards, tuatara, small seabirds, landbirds, and bats. Probably the most damage to wildlife results from large numbers of kiore eating fruit, seeds and leaves, leaving the native animals without a sufficient supply of food. The Department of Conservation (DOC) recommends eradication on islands where the rat is considered a threat to native wildlife.

When the black rat (*R. rattus*) and the Norwegian rat (*R. norvegicus*) arrived in New Zealand with Europeans, kiore found themselves outcompeted by their more aggressive relatives. Today kiore occur on the mainland only in Fiordland where they are in low numbers.

Until 1983 they were present on about 50 islands but since then have been eradicated from 16. The latest eradication attempt was on Kapiti Island in 1996. Codfish Island, home to the endangered kakapo, is to be the next major target for eradication.

The response of native wildlife once kiore are removed has been remarkable. For example, on Korapuki Island off the Coromandel coast and Motuopao Island near Cape Reinga, lizard numbers have bounced back to 30 times higher than when kiore were present.

*The damage that kiore have done to the environment has become evident following a number of eradication programmes on islands. Kiore have a reputation as vegetarians, and therefore are assumed to be less harmful than other rats; however, these opportunists will eat whatever food is available, such as fish.*

Kiore occupied a position in Polynesian society that was not matched by the black rat or the Norwegian rat in Europe. Once fattened on a diet of berries and other vegetarian fare, especially miro—the flavour of which permeated the animal—the kiore was considered a delicacy by Maori. In *The Coming of the Maori*, Sir Peter Buck explains how the rat was captured and preserved: 'The rats became very fat in the berry-bearing season and they were trapped in sufficient numbers to be plucked, grilled, and preserved in their fat as huahua like pigeons.' That taste for kiore has now helped Auckland University anthropologist Lisa Matisoo-Smith to answer a question that has puzzled people for years: where did Maori come from? By comparing the DNA of kiore in New Zealand with that of kiore in a number of South Pacific islands, she has concluded that Maori most likely came from the Cook and Society islands.

Of the animals that came in the canoes—humans, kuri (dogs) and kiore—only kiore remain as potential indicators of migration patterns as no hybridisation has occurred with the two rat species introduced by Europeans.

Some iwi claim the kiore as a taonga (treasure). Advancing the claim most strongly is Northland's Ngatiwai, whose rohe (tribal area) encompasses a number of islands including the Hen and Chickens group, Little Barrier, and Mokohinau islands—islands where kiore eradication is likely some day.

DOC plan to relocate kiore from the Hen and Chickens to Ngatiwai islands of Rapahoe, Nikora and Ipurau in Ngunguru Bay, which at present have mice but no vulnerable native species.

Kiore were useful not just for food. Often they were skinned and their pelts converted into fine kakahu (cloaks), few of which remain today. People of great mana owned these cloaks, which were frequently buried with their owners.

In 1996 palaeoecologist Richard Holdaway rocked the scientific world with his contention that kiore arrived in New Zealand perhaps 2000 years ago, implying that humans must have arrived at the same time. He assumes these early human immigrants died out but the kiore lived on to wreak havoc on birds and insects. Although Holdaway's theory has been discounted by archaeologists, radiocarbon dating appears to support the speculation.

### KIORE MIGRATION

*The arrows show the route of probable migration from the Cook Islands and Society Islands to New Zealand, based on the fact that kiore from these islands are genetically closer to New Zealand kiore than those from any other island group.*

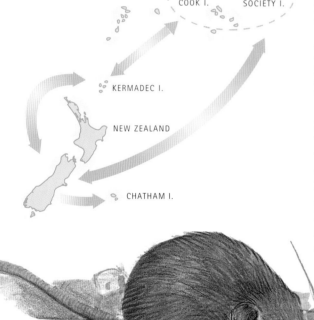

COOK I.  SOCIETY I.

KERMADEC I.

NEW ZEALAND

CHATHAM I.

*Kiore are now largely restricted to offshore islands where they prey on weta (pictured) and other insects which are important food for birds and lizards. Kiore also have an appetite for tuatara and birds' eggs.*

*Today the little spotted kiwi is known to exist only on islands. Smallest of the kiwi species, it may still survive on the West Coast and in northwest Nelson but none have been seen there for decades.*

# Kiwi

Since 1991 New Zealand's national symbol has been the subject of intense scrutiny. Surprisingly little was known about the kiwi, especially its conservation status, until a recovery programme was launched that year. Population counts have since been carried out and DNA testing done to determine the number of species.

There was widespread concern that the kiwi was in decline, but little hard and fast data existed to enable comparison of numbers in previous decades with today. As was feared, the new counts pointed to an alarming collapse in the population of the bird that Maori also called te manuhuna a Tane (the hidden bird of Tane, god of the forest), so named for its nocturnal habits. The kiwi's name is not derived from its call, as is often believed, but rather from the Polynesian name for the bristle-thighed curlew, the kivi. This tropical seabird has a similar habit of poking for food with its long beak, albeit along the coast.

Maori hunted the kiwi for food, but favoured it less than other game such as moa. The bird was most esteemed for its feathers, from which were fashioned beautiful cloaks worn by chiefs. To preserve the traditional cloak-making practice, Maori today are given feathers from kiwi which have been killed accidentally.

When Europeans found the kiwi, they identified it as a distinctive bird, an appraisal that has been reinforced by a succession of scientists fascinated by aspects of its biology and behaviour.

*North Island brown kiwi males take sole responsibility for incubating an egg over a period of 70–85 days.*

## An honorary mammal

A ratite, and therefore related to the moa, emu, ostrich, cassowary and rhea, the kiwi has been described by US biologist William Calder as 'an honorary mammal' and by others as the most unbirdlike bird in the world. The description has some basis in fact: the kiwi occupies niches that elsewhere are the domains of moles or badgers; it maintains an average body temperature of 38°C, two degrees below that of most birds and closer to the mammal range; instead of having hollow bones, as most birds do, kiwi bones are filled with marrow; and the female has a pair of functional ovaries instead of the one that most birds have— again a feature typical of mammals.

The kiwi also stands apart from other birds because of its superior sense of smell. Some birds, for example seabirds and vultures, have a well-developed sense of smell, but generally birds do not. Equipped with an olfactory (smell) bulb in its brain much larger than that of other birds, the kiwi snuffles like a hedgehog as it shuffles through the bush, continuously probing the soil for worms and invertebrates.

Two species—the great spotted and little spotted kiwi—are holding their own better than the brown, even though there are more individual brown kiwi. The little spotted kiwi occurs only on islands, mainly Kapiti, while a portion of the great spotted kiwi population lives in alpine areas less hospitable to predators. The brown, on the other hand, lives at low altitude, often close to human settlement where it has to cope with a variety of enemies.

Prior to human arrival in New Zealand about 1000 years ago, there may have been up to 12 million kiwis rustling about in the rainforests at any one time.

For the moment the brown and the great spotted kiwi survive on the North, South and Stewart islands, but dogs, pigs, cats, stoats, ferrets, possums and humans threaten them—a formidable list of enemies.

## A life-long struggle for survival

Although the sturdy, flightless kiwi, equipped with strong legs and sharp claws, is a match for some predators, it is especially at risk at the juvenile stage of its life.

Predators make life difficult for the kiwi from the time the huge egg—about six times the size of an egg from a domestic hen—is laid in the bird's burrow. Possums wander into the nest, sometimes breaking the egg by accident or, if they are hungry, by design.

The kiwi egg is the richest of any bird in the world—60 percent of it is yolk compared with 40 percent for a domestic hen's egg. For the first week of its life the chick is sustained by this nourishment without any other food and is then able to start foraging independently. Scientists reason that the enormous investment kiwi parents put into the energy-rich egg relieves them of parental obligations once the chick is hatched, although the male broods it during the day for the first 10–20 days.

However, in the first 9 months of life the kiwi is at its most vulnerable. The present chick mortality rate is around 90 percent. Cats and stoats prey on the juveniles as they range, parentless, away from the home burrow in search of food. When the chick is 15–20 days old, it is truly on its own, for by then its father has moved to a new nest and is incubating a second clutch of eggs. The juvenile kiwi roams within a kilometre or two of its parents' burrow, setting up home in

## *Sunny side up*

Until recently it was thought kiwi eggs were not turned by parents so they were not turned in hatcheries; wildlife managers also did not know the optimum temperatures at which to keep the huge eggs. Consequently the numbers of chicks hatched in captivity were low, stalling efforts to safeguard the vulnerable bird.

Kiwis do not lay a lot of eggs in a season—the North Island brown is the most prolific, at two clutches of two eggs, but the three other species lay on average only one egg. With so few eggs available to be taken from nests, a reasonable hatching rate is even more important.

Scientific officer Rogan Colbourne experimented by placing dummy eggs under nesting kiwis and the tests showed that in fact kiwis do turn their eggs to provide them with an even heat. It is known from studies of other birds that this practice also assists embryo development by orienting the eggs right way up. Temperature transmitters placed inside the artificial egg demonstrated that the temperature where the parent kiwi came into contact with the egg was 2°C higher than had been recommended for hatchery-reared eggs.

In 1995 hatcheries involved with the kiwi recovery programme turned their eggs and increased the temperature on top of the egg. The result: an 80 percent hatching success rate, double that of previous years.

(Left) A week after hatching, this brown kiwi chick will be foraging independently of its parents.
(Below) A male kiwi in its burrow turns an egg to ensure it is evenly heated.

regenerating vegetation such as bracken or toe-toe. In 5 months it doubles its hatching weight; males become sexually mature at the end of their first year and females sometime later.

The kiwi's worries are not over once it becomes an adult. Even though large, it cannot withstand the attentions of pigs, dogs, and occasionally ferrets. In one well-documented case in 1987, a German shepherd on the rampage in Waitangi Forest killed 500 birds out of a population of 900. Because kiwi lack a reinforcing ridge on their breastbone, they are easily killed by dogs. Land clearance could be the final nail in the coffin for kiwi. Fortunately the clearance of native forest, where the birds are found in greatest numbers, has mostly stopped. Kiwi also live in pine plantations if there is native forest nearby.

Just after dusk and in the hours before dawn kiwi utter their harsh, shrill call. Although generally nocturnal, the Stewart Island brown kiwi also forages during the day. The kiwi diet is a mixture of worms, spiders, insect larvae and sometimes fallen fruits.

Kiwi are fiercely territorial, with some individual territories up to 40 ha in size, although others are as small as 2 ha—size is dependent on food supply. Andrea Reischek, a 19th-century Austrian bird collector, described a fight between two kiwi males: 'The fight was a combination of sabre duel and boxing match. They attacked each other

*High in the mist-shrouded forests and tussocky subalpine areas of northwest Nelson and Westland lives New Zealand's largest and arguably most handsome kiwi—the great spotted or roa.*

ferociously with their bills, so that the feathers flew from their breasts; and they rose up on one leg, letting fly at one another with their sharp-clawed feet. In the excitement they pawed the ground and uttered grunting noises.'

The Department of Conservation's strategy to preserve kiwi is twofold: to intensively manage populations by protecting nests from predators, and to raise chicks in captivity before releasing them in the wild at an age when they are able to defend themselves.

Recent experiments with kiwi in the forests around Lake Waikaremoana point to the magnitude of the challenge of maintaining kiwi on the mainland. In one area, predators were trapped and killed along 20 kilometres of track while another area was left untrapped. By the end of the season 90 stoats, ferrets, weasels and cats had been caught and catch rates slowed down, implying that most predators had been caught. Of the seven kiwi chicks hatched, one was known to have been killed by a ferret, and the remainder survived. However, in the untrapped forest, four out of six chicks were killed.

Promising as this trial has been, it has brought home the fact that keeping kiwi on the mainland will be successful only with intensive control. Mustelids especially have proven to be wily foes; breakthroughs in dealing with them could prove the key to mainland kiwi survival.

## Kiwi family ties

DNA testing has shed new light on kiwi taxonomy. Until now it was thought there were just three species; there are in fact four, and six different varieties.

The brown kiwi is now divided into _Apteryx mantelli_ (North Island and Okarito brown) and _A. australis_ (Haast, Fiordland and Stewart Island brown, also known as tokoeka). The Okarito birds are a separate subspecies and the Haast kiwi represents a subspecies different from the rest of the tokoeka in Fiordland or Stewart Island. It is possible the Okarito and Haast birds are species in their own right—a theory awaiting confirmation by further DNA testing.

Southern tokoeka on Stewart Island behave differently from other kiwi. Their daytime foraging habit has been attributed to a poor food supply—forcing them to search for food for longer periods—and a high population density. This kiwi is further differentiated by the fact that ex-

> ### _Did you know?_
>
> In 1968 Dr Bernice M Wenzel of the University of California tested the kiwi's ability to detect its food by smell. A number of tapering aluminium tubes were set into the ground, some imbued with strong smells, others containing food and others just earth. Each time, the kiwis went unerringly for the food tubes, proving beyond doubt that the kiwi (like the Okarito brown below) could detect the smell of food more than 50 mm below the surface.
>
>

tended family members help with incubating—an offspring of a Stewart Island pair has been observed sharing nesting duties.

It is impossible to be accurate about brown kiwi numbers, other than the very small Okarito and Haast populations which are 60–100 and 200–300 respectively. There are certainly fewer than 100 000, and possibly no more than 20 000.

The three populations of the great spotted kiwi or roa (_A. haasti_) occur in northwestern Nelson, the Paparoa Range and the Southern Alps from Lake Sumner to just south of Arthur's Pass. Unusually, many of these kiwi live in the subalpine zone and can be seen in winter foraging for food in the snow or scaling glacial valleys in the middle of the night. Some birds which are less alpine-inclined live in warmer forests at lower altitudes, but they are comparatively few. Scientist John McLennan estimates there are more than 10 000 great spotted kiwi.

Around 1000 of the little spotted kiwi (_A. owenii_), the smallest species, live on Kapiti Island. It is also now well established on Hen Island, Red Mercury Island and Long Island (Marlborough Sounds), and a new population is being started on Tiritiri Matangi Island where numbers should grow to about 40 pairs.

In 1992 a kiwi found near Franz Josef was initially considered a little spotted, but DNA testing revealed it was in fact an Okarito brown kiwi. The bird was a hybrid—not necessarily first generation—of a little spotted male and an Okarito brown female. The bird has been placed on Mana Island pending a decision on its future.

## Kiwiana

Within New Zealand the kiwi's popularity as a symbol increased from the 1880s. However, outside ornithological circles, the kiwi's international reputation was first created in 1906 by Australian shoe polish manufacturer, William Ramsay, who featured the name and outline of the bird on his round tins in honour of his wife, who was a New Zealander.

During World War I, Australians, with their penchant for nicknames, labelled New Zealand soldiers 'kiwis'. From that point on kiwis and New Zealanders became synonymous.

### DISTRIBUTION OF KIWI IN NEW ZEALAND
*Kiwi have noticeably declined in Northland, Hawke's Bay, Bay of Plenty and the West Coast since surveys carried out in the 1970s.*

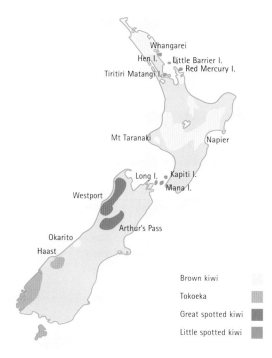

| | |
|---|---|
| Brown kiwi | |
| Tokoeka | |
| Great spotted kiwi | |
| Little spotted kiwi | |

# Kokako

Until the early 1990s the North Island kokako (*Callaeas cinerea wilsoni*) appeared to be destined for a slow slide into extinction, but an innovative rescue programme in the King Country has given rise to renewed hope that this beautiful songster will survive.

Mapara Forest on the edge of Pureora Forest seems at first glance an unlikely area to be at the cutting edge of international conservation efforts. Surrounded on all sides by pastureland, the forest has been heavily logged and until recently swarmed with introduced pests. Yet in this 1400-ha cutover remnant of a formerly vast podocarp and hardwood forest, scientists have proved with spectacular results the concepts of 'mainland island' restoration and 'research-by-management' work.

Until 1989 the main focus had been on restoring offshore islands to safeguard native species against predators or the consequences of habitat destruction. But in that year conservation managers decided to set up a programme in Mapara to protect the kokako.

Reduced to around 1000 individuals in scattered forests, the kokako is a poor flier whose nests are raided for chicks and eggs by ship rats and the harrier. Infrared, time-lapse cameras captured the startling evidence that the supposedly vegetarian possum also has a taste for kokako chicks and eggs, and mustelids, especially stoats, occasionally also prey on the birds.

Scientists decided to study populations in three different central North Island forests: in one (Rotoehu, in the Bay of Plenty) they monitored the birds but carried out no predator control; in the second, Kaharoa (in the King Country), they killed as many goats, pigs, ship rats, possums, mustelids and feral cats as possible for 3 years, and recorded how many chicks fledged (management was then discontinued). A similar regime was followed at Mapara, except that pest control has continued.

For the first 2 years the 65-strong kokako population in Mapara actually decreased. One of the reasons for the slow recovery soon became evident: because of high predation rates on females, 75 percent of the pairs were male-male. By 1997 only 10 percent were male-male. In 1990–91 five birds fledged, followed by seven the next year.

*The North Island kokako is not a strong flier, instead adroitly bounding from branch to branch.*

Even more encouraging was the fact that around 80 percent of fledglings were surviving. Not only was there an increase in bird numbers, but the forest itself was showing signs of being restored to health.

Success built on success; by the summer of 1994–95, 18 breeding pairs were established and some pairs were fledging the unheard-of number of three broods in a season. That year 54 fledglings were added to the Mapara population, doubling it and rescuing it from near-certain extinction. In 1996–97 an even more successful year saw 64 fledglings from 19 pairs.

Meanwhile, at Kaharoa where predator control had produced a 160 percent increase in the population of kokako pairs by 1993, the birds were abruptly left to fend for themselves. The response was almost immediate as the rats and possums reasserted themselves; by 1996–97 no chicks at all fledged and the adult population was declining.

Finally, in Rotoehu Forest, which had been monitored with no pest control during this time, predator control was begun in 1994–95. That

season 40 percent of monitored pairs fledged young, the highest recorded in the 5 years of study there, and this rose to 66 percent the year after. By 1996–97, more chicks fledged in one season than in the entire 4 years of no pest control.

Partly over concerns of too many toxins entering the Mapara ecosystem from the 1080 poison used to kill predators, management is now 'pulsed'—that is, switched off and on. For the future the long-lived kokako (its life expectancy is 20 years) will be monitored so scientists can decide when predator control is again needed.

The challenge now is to broaden the mainland restoration concept to larger areas. In Urewera Forest, where the largest population of kokako (around 600) live in a 60 000-ha area, sections of forest will be managed as 'islands within a sea of forest'. In time the juveniles will expand out to occupy new territories.

### Kokako Facts
• The kokako is one of New Zealand's most ancient bird species. Like the saddleback and the

## DISTRIBUTION OF NORTH ISLAND KOKAKO

*A rescue programme in the 1990s has dramatically increased kokako numbers.*

Mataraua
Trounson Park
Little Barrier I.
Hunua Ranges
Kaharoa
Rotoehu
Pureora
Mapara
Te Urewera
National Park
Kapiti I.

*For obvious reasons the kokako has also been called the 'blue-wattled crow'.*

extinct huia it is a wattle bird, named after the pair of brightly coloured, fleshy 'wattles' that extend from either side of its gape and meet below the neck.

• The kokako can fly but not very well, preferring to bound from branch to branch. It is incapable of sustained flight further than 50 metres.

• Kokako territories are about 8 ha in area, guarded by birds which zealously protect their home 'patch'.

• Kokako eat leaves, fern fronds, flowers, fruit and insects.

• Kokako occur in the Northland kauri forests of Puketi, Raetea and Waipoua, the Hunua Ranges, southern Waikato and northern Taranaki, the King Country, Bay of Plenty forests, northern Urewera Ranges, Little Barrier and Kapiti islands.

• In Maori myth the kokako filled its wattles with water and gave it to Maui as he fought the Sun. His thirst quenched, Maui rewarded the kokako by making its legs long and slender, enabling the bird to bound through the forest with ease in search of food.

### Missing: the South Island kokako

One of the most intriguing bird mysteries of recent times surrounds the whereabouts of the South Island kokako (*C. cinerea cinerea*). Once presumed extinct, the orange- or yellow-wattled crow continues to tantalise bird lovers with unconfirmed reports of its existence on Stewart Island and in the beech forests of Mount Aspiring National Park, Nelson Lakes and Marlborough's Richmond Range.

Typical of the sightings is this by Timothy Hurd who claimed to have seen a kokako in the Nelson Lakes area in 1987: 'I came round a sharp bend and surprised a very large bird (est. 40 cm) sitting about 8 m up in a tree. The bird gave two sharp, but not very loud alarm calls, hopped off the branch and appeared to make a laboured "surge" to get airborne. The bird then glided effortlessly across the creek, and disappeared into thick tree and fern. The flight colour was a soft but pronounced steely bluish-grey, the beak black and moderate in length. Most importantly, the wattles were clearly visible throughout the flight: dusky, orangish-red.' Expeditions to search for the lost bird have failed to find any, but many authorities admit there may be a few solitary South Island kokako surviving.

# Kotuku

Even though kotuku, the white heron (*Egretta alba*), is common in Australia, the South Pacific and tropical Asia, in New Zealand it has always been rare, and hence has attained almost mythical status in both Maori and Pakeha eyes.

At present the population is stable at between 100 and 120 birds, of which around half are non-breeders. Breeding at Okarito in south Westland, the colony originated from birds blown across the Tasman Sea from Australia several hundred years ago. Today wayward herons are still blown in. In the winter of 1957 more than 200 birds were counted in Northland, Waikato, Bay of Plenty, Canterbury and Otago. Presumably some of these birds had come from Australia.

'Rare as the kotuku' became a Maori saying; to compare a visitor to a kotuku was the highest compliment, while North Island Maori regarded the bird as so rare that it was seen only once in a lifetime (te kotuku-rerenga-tahi; the rare white heron of a single flight). Its feathers were highly prized, ranking just below those of the huia and alongside those of the albatross. In the 19th century Pakeha women also admired kotuku plumes, wearing them in their hats, but fortunately this practice did not lead to the bird's extinction, as with the huia.

While the kotuku has always been rare, by 1940 it was alarmingly so. Only four nests remained at Okarito, provoking the New Zealand Government to create the Waitangiroto Reserve (the birds breed in the stately forest on the banks of the Waitangiroto River). Today the number of breeding pairs in the area, which can be visited by permit, is a constant 25. Unlike the neighbouring royal spoonbills, which nest in kahikatea, kotuku prefer to build their heavy constructions in kowhai and kamahi or in the crowns of tree ferns.

The breeding time of September–October matches that of the upstream migration of whitebait, the juvenile form of the native fish inanga, so there is a plentiful food supply for the offspring. Sometimes kotuku have been observed dining on more exotic fare such as mice or small birds. By December the breeding season has ended and the birds scatter around the country to winter feeding grounds.

*Kotuku numbers in New Zealand remain remarkably consistent at 100–120. Why the elegant white heron has not colonised wider breeding areas is a mystery, but its rarity has guaranteed it a special mystique.*

_Unlike saltwater crayfish, koura have a pair of large pincers on their first abdominal limbs and clasping claws on each of their four pairs of walking legs. Some koura are deep-lake dwellers, having been discovered below 60 metres in clear South Island lakes._

# Koura

Like its saltwater cousin the crayfish, the koura or freshwater crayfish is a crustacean. In New Zealand there are two species: _Paranephrops zealandicus_, the larger of the two at 80 mm long, is found on the east coast of the South Island from north Canterbury southwards and also in Stewart Island, while _P. planifrons_ occurs in Nelson, Marlborough, the West Coast and throughout the North Island.

Koura live in streams, lakes, ponds and swamps to relatively high altitudes. They have been found at an altitude of 1200 metres in Tongariro National Park and 1300 metres in the Paparoa Ranges. As an important scavenger in freshwater ecosystems, their favourite foods are insects and leaves. Not only do they recycle plant material but they also act as ecosystem 'engineers', stirring up fine sediments and flushing them away. This action improves conditions for other invertebrates. Because of their vital role in stream ecosystems, koura have been described as a 'keystone' species: their activities are critical to the structure of the community in which they live. As a result, it is important to know their natural densities and whether they are vulnerable to human impact. A recent census of a native forest-bordered stream showed koura densities of three per square metre.

Instead of hunting for a living, koura wait for old leaves or insects to float by, then seize them with their pincers and push them into their mouths. Secretive animals, koura generally stay hidden during the day then come out at night to feed. If alarmed they flick their tail forward violently, shooting backwards into shelter.

Between April and December the female koura produces eggs which lie under the side flaps of its abdomen. Newly hatched koura ride piggyback on their mother until nearly 4 mm long. At 20 mm long, in their fourth year, the new generation become sexually mature adults.

To Maori, koura were an important food resource. Attempts have been made for some years to farm them, but with little success. Large trout and shags are their major predators.

# Kowhai

Kowhai seeds are nothing if not hardy—it is believed that the kowhai trees growing in southern Chile have germinated from seeds which have floated thousands of kilometres across the ocean from New Zealand.

Sometimes described as the national flower, the kowhai was the first New Zealand plant to be grown in Europe, after Banks and Solander brought back seed, and by 1783 it was appearing in London plant catalogues.

The most widespread of the three species of kowhai is the small-leaved *Sophora microphylla*, which, although it takes some years to flower, has the most striking blooms. There are a number of different forms of *S. microphylla*, including varieties with a weeping habit and two varieties from Stephens Island which are hardy against wind and salt spray.

*S. tetraptera*, a large-leaved species, is the most commonly grown in gardens, although it grows in the wild only in the North Island, from East Cape to the Ruahine Ranges. The kowhai is one of New Zealand's few deciduous plants, even if for a short time; no sooner does *S. tetraptera* shed its leaves at the end of winter than golden flowers appear, followed soon after by new leaves.

A dwarf cultivar, 'Gnome', at first considered a form of *S. tetraptera*, has been revealed not to be a native, but to originate from Lord Howe Island.

The third kowhai species is *S. prostrata*, found in open rocky or grassy locations in the South Island from northwest Nelson to Canterbury. The prostrate kowhai forms a small dense mound of twiggy shoots with tiny leaves.

Maori had a number of uses for kowhai. When flowers started to bloom, it was a sign to plant kumara. As a medicine, the bark was said to cure various skin diseases, bruises and fractures. A recipe for colds and sore throats was to steep kowhai in boiling water and drink the infusion. The tree's tough wood provided axe handles.

*Chief pollinators of kowhai are birds such as tui, bellbirds and silvereyes.*

## Did you know?

In 1925 famous Maori All Black fullback George Nepia burst a blood vessel in his leg while playing rugby. A doctor advised him he would need an operation to avoid blood poisoning, but Nepia visited an elderly Maori woman who gave him a 'kowhai cure'. Two sackfuls of bark, from trees facing the rays of the sun, were taken, beaten with a hammer then placed in boiling water. Nepia lay in a bath of the concoction for 2 hours; at one point the old woman made a series of small nicks in the bruised leg. The treatment drew the affected blood out of the leg and in a week Nepia was back playing. From then on, whenever he suffered an injury, Nepia took the same cure. As a result, in his retirement he never suffered from old injuries.

# Lakes

The North Island and South Island, divided by fault-ridden Cook Strait, are also separated by the fact that their most distinctive lakes owe their origins to completely different processes. Volcanic lakes occur only in the North Island and glacial lakes only in the South Island.

The best known of the 29 volcanic lakes are Ruapehu crater lake, Rotoaira, Rotoiti, Rotorua, Tarawera and Taupo. Along the west coast, small dune lakes formed by wind-blown sand are the most common type of North Island lake (106 in number). The second most common category are lakes which have been created adjacent to rivers in flat country.

Only rarely in the North Island have lakes been caused by landslips (in the South Island they are slightly more common, especially in earthquake-prone areas of north Westland and Nelson). Lake Waikaremoana has been formed by a series of huge sandstone landslides which dammed the headwaters of the Waikaretaheke River, and Lake Wairarapa is one of only three North Island lakes (but by far the largest) that have resulted from earthquakes.

South Island lakes are generally glacial (268 out of 475), many lying at altitudes higher than 600 metres. New Zealand's largest bar lake (182 square kilometres) is Lake Ellesmere, formed by a large shingle spit separating it from the sea.

Thirty South Island lakes are man-made, for irrigation, water supply or hydroelectricity generation. Benmore, made by damming the Waitaki River, is one of the largest lakes in the country. Just as glaciers carved below sea level to create the western fiords, so were the eastern valleys of Fiordland excavated. Water filled these to form lakes such as Hauroko and Manapouri, New Zealand's deepest lakes at 462 and 443 metres, respectively.

*The sun sets on kahikatea-fringed Lake Mahinapua, a sea-level lake formed by a glacier, just south of Hokitika in Westland.*
*(Inset) Nestled among the folds of the Central Plateau's volcanic landscape lie the mineral-rich Emerald Lakes. This region has several such crater lakes.*

*The spindly juvenile lancewood contrasts markedly with the adult tree behind it.*

# Lancewoods

So different is the juvenile lancewood from the adult form of the plant that early botanists believed they were separate species. Like a half-opened umbrella, the rigid leaves of the juvenile form bend downwards. At this stage the stem can be bent over double and will not break. Once the plant reaches maturity in 15–20 years, it changes shape completely. Instead of having just one stem, the tree branches freely into a round crown and the small leaves point upwards.

Several theories have been put forward to explain this striking habit. One early botanist, Dr Leonard Cockayne, believed the plant was a survivor from a time when climatic conditions were much harsher, surmising that until the climate improved, the lancewood remained in the juvenile form. Others contend the tree's juvenile stage was a response to moa browsing; once it had grown taller than the moa could reach, it transformed into adult form. A further theory says lancewoods put their early growing effort into height in order to outcompete other species.

There are two lancewood species, *Pseudopanax crassifolius*, and the less common *P. ferox*. Both are called horoeka by Maori. Another related plant, *P. edgerleyi*, or raukawa, was used by Maori as a perfume. They rubbed themselves with the fresh leaves, or mixed the leaves with fat or oil to anoint their bodies.

The largest known lancewood grows at Cambridge, near the Waikato River. Planted in 1897, it has a diameter of 700 mm—50 percent greater than the normal size—and a height over 12 metres. In the 1940s when a telephone was first installed in the house behind the tree, linesmen informed the owner she would have to cut the lancewood down to make way for the lines. She refused and the telephone was not connected.

# Leeches

It must be one of New Zealand's rarest invertebrates: the Open Bay Island leech (*Hirudobdella antipodum*), found under just one boulder on Taumaka, the largest of the Open Bay Islands in south Westland. New Zealand has only two known land-based leeches. Fortunately neither are the variety that plague humans, as do tropical

*An Open Bay Island leech feeds on the foot of a Fiordland crested penguin.*

leeches; nevertheless they are fond of the blood of penguins and albatrosses. The Taumaka leech, first recorded in 1903, was thought to have become extinct when weka were introduced onto the islands but somehow managed to survive and was rediscovered in 1987.

The southernmost leech in the world is the other land-based species, *Ornithobdella edentula*, confined to the Snares Islands and Little Solander Island. It also lives off penguins. Leeches have been seen on Big South Cape, an island southwest of Stewart Island, but they have not been identified. New Zealand also has a number of freshwater leeches which feed on waterfowl, and marine leeches which are parasitic on fish.

# Lichens

New Zealand has one of the richest collections of lichens in the world. So far about 1000 species have been described, but at least that many again remain to be studied. The fact that so many exist in New Zealand is an indicator of the relatively unspoiled nature of the country—pollution is a destroyer of lichen, and in many parts of the world lichens have not survived.

A lichen is two plants in one, a fungus and an alga which live together and help one another to survive. The fungus protects the alga from the elements and predators, and supplies it with water and nutrients, while the alga provides the fungus with the sugars it needs. The fungus also furnishes a place for the alga to grow. Such a symbiotic relationship is described as mutualism. Lichens spread either by the fungus producing spores which must then find algal partners, or by the less uncertain method of the lichens splitting into fragments when they are dry and blowing away to a new rock or tree where they take hold and slowly grow.

Lichens flourish in deserts, on mountain tops or in rainforests. They can put up with a variety of climatic conditions, from above boiling point to well below freezing level. In many locations they act as a pioneering plant, weathering the surface of a rock and preparing the way for other plants. However, rooted plants, not lichens, usually win the race to settle on unstable surfaces such as scree slopes.

Scientists divide lichens into three types: crustose lichens which grow on rocks and other surfaces; foliose lichens which resemble leaves; and fruticose lichens which look like shrubs. The last are sometimes used by model enthusiasts as make-believe trees.

## Did you know?

Lichens are the slowest growing of all plants. The average lichen enlarges its diameter by only a few millimetres a year. It has been estimated that some *Rhizocarpon* lichens growing on rocks in the Arctic are as old as 4500 years. The *Rhizocarpon geographicum* shown below is a very slow-growing and long-lived lichen that is widespread throughout the world.

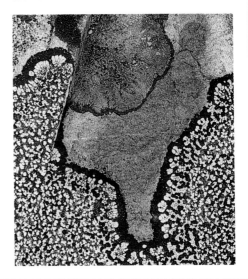

In order to survive in extreme conditions, lichens dry out and become dormant, then once conditions become favourable, they begin to take up moisture and resume growing.

One of the few New Zealand lichens known by its popular name is old man's beard (not to be confused with the destructive introduced climber which goes by the same name). This lichen grows abundantly on forest trees in wet and humid areas such as the West Coast.

Some New Zealand lichens are useful sources of dyes and potentially have medicinal properties. A common native, *Pseudocyphellaria coronata*, contains polypric acid which has been shown to be active against leukaemia in experiments on mice. Lichens have antibiotic properties and usnic acid found in them is strongly antibacterial.

*Cladonia coccifera produces bright red spore-bodies on tall hollow stalks.*

*Lichens of the* Pseudocyphellaria *genus are New Zealand's most common foliose lichens.*

# Limpets

Throughout the intertidal zone limpets clamp on to rocks, grazing algae on the rock surface with their rasping tongue or radula. As fast as this tongue is worn down by the abrasive rocks, its tissue is replaced.

The most common limpets are the ornate (*Cellana ornata*) and the radiate limpet (*C. radians*), which occur from north to south. There are more than 20 other limpet species, some of them restricted in their range by temperature. The Otago limpet (*C. strigilis redimiculum*) is found south of Kaikoura, while the Cook Strait limpet (*C. denticulata*) is most abundant around the centre of the country.

New Zealand can claim the largest living limpet in the world, *Patella kermadecensis*. Grazing the rocks around the Kermadec Islands, the Kermadec limpet grows to the size of a dinner

## *Staying in the groove*

For an animal with such a primitive brain, the limpet has an astounding ability to find its way back to its home patch. This homing instinct remains a mystery—limpets cannot see and when they head out on a feeding trip they do not appear to lay chemical trails to guide them back. In fact, as often as not they return home by a completely different route.

When the tide is full, a limpet moves about 10 mm a minute, grazing on algae and tiny seaweeds. Once the tide starts to turn, the limpet speeds up to 30 mm a minute in order to return to its oval groove in the rock, where it will seal itself to prevent drying out.

To test their homing abilities scientists have tried to confuse limpets in a number of ways: chipping away landmarks, cutting new scratches in rocks and placing bricks in their path, but still the limpets make it back. Not all limpets home (the ornate does, but the radiate does not), and among the homing species, some individuals home only some of the time, and some never.

*This limpet has made a substantial inroad into the green seaweed 'pasture' surrounding its home base.*

plate. This homing species is also territorial, occurring in a distinct band low on the shore, extending down to 3 metres subtidally. Kermadec limpets are very slow growing and large individuals may be several decades old.

Some limpets do not have to hunt for food. Cave limpets (*Gadinia conica*) remain immobile, suspended on cave ceilings waiting for plankton to be washed in by strong currents. This white-shelled species has a curtain of secreted mucus which entangles the plankton.

The filter-feeding slipper limpet (*Maoricrypta costata*) is often seen in pairs, the smaller male on top of the female. Its North Atlantic relative stacks in piles of more than two with a young male at the top of the heap and females at the bottom. The male has a long penis to fertilise the females beneath him; a fresh recruit to the pile is a male, but as female limpets die off at the bottom, males on top change sex.

Another limpet curiosity is the only light-producing freshwater limpet in the world, *Latia neritoides*, which makes its home on boulders of fast-flowing North Island rivers. Like the glow-worm, this limpet is bioluminescent.

The shield limpet or duck's bill limpet (*Scutus breviculus*) is actually a sea slug closely related to the paua. About the size of a person's palm, it has a narrow shell which resembles a duck's bill, but this is usually hidden by a fold of skin.

*All spore plants are survivors of a time when liverworts, mosses and ferns dominated the Earth. This* Schistochila *species is a leafy liverwort, its spore sacs contained within the black heads.*

# Liverworts

Liverworts are the little-recognised plants that, along with mosses and lichens, form the forest 'carpet'. Plants thought to be mosses are often liverworts. Modern liverworts look like the earliest and simplest land plants that emerged from the water 400 million years ago—then they were little more than a layer of green cells on the wet mud. Today their habitat requirements are not much different; without plenty of moisture, they cannot grow. Their curious name, meaning 'liver root', arises from a mediaeval practice of assessing a plant's medicinal value by comparing its appearance with human organs. Because some liverworts resemble livers it was thought they must be beneficial to the liver.

New Zealand's more than 500 liverworts come in two main forms and in many different sizes. By far the majority are described as leafy liverworts and are easily confused with mosses or filmy ferns. The other group are thallose liverworts which have liver-shaped leaves.

Like many plants, liverworts use chemicals to defend themselves against grazing enemies. Some liverworts have aromatic molecules called monoterpenoids which repulse insects and slugs.

# Lizards

New Zealand's lizard fauna, which is more diverse than its landbird fauna, has been described as one of the country's best-kept secrets. Victoria University scientist Dr Charles Daugherty believes 'New Zealand has the most diverse lizard fauna of any temperate archipelago on Earth'.

Lizards are also highly specialised ecologically and are found in a wide range of habitats: warm Northland beaches, rocky Fiordland shores, high-altitude grasslands, treetops, alpine scree and rock faces.

Our knowledge of lizards has expanded dramatically in the last two decades with intensive scientific study. In 1955 just 28 species were identified, but by 1994, 59 species of lizard were recognised. Partly this increase was a result of new finds, but also recently developed genetic techniques have demonstrated that lizards once thought to be the same species are in fact distinct from one another.

New Zealand lizards are unique in the diversity of species found in small areas. For example, there are 13 species on Great Barrier Island (27 761 ha); more remarkable still, 10 species of lizards and the tuatara squeeze onto 13-ha Middle Island in the Mercury group.

New Zealand lizards are divided into geckos and skinks. Geckos have a soft, loose skin covered with granular scales, while the skin of skinks is shiny and smooth. Geckos' eyes are permanently open but skinks have small blinkable eyes.

Except for one skink, New Zealand's lizards give birth to live young rather than laying eggs as tropical species do. This ensures that the young survive in the cooler temperate climate, whereas eggs would be at the mercy of the weather.

Geckos arrived in New Zealand before skinks, but exactly when is uncertain. It is assumed that both were here at least 25 million years ago, at a time when a rising sea level reduced the land surface to about 22 percent of its present area, and that they were likely to have been on board New Zealand when it floated away from Gondwanaland around 80 million years ago.

Both geckos and skinks can lose their tails. This has the advantage of distracting a predator, which concentrates on the twitching tail while the lizard escapes, although the loss of the tail does mean loss of valuable fat stores.

## Geckos

Among the oldest in the world, New Zealand geckos fall into two groups: the grey-brown *Hoplodactylus* genus and the green *Naultinus*. The *Hoplodactylus* is a night-time hunter, numbering 22 species. By contrast the seven species of *Naultinus* geckos are active by day, crawling among foliage where they stalk their insect prey, often catching them on the wing.

Geckos eat mainly invertebrates, but also carrion, nectar and berries. They communicate through a variety of chirps, squeaks and barks, most of which are audible to humans. Little is known about how long they live. One Auckland green gecko is believed to have lived 45 years, and a record exists of a 36-year-old Duvaucel's gecko.

The common gecko, once considered one species, has been reappraised by experts who now recognise a group of closely related but distinct species which are distinguished by minute differences such as the size and shape of their scales. Until 1996 the common gecko and the forest gecko were the only geckos not protected legally and fears were held that collectors might threaten some of the yet-to-be-described species which have restricted ranges. Wild populations of geckos cannot withstand intensive collecting because of their slow breeding rate; some species breed once a year but in colder areas breeding occurs only every second year.

### NEW ZEALAND'S GECKOS

Goldstripe gecko (*Hoplodactylus chrysosireticus*)
Duvaucel's gecko (*H. duvaucelii*)
Forest gecko (*H. granulatus*)
Black-eyed gecko (*H. kahutarae*)
Common gecko (*H. maculatus*)
Cloudy gecko (*H. nebulosus*)
Pacific gecko (*H. pacificus*)
Harlequin gecko (*H. rakiurae*)
Striped gecko (*H. stephensi*)
Common green gecko (*Naultinus elegans*)
Jewelled gecko (*N. gemmeus*)
Northland green gecko (*N. grayii*)
Marlborough green gecko (*N. manukanus*)
Rough gecko (*N. rudis*)
Nelson green gecko (*N. stellatus*)
West Coast green gecko (*N. tuberculatus*)

A further 13 species of *Hoplodactylus*, most presently known as *H. maculatus* or *H. granulatus*, are awaiting description.

*Mahoe berries cram the brightly coloured mouth of this jewelled gecko.*

*Green geckos live on the outer branches of shrubs where they gain protection from predators.*

## Kawekaweau gecko

**A**re the forests of Urewera National Park or the East Cape home to the largest gecko that ever lived? Lizard enthusiasts have been harbouring hopes of discovering a live example of the 620-mm-long kawekaweau ever since the only known specimen was discovered in the dusty basement of a Marseilles museum in 1979. The undescribed endemic gecko is presumed to have been shipped to Europe in the 19th century.

In 1986 the lizard was named *Hoplodactylus delcourti,* after the museum curator who rescued it from the basement; the specimen travelled to New Zealand in 1990 for a 'Forgotten Fauna' exhibition at the Museum of New Zealand and sparked interest among people who believed they may have recently sighted the large gecko in this country.

The last reliable account of a sighting was in 1870 when surveyor Gilbert Mair reported how a Urewera chief caught and killed a kawekaweau near Whakatane, 'about two feet long, and as thick as a man's wrist; colour brown, striped longitudinally with dull red'.

Sightings have been reported from the 1950s up to the present day, in the vicinity of Tolaga Bay on the East Cape. A motorist recalled running over a lizard 'as long as a man's arm' in the region in the mid-70s, and in 1995 forestry workers near Rotorua reported seeing geckos longer than 300 mm. However, in the absence of solid evidence, it has to be presumed that the kawekaweau is extinct.

*Kawekaweau, the world's largest gecko, is lined up for size with the tuatara (see page 341).*

One *Hoplodactylus* species, the black-eyed gecko, lives in the mountains of the Kaikoura Ranges as high as 2180 metres. Only a few dozen of this species have been discovered. Just how this gecko has adapted to the harsh alpine environment is as yet little understood. For months of the year its habitat is snow covered, with temperatures below zero. It is suspected that the gecko takes advantage of the way the greywacke rocks store solar energy, so that their surface temperature is raised 2–4°C above that of the surrounding air.

Geckos have been discovered to be plant pollinators, with flax and pohutukawa their favourite sources of pollen. In the days when lizards occurred in much greater densities than at present they would have played a key role in pollination; their importance on islands continues today. At times plants in bloom are blanketed by masses of geckos. The pollen accumulates on the animals' throats from where it is easily transferred to other plants for pollination. Lizards are also fruit eaters and thus play a role in spreading seeds. More than half of a group of common geckos studied near Wellington ate coprosma and pohuehue fruit, while during summer 30 percent of the robust skink's diet is fruit. It has been speculated that geckos, rather than birds, feed on divaricating shrubs, based on the fact that birds cannot reach the berries, which are borne on the inside of a dense tangle of branches and twigs.

### Skinks

There are two skink groups: the *Oligosoma* skinks have pointed heads, long fingers and toes, are active during the day (except the egg-laying skink) and enjoy resting in the sun. The *Cyclodina* skinks have blunter heads, shorter fingers and toes, are active at night, and prefer shaded areas.

The egg-laying skink, which lives on islands in the north from the Three Kings to the Aldermans off Coromandel, is an odd skink for two reasons: of all the lizard species, it is the only competent swimmer and is often seen in saltwater rock pools; and it is the only lizard to lay eggs.

Two skinks inhabiting Otago tussocklands are the Otago skink and the grand skink. Collectively the two are known as 'giant' skinks but at 300 mm in length they are just half the size of the kawekaweau gecko (see box). Found only in Central Otago, they live in the crevices of schist outcrops and tors. Both are strikingly coloured jet black with yellow or gold markings in the form of blotches on the Otago skink and flecks on the giant skink, which camouflage them well on the lichen-encrusted rocks where they live.

The decline of the Otago skinks has been well documented. In the mid- to late 1980s scientists pored over 1.46 million ha of potential habitat, uncovering populations in only 140 000 ha. A complex series of events has led to the significant reduction in numbers, triggered by conversion of tussocks to farmland. When shrubs surrounding outcrops were removed, the skinks lost a source of berries, and with the disappearance of the scrub cover, wild cats found skinks easier to catch.

The present distribution of some lizards provides a clue as to how widespread they were in the past. For example, the rare 200-mm long Whitaker's skink hangs on at one site at Pukerua Bay, near Wellington, but its next appearance is 500 km north on the Mercury Islands off the Coromandel coast.

Lizards have suffered from the effects of introduced cats, rats, dogs and stoats, as well as destruction of their habitat. Scientists consider that 24 of the country's 59 lizards are rare. Without islands, New Zealand would have lost even more species.

## NEW ZEALAND'S SKINKS

Copper skink (*Cyclodina aenea*)
Robust skink (*C. alani*)
McGregor's skink (*C. macgregori*)
Marbled skink (*C. oliver*)
Ornate skink (*C. ornata*)
Whitaker's skink (*C. whitakeri*)
Fiordland skink (*Oligosoma acrinasum*)
Green skink (*O. chloronoton*)
Falla's skink (*O. falla*)
Grand skink (*O. grande*)
Chevron skink (*O. homalonotum*)
Cryptic skink (*O. inconspicuum*)
Speckled skink (*O. infrapunctatum*)
Spotted skink (*O. lineoocellatum*)
McCann's skink (*O. maccanni*)
Small-scaled skink (*O. microlepis*)
Moko skink (*O. moco*)
Chathams skink (*O. nigriplantare nigriplantare*)
Common skink (*O. nigriplantare polychroma*)
Southern skink (*O. notosaurus*)
Otago skink (*O. otagense*)
Shore skink (*O. smithi*)
Small-eared skink (*O. stenotis*)
Striped skink (*O. striatum*)
Egg-laying skink (*O. suteri*)
Scree skink (*O. waimatense*)
Brown skink (*O. zelandicum*)
  Two *Cyclodina* and two *Oligosoma* species are in the process of being described.

*The scale patterns of the common skink blend in with the rocks on which it basks.*

*Amphibious by nature, mangroves breathe through pencil-like roots protruding through clogging black mud, also home to mud crabs. New life asserts itself in the shape of hundreds of seedlings.*

DISTRIBUTION AND RANGE OF
NEW ZEALAND MANGROVES

---- Natural southern
     limit of mangroves
     (some mangroves
     have been planted
     south of this line).

# Mangroves

Only in Victoria, Australia, do mangroves or manawa grow further away from the equator than in New Zealand. From a line south of Kawhia Harbour in the west and Opotiki in the east, mangroves' march further south is restricted by winter frost.

There are about 19 500 ha of mangroves in New Zealand, a fraction of the area they occupied in pre-European times. The largest areas of mangrove distribution include Kaipara (5500 ha), Raungaunu (2400 ha), Hokianga (1900 ha) and Whangarei (1200 ha) harbours.

Often serving as a border between land and sea, mangroves are formed on the mud of estuaries that are regularly inundated by the tide. Of the world's 55 species, just one, *Avicennia marina* var.

*resinifera*, is found in New Zealand. In naming it *resinifera* (resin bearing), early botanists mistakenly assumed the lumps of resin floating among mangroves had been produced by the plants, but in fact they had come from kauri trees.

Although mangroves will survive in fresh water, they do best where salt water is diluted to 25–50 percent of its normal salinity. The plants have several ways of coping with their salty and muddy environment.

Because the mud that mangroves grow in is anaerobic (does not have any oxygen), they have to take oxygen from the air, either through aerial roots or breathing roots called pneumatophores. These peg-like roots rise out of the mud around the base of the tree. To avoid being overloaded with salt, the mangrove secretes salt through tiny glands in the surface layer of its leaves.

Mangrove estuaries are among the most fertile ecosystems in the world, producing four times as much plant matter as good pasture and 20 times as much as the open ocean. Shedding about 8 tonnes of dry leaf litter per hectare each year, the taller trees boost the estuaries' productivity.

Invaluable though mangrove estuaries are for a host of reasons—including acting as nursery grounds for fish, preventing coastal erosion, and providing a home for hundreds of animal species—they have not been well respected. Too often have they been favoured dumping grounds or candidates for reclamation.

Mangroves produce some of the hottest-burning firewood of all plants. Maori avoided using dried mangrove wood to heat hangi stones because it made them too hot and also gave out a pungent smell.

# Manuka

Depending on where it grows, manuka (*Leptospermum scoparium*) adopts a number of different forms: in sheltered, wet locations it can attain a height of 12 metres, but in areas of poor soil it creeps along the ground. Sometimes it barely flowers at all, while in some areas it flowers as a seedling just a few centimetres high.

Hardy and versatile, manuka has spongy, air-filled root tissue which enables it to grow in sour, nutrient-deficient and waterlogged soils. Yet it also thrives in very dry, exposed sites. Botanists have used the term 'plastic' for manuka's ability to grow differently according to its surrounding environment. However, in a recent study a number of seedlings gathered from around the country were grown in Dunedin, and over time retained many of their original characteristics, proving another theory: that there are some genetically determined and permanent forms of manuka adapted to different habitats.

Manuka and kanuka (see page 173) are sometimes confused; manuka is smaller in stature, its leaves are prickly compared to kanuka and its capsules and white or pink flowers are larger and borne singly, not in a cluster. Both are important in the early stages of forest succession, providing shelter for slower-growing canopy species such as totara, rimu, beech and broadleaf trees. They are also a key wildlife habitat for species such as kiwi, fernbirds and green geckos. The coral mistletoe can live only on kanuka and manuka.

Captain James Cook dubbed the plant 'tea tree' after brewing a cuppa from its leaves. Maori used different parts of manuka to cure a variety of ailments including sore throats, back pains, and mouth, throat and eye troubles. Manuka honey has been found to be one of the most effective honeys in preventing bacterial growth. Researchers have identified a group of aromatic acids, present in the honey along with hydrogen peroxide, as being minor antibacterial agents, and further research is being undertaken to discover the major antibacterial component. The Cawthron Institute, a research organisation based in Nelson, tested manuka oil against 39 micro-organisms and found it to be active against all of them. New Zealand's manuka oil is 20–30 times more active than Australian tea-tree oil.

*Manuka is a key pollen and nectar plant not just for honey bees, but also for native bees, flies, moths, beetles and green geckos.*

# Marine reserves

Marine reserves are protected-area latecomers. In the 1970s campaigners and scientists promoted the concept of a marine reserve near Leigh, north of Auckland, to protect an area of representative coast; in an unheard-of move, people were prohibited from taking fish or shellfish.

Today the Cape Rodney-Okakari Point Reserve, established in 1975, attracts thousands of people who delight in being able to feed fish by hand and see plentiful numbers of species which are rare elsewhere.

Gradually the idea of marine reserves is taking hold. New Zealand's diverse coastal marine environment, characterised by long ocean beaches, exposed cliffs, bays, drowned valleys, and numerous islands, provides many opportunities for reserves. Some of the special features protected include kelp forests, sponge gardens and dense scallop populations (Whanganui-a-Hei), underwater hot springs and areas of black volcanic glass (Mayor Island), and mangroves, fernbirds and New Zealand dotterels (Pollen Island).

A total of 14 marine reserves have now been gazetted, covering 4 percent of the 0.16 million square kilometres of territorial sea (extending 12 nautical miles from the coast). However, the Kermadec Islands Marine Reserve, covering 7350 square kilometres, dwarfs all the others in size.

Unusually for protected areas, any individual or organisation, and not just the controlling body (the Department of Conservation), can propose that an area become a marine reserve. The Federation of Commercial Fishermen and Fiordland fishing interests nominated reserves in Milford and Doubtful Sounds to protect black coral and sea pens, while the Royal Forest and Bird Protection Society advanced the Kapiti Island reserve.

*Horizontally striped mado swim in schools down to 40 metres, feeding on worms, amphipods, shrimps and seaweed.*
*(Inset) Fed by warm subtropical currents, Nursery Cove at Poor Knights Island contains a profusion of schooling fish, reef fish, sponge gardens, submarine caves, archways and steep walls, making it one of the world's premier dive spots.*

# Marlin

Striped marlin (*Tetrapturus audax*), though not the largest of the billfish—that honour goes to the black marlin and the blue marlin—grow to their greatest size in the food-rich coastal waters at the top of the North Island. Each year they migrate there from spawning grounds at the equator, feeding on fish and squid which they kill with a side-to-side slash of their bill.

Black and blue marlin also go south, but the record sizes are found elsewhere, such as off the Australian Great Barrier Reef, Hawaii and Peru. Some black marlin caught by commercial fishers have weighed as much as 1.5 tonnes, and blue marlin 1 tonne. The world record for a striped marlin, 224 kg, is for a fish taken off Whangarei in 1986.

New Zealand gained its reputation as a mecca for big-game fishers after US author and angler Zane Grey wrote *Tales of the Angler's El Dorado: New Zealand*, a book about his experiences when he hooked 34 marlin during a 5-week stay at the Bay of Islands in 1926.

Marlin began to decline when commercial longliners first started to fish in New Zealand waters in 1961. Even though they were after tuna, they inevitably caught marlin as well. By 1971, Japanese fishers were taking about 6000 marlin a year; during the 1960s and 70s, anglers were catching fewer than 100 a season.

Persuaded that some form of control was needed, in 1987 the New Zealand Government banned foreign longliners from fishing in northern waters. As a result, recreational fishers began to see a dramatic increase in the numbers of striped marlin. In the 1995–96 season the catch was estimated at 1600 marlin, of which 1090 were tagged in a programme that began in 1975. One striped marlin tagged just northeast of the Three Kings Islands on 11 May 1996 was recaptured near Fiji on 28 June. In 48 days it had swum 930 nautical miles, an average of 19.3 nautical miles a day.

*Taking the bait: although striped marlin are the smallest billfish, their bills are the longest of the marlin species.*

At the same time as commercial fishers were denied marlin, a change in attitude by anglers towards catching the large fish became apparent. Before 1987, less than 1 percent of marlin were set free, but now a large proportion are released.

Although whales need fear few animals in the ocean—humans, orcas and sharks are their only predators—they can expect attack from an unusual quarter. Billfish such as striped marlin are very territorial and will charge a whale swimming through their feeding grounds. A sei whale captured in 1969 had the bill of a billfish stuck deep in its throat.

Striped marlin and other billfish are said to use their long bills to attack and stun fish. Often tuna and mako sharks found in marlins' stomachs have been speared. Obviously this is an optional hunting method, as observers on fishing boats have reported that around 20 percent of marlins caught had lost their bills yet invariably remained in good condition.

Much remains to be discovered about marlin. The latest development in big gamefish research is satellite tagging. Transmitters, attached to the fish and powered by lithium battery packs which can last for a year, send information to satellites each time an aerial breaks the surface. A more up-to-date development will incorporate the use of tags which gather information for a predetermined period, then break free from the marlin and float to the surface, from there downloading their data to satellites.

# Matai

'We cut down a young one of these trees; the wood proved heavy and solid, too much so for the mast but would make the finest Plank in the world.' Captain Cook's prediction of the fate of matai, made following an overnight journey up the Thames (Waihou) River in 1769, proved to be accurate, although in fact Cook and his botanist Joseph Banks thought that what they were cutting down was another podocarp, the kahikatea (see page 165), larger versions of which grew along the Waihou.

Also known as black pine, matai (*Prumnopitys taxifolia*) possesses strength and durability, qualities that have earned it popularity as a flooring timber especially. Matai are slow-growing, long-lived trees, reaching maturity at between 300 and

*Did you know?*

Resembling hammer marks, the depressions on this matai trunk are left where the bark has flaked off, and discourage climbing plants from attaching themselves to the tree. Maori legend has it that the red marks on matai trunks are splashes of blood from a fight between Maui and an eel.

600 years and enduring at least 900 years. Their purplish berries are an important food for kereru and kaka, and were eaten by Maori. The tree is the only podocarp with a juvenile divaricating form. Like totara and kahikatea, it thrives in younger, fertile soils such as those alongside rivers or created by volcanic eruption, growing to a maximum of 30 metres.

Matai that have achieved a degree of fame include the wishing tree, Te Rakau-tipua a Hinepou (the magic tree of Hinepou) near Lake Rotoiti in the North Island, which commemorates the marriage of the chieftainess Hinepou and her husband Pikiao. Another is the largest known matai, near Lake Ianthe in Westland, estimated to be more than 1000 years old, with a squat, massive trunk 2.35 metres in diameter.

Before matai were felled, loggers used to tap into the sap in the heart of the tree. The liquid, known as matai beer, was refreshing with a bitter aftertaste, and was believed to be effective in checking tuberculosis.

*Black glass formed from the rapid cooling of rhyolitic lava, obsidian was fashioned into razor-sharp tools by Maori. Mayor Island, Bay of Plenty, was a key site for the high-quality mineral.*

# Minerals

Depending on their atomic structures, minerals can vary from soft talc to hard diamonds. Scientists have identified more than 2000 minerals, ranging from gemstones treasured for their beauty and rarity, to more mundane minerals which are nevertheless valuable for their use in our everyday lives. Only about 20 of them make up more than 95 percent of the Earth's crust.

But what exactly is a mineral? Many people use the terms 'mineral' and 'rock' interchangeably but there are major differences between the two. Minerals are the basic chemical compounds of the solid earth, whereas rocks are physical mixtures of minerals, usually in the form of interlocking crystals. Some rocks may consist of just one mineral, but most consist of several.

Ever since Maori settlement of New Zealand, humans have made use of minerals: greenstone for ornaments, tools and weapons, argillite and obsidian for tools, and clays for decorating bodies. Obsidian from Mayor Island has been found in most archaeological sites, including Stewart Island. Early European settlers mined coal and copper ore, and dug for gold. Today many minerals are used as the raw materials of industry.

Minerals are divided into three broad groups: metallic, non-metallic and energy minerals. Non-metallic gemstones such as jade, garnets and rubies are regarded as the 'glamour' minerals, although it is the hard-working metallic minerals such as copper and iron that have played a more important role in human history.

Scientists have devised a hardness scale for minerals, called the MOHS hardness test. The test method is rudimentary; if a fingernail can scratch the rock, it is given a hardness of 1 (talc or gypsum come into this category); a pocket-knife scratch means a hardness of 4 or 5 (fluorite or calcite); and to test for diamonds (hardness of 10), the rock is scratched across glass to see whether sparks are produced.

## How minerals are formed

Minerals are formed in a variety of ways. A simple example is pools of seawater at Lake Grassmere drying in the sun to manufacture sodium chloride or salt. What this mineral has in common with other crystalline minerals is the way in which it is created: a crystal is formed out of a type of liquid.

Some minerals are created on the Earth's surface, while others are fashioned kilometres down in the crust. Because rocks are composed of minerals, the story of the creation of many minerals cannot be separated from that of the creation of rocks, whether they be igneous, sedimentary or metamorphic types.

Many minerals are hard to find. Some are in rocks at the surface, but, as in the case of jade, masked by the rock that contains them. Other minerals are buried deep down. Geologists gain clues about the possible whereabouts of minerals by studying the geological processes in an area. They know that in areas of past hydrothermal activity they can expect to find gold, silver, copper, zinc and lead, in magmatic regions chromium, iron and platinum, and among metamorphic rocks, marble, garnet and serpentine.

Only small areas of the world are mineral-rich. Commercially valuable concentrations of minerals are called ore deposits. Hard to find because they are often covered by plants or are beneath the surface, ore deposits can be very small—10 million tonnes of ore can be contained in an area 300 metres in diameter and 50 metres thick.

## Metallic, non-metallic and energy minerals

The most important metallic minerals mined in New Zealand are gold, iron and silver. Historically lead, zinc, manganese and mercury have been exploited, but supplies are limited. The mining of titanium from several sites is at present being investigated.

By far the most-used minerals and rocks are non-metallic. They include aggregate (rock fragments) used in roading or for concrete, clays (for bricks, tiles and pottery), dolomite (fertiliser), limestone (fertiliser and cement), marble (building), and silica sand (glass).

Coal, petroleum and gas—the energy minerals—are derived from plant remains deposited over millions of years, but each is formed in a

## Gemstones

New Zealand has no precious gems such as diamonds, emeralds, rubies or sapphires. Some of these exist here, but the stones are generally too flawed to be of gem quality. Nevertheless a number of New Zealand stones qualify as gemstones because of their beauty, rarity, or durability. The most obvious example is jade (see page 145).

Other New Zealand gemstones include varieties of agate, amethyst, flint, garnet, jasper, onyx, opal, quartz and topaz. Most of these have a hardness rating (see above) of 5–7; below 7 the stone is liable to fracture.

*Jasper*

*Kyanite (blue) and green mica*

*Moss agate*

*Grossular garnet*

*Sapphire-bearing vein*

different way. During the late Cretaceous period around 100 million years ago, massive beds of peat and plants accumulated and over time were buried. First the carbohydrates and waxy materials of the plants were attacked by swamp bacteria and fungi, producing volatile gases such as methane and carbon dioxide. Successive layers built up, squeezing out water from the material lower down.

Coal was then created by the 'cooking' action of the Earth; temperatures increase by about 1°C for every 32 metres, and the quality of the coal depends on the depth at which it is buried. Top-quality bituminous coal—the kind produced on the West Coast—requires a temperature of 200°C at a depth of 5 km. The next grade up, called sub-bituminous, lies 2 km below the surface; important deposits are in the Waikato and Taranaki. The lowest-quality coal, lignite, formed at 1 km deep, is found in Otago and Southland.

Gas and petroleum are at first formed in the same way as coal, but at some point, instead of becoming a solid element they change into a gas or liquid and are trapped between layers of rocks. In New Zealand, gas is produced in Taranaki, chiefly from the offshore Maui and onshore Kapuni wells, which tap into reserves 3–6 km below the surface.

New Zealand imports more minerals than it exports. Main imports include oil (for transport), bauxite (for making aluminium), rock phosphate and sulphur (for farm fertiliser).

*Remains of 19th-century gold workings are still to be found in the Clutha Gorge, Otago.*

# Miro

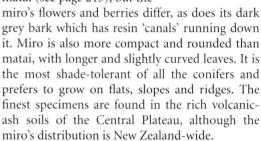

A podocarp, the miro (*Prumnopitys ferruginea*) is a handsome tree growing as tall as 25 metres. Some features are difficult to distinguish from matai (see page 213), but the miro's flowers and berries differ, as does its dark grey bark which has resin 'canals' running down it. Miro is also more compact and rounded than matai, with longer and slightly curved leaves. It is the most shade-tolerant of all the conifers and prefers to grow on flats, slopes and ridges. The finest specimens are found in the rich volcanic-ash soils of the Central Plateau, although the miro's distribution is New Zealand-wide.

During late autumn, birds, particularly kereru, wax plump on the small-plum-sized, bright red miro berries, to the point where they can hardly fly. Maori took advantage of the kereru's thirst after gorging itself on the berries by placing snared water troughs near the trees; when drinking, kereru caught their heads in hidden nooses.

The tree was considered to have healing properties. Maori used oil from the berries to cure fevers, gum to stop the loss of blood from wounds, and a drink made from leaves and bark to treat gonorrhoea.

Today there are few large miro left, most having been cut for their durable timber used in housing. The largest tree recorded in recent times had a trunk diameter of 1.32 metres.

# Mistletoes

When comic hero Asterix needed a burst of superhuman strength, he used to visit the druid Getafix who would brew him up a potion based on a European variety of the mistletoe *Viscum album*. In New Zealand, honeyeaters such as tui and bellbirds also gain energy by drinking from native mistletoe flowers, even if the results are less dramatic than those experienced by Asterix and his fellow Gauls.

There is a two-way benefit: without honeyeating birds twisting ripe buds, some mistletoe flowers cannot open and thus release their seeds to germinate. Only in 1993 was the role of birds in mistletoe pollination revealed. In Africa and Asia the phenomenon of 'explosive' or animal-opened mistletoes is well known. However, it appears the New Zealand *Peraxilla* species—*P. colensoi* and *P. tetrapetala*—are the only Australasian mistletoes to be pollinated in such a way.

These two species are also the showiest of New Zealand's nine mistletoes, their scarlet blooms an eye-catching sight among the predominant sombre green of the forest. Maori called the red mistletoes pikirangi, meaning 'climb to the sky'. Another conspicuous mistletoe is the yellow-and-orange-flowered *Alepis flavida*.

However, in many forests the once-common spectacular flowers light up the trees no more. Wherever possums have set up residence for a long time, mistletoes are largely absent, and with possums distributed over 92 percent of New Zealand, few forests are untouched by them. In Australia, mistletoes have learned to mimic their host plants to avoid being eaten by possums.

Other mistletoes include the small greenish-yellow-flowered *Ileostylus micranthus* and *Tupeia antarctica*, and three dwarf species: *Korthalsella clavata*, *K. lindsayi* and *K. salicornioides*.

One of the greatest losses to the New Zealand plant world was that of the beautiful red mistletoe, *Trilepidea adamsii*, which was last seen in 1954. Forest destruction, overenthusiastic collecting, and possum browsing are likely to have hastened this mistletoe's end.

## Did you know?

New Zealand mistletoes are semiparasitic, making their own food and synthesising like other plants, but also relying on a host tree for water and nutrients.

Once the sticky seed, usually transported by a bird, lands on a tree branch, it glues itself on and sends down a special root to tap into the tree's water and nutrient supply. The mistletoe may eventually kill its host.

*Mistletoe* P. tetrapetala *grows on mountain beech near Lake Ohau.*

# Moa

No one knows quite when the last moa disappeared, but if Abel Tasman and his crew had landed in New Zealand in 1642 they may have seen the now-extinct bird, though it would have been an extremely lucky sighting for by that time there would have been few of the large birds left.

To this day people report possible sightings of moa, but most authorities believe that the last moa died between 300 and 500 years ago. It first disappeared from the far north, then from progressively further south; its last refuge was likely to have been the dense bush of south Westland where few humans ventured.

In the last 40 years techniques such as radiocarbon dating have clarified our understanding of the moa, and along the way cherished beliefs about many aspects of the bird have been overturned. Take the way the moa stood: what never fails to impress people today is the height of *Dinornis giganteus*—3 metres—making it the tallest bird ever to have lived.

In reality, the moa reached that height only when straining for a succulent high branch; in its normal posture it was around 2 metres tall. Early moa enthusiasts used to exaggerate the moa's

*A height-exaggerated moa skeleton compared to a human skeleton, from an early-20th-century Canterbury Museum display. Moa necks tended to be S-curved, so that rather than being twice as tall as a human, as depicted here, they were about two-thirds as tall.*

## *Moa questions and answers*

**What family of birds did the moa belong to?**
*Ratites, the same family as the flightless kiwi, emu, cassowary, ostrich and the rhea. Except for the kiwi, all ratites are large birds.*

**What did moa taste like?**
*If it tasted anything like its relative the cassowary, it was gamey, rich, tasty, and to judge by midden remains, fatty.*

**How did Maori hunt moa?**
*In a variety of ways: with spears, nooses, snares, by chasing them to exhaustion, herding them into pits, running them into lakes where they were beheaded. Kuri, or dogs, would sometimes have been used in the hunt.*

**Did moa have wings?**
*Moa had no wings whatsoever nor any traces of them. Even the flightless kiwi has small vestigial stubs of wings.*

**Before the arrival of man, did moa have any enemies?**
*The giant eagle* Harpagornis *would have eaten medium-sized adult moa, while the large extinct harrier would have preyed on chicks.*

**How heavy was the largest moa?**
*More than 250 kg. While that is weighty, the dromornithids of Australia, massive birds now extinct, are estimated to have weighed more than 500 kg.*

height by elongating the neck when making reconstructions from bones.

For many years scientific debate raged over the number of moa species. One count went as high as 38, but the figure of 29 species put forward by bird authority W R B Oliver in 1949 remained largely undisputed until 1976 when the number was reduced to 13. Today most scientists accept that there were 11 species in two families: three belonged in the Dinornithidae while the remaining eight have been classified in the Emeidae family, and included the smallest moa of all, the 20-kg *Eurapteryx curtus.*

Because so many moa remains were uncovered on the east coast of the South Island, where today there is little if any forest, early researchers came to the conclusion that the moa was a bird of the open plain or tussockland. However, botanists in recent decades who have studied the moa diet have discovered it consisted largely of twigs, leaves, fruits and seeds—not grasses or tussock. This confirmed that the South Island east coast was mostly forested in the recent past, and that moa were forest or forest-margin birds.

The question that was not satisfactorily answered for many years was: how did the moa become extinct? Up until the 1960s the received wisdom was that moa had died out because of a change of climate, and any moa species surviving when Maori arrived were a remnant population on the verge of extinction.

From the 1950s onwards archaeologists began to closely scrutinise moa bone sites and soon came to a quite different conclusion. Hundreds of such sites covering large areas are known. They showed that Maori carved up prodigious numbers of moa, ate the meat, made jewellery from the bones, used the skins for clothing and fashioned water containers out of moa eggs.

At the mouth of the Shag River in Otago, wagonloads of bones were carted away in the 19th century to the local bone mill where they were crushed into fertiliser.

It is now clear that Maori exterminated the moa, both directly, by simply killing them, and indirectly by robbing their nests of eggs and burning the forests on which they depended. A few centuries of hunting ended millions of years of moa history.

*These species of moa represent the three families:* Dinornis giganteus *was the largest moa, the medium-sized* Pachyornis elephantopus *was one of the heavier-built moa, and* Anomalopteryx didiformis *was a 30-kg species of the North and South islands.*

*The Moeraki boulders are the stuff of legend.*

# Moeraki boulders

About 60 million years ago, the giant cannonball concretions known as the Moeraki boulders began to form, and today are able to tell us the story of one of the greatest extinction events to have occurred in the Earth's history. Wrapped up in the 2-tonne, 2-metre, perfectly spherical concretions are the bones of mosasaurs and plesiosaurs, and the shells of ammonites and belemnites.

The boulders were formed in sediments lying on the sea floor. Lime-rich minerals that accumulated around a reptile bone, a fossil shell or a piece of wood gradually transformed the soft and pliable sediments so that they grew evenly outwards. Maori legend attributes a more picturesque origin, claiming that when the Araiteuru canoe was shipwrecked near Palmerston, its cargo of kumara, gourds and eel pots was transformed into the Moeraki boulders.

# Morepork

Now that the kiwi's range has shrunk, the haunting call of the native owl, the morepork (*Ninox novaeseelandiae*) is the night-time sound associated more than any other with the New Zealand bush. Today moreporks live not only in native forests but also pine plantations and open country where there are large trees providing shelter.

Compared with many native bird species, the morepork has managed to hold its own in the face of introduced predators and habitat destruc-

tion. Itself a predator, it is capable of warding off enemies with its sharp talons and beak. In fact, some scientists believe that, greeted by the bonanza of introduced prey such as rats and mice, moreporks might have actually increased since human arrival.

The only other owl in New Zealand is the little owl (*Athene noctua*), introduced from Germany.

A morepork has played a successful role in the attempt to rescue its endangered cousin, the Norfolk Island boobook (also called morepork). Two New Zealand moreporks were enlisted to mate with the sole surviving female boobook in 1987; one succeeded and the result is more than a dozen progeny so far.

In Maori tradition the appearance of a morepork or ruru could be a good or a bad sign. A morepork flying along a path was there as a protector, but one that perched in a prominent place, fluttered against a wall or entered a house might be indicating an imminent death.

*An expectant morepork chick awaits a delicious snack.*

# Mosquitoes

The whine of a mosquito about to home in on a bloody meal is a familiar, if unwelcome, sound to people living in the more humid parts of the North Island. Further south, mosquitoes tend not to invade homes, although they are a pest outside in wetter areas such as the West Coast.

The incessant drone of a female searching for a mate is produced by the beating of the insect's wings at up to 600 times a second. Male mosquitoes—fooled into thinking they were homing in on females—have been known to fly into the mouths of opera singers who were simply holding a note at the crucial pitch.

In some species (not found in New Zealand), during mating the female sinks her mouthparts into the male's head, draining the insect dry. In this way the female immediately gains nutrients for the egg-laying process. The male of another mosquito species is careful not to mate until after the female has taken a meal of blood. Females need to ingest blood before they can reproduce, but males, whose mouthparts are too weak to jab through the skin of an animal, generally feed on plant juices.

Of New Zealand's dozen mosquito species, the common mosquito (*Culex pervigilans*) breeds all year round in warmer regions. It feeds at night, refusing to be shooed away, driving victims to distraction with its persistent attacks.

The winter mosquito (*Aedes antipodeus*) is not limited by cool temperatures. A biter day and night, it lays its eggs in slime and mud where they hatch at temperatures as low as 5.5°C.

One of the most unusual mosquitoes is the coastal species (*Opifex fuscus*), a large black insect which breeds in seawater rock pools and bites during the day. The male flies over the water waiting for the moment when a female starts to emerge from her pupa. Even when she is only half-emerged he will haul her over to the side of the pool to mate with her. Occasionally the male makes a mistake and seizes another male but does not find out until the young mosquito has finally emerged.

Fortunately none of the world's 200 species of malaria-carrying *Anopheles* mosquitoes live in New Zealand. Global warming, however, could see some of them become established.

*A female mosquito's proboscis works like a two-way hypodermic syringe, one tube pumping in anticoagulant saliva while the other sucks up the freely flowing blood.*

# Mosses

Without mosses to soak up the copious rainwater that falls in New Zealand, the resulting runoff would be extremely damaging, flooding down-stream areas. The most common moss, sphagnum, is able to absorb up to 25 times its dry weight in water. Mosses also play an invaluable role in providing habitats for insects and other small animals. Compared with flowering plants mosses are primitive, without a well-developed system for transporting water from the roots to the leaves. In fact, mosses usually obtain water simply by soaking it up.

Like ferns and liverworts, mosses are spore plants, that is, they produce microscopic particles that grow into new plants, and water is crucial in their reproduction. The sperm are produced on different branches from the eggs, so the sperm has to swim to reach the egg and fertilise it, hence the need for water. Once the egg is fertilised, a stalked capsule full of spores pushes above the plant and the spores settle on the ground to start the cycle again.

More than 550 moss species have been recorded in New Zealand and new species are still being discovered. They occur in a variety of habitats: moist, shady sites, swamps, as epiphytes, in dry areas and on tree trunks. There are three different groups of mosses: the sphagnums, the

*Sphagnum moss harvesting, West Coast. Most sphagnum exported from New Zealand ends up in Japan where it is used for growing indoor plants.*

'true' mosses (most species belong in this group) and the granite mosses (sometimes called lantern mosses because their spore capsules resemble Chinese lanterns).

Only 30 species of mosses are endemic to New Zealand. Because their spores are very resistant, mosses are able to spread themselves far and wide around the globe. Often they travel thousands of kilometres in the upper atmosphere before landing to germinate.

Sphagnum moss is the plant that dominates peat bogs, which cover about 1 percent of the Earth's surface—or half the area of Australia. In fact, the peat is partially rotted sphagnum. New Zealand's great peat regions are the Hauraki Plains, the Chatham Islands and a few sites in Southland. One of sphagnum's valuable properties is that it is an antiseptic; it was used during World War I to heal wounds caused by shrapnel and poison-gas. Its more innovative uses have included serving as babies' nappies and mopping up oil spills.

A hectare of land can yield 12 tonnes of sphagnum a year; the industry earns $12 million annually and employs 500 people. West Coast sphagnum, which is harvested from areas which have been previously logged, mined or burned, is particularly valued because it is uncontaminated.

Of the 11 species of sphagnum moss in New Zealand, the one targeted for harvesting is *Sphagnum cristatum*, which grows in extensive carpets or as hummocky cushions.

## Did you know?

Claimed by some to be the largest moss in the world, *Dawsonia superba* grows on the forest floor throughout New Zealand. Reaching a height of half a metre, it is sometimes mistaken for a pine seedling.

*A 'river' of sphagnum moss flows through the Sabine Valley, Nelson Lakes National Park.*

# Mountains

On a geological timescale the Southern Alps and the North Island axial ranges (the Raukumara, Kaweka, Kaimanawa, Ruahine and Tararua) are youthful upstarts. It is only in the last 5 million years, from the onset of the Kaikoura Orogeny (mountain-building phase) which continues to this day, that they have been raised to their present position. The rocks of the Southern Alps were first laid down on the sea floor more than 300 million years ago as muds, sands, pebble beds and underwater volcanic rocks, before being reconstituted into stable rocks.

The Kaikoura Orogeny was the third of New Zealand's mountain-building periods. The first, the Tuhua Orogeny, occurred 395–345 million years ago, uplifting the most ancient parts of Fiordland; the second, the Rangitata Orogeny, is dated to 140–120 million years ago.

New Zealand's mountains owe their existence to the action of two continental plates crashing into one another, the force of the collision thrusting the land skywards, and in places shifting rocks that once lay side by side 450 km apart. So violent and swift has this uplift been, that Mount Cook and its neighbours have been raised an awesome 18 000 metres over the last few million years. At present parts of the Southern Alps are being hoisted up at a rate of 10 mm a year, but counteracting this upward mobility are the equally powerful erosive forces of wind, rain and frost.

Although Mount Cook is always being pushed up, devastating events such as the December 1991 rock avalanche are also at work to cut the growing mountain down to size. This avalanche lopped off 20 metres from Mount Cook's former 3764-metre summit, sending 14 million cubic metres of rock and ice down a steep slope at speeds of 400–600 km/h.

*The razor-edged summit ridge of Mount Cook thrusts above the milky glacial waters of Lake Pukaki.*
*(Inset) Erupting at intervals of 2–7 years, Mount Ngauruhoe is one of the world's most active volcanoes. It was formed only in the last 2000 years as magma forced its way to the surface.*

# Mudfish

Lying buried in mud for up to 5 months at a time, the mudfish is one of the most bizarre and obscure of animals. Like the lungfishes of South America, Africa and Australia, New Zealand's three species of mudfish aestivate for part of the year—the summer equivalent of hibernating. So well do they conceal themselves that for over a century it was thought the brown species might have become extinct on the West Coast, until it was 'rediscovered' in the 1960s.

Since then scientists have ascertained that both the brown (*Neochanna apoda*) and the black mudfish (*N. diversus*) are present in good numbers. Their capacity to breathe air and to burrow into mud allows the fish to tolerate extreme conditions, which explains why populations have managed to hang on in areas where their habitat has been modified.

Brown mudfish numbers are unknown, but they are relatively abundant in a diversity of habitats on the West Coast and in Taranaki, Wanganui,

Wellington and the Wairarapa. Department of Conservation staff who recently 'went fishing' in the Ngaere wetland near Stratford—a 10-ha remnant of a former 4000-ha swamp—found 57 mudfish in 3 nights, and on the West Coast mudfish have been found where experienced bushmen vowed there were none. The fish can burrow a metre down into the ground, and often occupy holes around the buttresses of trees. One was discovered aestivating under a Karamea house when the piles were being replaced.

Black mudfish are found in wetlands, swampy streams and drains in the northern half of the North Island. A study carried out in the early 1990s unexpectedly showed that black mudfish were present throughout the Waikato in a variety of habitats. Before then they were known to be in only a few locations such as the Kopuatai Peat Dome and the Whangamarino wetlands. Nevertheless, they showed up in their highest numbers in unmodified habitats.

The Canterbury mudfish (*N. burrowsius*), which has suffered more from habitat destruction, is a threatened species. Found from the

*A little larger than a goldfish, the Canterbury mudfish is rarer than the brown or black mudfish, but is not legally protected. It has small pelvic fins, whereas the brown and black fish have none.*

## A breathtaking experience

What makes a fish leave water for as long as the mudfish does? Studies have shown that as soon as the water becomes too acid (that is, its pH levels are too low), and when temperatures climb higher than 15°C, the mudfish finds it difficult to obtain sufficient oxygen from water. The environmental changes may act as a trigger for the fish to leave water and start aestivation.

Mudfish which are removed from water and held in the air have a 60 percent reduced metabolic rate, pointing to the fact that at certain times of the year more effort is needed to take up oxygen from water than from air. When they gulp in air, they hold it in the mouth. Unlike lungfish, mudfish do not enter a state of torpor when aestivating; if returned to water they immediately swim away.

Ashley River in the north to the Waitaki River in the south, the Canterbury mudfish today lives in weedy springs, drains and irrigation races; originally it would have occurred in the numerous wetlands found throughout Canterbury. Lowland kahikatea forest, ideal mudfish habitat, once covered substantial areas of the province. This mudfish is now known at fewer than 20 localities, with approximately 100 fish at each, although numbers fluctuate considerably.

Besides having to cope with habitat destruction, the Canterbury mudfish is preyed upon by brown trout, eels and perch.

Whether the Canterbury mudfish burrows into the mud or is simply left stranded at the beginning of a drought is a matter of circumstance. Ample fat reserves in its abdomen allow it to aestivate for up to 20 weeks. Its main foods are aquatic invertebrates.

A fourth species of mudfish was discovered at Kerikeri and near the Ngawha hot springs in 1997, neither population large. No juveniles could be found at Ngawha, but the Kerikeri site is more promising. The new species, in the process of being described, differs from the other three by virtue of its spotted appearance.

# Mussels

New Zealanders tend to think of mussels as the commonly cultivated greenshell (*Perna canaliculus*), available fresh or marinated at most good supermarkets. However, there are another nine species of mussel which grow around the coastline, and even a freshwater mussel. Attaching themselves by strong threads to rocks, hardy mussels persist on windy and wave-washed shores where weaker animals cannot survive.

Mussels with the widest-ranging distribution include the green, the blue (*Mytilus edulis aoteanus*), the black (*Xenostrobus pulex*) and the ribbed (*Aulacomya ater maoriana*). Another common mussel, the horse mussel (*Atrina zelandica*), is also the country's largest, growing to 300 mm in length, compared to 200 mm for the greenshell. Horse mussels live upright, partially buried in mud or sand.

Lauded not just for its taste but also its medicinal qualities, the greenshell mussel is a widely cultivated native shellfish. Thirty years ago mussel farming in New Zealand was unknown, but

*Black mussels and barnacles compete for space on rocks at the middle and upper tidal shore.*

today almost 50 000 tonnes are processed a year, for an export return of $55 million. Various claims have been made for the therapeutic properties of mussel extract: it was first touted as a possible anticancer cure, but medical tests proved inconclusive. However, the tests did indicate anti-inflammatory action, and it has been marketed as a product to help arthritis sufferers. Again investigators have been equivocal about its effectiveness. Japanese researchers have tried to tap into the mussel to see if it contains a cure for osteoporosis. Whatever the specific claims made for greenshell mussels, like all fish and shellfish they are a high-quality food, so undoubtedly contribute to all-round good health.

The freshwater mussel (*Hyridella menziesi*) is only distantly related to the coastal species. These mussels have an ingenious method of moving upstream: instead of producing sperm and eggs at spawning as coastal mussels do, the freshwater variety bears larvae inside its shell until these reach a two-shelled stage. Armed with special teeth, the larvae fasten themselves to the fin of a native fish and in that way hitch-hike to an upstream home.

In the early 1990s, mussels were affected by toxic algae, making the shellfish poisonous to humans. Mussels appear to be more susceptible to accumulating toxins than other shellfish; the toxins have little effect on the mussels themselves but can be passed on to predators.

Because mussels are efficient filter-feeders, processing as much as 50 litres of water a day, they are ideal monitors of water pollution and have been used in programmes around the world including one based around South America and another in the Pacific.

Oil companies have long used mussels for spotting oil leaks, as have water authorities to warn of excess sewage in inshore waters. In Holland baskets of mussels are placed at intervals in rivers and coastal waters to monitor pollution trends. The Dutch have also developed early-warning systems based on the mussel's reflex shutting of its shell at the first sign of danger—an alarm is sounded when several mussels shut their shells. In New Zealand a number of local authorities—Bay of Plenty, Taranaki and the Auckland Regional Councils—use mussels as bio-indicators. Freshwater mussels have also been employed in the Waikato River to monitor pollutants such as heavy metals and pesticides.

# Muttonbird

The muttonbird or titi (*Puffinus griseus*) is one of the great bird migrators, heading for the northern hemisphere each year between March and May. Eventually it reaches subarctic waters between Japan and North America to take advantage of abundant food during the northern summer. At every stage of the journey, the birds make use of prevailing winds to assist their flight.

Because the parents leave the nesting burrows several weeks before their chicks, the young have to make their own way north, the instinct to migrate somehow imprinted on them from birth. These juveniles will not return to the island of their birth for 3–4 years, and they will not start breeding until several years after that.

In September huge numbers of muttonbirds make their way southwards again to breed, mainly to islands around Foveaux Strait, the Chatham Islands, and the subantarctic Snares, Auckland and Campbell islands. However, they are not restricted to cooler latitudes, occurring on islands from the Three Kings northwest of Cape Reinga, along the Coromandel coast and on Kapiti and Mana. As many as 500 000 birds in a single flock have been seen at sea. Muttonbirds lay only one egg a season. This low productivity is

*Muttonbirds have become expert at underwater pursuit, using their strong, streamlined legs and compact plumage to sink more easily.*

# *Titi take*

Raised on a rich diet of fish and squid, young muttonbirds put on weight rapidly to reach 1 kg about 50 days after hatching. Some chicks have been observed to gain 300 grams in a single night. As they might not receive the next meal from their parents for a long period, they need to eat as much as possible at one time.

As well as increasing in size, the chick also builds up stockpiles of body fat, and a special stomach oil which allows it to fast after its parents have migrated north, before its own feathers are developed enough for flying. The juvenile's weight drops to about 750 grams by the time it is ready to follow its parents.

For centuries Maori have taken the juvenile titi when they are at their plumpest, and the practice continues today. The take of muttonbirds is one of the few harvests of a wild species that remains in the control of Maori. Every year between 15 March and 31 May, Rakiura Maori (a hapu of the Ngai Tahu tribe) travel to islands surrounding Stewart Island and collect around 250 000 of the fatty chicks.

In the past, the harvest provided food for families to last a year. People crossed from the mainland on sometimes arduous and dangerous journeys to gather the titi. Once captured, the birds were cooked in their own fat (titi tahu) and preserved in kelp bags (poha). Not only were they an important food for the Ngai Tahu, but titi were also sold or traded with other tribes.

In premodern times, the Ngai Tahu developed their own 'environmental code of practice' in order to preserve the resource. People were discouraged from living on the islands outside the harvesting period, as it was felt the adult birds would not return to nest.

Today, while harvesting continues, questions are being raised about the sustainability of the take on the titi islands. Muttonbirds are long-lived, slow-producing birds and fears are held that they are not replacing themselves, although no long-term studies have been carried out. Fortunately they are protected elsewhere, so the overall population is probably secure.

*This juvenile muttonbird has lost much of its plumpness now that it is ready to start its migration north.*

compensated by their relatively long life; the oldest bird recorded lived over 25 years.

In New Zealand waters muttonbirds eat squid, small fish, krill and small crustaceans; in the north Pacific their diet includes squid, anchovies and sand eels. They dive up to 8 metres below the surface to take their prey, propelled by powerful wing strokes.

Termed muttonbirds because the nestlings are taken for oil, feathers and meat—products that compare with those from sheep—scientifically the birds are known as sooty shearwaters, and are one of the seven shearwaters (see page 311) that breed in the New Zealand region.

With a population estimated at more than 20 million, the muttonbird is the most abundant seabird around the New Zealand coast. The largest colony is on the Snares where about 2.75 million pairs breed.

Muttonbirds are not unique to this country; they also breed in subantarctic South America and on islands in the southern Atlantic.

# National parks

In the public mind national parks are New Zealand's pre-eminent reserves, providing a trusted level of protection above that of any other designation, although the distinction between a national park and other type of reserve is a fine one. By definition, a national park is at least 10 000 ha in size, containing scenery of such distinctive quality and ecological systems or natural features so beautiful, unique or scientifically important that their preservation is in the national interest. Today there are 13 parks, covering 9 percent of New Zealand's land area (see page 376).

New Zealand's first national park, Tongariro, was created in 1887, following close on the establishment of the world's first national park, Yellowstone, USA, which came into being in 1872. Tongariro was a gift to the nation by Tuwharetoa chief Te Heuheu Tukino IV.

The first New Zealand national parks were created from a mix of motives: Egmont (1900) in order to protect the forest surrounding Mount Taranaki at a time when the rapid expansion of dairying was sweeping away large areas of native forest; Fiordland (1905) in order to safeguard the area for tourism and provide a magnet for visitors; Arthur's Pass (1929) on ecological grounds, as providing important examples of alpine flora.

National parks have largely been created in remote, mountainous areas, but pressure to include lowland forests, wetlands and tussocklands has seen the recent gazetting of forested parks such as Paparoa and Whanganui. The latest addition to the park network is 452 000-ha Kahurangi National Park; its varied geology has given rise to a wide variety of plants and animals within its borders.

*Morning light filters through beech forest, Fiordland National Park. At 1.2 million ha, Fiordland is one of the largest national parks in the world.*
*(Inset) Golden sands and granite boulders are a feature of Abel Tasman National Park. This park owes its existence largely to the efforts of Nelsonian Perrine Moncrieff, and the year of its creation (1942) coincided with the tercentenary of Tasman's arrival in Golden Bay.*

# Nests

Some birds construct much more elaborate nests than others, usually because their chicks are less well developed when they hatch and need the protection of a secure and warm home. Well-built nests protect eggs and young from excessive heat and cold, and permit young birds to develop in comfort and safety during the period when they are totally dependent.

## Rifleman

Because they are so small, riflemen (see page 289) are in greater danger of succumbing to the cold than larger birds. Born blind, naked and totally dependent on their parents for food, riflemen chicks require a cosy nest to grow up in. Master nest builders, riflemen choose a ready-made cavity such as a small knot hole in which they weave an outer structure of tightly twined twigs and straw. Inside this they place a layer of coarse feathers followed by an inner layer of down feathers. When a parent leaves the nest, if its mate does not immediately take over incubating the bird covers the eggs with down and blocks the entrance with feathers. The diligent parents are also careful to remove any moisture from feathers lining the nest, sometimes brushing it off on a perch before carefully returning the feathers to the nest.

## Wrybill

The wrybill (see page 371) does not need to create a complex nest, so well camouflaged are its eggs in a South Island braided riverbed. By nesting on a shingle 'island' in the river, the wrybill avoids predators such as stoats, cats and rats, but it has to be constantly on guard against black-backed gulls flying overhead.

## Royal albatross

Moulded out of mud and grass, royal albatross (see page 46) nests are cup-like forms which rise out of the surrounding boggy peat. Some albatrosses shuffle backwards to the nest while repeatedly throwing lumps of soil and vegetation over their shoulders until they have piled up a mound. Most of these nests last for many years, accumulating moss and algae at their base.

## Pied shag

Pied shags (see page 306) build the simplest types of tree nests, assembling sticks, twigs, plants and debris which the birds work into a compact structure. Although flimsy looking, the untidy nests are quite strong.

## Grey warbler

The grey warbler (see page 350) nest is built entirely by the female, and is arguably the most intricate of New Zealand bird nests. Suspended from a light branch at the top, it is kept from swaying by light 'guys' fastened to the surrounding twigs. A variety of materials—moss, grass, wool, cotton, tree-fern scales—are pressed into service and the nest is furnished with refinements such as a porch to guard against the rain and a ledge for the incubating parents to alight on when passing to and from the interior.

*Wrybill*

Pied shag

Rifleman

Royal albatross

Grey warbler

# Nikau

The southernmost palm in the world, the nikau (*Rhopalostylis sapida*) grows down to Banks Peninsula on the east coast and Greymouth on the west. Reaching 10 metres in height, it is New Zealand's only palm.

Closely related to the tropical betel nut, date palm and coconut, the nikau's ripe berries are an important food source for kereru and kaka.

Several parts of the nikau were eaten by Maori: the immature flower (the *sapida* in the scientific name, meaning savoury, refers to the flower); the berries when green; and the 'heart' of undeveloped leaves, the cutting out of which unfortunately killed the plant. In Polynesia a similar meal made of coconut palm hearts was referred to as a 'millionaire's salad' because it meant destroying the plant so valuable in Polynesian culture.

Nikau leaves were traditionally used to thatch the top and sides of whare, and for weaving into bags or kete.

Nowhere does the nikau grow more luxuriantly than around Punakaiki where a unique geography has created optimum conditions for the palm. The mountains behind the coastal flats are not elevated enough to hold perpetual snow, thus during winter the winds are not cold enough to curb the nikau's growth.

Attractive though the nikau is, with purplish-pinkish flowers produced in large bunches, it is seldom seen in gardens because it is slow growing, taking 30 years before bursting into flower.

*The feathery-fronded silhouette of nikau palms is unmistakable against an evening sky.*

*The head of the midget octopus is the size of a human fist.*

# Octopuses

Octopuses are the most advanced of the molluscs, and like squid of the same family, have no shell. Their frightening reputation is unjustified as they are more likely to flee from humans than attack them. If cornered they may bite, but usually they release a cloud of dark ink to mask their escape.

In New Zealand the two main species are the common octopus (*Macroctopus maorum*) and the midget octopus (*Robsonella australis*), both occurring among rocks and in crevices at the low-tide mark. The common octopus occurs throughout the country down to Campbell Island. Octopuses are adept at moving in and out of confined spaces, being able to flatten their body and tentacles to wafer-thin size. With an arm spread of up to 2 metres, the common octopus is the larger of the two species, although the midget octopus is the less timid.

Using their eight tentacles, octopuses grasp hold of scallops, crabs and crayfish, biting them with their powerful beak and injecting a poisonous saliva before devouring them.

Often the first a diver knows of an octopus is when he brushes against one. The octopus is a camouflage specialist, changing colour to suit the background, be it the brown of a seaweed or grey of a rock. The secret of its camouflage skills lies in how it uses chromatophores, the sac-like cells in its skin, which carry red, yellow or black pigments. By contracting or relaxing these cells,

*During the breeding season, one of the male octopus's eight tentacles, called a hectocotylus, is used to fertilise the female. The specially modified hectocotylus carries tubular sperm-filled packages down a groove in the tentacle and into the female's body cavity where the eggs are. The female then lays about 75 000 eggs.*

the octopus changes colour. In addition, octopuses can alter their skin texture to match the environment. On flat sand their bodies appear smooth, but among rocks their muscles can pull the skin into pimples and peaks.

Of all the invertebrates, octopuses have the most highly developed eyes, with a structure similar to that of human eyes, but with an important difference: the lens of the human eye changes shape to focus, whereas in octopus eyes the lens moves backwards and forwards, akin to the focusing mechanism of a slide projector.

Like a number of large, complex animals, octopuses invest a great deal of time and effort in reproduction. The females of both New Zealand species lay their eggs in sheets on rock faces and carefully guard them while they develop, sweeping their arms across to keep intruders clear. During the 6–8 weeks of incubation, the mother forgoes food. Periodically she cleans the eggs of debris with her tentacles and flushes clean water over them. The midget octopus is even more attentive than its larger relative, frequently siphoning water across the eggs.

The octopus has the largest brain, in proportion to its size, of any invertebrate. In an experiment carried out at the Yerkes Laboratories in Florida, USA, an octopus was presented with a crab to which a white card and an electric wire were attached. When the octopus touched the crab, it got an electric shock. Then it was fed a crab without a card or wire and received no shock. After only three experiments it learned to leave the crab with the white card alone.

# Ongaonga

Ongaonga's scientific name, *Urtica ferox* (fierce nettle), says it all. Undoubtedly the most unpleasant plant in the bush, ongaonga, the tree nettle, has been known to kill dogs, horses and even a human. The extract of just five of the plant's hairs can kill a guinea-pig. The merest touch can produce a sting lasting several days.

Just what it is that makes ongaonga so toxic is unclear. The same chemicals are present in its hair fluid in the same quantities as those found in the common European nettle, which stings but is not life-threatening.

A lowland plant that grows in forested areas near the coast, the tree nettle is found throughout New Zealand, although it is not common in western parts of the South Island. Ongaonga is a host plant for the red admiral butterfly (see page 75) which appears to be impervious to its venom.

(see page 75)

> ## Did you know?
>
> On 26 December 1961, two young men hunting in the Ruahine Ranges stumbled into a thicket of ongaonga. About an hour later one of the lightly-clad men complained of a stomach ache. Soon he became partially paralysed and then blind. His companion ran for help and the sick man was airlifted to hospital, but died 5 hours after arrival.

*On his travels around New Zealand Kupe is said to have left behind him several barriers to foil angry pursuers whose wives he had stolen; among these obstacles was the stinging ongaonga.*

*Ongaonga is the chief host plant for caterpillars of the red admiral butterfly and the nettle moth. Often the red admiral pupa is attacked by the ichneumon wasp, introduced to control white butterfly.*

Chrysalis

Ichneumon wasp

Caterpillar

Pupa

Nettle moth

Red admiral

# Orange roughy

While hundreds of thousands of tonnes of orange roughy (*Hoplostethus atlanticus*) have been caught since large-scale trawling began in 1979, much is as yet unknown about the biology of this mainstay of the New Zealand deepwater fishing industry.

Orange roughy are not exclusively fish of the New Zealand region. They are widespread in most temperate oceans, from the north Atlantic to South African and Australian waters, although commercial fisheries appear to be confined to New Zealand and Australian waters.

Living at depths of up to 1.5 km, where the pressures are up to 150 times those at sea level, orange roughy are difficult, if not impossible, to study in natural conditions. Scientists have learned what their diet is, how many eggs the females produce and what age the fish might reach. They have also pinpointed very accurately the time when they start to spawn, and where, but many other aspects of their lives are shrouded in mystery. For example, it is uncertain which are the chief predators of orange roughy. The fish have been found in the stomachs of seal sharks; and sperm whales, which can dive to the depths where orange roughy live, have also been observed in the same areas as the fish.

Perhaps the most intriguing aspect of orange roughy is the great age they can reach. By measuring ear bones, or otoliths, which have annual growth rings comparable to the growth rings in trees, scientists can assess fishes' ages. Australian and New Zealand researchers have estimated that some orange roughy may be as old as 150 years, and that the average fish takes 30 years to reach sexual maturity.

Orange roughy are punctual spawners, a convenient feature for the fishing industry which can depend on the fish being in a particular place at a

*The size of orange roughy aggregations is staggering—a 60-second trawl of the sea floor at spawning time can bring up a haul of 50 tonnes of the high-value fish.*

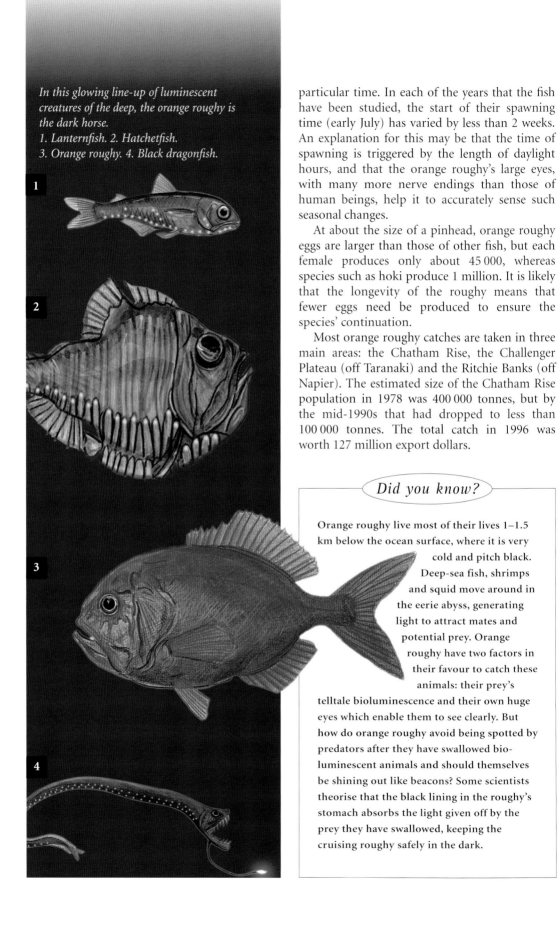

*In this glowing line-up of luminescent creatures of the deep, the orange roughy is the dark horse.*
*1. Lanternfish. 2. Hatchetfish.*
*3. Orange roughy. 4. Black dragonfish.*

**1**

**2**

**3**

**4**

particular time. In each of the years that the fish have been studied, the start of their spawning time (early July) has varied by less than 2 weeks. An explanation for this may be that the time of spawning is triggered by the length of daylight hours, and that the orange roughy's large eyes, with many more nerve endings than those of human beings, help it to accurately sense such seasonal changes.

At about the size of a pinhead, orange roughy eggs are larger than those of other fish, but each female produces only about 45 000, whereas species such as hoki produce 1 million. It is likely that the longevity of the roughy means that fewer eggs need be produced to ensure the species' continuation.

Most orange roughy catches are taken in three main areas: the Chatham Rise, the Challenger Plateau (off Taranaki) and the Ritchie Banks (off Napier). The estimated size of the Chatham Rise population in 1978 was 400 000 tonnes, but by the mid-1990s that had dropped to less than 100 000 tonnes. The total catch in 1996 was worth 127 million export dollars.

## Did you know?

Orange roughy live most of their lives 1–1.5 km below the ocean surface, where it is very cold and pitch black. Deep-sea fish, shrimps and squid move around in the eerie abyss, generating light to attract mates and potential prey. Orange roughy have two factors in their favour to catch these animals: their prey's telltale bioluminescence and their own huge eyes which enable them to see clearly. But how do orange roughy avoid being spotted by predators after they have swallowed bio-luminescent animals and should themselves be shining out like beacons? Some scientists theorise that the black lining in the roughy's stomach absorbs the light given off by the prey they have swallowed, keeping the cruising roughy safely in the dark.

## *Safeguarding the wealth of the sea*

In 1986 the New Zealand Government established a quota management system to improve sustainability of the fishing industry. This sets a Total Allowable Commercial Catch (TACC)—the tonnage of fish which may be caught in a given year. Individual fishers are allocated a proportion of that TACC by the Ministry of Fisheries. In theory a good system of maintaining fish stocks, in practice it has not always worked, and some fisheries are seriously depleted (orange roughy, snapper, kahawai).

During the 1980s the discovery of commercial quantities of orange roughy, along with deep-sea species such as hoki, alfonsino and oreo dory, launched the fishing industry into a new era. Seemingly overnight, a small owner-operator enterprise was transformed into a billion-dollar export business, but in some fisheries the boom has relatively quickly turned to bust.

Scientists measure the health of a fishery in several ways. One of the most important is to keep an eye on fish biomass, that is, the tonnes of species in the water. An undisturbed fishery has a biomass of 100 percent, and a fishery that is well managed and produces good numbers of juveniles should have a biomass of between 25 and 50 percent. The orange roughy fishery off the Chatham Rise has been reduced after almost two decades of exploitation to a biomass of 20 percent; the snapper fisheries in the Hauraki Gulf and Bay of Plenty have a biomass of only 15 percent.

Researchers are concerned that overfishing of orange roughy has led to a loss of genetic diversity in the fish. Fishing has selectively removed the largest and most genetically variable individuals, leaving the less variable to breed.

# Orca

Historically orcas (*Orcinus orca*) have been called 'killer whales', but while they have a well-merited reputation as hunters, there is no record of an attack on a human; and in captivity orcas demonstrate an astounding gentleness. In the past they were accurately described as 'whale killers' but in recent times the words have been transposed, giving them an undeserved reputation.

The orca is the largest member of the dolphin family, itself a member of the grouping called 'toothed whales'. Growing to an average length of 7 metres and weight of 5 tonnes (females 6 metres and 3 tonnes), orcas are toothed predators which need fear no other creatures except humans. Male orcas can be readily differentiated from females by the size and shape of their dorsal fin which is an impressive 1.8 metres high.

Female fins stand about 1 metre tall and are hooked rather than straight like the male fin. Many orcas live in Antarctic waters where they feed on large quantities of fish, penguins and marine mammals. Exactly how many live around the New Zealand coast is unknown, although researcher Ingrid Visser has identified 100 so far and estimates there could be 200. Orcas have distinctive dorsal fins, some with large notches or with the tops missing. This characteristic has allowed Visser to trace the orcas' movements.

In Canada, orcas have been divided into three distinct groups, or ecotypes: the first, 'residents', congregate in pods of eight to 25, are very vocal and often leap out of the water to slap their tails. Their main diet is fish. The second group are 'transients' in pods of up to five and are stealthy, omnivorous hunters. 'Offshore' orcas make up the third grouping. Comparing these categories with New Zealand orcas, Visser believes she has

# Of men and orcas

Since ancient times dolphins have been reported to co-operate with humans in fishing. The most famous recent account involving orcas centred on Twofold Bay in southern New South Wales, Australia, where for 80 years, until the 1930s, the big dolphins used to assist whalers to catch the great whales migrating along the coast.

Whenever a whale—often a humpback— swam past the coast, the orcas would 'tail-lob' or breach in such a way that lookouts were alerted by the commotion. (Tail lobbing involves slapping the flukes against the water, while a breaching whale leaps with its whole body clear of the water.) While the whalers rowed out to harpoon the whale, the orcas would harass it so it could not escape out to sea. Once the whale was harpooned, the orcas would grasp the cables and drag the whale underneath to drown it. They would then prise the whale's jaws open and take out its tongue and eat it—their reward for assisting the whalers—before releasing the remainder of the whale for processing.

*A male orca is readily identified by its spectacular dorsal fin which rises about 1.8 metres above the body.*

identified a fourth ecotype, 'opportunistic feeders' which eat whatever comes their way.

The sleek predator is renowned for its hunting abilities. This account of an attack by a pod of 29 orcas on a blue whale in the Gulf of California shows why they are called 'the wolf of the sea': 'For five hours over a distance of 20 miles, marine researchers watched a bloody, one-sided battle that had begun before they arrived on the scene. Like bees swarming on a bear, but with deadlier intent, the killer whales completely surrounded the 60-foot-long blue whale, preventing its escape. They tore off its dorsal fin, shredded its flukes, and gouged a gaping hole, 6 feet square, in its side. Then, inexplicably, they swam away, leaving the leviathan mortally wounded.'

Each of an orca's 40–50 teeth is 50 mm in diameter. The stomach of one orca was found to contain the remains of 24 seals, in that of another were traces of 13 porpoises and 14 seals. Whale tongues are high on their list of delicacies. During the height of whaling in the Southern Ocean, orcas used to attack baleen whales tied to the sterns of factory ships, and take the whale tongues, some of which weigh several tonnes.

Ingrid Visser's study of orca feeding behaviour has exploded the myth that they do not strand— a myth furthered by spectacular footage of orcas seizing seal pups off the coast of Argentina. Only 17 individuals hunt in this fashion and, taught by their mothers, have refined the technique over many years. The coastline where they catch the seals is deeply shelving, so even though some of an orca's body might be out of the water, the rest is still in relatively deep water.

In New Zealand orcas often feed on stingrays, facing the danger of stranding because the stingrays live in shallow waters. Two orcas in particular, possibly brothers, have been observed hunting rays and sharing their catches. One was seen to take 18 in a day, while in one mid-1990s incident an 8-year-old became stranded after being tempted into the shallows of Mangawhai Beach by a meal of stingrays. New Zealand has one of the highest rates of orca strandings in the world, and holds the record for the number of orcas stranded in a single incident—17 at Paraparaumu Beach in 1955.

Researchers theorise that there may be two species of orca, distinguished by their preferred prey. Some groups are predominantly fish eaters, while others commonly eat dolphins or seals.

*A trio of orcas spy-hopping—perhaps to get their bearings, take a better look at their surroundings or keep an eye on other members of the group. Orcas are more visually oriented than other cetaceans.*

Orcas are long lived, possibly reaching an age of 80 years, and are sexually mature at 12–15 years. Orcas are also well travelled: A1, a female first photographed in 1977 in Waitemata Harbour, has been seen in locations as far apart as the Bay of Islands and Kaikoura, and at various places in between, including Warkworth, Gisborne, Whakatane and the Marlborough Sounds. She has also been seen on the North Island's west coast, in Kaipara Harbour.

For many years scientists believed that orca pods were ruled by a dominant male with a harem of females, but long-term studies have shown females to be in charge. Sometimes orca pods team up with others, but only if they belong to the same community. Each pod has a common 'language' of sounds.

## Did you know?

Around Kaikoura orcas have been seen eating dusky dolphins and, in the Bay of Islands, common dolphins. Over a 12-day period near Kaikoura observers saw 13 dolphins captured. Two male and two female orcas co-operatively hunted for the dolphins; in one incident, a female orca threw a dolphin clear out of the water. Orcas have also learned that dolphins surfing the bow waves of motor boats cannot hear their approach, and have been seen diving under boats in order to catch the unsuspecting joy-riders.

# Orchids

New Zealand orchids, like those from other temperate countries, are less spectacular than the large and showy varieties of tropical countries; nevertheless, close up they reveal a wide range of flower shapes and colours. They are also a highly diverse group whose species almost match those of grasses and daisies in number.

Orchids are the most colourful of New Zealand native flowers, which, be they alpine, forest or wetland, are predominantly white, red or yellow. While orchids mainly blossom in shades of green, they also come in tones of white, red, yellow, violet, blue and black.

There are more than 80 species of New Zealand orchids, growing from mountain top to sea level. One, *Corybas macranthus*, grows on subantarctic Macquarie Island and is believed to be the southernmost orchid in the world. Most resemble bulbs such as daffodils, emerging through the soil from autumn to spring, flowering then dying back until the next season; a few which grow in the ground, such as *Spiranthes sinensis*, are evergreen, as are perching orchids.

Perching orchids have evolved an effective way of conserving moisture. Unlike other plants which open their leaf pores during the day,

*The diversity of New Zealand's orchids is indicated by these photographs of* Earina autumnalis *(top left),* Thelymitra ixioides *(top right),* Pterostylis alobula *(inset) and* Caladenia lyalli *(bottom).*

perching orchids close their pores during daylight hours, absorbing water and nutrients directly through their spongy root sheaths.

Most orchids, however, function like other plants, drawing up moisture and nourishment from the soil and opening their pores during the day. One of several exceptions is the rare *Yoania australis*, which relies on fungi to manufacture its food. Although once thought to occur only in kauri forests, *Y. australis* grows in association with a puff-ball fungus living in close contact with the roots of the taraire tree, and recently was discovered near Collingwood, associating with the kohekohe.

Some pine plantations provide ideal habitats for native orchids. One example is the Iwitahi native orchid reserve in Kaingaroa Forest, where 31 species have been discovered in just 6 ha of *Pinus nigra* forest. Thousands of orchids of these species, many of them rare, grow under the pines. Other species of pine do not appear to be as conducive to orchid cultivation.

Flowers of *Gastrodia cunninghamii* can vary in colour from yellow to black. Up to 40 flowers are supported on a long, leafless spike.

The *Thelymitra* orchids, the second largest genus of native orchids, are known as sun orchids because they grow in open areas; the blooms of many, such as *T. ixioides,* will not open unless the sun is shining.

The best-known New Zealand orchid is the Easter orchid (*Earina autumnalis*), which produces highly perfumed flowers in autumn. A perching plant found either on trees or cliffs, the Easter orchid was called raupeka by Maori. Perching orchids are not parasitic but use trees as a platform to grow on.

The highly ornamental lip of *Caladenia lyalli* is a feature of this group of orchids. *C. lyalli* thrives in high-altitude forests and subalpine areas up to 1500 metres. *Pterostylis alobula* is a winter-flowering greenhood orchid featuring prominent wings or antennae.

# Oystercatchers

New Zealand has three species of oystercatchers, two of which occur nowhere else and are rare. Most common is the pied oystercatcher (*Haematopus ostralegus*), a bird which is also found worldwide. Here it breeds almost exclusively alongside South Island braided rivers but since the 1980s a few have set up breeding quarters in Hawke's Bay and the Wairarapa.

Until 1940, when it became legally protected, the pied oystercatcher was a popular gamebird, and as a result its numbers plummeted. The population has since climbed to 85 000, an increase of about 75 percent from 1971.

Like all oystercatchers, the pied variety aggressively defends its nest. One Central Otago farmer ploughing his paddock avoided a running chick, only to have an adult land on his head and beat him about the ears with its wings. Birds often make low-level attacks on people strolling along beaches, pulling away at the last moment.

The world's rarest oystercatcher is the Chatham Island species, *H. chathamensis*, (see photo page 57) whose population stands at around 100, double that of 1970. Stockier than mainland oystercatchers, it uses its solid bill to lever limpets and chitons off rocks.

Conservationists have attempted to boost numbers by artificially incubating eggs, but a high proportion of the eggs taken from the oystercatchers' nests are infertile, implying that the population is old. Nests have also been protected from predators and sea storms. Such conservation efforts are paying off, with better breeding success in recent years.

Variable oystercatchers (*H. unicolor*) are so named because they come in varying shades of black and white, the degree of colour difference

*A variable oystercatcher parent and chick. Adults are attentive parents, feeding their young for longer than other bird parents.*

depending on the region. The further south, the blacker the birds; in the North Island 43 percent are totally black, in central New Zealand 89 percent and in the southern South Island 94 percent.

The colour-phase gradient in New Zealand is paralleled in North America, where totally black oystercatchers occur from Alaska to southern California; further south they become progressively more pied, and on the Mexican coast of the Gulf of California pied birds make up 100 per-cent of the population. Black colouring absorbs the sun's rays better, an important factor for species at cooler latitudes.

Like the pied oystercatcher, the variable oystercatcher is enjoying a comeback. Since the early 1970s numbers have doubled to 4000—a jump that in part could be attributed to the protection work carried out on behalf of several dune-nesting birds such as the New Zealand dotterel (see page 100).

## *Hammerers and stabbers*

Few birds are capable of attacking molluscs and crustaceans with as much skill as oystercatchers, which make short work of tough-shelled oysters, limpets, barnacles and chitons. Long, stout and flattened at the end like a chisel, an oystercatcher's beak is an efficient tool for opening two-shelled molluscs.

The oystercatcher exploits the eating habits of oysters, which open their shells to feed in shallow water when the tide is out, allowing the bird to insert its beak between the shells, using it like a lever, and cut the muscle uniting the two halves. It then eats the succulent meat inside. Mussels exposed to the air keep their shells shut tight so the oystercatcher has to hammer at them with repeated blows until the shells are broken. However, when the mussels are under water the oystercatcher stabs at them to sever their abductor muscles. Limpets and chitons are prised off rocks and eaten.

Young oystercatchers take time to pick up such skills, and so, unusually among waders, adults feed chicks for a lengthy period. Six-week-old juveniles are as proficient as their parents at digging for worms, but it takes up to 3 years to master the technique of shellfish feeding. Depending on its upbringing, an oystercatcher will become either a hammerer or a stabber.

*A pied oystercatcher's sturdy beak enables it to break open most shells, either by hammering them against rocks or stabbing at them. It can take some years for the bird to become accomplished at this art.*

# Oysters

Oysters have a wide appeal. For many people they are a gourmet food without parallel, while fish eat their spat (larvae), and starfish and crabs prise open their tough shells in order to get at the tender flesh inside. A bird (the oystercatcher) has been named for its adeptness at capturing the creatures (see page 244), even if oysters do not make up a large proportion of its diet.

In New Zealand the most common oysters are the Bluff or dredge oyster (*Tiostrea chilensis*), the rock (*Saccostrea glomerata*), and the Pacific (*Crassostrea gigas*).

Most celebrated of New Zealand oysters is the Bluff oyster, although it is not restricted to the Bluff region—that is simply where the main fishery is located. Elsewhere they turn up in the South Island around Timaru and Akaroa, and off the North Island along the Taranaki and Wairarapa coasts, Hawke's Bay, Bay of Plenty and the Firth of Thames. The first Bluff oysters harvested in the 1880s came from intertidal areas around Stewart Island, but today they are all taken in deep water.

By nursing their larvae inside their shells for a month, Bluff oyster females ensure their young's survival better than if they were left to float about; as a consequence, these oysters produce fewer larvae than other oysters—from 7000 to 120 000 eggs. Pacific oysters, on the other hand, are prolific egg producers, capable of releasing 55 million in an hour.

*Rock oysters, one of two native species, grow mainly in the far north of the country.*

In the late 1980s Bluff oysters were crippled by a parasite called bonamia and the fishery had to be severely curtailed, then closed until 1995. Fishermen first knew of the problem when they hauled up oyster shells with no oysters inside them. The oyster population was cut back from an estimated 1500 million in 1985 to a mere 365 million in 1992.

Bluff oysters are targeted by bonamia during the process of reabsorbing their eggs; the damage leads to a loss of reproduction and sometimes death, depending on the severity of infection. In Europe and elsewhere bonamia has devastated similar oyster fisheries. Initially scientists thought bonamia had been introduced, but they now believe it occurs naturally and has struck the oysters in the past.

The Pacific oyster arrived in New Zealand on ships' hulls from its native Japan around 1970 and since then has rapidly spread to become the dominant cultivated oyster. Its razor-sharp shells make barefoot walking hazardous in some areas. Initially it was feared that the Pacific oyster would replace the native rock variety, but in fact it occupies different habitats.

The rock oyster is a warm-water species of the middle shore not found much further south than Auckland. It prefers hard clean surfaces and can tolerate being without water for a period. By contrast, the Pacific oyster prefers the upper reaches of estuaries, does not like to dry out and has spread further south than the native species.

## Did you know?

Oysters are filter-feeders, remaining stationary in the water, taking in small particles which pass over them. The modified gills they use for feeding, also employed in respiration, are so large they take up all of the creature's body. As the oyster snaps its shell shut, it ejects unwanted large food particles and draws small particles down into its gut, wrapping them around a rotating crystalline organ called a style. The only rotating organ in any animal, the style revolves the food, which is then digested by stomach enzymes.

*Though scarce on the mainland, red-crowned parakeets remain in good numbers on islands such as Macauley in the Kermadecs, South-East and Mangere in the Chathams, and on the Antipodes.*

# Parakeets

In mainland forests the appearance of a parakeet is a relatively rare event: the small parrots are usually heard rather than seen, their loud chatter of ki-ki-ki-ki giving them away. In reference to this call, Maori coined the phrase 'just like a nest of kakariki' to describe noisy talk or gossip. The Maori name for the parakeet (meaning little kaka) also came to be the word for the colour green, in recognition of the striking coloration of the bird.

Parakeets are long-tailed parrots, found throughout the world, especially in tropical countries. In New Zealand there are three native species: the Antipodes Island parakeet (*Cyanoramphus unicolor*), the red-crowned parakeet (*C. novaezelandiae*) and the yellow-crowned parakeet (*C. auriceps*).

The Antipodes Island parakeet, numbering up to 3000, is the rarest of the three species. Occupying an island of only 2100 ha in the Southern Ocean, this parakeet is widely raised in aviaries and appears to have adapted well to captivity. In its native habitat it feeds mainly on tussocks, seeds and flowers, and sometimes scavenges for the fatty remains of skua-killed penguins. Its habit of roosting in burrows proved to be a problem when birds were transferred to Stephens Island in 1986 in a bid to start another population: tuatara, also burrow dwellers, made short work of some of the parakeets.

Red-crowned parakeets were once abundant on the mainland, gathering to feed in such large flocks that early European settlers regarded them as crop and orchard pests and shot thousands. This profusion of parrots was not to last long, however, as cats, ship rats and stoats started to reduce their numbers in the 1870s and 80s. Their characteristic of feeding on the ground and nesting near the ground makes them easy prey. It is possible there are none left in the South Island; in the North Island they are in low numbers in western Northland forests, the central North Island and the Ruahine Ranges.

Attempts during the 1970s and 80s to re-establish red-crowned parakeets in the Waitakere Ranges failed, indicating how vulnerable these birds are to introduced predators. However, the presence of red-crowned parakeets on a number of offshore islands in good numbers (more than 10 000 in the Kermadec Islands, and up to 5000 on the Antipodes) is evidence that the species will survive where there are no predators.

Less inclined to feed and breed at ground level, the yellow-crowned parakeet is widespread on the mainland but rarer on islands. A subspecies, Forbes' parakeet (*C. forbesi*), is found on the Chatham Islands and numbers less than 100. Until recently a colour variation of the yellow-crowned parakeet—the orange-fronted parakeet—was thought to be a separate species. Very rare, it has been seen only in northwest Nelson, southern Nelson and inland North Canterbury.

Since the 19th century, ornithologists have argued about the orange-fronted parakeet's status. It was long considered to be a distinct species because of its different ecology and behaviour, its coloration, and its size and shape. However, until populations were 'rediscovered' in 1980, scientists did not have an opportunity to study the orange-fronted parakeet closely.

Latest re-evaluations confirm little difference in ecology and behaviour between yellow-fronted and orange-fronted birds, and early authorities may have been confused about size because they were comparing captive with wild birds—captive birds are invariably larger. But until the orange-fronted parakeet is officially downgraded to a

subspecies, its preservation remains a top priority for the Department of Conservation.

Both the red- and yellow-crowned parakeets have suffered as a result of habitat destruction. Like the kaka, they nest in knot holes in old trees and although New Zealand forest regenerates swiftly, saplings are not adequate to breed in.

Two species often confused with New Zealand parakeets by inexperienced observers are the Australian rosellas. Larger than parakeets, their colouring is quite distinct. The eastern rosella (*Platycercus eximius*) was introduced from Tasmania and southeastern Australia and kept as a caged bird before it first escaped in the Dunedin area around 1910. Two populations have established in the North Island, the first starting in Auckland in the 1920s and spreading into Northland and as far south as Taranaki. The 1960s saw a population establish in the Wellington region. Today the bird is considered common. Crimson rosellas (*Platycercus elegans*) are in much smaller numbers around Wellington. Some can be seen in the inner-city Botanical Gardens and Central Park, but there are not many more than a dozen of these attractive birds.

*Yellow-crowned parakeets, solitary for much of the year, form small flocks during autumn and winter.*

*The Antipodes Island parakeet is the rarest of New Zealand's parakeets.*

# Paua

Paua (abalone) occur throughout the world but nowhere are their shells as exquisitely coloured as in New Zealand. The rainbow-hued shellfish has long been prized for ornament making and for its meat. Early explorer Charles Heaphy wrote: 'The muttonfish or pawa, although resembling india rubber in toughness and colour, is very excellent and substantial food for explorers.'

A univalve mollusc, generally found under boulders in shallow waters, the paua is a gastropod of ancient lineage, related to limpets, catseyes, neritas and sea snails. Although paua appear to be sedentary creatures, they can move with unexpected agility if threatened.

Paua derive the colour of their shell from the dominant food they eat. A diet of brown algae furnishes the iridescent blue-greens, while bladder kelp and red algae are responsible for the deep red-browns.

The three New Zealand paua species are the 175-mm rainbow or common paua (*Haliotis iris*), the 125-mm silver paua (*H. australis*) and the virgin paua (*H. virginea*), the smallest at only

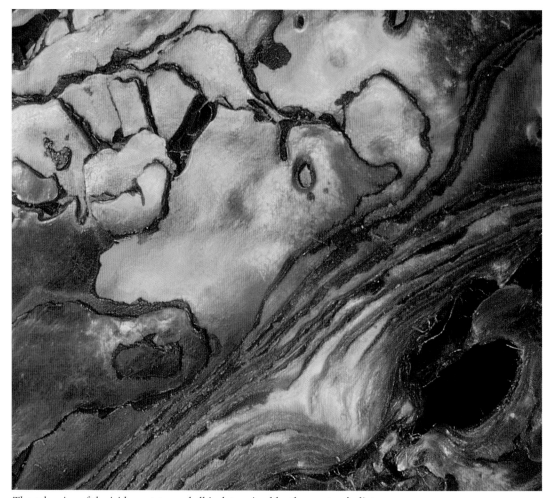

*The colouring of the iridescent paua shell is determined by the creature's diet.*

60 mm. The first two occur all round the coast, but the third is concentrated in the South and Stewart islands.

When commercial paua fishing began after World War II, the meat was discarded and only the shell used. Now paua meat is an important export, mainly to Asian markets, but the flesh has to be bleached to be acceptable to those consumers. Paua are rich in iodine, essential in the human diet for the health of the thyroid.

The deep-velvet black-foot rainbow paua is especially esteemed for its flesh, making up the entire export catch. Most (424 tonnes a year out of a total of 1120 tonnes) comes from the lower part of the South Island including Stewart Island. Around large population centres, black marketeers have plundered stocks and conservation measures have failed.

*The foot of the medium-sized silver paua is yellow soled, in contrast to the black feet of the other two species. Silver refers to the shell's colouring.*

# Penguins

No other country has as many penguin species as New Zealand. If the New Zealand region is taken to include not only the subantarctic islands but also the Ross Dependency (a large uninhabited area in the Antarctic), a total of 13 of the world's 18 penguin species have been recorded in New Zealand.

Located close to the boundary of the subtropical convergence, where subantarctic waters meet warm northern currents to provide rich feeding grounds, New Zealand is a prime site for penguins. Of the 13 species of penguin, nine breed here: the blue, yellow-eyed, Fiordland crested, Snares crested, erect-crested, rockhopper, emperor, Adélie, and the chinstrap. The remaining four species (the king, gentoo, macaroni and magellanic) are referred to as 'stragglers' or 'vagrants', birds which rarely come ashore in New Zealand.

New Zealand penguins can be divided into those that occur on the mainland, those on subantarctic islands and those around Antarctica. The penguins that survive in temperate waters have evolved under different conditions to those of their Antarctic cousins. For example, they do not gather in massed throngs, but breed alone or in small groups. There are three mainland penguin species—the blue, yellow-eyed and Fiordland crested.

Crested penguins are well represented in New Zealand. Of the world's six species, five breed here, and three—the Fiordland crested, the Snares crested and the erect-crested—breed nowhere else. Besides their crest, which grows during the first few years of the birds' life, these penguins differ in other significant ways from other groups. The males are markedly larger than the females, with heavier bills, longer flippers and larger feet. Unique among penguins, cresteds produce two eggs a season, the first much smaller than the second. This first egg is often poorly incubated and invariably fails to hatch or is eaten by skuas. If it does hatch, the resultant chick is a runt which fails to thrive.

One of the crested species, the aggressive rockhopper, lives on subantarctic islands around the Southern Ocean, and in New Zealand on the Antipodes, Campbell and Auckland islands. The main breeding site is Macquarie Island. Since 1942 scientists have documented a disturbing decline in rockhopper numbers on Campbell Island, down from about 1.7 million birds to 100 000 today. The most likely cause of the drop is a change in sea temperature.

On other islands, rockhoppers eat mainly krill, but on Campbell Island their diet is dominated by less nutritious fish. It has been suggested that a rise in sea temperature has forced krill further south, out of the reach of the penguins. A population increase during the 1970s coincided with a fall in sea temperature, presumably inviting the temporary return of the krill.

### NEW ZEALAND'S PENGUINS

**Mainland breeding**
Yellow-eyed (*Megadyptes antipodes*)
Fiordland crested (*Eudyptes pachyrhnchus*)
Blue (*Eudyptula minor*)

**Subantarctic and Ross Dependency breeding**
Snares crested (*Eudyptes robustus*)
Rockhopper (*E. chrysocome*)
Erect-crested (*E. sclateri*)
Emperor (*Aptenodytes forsteri*)
Chinstrap (*Pygoscelis antarctica*)
Adélie (*P. adeliae*)

**Vagrants**
King (*A. patagonicus*)
Gentoo (*P. papua*)
Macaroni (*E. chryolophus*)
Magellanic (*Sphenicus magellanicus*)

*Insulated from the ice on its parent's toes, and cosy under the brood patch that warmed it as an egg, an emperor penguin chick surveys its world.*

Exactly when penguins evolved is unknown, but scientists have been able to hazard a guess (give or take a few million years) by studying fossil remains on the South Island east coast, mostly around the Waitaki River in north Otago and Waipara in north Canterbury. The oldest of these fossils of birds resembling the modern penguin have been dated to 45–50 million years ago, although a recently found fossil of a proto (primitive) penguin may be more than 55 million years old (see box, page 253).

The ancestors of penguins were flying birds, possibly from the petrel or grebe family. But today, instead of flying through the air, the penguin uses its specially adapted flippers to propel itself through the ocean at speeds of 10–12 km/h. Some species take to the air momentarily, leaping in and out of the water in an energy-saving method of travel called 'porpoising'.

Unlike the wings of flying birds, which are hollow, the penguin's flipper is a rigid but thin paddle which provides remarkable propulsion. Other adaptations the penguin has made to a life spent primarily at sea and in cold temperatures are a waterproof plumage and thick deposits of fat. These latter adjustments serve penguins well in the cold Antarctic, but what of species in warmer climes? Penguins have a variety of cooling-off techniques. One is to fluff out the feathers to ex-

*The golden gaze of the yellow-eyed penguin whose unique colouring makes it easily identifiable.*

pose the warm skin to the air; another is to expel heat from places where there are no feathers, such as the feet. For this reason, on hot days yellow-eyed penguins have bright pink feet.

## Blue penguin

The blue or korara is the most common New Zealand penguin, occurring from Northland down to Stewart Island and surviving near populated areas such as Wellington and Oamaru. It is also the only penguin to inhabit mainland Australia, where it is known as the fairy penguin. At just 300 mm in height the blue is the smallest of all penguins. In New Zealand it is divided into five subspecies: the northern, Cook Strait, white-flippered, southern and Chatham Island.

Despite its small size, the blue is an impressive ocean traveller, having been recorded swimming 113 km in 34 hours. Some birds occasionally reach the Snares Islands, several hundred kilometres to the south of Stewart Island. Unlike most other penguin species, the blue tends to remain in one area, rather than disperse across the Southern Ocean during its non-breeding period. At night birds can often be seen in huddles of loose colonies.

Blues have a reputation as noisy revellers during the breeding season and can be unpopular neighbours. If the basement of a house offers sanctuary to a nesting pair they will use it, often at the cost of sleep to the human occupants. While relatively common compared to the other mainland penguin species (for example, there are around 5000 on Motunau Island off the north

*Caves and rock cavities at sea level are favourite blue penguin nesting places, although some birds have been seen near the summit of Kapiti Island.*

Canterbury coast), the blue has dropped in numbers close to large centres of population. The traditional causes of their decline—stoats, dogs and vehicles—still exact a toll, although efforts at conservation such as providing nesting boxes have had some success.

## Yellow-eyed penguin

Research in the early 1980s showed that predators and the clearing of their habitat have meant a decline in the number of yellow-eyed penguins. With a population estimated at 5000 (1200–1600 breeding pairs and 2000 non-breeders in 1996) it has been declared 'the world's rarest penguin'.

Although its Maori name, hoiho, means noise shouter, the yellow-eyed penguin is naturally publicity shy, yet since the mid-1980s it has been increasingly in the spotlight. In the south the Yellow-eyed Penguin Trust has been set up to safeguard this most unusual of all penguins, and the Mainland Cheese Company sponsors it. As confirmation of its singularity, the yellow-eyed penguin has been placed in a genus all of its own.

For a temperate penguin, the yellow-eyed is large; in fact only the emperor and king can top its maximum height of 680 mm. It occurs on the east coast of the South Island, from Banks Peninsula down to Stewart Island, as well as on Campbell and the Auckland islands. The Banks Peninsula population is tiny at just over 30, but the greatest mainland concentration is from Otago south. On the Otago Peninsula there are around 1000 of this species.

Sociability is not the yellow-eyed's strong suit. Not only is it extremely wary of humans, it also prefers to keep other yellow-eyeds at a distance, especially during the breeding season when it will seek out a nesting site that cannot be seen by its neighbours. Each day the penguins leave their sheltered nesting sites to go on deep-sea fishing

*Survival rates for Fiordland crested penguins are higher on islands than at mainland sites because there are fewer predators on islands. This penguin is one of six crested species, four of which are found in the New Zealand region.*

*Emperor penguin parents are visually identical, but family members recognise each other's voices.*

# *In search of the missing link*

The 18 penguin species that live today are just a few of the many species that have existed since penguins first evolved more than 55 million years ago. Fossil scientists have unearthed the bones of 30 extinct species, 14 of which come from New Zealand. Some of those species appear to have attained remarkable heights; one fossil found near Oamaru in the 1850s, and named *Palaeeudyptes antarcticus* by eminent biologist Thomas Huxley, is estimated to have stood 1.45 metres tall—close to human height.

Within the fossil record, though, there is a frustrating gap of 10–15 million years between the oldest penguin fossils which most resemble modern species and a primitive or proto penguin, dated as existing 55–62 million years

ago. The ancient bones of this proto penguin were found near Waipara, north Canterbury, in 1982. Scientists describe it as proto because it had many of the characteristics of modern-day penguins but also showed some significant differences. For example, it had a long, delicate bill and a wing more like that of a bird than the flipper of a penguin. Its height was between that of a yellow-eyed and a king penguin.

The fact that other fossils linking the proto penguin with later species have not been found does not mean they do not exist. Limestone sites along the east coast from north Canterbury to north Otago are unlikely to have yet yielded all their fossil penguin secrets to the inquiring gaze of palaeobiologists.

expeditions (the scientific name *Megadyptes* means deep diver), which take them down 144 metres below the surface. Returning to land in the late afternoon or early evening, they patrol along the shore until, satisfied there is no danger, they head towards their roosts.

Adult yellow-eyeds generally remain all year round in the area they were born, but adventurous fledglings swim as far as Cook Strait before returning to their home patch to breed. Given the chance, yellow-eyeds will lead a long life; the oldest bird recorded was 30 years old. Without human intervention the yellow-eyed will not

remain on the mainland. The rescue effort is concentrating on replanting areas and fencing them off from cattle, sheep and goats, and trapping or poisoning ferrets and stoats. A major setback occurred in 1995 when a fire killed more than 60 penguins at one of the most important reserves in the Catlins.

## Fiordland crested penguin

Our knowledge of the Fiordland crested penguin or tawaki is patchy, partly because it occurs only on remote coasts and islands where humans rarely venture. As its name implies, the penguin

occurs mainly in the Fiordland region, although it also inhabits south Westland, Stewart Island and other islands in the vicinity.

Along with the yellow-eyed and the Galapagos penguins, the Fiordland crested shares the dubious distinction of being one of the rarest penguins in the world. A 5-year census completed in 1995 estimated that there were 2000–2500 nests, a major decline since the 1890s when naturalist Richard Henry reported thousands of nests in the Dusky Sound area alone.

Unusually timid for a crested penguin, the smallish (550 mm) Fiordland species comes ashore each June on boulder beaches and laboriously makes its way up to the heavy undergrowth of the Fiordland rainforest to breed. Once there, the penguins form colonies of up to 10 pairs where they raise their chicks until these depart in November at around 10 weeks old.

Perhaps the greatest mystery surrounding the penguin concerns its whereabouts between March and June, after it has moulted and before it starts nesting. Not much evidence is available, but scientists assume that during this time it remains at sea, eating and sleeping, until it comes ashore again.

The Fiordland crested suffers a battery of threats: stoats, dogs, wekas and human disturbance are a constant danger, while the heavy rainfall characteristic of Fiordland sometimes washes nests away.

# Peripatus

The curious, caterpillar-like peripatus has been described, like the tuatara (see page 341), as a 'fossil in the flesh'. This insect-worm belongs to an order of animals that has been around even longer than the tuatara—around 550 million years. A fossil of that vintage unearthed in British Columbia closely resembles the animal that lives in New Zealand today.

When zoologists first discovered the peripatus they believed it might be a 'missing link'—a sort of intermediary stage—between worms and insects. On the one hand it has some of the features of worms, such as a segmented body, but, like crayfish, woodlice and other insects, it also boasts jointed legs. It has now been decided that it has followed its own evolutionary bypath.

Each segment of the peripatus's body bears a pair of fleshy legs with two tiny claws. Two pairs of legs have been modified: one forms jaws with hard claws on the end and the other forms a 'gun' that shoots out a sticky thread to capture prey.

*The peripatus is a living link with an ancient past.*

# Pests—animals

It could be argued that every introduced animal—humans included—which impacts adversely upon native animals is a pest. Some, though, are regarded as more of a menace than others, and sizeable amounts of taxpayers' money are spent on controlling them.

Cats, rats, stoats, ferrets, possums, rabbits, goats, deer and wasps (see individual entries) are the species most targeted because of the proven damage they cause. However, there are a number of other animals which are also considered pests, even if this view is not shared by some groups (hunters, for example, who contend game animals such as deer are a 'resource').

Wallabies, chamois, tahr, dogs, pigs, hedgehogs and mice have all played their part in the country's loss of diversity. Even dogs, which are not feral animals, can wreak havoc on wildlife on weekend excursions or when they occasionally 'go walkabout'.

There are two New Zealand species of peripatus, one which gives birth to live young (*Peripatoides novae-zelandiae*) and one which lays eggs (*Ooperipatus viridimaculata*). The former is relatively common throughout the country, and although it occurs more often in bush it can also be found in suburban gardens. Grey or green in colour and sporting a velvet coat, the peripatus is a nocturnal animal. The egg-laying species is found in South Island beech forests. Both species live under rotten logs, moss or stones, or anywhere damp.

One of the intriguing features of the peripatus is its ability to capture prey by shooting out a jet of sticky saliva from the glands on either side of its mouth. Some species can squirt the slime as far as 30 mm.

Once its prey—usually an insect—is immobilised by the gluey threads, the peripatus punctures the body wall with its jaws and sucks out the contents. As this is an energy-sapping way of obtaining food, the peripatus eats its saliva as well as the insect to recover some vigour.

## Wallaby

Of the seven species of wallaby released in New Zealand, five still survive—the dama wallaby (*Macropus eugenii*), Bennett's wallaby (*M. rufogriseus rufogriseus*), the parma wallaby (*M. parma*), the swamp wallaby (*Wallabia bicolor*) and the brush-tailed rock wallaby (*Petrogale penicillata penicillata*).

Three of the wallabies—the parma, swamp, and brush-tailed—are confined to Kawau, Rangitoto and Motutapu islands in the Hauraki Gulf. The brush-tailed rock wallaby eats colonising pohutukawa, Kirk's tree daisy and *Astelia banksii* on Rangitoto.

Ironically the parma wallaby was considered possibly extinct in Australia in the 1960s, and New Zealand was asked to legally protect it. In 1969 a number of this smallest of wallaby species were sent to Australia or to zoos worldwide, in an effort to restore the population. However, in 1972 the species was confirmed to be still in relatively good numbers in its homeland, and protection in New Zealand was removed.

The dama wallaby has gradually spread in the Rotorua region until now it threatens to enter Urewera National Park. Bennett's wallaby, the only South Island species, has its main population centre in Hunters Hills, south Canterbury.

# An expanding menace

Chamois currently occupy a third of the South Island and are continuing to disperse into remaining available habitat such as northwest Nelson, Marlborough and Fiordland. Although predominantly alpine and subalpine browsers, in central Westland they have moved down to low altitudes. There are unsubstantiated reports of liberations of one or both of these species in the North Island.

Wallabies are less of a menace. With the exception of dama wallabies around Rotorua, other wallaby species are either contained on a number of small islands near Auckland or marooned by pasture in South Canterbury. A small number of illegal liberations of Bennett's and dama wallabies have been made in recent years well outside their existing range.

*AHB, Landcare Research, DOC*

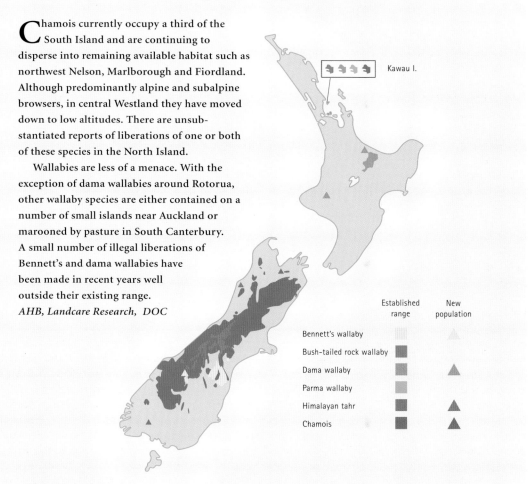

Kawau I.

|  | Established range | New population |
|---|---|---|
| Bennett's wallaby |  |  |
| Bush-tailed rock wallaby |  |  |
| Dama wallaby |  |  |
| Parma wallaby |  |  |
| Himalayan tahr |  |  |
| Chamois |  |  |

*The Himalayan tahr is also present on Table Mountain in South Africa, in California, USA, and Ontario, Canada. In New Zealand tahr eat out most vegetation at sites where they camp.*

## Chamois and tahr

Chamois (*Rupicapra rupicapra*) and the Himalayan mountain tahr (*Hemitragus jemlahicus*) are more glamorous introduced mammals, though no less destructive. Both related to goats, the two species arrived in the South Island in the early 1900s, chamois from Europe where it has long been a prized game trophy, and tahr from the Himalayas where it lives at heights of up to 4500 metres, making it one of the highest-living large animals.

In a few decades, tahr and chamois numbers exploded as the animals spread out from their release point near Mount Cook. More damaging was the gregarious tahr which concentrated in a smaller area, whereas chamois expanded as far as Nelson and Fiordland, but in less dense aggregations. Snow tussocks cannot tolerate severe grazing by tahr, and attractive alpine flowers such as Godley's buttercup (see Plants—endangered, page 271) were devastated by both species. Government-paid hunters carried out intense control operations during the 1950s–60s, considerably reducing tahr and chamois numbers.

Conservationists and hunters are sharply divided over what to do with chamois (population 30 000) and tahr (around 15 000). Department of Conservation strategy is to keep their numbers as low as possible in special areas such as national parks, and to use recreational hunters as the control agents elsewhere. Some conservation groups want to eradicate them, but sportsmen argue they are an economic resource—wealthy hunters will pay $5000 to shoot a trophy bull.

## Hedgehog

In their native Europe, hedgehogs (*Erinaceus europaeus occidentalis*) are regarded with affection—as they are by many New Zealanders. At first introduced as a reminder of 'home', they were later also welcomed because they ate slugs and snails. Hedgehogs have about 16 000 sharp spines on their bodies with which to defend themselves, but these are no protection against motor vehicles. At least 10 times more (and in certain areas up to 60 times more) hedgehogs die on New Zealand than on English roads, indicating how much denser the hedgehog populations are here. At Tawharanui, a key breeding area of the endangered New Zealand dotterel, hedgehogs have eaten the bird's eggs, causing major breeding failures several years in a row.

*Several thousand Bennett's wallabies are shot or poisoned in New Zealand each year. A forest and pasture pest, this species is largely restricted to hills near Waimate in south Canterbury.*

## Pig

Although important in Polynesian culture, pigs (*Sus scrofa*) did not arrive in New Zealand with early Maori, but European explorers soon made good the deficiency, and by 1840 feral pigs were well established throughout the country. They were also released on islands as food supplies for castaways. Today's wild pig is likely to be a mix of animals released by explorers and semi-feral species which escaped from early settlers' farms. Pigs are believed to have played a role in the reduction of kakapo, and are known to destroy the spectacular, large native snails—their habitat, eggs and the snails themselves.

## House mouse

Of the mammals, only man has proved to be a more successful coloniser than the house mouse (*Mus musculus*), which is now present in almost every country in the world. In New Zealand it is as rural as it is urban, being found in forests, pasture and tussock grasslands.

Wild mice eat insects and seeds, competing with native species for food and inhibiting natural regeneration of plants. They also eat bird and lizard eggs. In 1989 conservationists eradicated all 5 million mice on 217-ha Mana Island, north of Wellington—the largest island in the world where such a feat has been accomplished.

*Spreading an insidious green blanket over a reserve near Mangaweka, old man's beard smothers even tall trees.*

# Pests—plants

The almost total conversion of lowland New Zealand from indigenous to predominantly introduced plants in the space of 150 years is an event unparalleled in world botany. At present more than 1500 species of exotic plants coexist with the 2200 species of native plants. Around four new species become permanently established here each year.

Many introduced plants are welcome, adding colour and variety to gardens and parks (just as New Zealand plants grace many overseas landscapes). However, planted in an alien environment, a number of exotic plants have become pests, threatening native plant ecosystems. Such weeds are more insidious than animal pests, because, while animals can modify an ecosystem, they do not necessarily destroy it, and once the animals are eradicated the plants recover. Weeds, on the other hand, have the potential to completely destroy indigenous vegetation, and programmes to kill weeds that involve sprays or large-scale cutting can also easily harm the plants they are designed to save.

Some plants such as old man's beard, contorta pine and wandering Jew have been recognised as pests for a long time; others such as ginger, jasmine and Boston fern are popular garden plants which have only recently appeared on the 'unwanted' list because of their destructive tendencies towards native ecosystems.

## Ling heather

During autumn the open landscape surrounding Tongariro National Park is drowned in a flowing purple wave. To the unsuspecting passerby the scene is attractive, but those with a knowledge of the effects of ling heather (*Calluna vulgaris*) realise that the diversity of the area is being smothered by a plant whose spread is accelerating.

The first heather seed was planted in 1912 by Tongariro's first ranger, John Cullen, who wanted to establish a hunting habitat for gamebirds. Although forbidden to release grouse in the park, in 1924 he liberated them on the other side of the road forming the park boundary. The birds failed to survive, but the heather took hold, and now grows better, stronger and higher than native vegetation. Heather is being controlled by pulling the plants out and spraying with herbicides, but in the long term a European heather beetle may have to be used to stop the plant's advance.

## Old man's beard

More than anyone, naturalist David Bellamy has alerted the public to the dangers of old man's beard (*Clematis vitalba*) which was introduced as an ornamental vine and continued to be widely

*Almost as far as the eye can see, ling heather clothes the landscape surrounding Tongariro National Park, suppressing native plants.*

sold in nurseries until the 1980s. In its native Europe it is dubbed traveller's joy, but in New Zealand it brings nothing but despair as it entwines itself around the tallest trees, strangling them in its embrace.

## Ginger

In its native India, ginger grows only in full sunlight along forest margins, but in New Zealand it manages to penetrate low-light areas under the forest canopy where it smothers existing occupants and prevents other plants from establishing. There are two species, kahili ginger (*Hedychium gardnerianum*) and yellow ginger (*H. flavescens*); kahili is much more destructive and is a major pest in the Waitakeres, the Coromandel and Northland; in the wild the plants have spread as far south as Christchurch.

## Water net

First recorded as a pest of Chinese rice paddies over 1000 years ago, water net (*Hydrodictyon reticulatum*) arrived here in 1986. It has rapidly spread throughout Bay of Plenty and Rotorua lakes, and into the Waikato River system. Water net has a fast and effective method of reproducing vegetatively, which allows populations to grow rapidly when temperatures are around 25°C.

# Petrels

New Zealand has been described as 'the seabird capital of the world'; the number of petrel species (36) which either visit or breed in the region justifies the description.

Petrels belong to the order of Tubenose seabirds, which also includes albatrosses and shearwaters. Their distinctive feature—the prominent nostrils—are not only useful for excreting excess salt, but also give the birds an acute sense of smell. It is believed they locate one another and their breeding places by smell.

Petrels are divided into three groups: the giant petrels, diving petrels and storm petrels. They spend most of their life at sea, coming to land only to breed. Many of the species now restricted to islands used to occur on mainland New Zealand, and many are taken on longlines in the same way as albatrosses (see page 45).

Another group belonging to the Tubenose order are the prions, small birds with a distinctive black M marking on their upper wings. Because they feed in the same way as baleen whales, filtering small animals from the water, prions were described by whalers as 'whalebirds'.

## Taiko

In 1867 the Italian research ship *Magenta* was sailing 800 km east of the Chatham Islands when

***Did you know?***

By some loose association, petrels take their name from the apostle St Peter, who, wanting to emulate Christ, attempted to walk on water (petrels appear to walk on water as they take off to fly). More accurately, Bay of Plenty fishermen describe the white-faced storm petrel as the 'J C bird'.

*Petrels share characteristics of both penguins and flying birds, having an ability to 'fly' through water as well as air.*

a beautiful white-breasted bird flew by. Duly shot and collected, and given the name magenta petrel (*Pterodroma magentae*), it afterwards languished in the University of Turin Museum.

During the 20th century, ornithologists such as Sir Charles Fleming visited the Chathams and heard stories of a similar petrel called the taiko which most locals had not seen for years, although a farmer thought he had spotted some on his property. Such reports fired up a young Christchurch schoolboy, David Crockett, who had been collecting seabird skeletons, some of which he could not identify. Could any of them be the taiko, he wondered? Later, during the mid-1960s, an English ecologist wrote a paper suggesting that the magenta petrel and the taiko were one and the same bird. Crockett decided the only way he could solve the mystery was to go to the Chathams—which he did in 1969. By now the farmer who thought the taiko was on his property was dead; the amateur ornithologist had to piece together scraps of evidence about 'odd birds honking up the gully' and spent three cold days and nights without success. Crockett returned the following year, but again without luck.

During the 1970s a further two expeditions—each more sophisticated than the last, with spotlights and taped calls to attract the bird—trekked to the Chathams, and each produced tantalising sightings of petrels which never landed. Finally, on 1 January 1978, a triumphant David Crockett got his reward. Hypnotised by the spotlight, a weary ocean traveller fluttered closer and closer

to the ground, landing finally in the bracken. Twenty minutes later a second exhausted taiko landed and the birds were confirmed to be indeed *P. magentae*.

Since that momentous occasion, expeditions have regularly returned to the southwest of Chatham Island in an attempt to mount a rescue programme for the taiko. Up to 1996, just 65 had been banded and six active nesting burrows had been found. The Department of Conservation is trapping cats, possums, rats and weka near the burrows. The 1996–97 breeding season was the most successful since the bird was rediscovered in 1978, with four chicks fledged.

The rarest petrel in the world at an estimated 50-100 birds, the taiko was once an important food for Moriori, the first human inhabitants of the Chatham Islands.

## Westland petrel

Until 1945 the unusual Westland petrel was unknown to science. In that year school pupils at Barrytown School just north of Greymouth were listening to a radio broadcast by ornithologist Dr Robert Falla about the life history of muttonbirds. But the description he gave did not match that of the muttonbirds they knew that lived in the forested hills along the coast; 'his' muttonbirds were the sooty shearwaters around Stewart Island which bred in spring and migrated in autumn; 'theirs' bred in autumn. The teacher sent the disbelieving Dr Falla a specimen, and it was soon confirmed that this was an unidentified species, now known as the Westland petrel (*Procellaria westlandica*).

In other ways the new petrel differs from other petrels. It flies like a harrier with continuous slow beats (other seabirds punctuate their sailing flight with rapid wing beats), and it nests on the mainland. The size and aggression of adults allow the petrels to cope with predators, even though some burrows are close to housing.

The petrel breeds along an 8-km stretch of the forested foothills of the Paparoa Range. On food forays it ranges widely, though concentrating on hoki fisheries off the West Coast and in Cook Strait where huge amounts of offal are the prize. Thanks to this abundant food source, petrel numbers have trebled since the 1960s to stand at 20 000 birds. However, such a level might not be sustainable, as the fishery could run out, or

ever-larger numbers of petrels might get killed in longline fisheries. Satellite tracking has confirmed that the birds' fishing trips are centred on the Tasman Sea, but one petrel travelled more than 2000 km in 9 days (from Punakaiki to the Chatham Rise via Cook Strait, return), an impressive distance for an animal weighing only about 1 kg.

After fledging, Westland petrel chicks fly to the east of the Chatham Islands, possibly to the rich Humboldt Current off the South American coast. There they spend 5–10 years before returning to the Paparoa colony.

Since 1952 around 20 petrels a year—mostly juveniles on their first nocturnal flights to sea—have been killed after colliding with power lines. Electricity supplier Transpower is putting some of its lines underground to stop the problem.

*Each morning in the breeding season adult Westland petrels fly out from their nests or burrows near Punakaiki to find food for their charges. This species of petrel, one of the few that still breeds on the mainland, is increasing in number because of the rich pickings around fishing boats off the West Coast.*

# Pingao

The tufted shoots of arched, orange-green leaves make the pingao (*Desmoschoenus spiralis*) the most colourful native sand-dune plant. Together with the native grass spinifex, pingao, which grows from North Cape to Stewart Island and the Chatham Islands, is a true sand-binding and dune-building plant. Airborne sand is trapped among its spreading shoots which grow upwards so as not to be buried by the sand gradually accumulating around them. In this way dunes are eventually created, although, being dynamic systems, continually shifting dunes are only partially stabilised by pingao.

Maori weavers value pingao leaves for making kete, cloaks, mats, hats and belts. When dried in the sun, pingao takes on a golden sheen that provides a vibrant contrast to the red and black fibres used in tukutuku panelling.

*Unrelated to any other plant in the world, pingao was once New Zealand's dominant sand-dune plant.*

Formerly widespread, pingao has been outcompeted by introduced marram grass, which grows more vigorously, and suffers from being eaten by rabbits, hares, cattle and sheep. Marram produces higher, steeper dunes which are more susceptible to erosion. Since the mid-1980s, conservationists have replanted extensive areas in pingao; some of these are set aside for harvesting, and others are reserves.

# Plants—alpine

One of the great puzzles of New Zealand botany remains to be satisfactorily solved: where did the more than 600 species of alpine plants originate?

Scientists have been perplexed by the fact that although present-day mountains did not exist in New Zealand until 2 million years ago, in the short time since then a breathtaking array of alpine plants have evolved. Another unusual feature is that very few of these occur elsewhere in the world; 93 percent are endemic.

Presumably some of the plants already existed in New Zealand, and exploited the niches that opened up for them as the mountains were uplifted. The evidence for this is the fact that a number of alpine species can be found down to sea level: spaniards, celmisias, anisotomes, and the ubiquitous flax (*Phormium cookianum*). The remainder of the alpine flora originated in Asia and may have grown from seeds or spores carried across the ocean by wind or birds from the mountains of New Guinea and Australia.

White, and to a lesser degree yellow, are the dominant colours of New Zealand alpine flowers. They would gain no advantage by producing other colours because New Zealand lacks long-tongued native bees and butterflies which can detect different colours. Instead, most alpine plants have short-tubed flowers which are effectively pollinated by flies, moths and beetles.

Above the treeline (which varies from 900 metres in the south to 1500 metres in the north) there are three distinct alpine zones: mountain shrubland, tussock herbfield, fellfield. Several niche habitats also support specialised plants: scree slopes, snow banks and cushion moorland. **Mountain shrubland:** Up to 300 metres above the treeline grow shrubs such as mountain ribbonwood, *Dracophyllum*, hebes, coprosmas, the mountain toatoa and leatherwood.

**Tussock herbfield**: Snow grasses and tussocks are the dominant plants in tussock herbfields, but dotted through the tawny landscape are the alpine plant gems that bring the slopes alive every spring and summer. Buttercups, alpine daisies, anisotomes, astelias, eyebrights, orchids and speargrasses mostly bloom during December and January. Gentians are an autumn latecomer.

**Fellfield**: Plants which grow in the fellfield must be specialised and tough to cope with the extreme conditions of the zone, which begins about 500 metres above the treeline. They have to contend with periods of intense cold, heat, drought, and wind. Hebes, buttercups, edelweiss and vegetable sheep are some of the flowering plants that endure and thrive in this hostile landscape.

**Scree slopes**: Parts of the Marlborough and Canterbury mountain ranges appear to be barren and desolate, but scree slopes harbour a surprising variety of plant and animal life. Typical scree plants are penwipers, cotulas (now known as *Leptinella*), willowherbs, lobelias and some buttercups.

**Snow bank**: Insulated by a blanket of snow, some alpine plants can even form flower buds, while others start to bloom under melting snow. The conditions under the snow, where temperatures are even, are often more favourable than those above the surface where temperatures are less predictable.

**Cushion moorland**: The Central Otago mountains, studded with rocky tors, are ecosystems quite distinct from other alpine regions. Even though they are nowhere higher than 2000 metres, these exposed summits are relentlessly battered by freezing winds and subject to severe frosts. Icy winds sweeping unimpeded across the flat summits combine with constant freezing and thawing to create a landscape which is New Zealand's equivalent of the arctic tundra. Even in summer, while the valleys below swelter in high temperatures, the freeze–thaw cycle continues on the mountains above. In an average year on the Old Man Range (1695 metres), on 113 days temperatures remain below freezing, frost occurs on 179 days, and there are only 73 frost-free days. Small, ground-hugging plants dominate the landscape and the continual influence of freezing and thawing creates regular hummocks and hollows.

A number of New Zealand alpine plants are botanical oddities with no equivalents elsewhere in the world:

• The bizarre-looking vegetable sheep, one of the

> ## Did you know?
>
> The alpine sundew receives no food from its immediate environment because the soils around the tarns where it grows are too cold, too high in acid or waterlogged. In order to obtain the nutrients it needs, the sundew grows hairs, attached to which are sticky droplets which hold fast an insect that comes in contact with them. The blue damselfly shown below has alighted on the edge of a leaf of the alpine sundew and become trapped by sticky tentacles which are triggered by touch to bend inwards. Glands at the tips of the tentacles release powerful enzymes which turn the insect's body into liquid so that it can be absorbed by the plant.
>
>

daisy family unique to New Zealand, is a tightly packed mass of thousands of plants. By itself each plant would struggle to survive in the cold, but by clustering close together all the different plants' vital growing parts are protected.

• A member of the carrot family, the handsome yet needle-sharp spaniard is armed with fearsome spines to ward off browsing animals.

• Penwiper plants are scree specialists whose leaves blend in with greywacke and argillite rocks to avoid being seen by hungry grasshoppers.

• 'Pineapple' forests of mountain neinei grow in subalpine regions between 800 and 1400 metres. In some areas such as Mount Arthur, Kahurangi National Park, there are whole groves of the plant, which also carries the name 'grass tree'.

• Some hardy species of fern tolerate the cold mountain climate, although most of the world's ferns are found in tropical or subtropical regions.

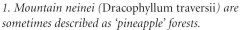

1. *Mountain neinei (*Dracophyllum traversii*) are sometimes described as 'pineapple' forests.*
2. *Gentians are the last flowers to appear during the brief high-country summer.*
3. *This* Myosotis traversii *ensures pollination by projecting its flowers up, to be noticed by insects.*
4. *Wind-blasted and sculptured hummocks of the Otago uplands are similar to Arctic tundra.*
5. *Unlike most ferns, the deciduous* Cystopteris tasmanica *is able to tolerate the alpine cold.*
6. *The leaves of the penwiper plant resemble the diamonds of felt on which quill pens were wiped.*
7. *The vegetable sheep is a New Zealand specialty.*
8. *A fellfield pincushion (*Aciphylla simplex*) forms bright orange-yellow hemispherical flowers.*
9. *The spiny spaniard (*Aciphylla *species) lies in wait for unwary trampers.*

# Plants—aquatic

Matching the situation on land, a variety of introduced plants have invaded many freshwater ecosystems, making it difficult to find areas where the vegetation is totally native. Unfortunately the exotics, such as the notorious oxygen weed species, infest lakes and crowd out beneficial native species.

Only a few lakes, such as some of Northland's dune lakes, have totally indigenous vegetation. These are characteristically fringed with tall emergent plants (*Eleocharis sphacelata* and *Baumea* species), with rich carpets of charophytes and occasional tall milfoils and pondweeds sprawling among marginal vegetation. Natives generally form a low-growing canopy which provides a rich habitat for invertebrates and fish.

A recent find in South Island lakes has been deepwater bryophytes, including many mosses and liverworts usually seen in streams and bogs. Growing as deep as 70 metres (this New Zealand record is from Lake Coleridge), the plants form small tangled clumps on silt or attached to rock or wood. So far 29 species of the bryophytes have been identified.

Remarkably, in twilight conditions with less than 1 percent of the light at the surface, the deepwater mosses manage to photosynthesise. Lake Wakatipu's bryophyte species have been

*At 35 metres and more below the surface of Lake Wakatipu, a surprising number of bryophyte species have been found.*

singled out as internationally outstanding in terms of their abundance and depth range.

Scientists consider that the plants survive at such depths—where light measurements are less than 1 percent of those at the water surface—because the waters are so clear, and cold temperatures reduce energy losses from respiration.

Despite having the clear water ideal for bryophyte growth, Lake Taupo and other seemingly suitable lakes do not support these plants. Scientists believe that the freshwater crayfish, koura, eats the bryophytes, preventing them from becoming established.

# Plants—climbing and perching

A newcomer to the New Zealand forest is immediately struck by its tropical appearance. In large part this is due to the profusion of tangled growth of ferns, vines and perching plants (epiphytes). Some vines, virtually all of them ferns, grow only below the canopy (see Ferns, page 113). Others either start life in the crowns of trees, or grow towards the sunlight with the help of different devices—with hooks or by entwining themselves around other plants.

Epiphytes come in a range of species. Shade epiphytes are generally ferns which fasten onto the lower parts of tree trunks, and many plants such as puka (*Griselinia lucida*) and five-finger (*Pseudopanax arboreus*) start life on trees or tree ferns before rooting in the ground.

### Vines

New Zealand's 'Tarzan' vines are those of the cable-like rata (see page 284) which starts life high in the crown of a tree and lowers its vines to the ground where they take root. The only other canopy vine whose roots are attached to trees is the kiekie (see page 183).

A member of the rose family, the bush lawyer (*Rubus* species) has hooked thorns that it uses to clamber up through to the canopy. The most common of New Zealand's five species is *R. cissoides*. In colonial times the plant earned the name 'bush lawyer' because of its tenacity.

Some twining vines climb in a clockwise direction, some anticlockwise. Best known of New Zealand's twining vines is the tough supplejack

1. Tied in a tangle, supplejack's twining growth bars all but the most determined tramper.

2. Related to the blackberry and raspberry, the bush lawyer is New Zealand's only prickly forest plant. Te Rauparaha's arduous 1822 journey from Kawhia to a new home on Kapiti Island was painfully remembered as te heke tataramoa, 'the bush lawyer migration'.

3. A collespermum epiphyte conserves its water supply in its plant 'vase'. A mosquito species develops its larvae exclusively in the water of these 'vases'.

4. Hanging gardens high above the forest floor, lily-related epiphytes poised on a rimu harbour a variety of insect and plant life. Sometimes growing to huge sizes, these epiphytes pose a danger to human life if they fall—as they occasionally do—during storms.

*Its seed having landed in a handy spot, a five-finger has sprouted and will eventually send a root to the ground to secure moisture and nourishment.*

(*Ripogonum scandens*) which climbs up small shrubs in an anticlockwise spiral, but as often as not falls to the ground, where it starts growing again. The tangled mess that results can make progress through the forest impossible.

The pure white, starry flowers of *Clematis paniculata* signal the arrival of spring. Maori called this clematis puawananga, the sacred flower. Its leaf stalks entwine themselves around supporting trees or shrubs.

## Perching plants

The most spectacular of the perching plants are the three species of lily—*Astelia solandri, Collospermum hastatum* and *C. microspermum*—which festoon large trees such as rata, kauri, kahikatea and rimu and contribute to the tropical look of New Zealand forests.

Called nest epiphytes, these tree passengers result from the gradual accumulation of humus in the crowns of trees or on their great limbs. Seeds germinate in, and draw nutrients from, the humus, which acts as an efficient sponge to soak up rainwater. In time the epiphytes develop water reservoirs at the base of their leaves.

Some years ago a scientist climbed into the Waipoua kauri, Te Matua Ngahere, and counted 36 epiphytes growing on it, while a 1993 study of a south Westland kahikatea revealed 28 types of perching plants. Intriguingly, humus was found to be deeper underneath, rather than on top of, horizontal branches, sometimes to a depth of 500 mm.

# Plants—coastal

The rocky cliffs, sand dunes, and salt marshes and meadows of the New Zealand coastline provide a wide variety of habitats for plants. In the subtropical north, mangroves and pohutukawa predominate, while in the deep south, tree daisies are common. Some plants, such as mountain flax and marram grass, occur on coasts throughout the length of the country.

Plants growing along the coast need to be able to tolerate salt and gales; in the North Island one plant especially is ready-made for New Zealand's sometimes boisterous weather: taupata or the mirror plant (*Coprosma repens*; see page 86) which grows in any niche. Another is *Hebe elliptica*, the coastal koromiko, whose strongly scented flowers bloom from Taranaki southwards to Stewart Island.

As light as cork and 150 percent lighter than balsa, whau (*Entelea aborescens*) grows on coastal cliffs from North Cape down to Nelson and Marlborough. Maori used the plant for fishing-net floats and rafts. Shining broadleaf (*Griselinia lucida*) often starts life as an epiphyte on top of a coastal rock and sends its woody roots down to the soil.

Ice plants are succulents, able to survive drought in the same way as cacti—by storing water in cells and sporting a waxy coat on their leaves which stops water from evaporating. There are two species in New Zealand: the introduced

1. Turning to follow the path of the sun, the attractive native ice plant is one of two species of ice plants; it readily hybridises with the other, a South African immigrant.

2. The spiked-ball female seeding heads of the silvery sand grass spinifex—a dune plant of the North Island and northern South Island—are lifted away by the lightest of breezes.

3. Euphorbia glauca *is the only milkweed native to New Zealand (the introduced swan plant, host to the monarch butterfly, is also a milkweed). Known commonly as Maori spurge,* E. glauca *has become something of a rarity, with its largest populations in Fiordland.*

4. Flushed with blue and strongly scented, the flowers of the hardy coastal koromiko bloom from late spring to early autumn.

*Although popularly termed the Poor Knights lily,* Xeronema callistemon *also occurs on Taranga, one of the Hen and Chicken Islands off Whangarei.*

South African *Carpobrotus edulis* and the native *Disphyma australe*. Other succulents along rocky shores include the glasswort *Sarcocornia quinque-flora* and the hardy, yellow-flowered shore groundsel *Senecio lautus*.

Different regions have their distinctive plants. Along the Marlborough coast the Marlborough rock daisy (*Pachystegia insignis*) is a spreading shrub with thick, leathery leaves. Foveaux Strait and Stewart Island have the coastal tree daisy or muttonbird scrub (*Olearia angustifolia*). So thick and large are its leaves that visitors to Stewart Island sometimes use them for postcards!

## Dunes

Marram grass (*Ammophila arenaria*), spinifex (*Spinifex sericeus*), tree lupin (*Lupinus aboreus*) and pingao (see page 262) dominate sand dunes. While useful as a sand binder, and therefore stopping dunes from migrating inland, the introduced marram displaces native binders such as pingao and spinifex. The large seed heads of the silvery sand grass spinifex can often be seen bowling along the beach. Lupin manages to colonise sheltered nutrient-deficient sand dunes by fixing nitrogen through nodules on its roots.

Growing back from the dune grasses are a number of plants such as the rare native sand spurge (*Euphorbia glauca*) with blue-green fleshy leaves and clusters of red flowers, the sand daphne (*Pimelea arenaria*) and the sand co-prosma (*Coprosma acerosa*). One of the rarest plants in the world, *Gunnera hamiltonii*, is known from half a dozen locations near Invercargill and on Stewart Island. There it is found in sand-dune hollows near the sea.

Dunelands are among New Zealand's most altered landscapes. Only in isolated areas such as Northland, Fiordland and Stewart Island are they relatively unmodified.

## Islands

Islands are a refuge for a number of unique coastal plants. Puka (*Meryta sinclairii*) is a rare, handsome-leaved tree which naturally grows only on the Three Kings and Hen and Chickens islands, but it is widely cultivated. Parapara (*Pisonia brunoniana*), the bird-catching tree, is mostly an island plant, although it also grows on North Island headlands. To ensure dispersal, the parapara has a sticky coating on its seeds, which attach to seabirds' feathers. In heavy fruiting years, birds become covered with the seeds; sometimes their plumage is so glued they cannot fly, and fall to the ground and die.

One of the most impressive flowering plants is the Poor Knights lily (*Xeronema callistemon*) which sports a flower stalk 80 mm long. From a distance the lily looks like flax, but it has no affinities with any other New Zealand plant and belongs in the same genus as a New Caledonian mountain species. Punui (*Kirkophytum lyallii*), whose leaves resemble rhubarb, is a Stewart Island and environs giant herb, a botanical foretaste of the megaherbs further south on the sub-antarctic islands.

# Plants— endangered

Native plants are threatened in a number of ways: people log or burn them; browsing animals such as deer and possums find them highly palatable; introduced plants outcompete and replace them; collectors like to hoard rare plants and in their misplaced enthusiasm put some at risk.

A total of 319 plants, or 19 percent of the New Zealand flora, are considered at risk. Using threat categories drawn up by the International Union for the Conservation of Nature, a Threatened Plant Committee regularly updates the list of New Zealand species.

The categories are: presumed extinct (9 plants); critical (20); endangered (37); vulnerable (62); rare (79); insufficiently known (28); and taxonomically indeterminate (84).

Because many plants are inconspicuous and do not have the 'cuddly' appeal of some animals, it has traditionally been an up-hill battle to find funds to rescue threatened plants. However, the Department of Conservation has introduced a new 'neutral' system of allocating money for projects, which has given plants a higher priority than before. Fortunately, saving plants is usually an easier job than saving birds.

No two plants could be more endangered (in the wild) than a pair from the Three Kings Islands which lie about 50 km off the northern tip of Cape Reinga. Like many of New Zealand's rare plants, both are grown widely in gardens. The climber *Tecomanthe speciosa* was discovered in 1946 and later cuttings were brought back to Auckland. In 1956 the plant finally set seed and now the glossy-leaved, vigorous *T. speciosa* is a favourite with many home gardeners.

On the Three Kings there is still only the one plant, which, after finally pushing through the forest canopy in 1995, collapsed to the ground after one of its main supporting trees died. On the positive side, the vine now receives more light, which should stimulate flowering.

Another single specimen on Three Kings is the small, glossy-leaved hardwood tree *Pennantia baylisiana* which appears in the *Guinness Book of Records* as one of the world's rarest plants. Found in 1945, it exists only as a female and cannot bear fruit, but is grown from cuttings. Botanists have

suggested that the pollen in some flowers may fertilise another flower on the plant, but this has not happened in the more than 50 years since the plant was discovered.

When tahr and chamois were liberated for recreational hunting near Mount Cook early in the 20th century, little thought was given to their potential effect on the environment. In the event, it was often disastrous, and attractive plants such as the 1-metre-high Godley's buttercup (*Ranunculus godleyanus*), were targeted by the browsing animals. Now known from only 20 alpine sites between Arthur's Pass and Mount Cook, the remaining populations of the buttercup are being monitored. Once the effects of tahr and chamois are known, specific action will be taken to protect the plant.

Two species of *Pittosporum* are among New Zealand's most threatened shrubs. *P. obcordatum* was once widespread on river gravel sites, but

*Tecomanthe speciosa, a Three Kings Island native, was eaten by goats until only one plant remained, but is now raised in nurseries as a popular garden plant.*

today grows in the wild only around Wairoa and Hikurangi north of Whangarei, in Wanganui, the East Cape area, and in the Catlins region and an area near Manapouri in the South Island. At the Cobb Saddle and Boulder Lake near Nelson, the attractive *P. dallii* grows in scattered numbers. As a cultivated plant it is appreciated more in Britain than in its native land.

One species that came back from the dead is the attractive *Hebe breviracemosa* from Raoul Island in the Kermadecs. Thought to have been wiped out by goats, it was last sighted in 1908. Then in 1983 a young shrub was discovered; a year later the last goat was killed on the island and the hebe has been replanted.

*Shore plover eggs are not hard to hatch; the difficulty in establishing a population lies in keeping birds on the island where they are released.*

# Plovers

Within the family of plovers are the dotterels and the famous wrybill (see individual entries), but to confuse matters there are some birds which are just plain 'plovers' (pronounced 'pluvver'). The common characteristic of the different species is that they are small- to medium-sized birds found in open country, such as beaches, estuaries or farmland. Some migrate to New Zealand from the Arctic, some, like the wrybill, migrate to the North Island in winter, and others stay in the same place all year.

Until rats and cats arrived in New Zealand, the shore plover (*Thinornis novaeseelandiae*) was common around New Zealand coasts, but its an-nihilation was so rapid that by 1871 the last had disappeared from the mainland. However, it hung on in the Chathams where a population of 100–140 remain on South-East Island. Incredibly, no rats have ever made it ashore on the island, making it one of the country's key nature re-serves. Until 1957 the island was farmed, but to-day it is unpopulated.

In 1991 the Department of Conservation launched a rescue programme for the shore plover, bringing eggs from the Chathams to the National Wildlife Centre at Mount Bruce and raising chicks to independence. More than 30 birds have been released onto Motuora Island in the Hauraki Gulf, with mixed success. More-porks have killed a number, while others have flown as far away as Kaipara Harbour and the

---

*Did you know?*

Besides being a great navigator, James Cook had a reputation for curing scurvy, a disease resulting from a deficiency of vitamin C, which was the curse of sailors for centuries. In New Zealand one of Cook's chief weapons against scurvy was the plant *Lepidium oleraceum* (pictured below), popularly known as Cook's scurvy grass.

Huge quantities of the plant were loaded aboard the *Endeavour* and served to the sailors. Today it is virtually impossible to find scurvy grass on the mainland; because it is highly palatable to sheep, cattle, goats and possums it is now confined to islands without those animals.

Coromandel Peninsula, making it difficult to establish a self-sustaining population on the island. It appears that a captive rearing programme may have to be started on Motuora to convince the plovers to stay there.

The spur-winged plover (*Vanellus miles*) is a raucous Australian immigrant which bred for the first time in New Zealand at Invercargill Airport in 1932, and since then has swiftly colonised the country, even as far as the Chathams. At home on farmland, where it eats copious quantities of worms, grass grubs and porina larvae, this plover is used to coping with predators such as harriers and magpies, which it does not hesitate to attack if they threaten its nest. Unfortunately it has revealed itself to be a predator on at least one threatened bird, the New Zealand dotterel, whose eggs it destroys.

Several other plovers are Arctic migrants, including the turnstone (*Arenaria interpres*) and the Pacific golden plover (*Pluvialis fulva*). Around 5000–7000 turnstones visit New Zealand harbours and estuaries, making the species the third most common migrant. In its breeding plumage the turnstone is one of the most colourful waders. Pacific golden plovers are less numerous (600–1200 birds).

# Pohutukawa

'The beach is fringed with pohutukawa trees, single and stunted in the gardens, spreading and noble on the cliffs, and in the empty spaces by the foreshore. Tiny red coronets prick through the grey-green leaves. Bark, flower and leaf seem overlaid by smoke. The red is of a dying fire at dusk, the green faded and drab. Pain and age are in these gnarled forms, in bare roots, clutching at the earth, knotting on the cliff face, in tortured branches, dark against the washed sky.' Bruce Mason, celebrating the New Zealand Christmas Tree, in his play *The Pohutukawa Tree*, was just one of many who have felt sufficiently moved by the tree's rugged grace to immortalise it in words or paint.

The pohutukawa (*Metrosideros excelsa*) is related to guavas, feijoas, and eucalypts; all are members of the myrtle family. There are two types of myrtles: trees with succulent berries, such as feijoas and guavas, and trees which produce dry, woody capsules with hundreds of small seeds, such as pohutukawa, rata, manuka and kanuka. A second species of pohutukawa, *M. kermadecensis*, from the Kermadec Islands, finds

*A pohutukawa, its silvery trunk gnarled and bent with age, on the edge of Houhora Harbour.*

favour in suburban gardens because of its smaller size. The two species can be told apart in other ways: the mainland tree has pointed-tipped leaves and its peak flowering time is December–January, while the Kermadec species has rounded-tipped leaves and flowers slightly earlier, in November–December.

In 1941 a yellow-flowered form of *M. excelsa* was found on Motiti Island in the Bay of Plenty and has since become a popular garden tree.

Close relatives of the pohutukawa grow throughout the Pacific, all varieties of *M. collina*. These look virtually identical to the New Zealand trees and have a similar flower.

As a coastal tree, pohutukawa is without peer, able to withstand salt-laden winds and drought. And while it can successfully gain a toe-hold in the poorest of soils, it also relishes sheltered gardens and rich soils.

Although it grows naturally only to Gisborne in the east and northern Taranaki in the west, pohutukawa have been planted as far south as Dunedin. Commonly regarded as a coastal tree, it grows inland on the shores of Lake Rotoiti near Rotorua. Presumably birds dropped seed there or Maori planted the trees.

The pohutukawa held a prominent place in Maori mythology. Legends tell of the young warrior Tawhaki and his attempt to find help in heaven to avenge his father's death. He subsequently fell to Earth and the pohutukawa's crimson flowers are said to represent his blood. A small, wind-beaten pohutukawa clinging to the cliff face near Cape Reinga is reputed to be 800 years old. Maori believed it guarded the entrance to a sacred cave through which disembodied spirits passed on their way to the next world. Other pohutukawa have cultural significance. One in

*Caught red-handed: possums have developed a taste for the nectar and fresh shoots of pohutukawa, contributing to a decline of this tree.*

Kawhia Harbour was said to be the tree to which the Tainui canoe was tied when it arrived after its voyage across the Pacific, while the Te Araroa pohutukawa honours Rerekohu, a notable 18th-century chief of the region. Opinion is divided as to whether this is the largest pohutukawa in the country; its spread is possibly the greatest, but a tree near Mangonui in Northland has a much greater timber volume.

One of Wellington's feature trees is a pohutukawa that grows opposite the Wellington Club on the Terrace. When the club was rebuilt during the 1980s, the tree was insured for $40 000 against damage. The tree is home to thousands of starlings whose guano spatters the footpath and, occasionally, passersby.

## Project Crimson

Concerned at the destruction of pohutukawa around the coast, the Department of Conservation and Carter Holt Harvey have created a trust fund to finance a programme dubbed Project Crimson, with the aim of restoring the species. The programme has extended its coverage to the pohutukawa's cousin the rata, also under pressure from possum browsing.

Today's pohutukawa are mostly elderly trees, facing myriad threats from possums, people (who light fires under them, use them for firewood or park cars on their sensitive roots), and weeds and grasses which prevent regeneration by smothering seedlings.

Since Project Crimson began in the early 1990s, more than 70 000 trees have been planted.

> ### Did you know?
>
> The pohutukawa was greatly favoured by early European boat builders. Its natural bends were ideal for boat construction, and the timber was immune to seaworms when exposed to salt water. The ribs of the largest sailing ship built in New Zealand, the 409-tonne *Stirlingshire*, were made from pohutukawa.

*The natural predators of possums—cats, stoats, moreporks and harriers—probably make little impact on the massive possum population.*

# Possum

The scale of New Zealand's possum (*Trichosurus vulpecula*) problem is staggering. Since the establishment of the first population in 1848 for a fur trade, the voracious vegetarians have multiplied alarmingly and fanned out across the country, stripping the trees in their path. Today the national possum population, numbering around 60 million, is distributed over 92 percent of New Zealand. Each night these pests gobble up about 20 000 tonnes of vegetation.

Up until 15 years ago a thriving trade in furs kept the animals in check, but international animal rights activists have largely succeeded in halting the trade, allowing the possum to proliferate. Most New Zealand possums came from Tasmania. Known as Tasmanian blacks (because

of the colour of their coat), they were preferred over the mainland Australian grey for their superior fur, which remains sleek after becoming wet, unlike the fur of the greys, which matts easily. Drier areas of New Zealand have many more grey possums, while the blacks thrive in wetter regions such as the West Coast.

Possums breed in autumn and spring, with most births occurring in autumn. In New Zealand the juveniles or 'joeys' are smaller than their Australian counterparts at comparable ages, and they grow more slowly.

It is not only the amount possums eat that is a problem, but also the way they do it. They are selective eaters, targeting tastier trees first before moving on down the list. After being browsed, a healthy tree will push out new shoots in order to survive. This new growth is the possums' preferred food, so again the tree is heavily browsed.

After two years of being subjected to possum browsing, the tree's old leaves fall and it dies.

Some New Zealand plants lack the natural toxins of Australia's eucalypts, which adversely affect the possums' digestive systems, limiting the amount they can eat, and here there are no predators—except humans—to check the possums' seemingly unstoppable advance. However, a number of plants, such as rimu, pepperwood, kawakawa, and crown and filmy ferns are left virtually untouched. Tests of the chemical composition of these plants revealed they had significant levels of terpenes (similar to turpentine) and also tannins. Other unpalatable plants include matai, miro and kahikatea. The leaves of beech, karaka, coprosma, rewarewa, lancewood, pukatea and nettle are also rarely eaten.

Often forests under attack from possums look superficially healthy, but the undergrowth consists of species which the pests find unpalatable, instead of regenerating trees. In a two-pronged assault possums eat the new growth on the trees while deer and goats chew through the undergrowth. The result is a collapse of plant diversity and a consequent threat to the food sources of native birds, many of which are endangered.

Also alarming is the threat posed by possums to the $5-billion beef, dairy and venison export trade. Possums are the major transmitters of bovine tuberculosis, a lung disease which has spread dramatically among cattle and deer in the 1990s. Possum control is a significant drain on the public purse. At least $40 million a year is

*A possum population explosion in Westland forests during the 1950s and 60s has resulted in these gaunt rata and kamahi skeletons in the Adams River Valley.*

devoted to killing possums, mainly by poisoning with the toxin 1080. A further $12 million is being spent on research into ways of halting the possum plague, much of it with a hi-tech focus. Currently under investigation are potential methods of biological control through interfering with the reproductive system or introducing deadly natural viruses which will spread through the possum population.

One of the most intriguing developments in current possum research is the attempt to trace just what caused 'wobbly possum syndrome', the graphic term coined by scientists in 1995 describing the behaviour of possums in the throes of dying from the unknown disease. The most likely scenario is that the disease is caused by a virus—a theory which caused a buzz in the marsupial scientific world, as viruses are virtually unknown in the animal. If the virus is responsible for the deaths, it has a formidable strike rate. Only three of around 40 possums which have been exposed in one way or another to it—either because they were inoculated with suspensions made from the organs of infected animals, or simply because they were in the same cage—have survived.

Australian scientists are investigating a number of biological control possibilities. One team is carrying out trials in which young animals are given drugs that interfere with the ability of the thyroid gland to regulate temperature, thus causing death. Another team is looking at the role that hormones from the pituitary gland play in growth and lactation, while a third is attempting to disrupt two hormones called oxytocin and vasopressin, both important in ovulation, the birth process and lactation.

However, even scientists are sceptical about the chances of introducing a successful biological control. They point out that should such control be developed over the next 10–20 years it might not be acceptable to the public.

One unanswered question is where a biological control can be safely tested. The New Zealand Government has spent millions of dollars clearing many islands of possums, so is unwilling to relocate animals there for experimental purposes. And the islands where possums are living, such as the Chathams, are also the habitats of endangered birdlife which may be affected by a biological control. Australians are concerned over the possible risks possum biocontrol presents to Australian marsupials.

# Praying mantis

Of the world's 1800 species of praying mantis, just one—*Orthodera ministralis*—occurs in New Zealand. The mantis is called 'praying' because its forelimbs appear to be raised in prayer, but given its abilities as a predator, 'preying' mantis might be as apt.

Blending in with its surroundings, the patient praying mantis can sit motionless for long periods. Although it has well-developed wings, the praying mantis rarely flies, instead waiting quite impassively until a meal happens along. Like the dragonfly, it has large compound eyes, stereoscopic vision and is able to swivel its head to follow its unfortunate victim. Its backward-directed, sharp-spined legs are specially designed to seize and hold onto prey.

In a fraction of a second the mantis reaches out and takes its prey, cutting it up into bite-sized pieces with its sharp jaws. The less tasty bits such as the wings and legs are discarded, allowing the mantis to concentrate on the nutritious body. In New Zealand, its main prey are flies, wasps, butterflies and spiders. Some mantises elsewhere take frogs and small lizards.

*After wintering over, praying mantis eggs hatch in spring, the small, delicate insects struggling to free themselves from the whitish membrane. They capture aphids and flies before graduating to larger prey.*

The least endearing feature of some species of praying mantis is the female's occasional habit of biting its mate's head off during or after mating. If the smaller, decapitated male has not succeeded in fertilising the female she will nonchalantly seek another mate. This is not a habit of the New Zealand species but is common in the European *Mantis religiosa*, a quarter of whose copulations end in decapitation.

*Plank-buttressed trees are a feature of tropical forests. The pukatea is the only one of New Zealand's trees with such well-developed planks to support growth.*

# Pukatea

Many New Zealand plants betray their tropical affinities in a number of different ways: the nikau, for example, closely resembles tropical palms. Other characteristics showing similarities to tropical plants are less obvious, such as the lack of overlapping scales to protect buds during winter. Of New Zealand trees, the pukatea (*Laurelia novae-zelandiae*) is one of the most obviously tropical. It is the only native tree to have plank buttresses and, like mangroves, it has pneumatophores or breathing roots.

Just what purpose plank buttresses serve is open to speculation; the leading theory says that, being triangular-shaped and extending for several metres up the trunks and out along the roots, they offer shallow-rooted trees more stability. Growing in damp places down to Banks Peninsula in the east and Fiordland in the west, pukatea reaches a height of 35 metres. Kahikatea, which is found in similar semiswampy habitats, also has buttresses, but they are not planked.

Pukatea bark has been found to contain pukateine, a substance with pain-relieving properties similar to those of morphine, but without its after-effects. Maori used a concoction made from the inner bark as a remedy for toothache.

# Pukeko

With a trademark flick of its snowy white undertail, the pukeko (*Porphyrio porphyrio*) advertises its presence in swamps and farmland. Pukeko can fly when forced to, but prefer to run or swim to cover, which makes it all the more extraordinary that they flew from Australia to make their home here some time within the last 1000 years. They have also been recorded making long-distance trips within New Zealand; one banded bird moved 240 km from a previous site and another alpine traveller was found at 2350 metres, approaching the Tasman Saddle.

Termed the swamphen or purple gallinule in southern Europe, Africa, Southeast Asia, Australia and New Guinea, in New Zealand the pukeko is widespread throughout the North, South and Stewart islands, as well as on a number of offshore islands such as Great Barrier, Kapiti and the Chathams.

Related to the rare takahe (see page 332), the pukeko resembles its more famous cousin in looks (although the takahe is three times heavier) and behaviour. Both species grasp food with their feet in a parrot-like way and takahe offspring, like pukeko youngsters, sometimes help their parents raise chicks. Conservation managers may be able to take advantage of the birds' similarity by using pukeko to raise takahe chicks. Pukeko have a better-evolved ability to avoid predators and it is hoped they may be able to pass on such advantageous traits to takahe. For example, pukeko give different alarm calls, depending on whether the threat is a ground animal such as a stoat, or an aerial one. They then lead their chicks to safety while other pukeko harass the predator.

Since European settlement the pukeko has expanded its range, especially onto farmland where from late summer onwards it enjoys eating clover and is regarded by farmers as a pest. Maori gardeners felt the same way after seeing their taro and kumara despoiled. Essentially, though, it is a wetland bird, and usually does not venture far from swamps or rivers. Its food includes insects, frogs, small birds and eggs.

An indication of the pukeko's abundance is the fact that birds can legally be shot during the duck-shooting season. As a gamebird it has a mixed reputation and is considered to be at its best in a stew or soup.

## Pukeko partnerships

The pukeko's social system, regarded as one of the most complex among birds, varies according to where it lives. In some areas birds are highly territorial and breed as pairs; in others, groups of up to a dozen occupy a territory and all help to raise chicks. The helpers are frequently offspring of the breeding pairs.

*Two adult pukeko are about to change the guard during incubation. Surrounded by water, this nest is less vulnerable to predators.*

Even more unusually, two females may lay and incubate eggs in the same nest. A few other species such as the ostriches, Tasmanian native hens, South American anis and Californian acorn woodpecker are known to share nests, but one female will usually throw the other's eggs out because there are too many to be incubated properly. Unaware of the pukeko's communal nesting behaviour, early ornithologists were fooled into thinking some females were highly productive because their nests contained up to 20 eggs instead of the usual seven.

Among some pukeko, communal life has gone one stage further and pair bonds have broken down so that males and females mate freely within the group. The males' uncertainty about which chicks they have fathered probably ensures that they stay around to help with raising all the chicks. Communal living also offers the advantage of having several males to defend a territory.

*Perched atop its parent, a 3-day-old pukeko chick gazes out confidently onto a new world. It will take at least a year for the youngster, already a competent swimmer, to acquire the scarlet bill and shield of the adult.*

# Puriri

The handsome puriri (*Vitex lucens*) belongs to a distinguished international family, the best known of its relatives being teak, a timber renowned for its durability. In New Zealand the puriri is the only representative of the genus *Vitex*; other members of this group occur in Fiji, Samoa, Indonesia and New Caledonia. With these tropical affinities it is no surprise that the puriri grows naturally in the northern half of the North Island, although good specimens have been cultivated further south.

Generally the puriri grows to about 20 metres in height and 1.5 metres in diameter. The largest recorded tree graces Reretiti Hill, Waimate North, with a height of 25 metres and a massive girth of 2.62 metres.

The puriri's ability to produce flowers and bright red fruit throughout the year makes it a favourite food source for birds, especially kereru. The tree was used by Maori for various medicinal purposes: the water from boiled leaves was good for sprains and backache, and the infusion was a remedy for ulcers and sore throats. Timber from the puriri is very dense and heavy but highly valued for use as a hardwood. Today puriri stands are too depleted to justify cutting down the trees for timber.

*The puriri flowers in winter, making it a valuable tree during a season of scarcity for nectar-eaters such as tui and bellbirds.*

# Rabbit

Introduced in the 1830s as game for sportsmen and a comforting reminder of home for European settlers, rabbits (*Oryctolagus cuniculus cuniculus*) were not initially regarded as a threat to the country's ecology. But by the 1870s they were swarming across the country in plague numbers, forcing farmers to walk off the land in frustration as the unwelcome guests stripped the countryside of vegetation. The damage to grassland caused sheep numbers to tumble in many areas. In an attempt to curb the rabbits, weasels, stoats and ferrets were introduced, which in turn decimated bird populations.

A battery of weapons was used against rabbits, including guns, traps, gas and poisoned bait. From the 1940s until the 1980s rabbit boards managed to keep the problem in check, with hunters paid by the taxpayer to shoot and poison rabbits. Several rabbit fences were built; one, the Hurunui fence in north Canterbury, which extended 80 km inland, is still partially in place.

However, during the 1980s, as the economy was transformed, subsidies were done away with and the responsibility for controlling rabbits fell back on individual landowners. For most, the job has proved too expensive; once more rabbits are winning the battle.

Rabbits are not a problem on intensively managed farms, but they continue to be a major pest on extensive sheep stations. In the South Island, an estimated 3 million ha are seriously affected, mostly in the high, semi-arid country of the Mackenzie Basin and Central Otago.

Although rabbit litters in New Zealand are no larger than elsewhere, the plant-growing season is longer, thus a female rabbit born early in the spring breeding season may herself be able to breed in autumn.

In desperation, farmers are turning to the rabbit calicivirus disease (RCD) as a means of control. The virus was first reported in domestic rabbits in China in the mid-1980s before spreading to other parts of Asia, Mexico and Europe. Since 1989 scientists on Wardang Island, Australia, have been conducting experiments on the effects of the virus. In September 1995 it slipped through quarantine precautions on the island and spread rapidly through the Australian mainland, killing millions of rabbits.

*Forget* Watership Down *or* Peter Rabbit*: in New Zealand rabbits are ecological pests, capable of producing six litters a year, with young rabbits breeding the year they are born.*

The virus was illegally imported into New Zealand in the spring of 1997 and first released on Mackenzie Basin and north Otago farms before the New Zealand Government approved its release throughout the country. Its feared effects on native bird species are unproven.

Doubts have been voiced about the long-term effectiveness of using a virus as a control mechanism. While up to 80 percent of rabbits will be exterminated, half the survivors might develop an immunity to the virus.

The rabbit's relative, the brown hare (*Lepus europaeus occidentalis*) has proved to be a less problematical introduction. Living in grassland, open country and alpine grasslands, the hare has never built up in large numbers. Scientists believe hare populations are self-limiting by an unexplained behavioural mechanism.

*Regiments of radiata grow alongside a North Island river. The latitude at which the pine does best in New Zealand neatly corresponds to its natural habitat in California.*

# Radiata pine

Planted in serried ranks throughout the country, radiata pine (*Pinus radiata*) is the tree upon which the New Zealand timber industry has largely been built. Today 1.3 million ha of the country is planted in exotic forest, 90 percent of which is radiata pine.

Radiata first came to prominence in Canterbury during the 1860s and 70s when it was planted for shelter belts. Impressed by the speed at which it grew and its tolerance of a variety of conditions, early foresters recommended plantations be sown in radiata.

The impulse behind the planting was to conserve native forests which were being fast logged out. From the 1920s the State Forest Service spearheaded a massive planting programme which saw Kaingaroa become one of the largest man-made forests in the world.

Radiata's reputation has changed over the years. Initially it was regarded as producing a knotty, low-quality timber, but improved growing and harvesting techniques have led to its acceptance as a high-value wood.

In the 1970s and 80s New Zealand timber companies and conservation groups were at continual loggerheads. However, in 1989, after long negotiation, Tasman Forestry Ltd (now Fletcher Forests) agreed to stop felling native forest and furthermore to contribute substantially to a programme to rescue the kokako. The kudos won by Tasman was eyed enviously by other timber companies and the way was paved for the 1991 New Zealand Forest Accord, in essence an agreement to move away from logging native forest and concentrate on plantation forests. Some conservation groups argue that plantations are more susceptible to pests and diseases, have poor soils and are inhospitable to birds, but most would prefer the disadvantages to felling native forest.

On the northwest coast of the United States, the natural home of radiata pine, the tree has a much lower profile than it does in New Zealand. Known as the Monterey pine, its total habitat amounts to only 7000 ha and trees grow to just over half the 60 metres common in New Zealand.

Following New Zealand's example, countries such as Chile (which now has more hectares in pine than New Zealand), Australia, South Africa and Spain have planted radiata.

# Rails

Apart from the pukeko and the weka (see individual entries), New Zealand rails are rarely seen. The takahe (see page 332) lives in remote Fiordland mountains, another rail is confined to the Auckland Islands, while the remaining three species are secretive birds which lurk in freshwater swamps and estuaries.

Because it is difficult to observe, little is known about the banded rail (*Rallus philippensis*). More common in the North than the South Island, it lives in mangrove forests and freshwater wetlands of Northland, Auckland, the Waikato, the Coromandel Peninsula and the Bay of Plenty. In the South Island there are only about 100 breeding pairs, concentrated in salt marshes around northwest Nelson and the Marlborough Sounds. The banded rail is also present on Stewart Island and adjacent islands. Like all rails, the banded rail's tail flicks continually as it searches for snails, crabs, spiders, beetles and worms. Its long toes give support and spread weight over a large area, like snowshoes.

The Auckland Island rail (*Rallus pectoralis muelleri*) must be one of New Zealand's most obscure birds—understandable perhaps in light of the fact that few people visit the subantarctic islands where it lives and because of the withdrawn nature of the species. Until a 1989 expedition discovered a population of about 1500 on 10 000-ha Adams Island (the largest of the Auckland Island satellites), the rail had been sighted only 10 times. Another healthy population of several hundred was then unearthed in 1993 on Disappointment Island. Cats most likely exterminated the rail on Auckland Island itself in the 19th century.

Under duress the rail can fly, but when the 1989 expedition members released five temporarily captured birds, none of them tried to fly, even though two were liberated from above head height. These simply dropped to the ground and ran for cover. Dr Robert Falla reported after a

*Banded rails occur not only in New Zealand but are also present throughout southeast Asia, Australia and Pacific island countries. Unwilling fliers, they prefer to run for cover.*

1966 trip that the rail could fly quite strongly and purposefully, but again in the ralline fashion that might be described as 'low gear'.

For the moment the rails are secure, even if their populations are not large. However, if rats were to accidentally come ashore on the islands the birds would be doomed.

Spotless crakes (*Porzana tabuensis*) and marsh crakes (*P. pusilla*) are mainland and offshore-island swamp-dwelling birds which are seldom seen but whose distinctive calls are often heard. Both at the small end of the rail spectrum (45 grams in weight compared with 1 kg for the pukeko and weka), the crakes are presumed to be relatively common, but because of their secretive habits it has been difficult to estimate numbers.

The Australian coot (*Fulica atra*) was a persistent but unsuccessful immigrant from 1875 until 1958 when it first started breeding at Lake Hayes near Arrowtown. Shooters did their best to stop the bird from settling, but it is now a protected self-introduced native which numbers about 2000; most live in the North Island.

Coots have outsized feet with flap-like lobes along the toes, which they use to scurry across the surface of the water, all the time beating their wings vigorously.

# Rata

Best known of the rata are the northern (*Metrosideros robusta*) and the southern (*M. umbellata*), both of them trees. The common names are not a strictly accurate indication of their distribution as northern rata grow as far south as north Westland and southern rata grow everywhere but Northland.

In 1975 a large, white-flowering rata around 25 metres tall was found at Te Paki, Northland. Named after its discoverer, Bartlett's rata (*M. bartletti*) is extremely rare with only about 30 specimens in the wild.

Except for one small tree, *M. parkinsonii*, the other eight rata are climbing plants. *M. parkinsonii* is one of the most striking examples of discontinuous distribution in New Zealand. First described in 1882 in the Nelson area, 34 years later it was spotted growing on Great and Little Barrier islands, 400 miles away.

Whether trees or climbers, rata are endowed with beautiful crimson flowers, important sources

*The rata vine* Metrosideros diffusa, *which flowers in November, is the most common flowering rata.*

of nectar for birds such as tui and bellbirds. Northern rata flower between November and January, and southern rata between November and March. Unfortunately the flowers which attract birds are also sought after by possums. More dangerous for the health of both species, though, is the fact that possums dine out on new season's leaves. After a few years of such selective browsing, the tree dies. During the 1950s and 1960s a possum population explosion on the West Coast resulted in the deaths of large numbers of southern rata. Possums show a preference for rata flowers and leaves over virtually every other plant.

Unlike the northern rata, which starts out as an epiphyte (see page 286), the southern rata grows from a seed in the ground. Shorter than the northern rata (one of which near Wanganui is 43 metres high), the southern grows to a maximum of 15 metres.

For those South Island forests that have been spared the worst of possums' attentions, early botanist Thomas Kirk's description still rings true: 'The colony has few more magnificent sights to offer than a mountain-slope covered with this species from base to nearly 4000 feet above sea-level, when the brilliant scarlet flowers are lighted up by the morning sun'. To Maori the rata was a significant tree. An important chief

*A rimu in the close embrace of a northen rata. As it ages, the rimu will decay and the rata will take its place.*

High in the forest canopy, the northern rata starts life when its light seed lands and germinates in an epiphyte or on the top branches of a suitable host such as a rimu (pictured) or kahikatea. From there its roots descend the tree, finally reaching the ground where the rata's great trunk takes shape. In time the mature rata will take the place of the host tree.

was often called a rata whakatau or rata whaka-marumaru (the shade-giving or sheltering rata, protector of his people). Maori explained the tree's crooked trunk by saying it had once been trampled by the moa. Its flowers (like those of the pohutukawa) were said to have come from the blood of the mythical Tawhaki.

# Rats

Virtually everywhere else in the world rats are human camp followers or 'commensal' animals, but in New Zealand many have made their homes in forests and other wild places far from human contact. There are three species of rat: the kiore (see page 185), the Norway or water rat (*Rattus norvegicus*) and the ship or black rat (*Rattus rattus*). While they can be nuisances in urban and rural areas, it is as predators on wildlife that rats are most reviled.

First of the 'Old World' rats to arrive in New Zealand was the larger Norway rat, which escaped from Cook's *Endeavour* in 1769 and was in the Bay of Islands by 1772, if a report by the Frenchman Crozet is to be believed. It quickly spread over the North and South islands, but towards the end of the 19th century people noticed its numbers were dropping. About that time the ship rat was beginning its rise to dominance as the most widespread rat, a status it enjoys today.

Uninvited passengers on sealing, whaling, trading and immigrant vessels, ship rats started to spread through the North Island in the 1860s and through the South Island in the 1890s. Ecologists believe the Norway rat may have lost ground to the ship rat through a combination of

# A New Zealand success story

When ship rats got ashore on Big South Cape, a small island off Stewart Island, in the early 1960s, the consequences shook the conservation world. In just a few years two native birds, a species of short-tailed bat and a flightless weevil became extinct. The ravenous rodents ate out much of the forest as well.

The events on Big South Cape confirmed fears about what might happen if rats got ashore on islands even more rich in wildlife, such as the Snares, and encouraged thinking about the possibility of eradicating rats on islands where they already existed. Scientists had assumed that, while it was possible to rid islands of possums, goats and deer, rodents would prove too small and wily to succumb to poisoning programmes.

During the 1970s and 80s rats were eliminated on a number of small islands—most less than 50 ha. But the two big breakthroughs occurred in 1988 when a Norway rat blitz was carried out on 170-ha Breaksea Island, off the Fiordland coast, and a year later 5 million mice were poisoned on 230-ha Mana Island near Wellington.

The success of these operations depended on sophisticated anticoagulant baits, and the ability to totally blanket the island with poison so all the rodents were killed in one fell swoop. In the past, cautious rats had eaten baits, suffered a small amount of poisoning and then become bait shy. But new delayed-reaction poisons meant rats could eat the toxic baits for 4 days before they showed signs of poisoning, by which time they had consumed many times the lethal dose and were guaranteed to die.

With an area of 1965 ha, Kapiti Island, which was plagued by Norway rats and kiore, was more of a challenge. In order to ensure a blanket cover on Breaksea, for example, baits were laid out in 743 stations at 50-metre intervals and replenished daily. On Kapiti this would have been impossible, and furthermore some areas were inaccessible. A complicating factor was the fact that there were two rat species on the island—trials had shown that dominant Norway rats entered bait stations and took bait, but the subordinate Pacific rats were repelled from entering at all. An aerial drop was more likely to succeed because all baits would be available to all rats at the same time.

In September and again in October 1996 a helicopter dropped poison on Kapiti, and in a few areas poison was applied from the ground.The results have been declared an unqualified success. An array of threatened species benefited from the rats being removed from the island, including birds such as the saddleback, stitchbird, and kaka, several species of lizard and a variety of invertebrates. The successful eradication has also cleared the way for species such as the tuatara to be reintroduced to Kapiti.

*Ship rats can detect by smell the kind of food eaten by their companions; if some rats show signs of illness, the healthy ones will avoid the food the sick rats have eaten. Rats which find certain food distasteful urinate over it to warn others.*

being outcompeted and preyed upon by stoats, which were introduced in 1884 to control rabbits. The two rats occupy different habitats: the Norway rat is not a good climber, spending most of its time in drains and sewers, but it is a good swimmer, able to cross 600-metre-wide sea channels. The ship rat is considered the most dangerous because it readily climbs trees and is more widely distributed than the other two rats.

Rats multiply at an astounding rate. The gestation period lasts 20 days, and they give birth to four to 10 baby rats on average four or five times a year. A rat is able to breed from the age of 6 months. Theoretically a pair of rats can produce a third of a billion offspring or descendants in just 3 years. In practice, however, environmental factors sharply reduce survival rates. A 6-year study in the Orongorongo Valley near Wellington showed females produced an average of only six young annually.

In a study on diet in the same valley, during autumn and winter ship rats ate mostly fungi and the fruit and berries of trees including hinau, miro, kawakawa, supplejack, karaka and nikau. In spring and summer the bulk of their food was insects, mostly tree wetas; cicadas, stick insects and spiders were eaten less often.

Rats are not long-distance travellers in the forest. In the Orongorongo Valley, the furthest a tagged male rat moved from its point of release was 190 metres, and a female rat ventured only 117 metres.

Few islands, apart from inaccessible ones in the Three Kings group or the Poor Knights, have escaped rats' attentions. But the good news is that rats have been eradicated from around 20 islands in the last 15 years.

*The largest of the three rat species in New Zealand, the Norway rat can kill some adult birds.*

*Food was not all the raupo provided; early European settlers gathered the fluff from the seed-heads and stuffed it into mattresses and pillows.*

# Raupo

One of the most versatile plants, raupo (*Typha orientalis*) or bulrush was used by Maori as a food, a medicine, for thatching and to make canoes. It grows in swamps throughout the country, forming a sausage-shaped seed-head at the height of summer. The most valued part of the plant was the pollen, which in various forms (depending on the tribe) was worked into sweet breads. Harvesting of the flower stalks was done in the calm of early morning and late evening, so that the light pollen would not be blown away; the stalks were left in the sun to dry and later the pollen was separated out from the down.

Colenso, the 19th-century botanist, compared the appearance of the processed pollen to mustard. Northern Wairoa Maori made a porridge from the pollen, but more commonly it was formed into cakes with water, then baked in an earth oven to create 'sweetish and light' cakes, according to Colenso. The Tuhoe concocted their own delicacy, a mixture of the pollen and crushed manuka beetles steamed in an earth oven. Also of some food value were the roots and fresh shoots of raupo. The roots were peeled and eaten raw or cooked, and sometimes made into cakes.

Medicinally, the ring of fine feathery hairs surrounding the seeds (called the pappus) was applied to wounds and old ulcerated sores to protect them against dust.

# Rewarewa

To find the modern relatives of the rewarewa (*Knightia excelsa*) one has to go to Australia, South Africa or South America, where proteas have developed into a magnificent array of forms. In New Zealand there are just two members of the protea group: rewarewa and toru (*Toronia toru*), neither of which produces the large, showy flowers of proteas on other continents. Rewarewa's link with plants in other countries tells us that they all had a common ancestor, living about 130 million years ago on Gondwanaland. Presumably the precursor to rewarewa came to New Zealand via South America.

Often growing abundantly in young forests or on hill slopes, the rewarewa is sometimes confused with young kauri because of its upright, poplar-resembling habit. However, viewed close up rewarewa is readily identifiable by its serrated leaves. It is common in the North Island but occurs only as far south as Marlborough and Nelson. Rewarewa nectar was eaten by Maori (the tree was also known as the honeysuckle tree) and today flavours a popular honey.

*A New Zealand tree flower unlike any other, the rewarewa bloom bears some of the protea's hallmarks but there are no petals and the 30–50 flowers are packed into a raceme.*

The tree's flowers appear in November and December and the seed pods, covered in a red-brown-coloured down, take a year to mature. When finally ripe the pods split in two, and bear a striking resemblance to a Maori canoe, complete with a prow and sternposts. They are said to be the original model for the Maori canoe.

# Rifleman

Weighing in at a minuscule 6 grams and measuring just 80 mm, the rifleman (*Acanthisitta chloris*) is the smallest of New Zealand birds and one of the wren family. Constantly on the move in its hunt for insects in the trunks and on the branches of trees, it gives out a high-pitched 'zitt'. Both the Maori and Pakeha names refer to the bird's colour: in Maori it is titipounamu (pounamu means greenstone), while 'rifleman' comes from the 19th-century New Zealand military riflemen's green uniform.

Riflemen are highly co-operative parents, and males are attentive fathers and caring mates, as recent studies at Kowhai Bush near Kaikoura have shown. The male, aided sometimes by non-breeding helpers, starts building several nests before the female finally joins in. Normally riflemen choose a knothole or crevice in a tree for the nest site, creating inside a cosy bed of leaves, twigs and feathers (see page 232).

For such a small bird, the female lays a relatively huge egg mass—on average 84 percent of her bodyweight (she may lay up to five eggs although the usual number is three). In order to build up her reserves, during courtship the male feeds her the rifleman staple diet of insects.

The female rifleman is larger than the male and from 3 days old, female chicks receive more food than males; the most likely explanation for the size difference is that because females produce relatively large eggs they need to be larger to cope with the physiological stress of laying.

Once the female has laid the eggs, the male does the lion's share of the daytime incubation, then at night allows the female to stay inside the nest where it is about 15°C warmer than outside. Overseas studies have shown that birds which roost inside the nest expend 15 percent less energy than those outside. A bird sitting on the nest usually does not leave until it hears a signal from its partner outside the nest that it is ready to take

*The rifleman is the smallest of New Zealand's birds.*

over incubation. If its partner is not available the departing bird covers the eggs and entrance hole with feathers. After the chicks have hatched, male riflemen provide more food for them than the females do.

While the young are still being fed, riflemen females frequently start laying eggs in a second nest. The male devotes more of his time to the first clutch, while the female incubates the second clutch, since feeding uses up more energy than incubation. This arrangement also allows the female more time to forage for food for herself, vital if she is to recoup the energy she has lost in laying a second time. When they are old enough, offspring of the first clutch occasionally help to feed the second clutch.

# Rimu

Of all the podocarps, rimu or red pine (*Dacrydium cupressinum*) is the most graceful and majestic, with pendulous, golden-green branchlets and purplish-black fruit. Rising as high as 50 metres (but usually 30–35 metres) above the forest floor, rimu is widespread throughout the country, although it is absent in some areas where rainfall is low and frosts severe.

Sometimes rimu is confused with kahikatea, to which it is related; it is generally shorter, with a brown wavy trunk (the kahikatea's trunk is grey). Many mature rimu have a pronounced spiral shape. As a juvenile, rimu's weeping habit is pronounced, making it attractive to home gardeners.

The evidence that ancestors of rimu existed over 100 million years ago can be found in abundant fossil pollen. Just when the modern rimu evolved is uncertain, although it was at least 1 million years ago. At the end of the last great Ice Age 10 000 years ago, rimu dominated the landscape, but beech has since expanded at its expense. By the time Europeans arrived, dense stands of rimu could be found only in Westland and the area of the central North Island affected by the Taupo eruption of 1800 years ago. In the great forests of Whirinaki and Pureora, rimu grows on a rich foundation of volcanic ash.

Rimu is a pre-eminent timber tree, the mainstay of the native timber industry over the last century once most of the millable kauri had been logged. So resinous is rimu heartwood that Maori used to split it into fine pieces, tie it together and use it for torches.

Podocarps, belonging to the family of conifers, evolved more than 200 million years ago, long before flowering plants. Rimu, totara, matai, miro, kahikatea, monoao, pink pine, bog pine, silver pine, yellow silver pine, pygmy pine, tanekaha and toatoa are the New Zealand representatives of the podocarp family. Instead of possessing cones like other conifers such as pines, cypresses, spruces and kauri, podocarps are distinguished by having a small succulent pedestal 'foot' or bright 'berry'. In their longevity, size and majesty they resemble the great redwoods of North America.

For nearly a century there has been debate on whether the great podocarp forests are in decline. Botanist Leonard Cockayne noted in the early 20th century that podocarp saplings rarely occurred under mature forests as did less light-demanding hardwood trees such as tawa in the north and kamahi in the south. Believing the demise of the podocarps to be inevitable, the now-defunct Forest Service argued during the 1970s that central North Island forests should be logged, contending this would allow juvenile podocarps to regenerate. Other botanists stated it was too simplistic to say the forests were in decline, that there was evidence for natural regeneration and the remaining podocarp forests should be left—a view which prevailed, at least in the North Island.

Although there are podocarps in southeast Australia, the southwest Pacific, Africa and South America, the finest range of species are found in

*(Left) The rimu's pendulous habit, marked in the symmetrically shaped juvenile, is retained throughout all stages of growth. (Right) At the beginning of 1997 tree sitters began their protest against rimu logging in north Westland. By 2006, when clear-felling is due to stop, between 50 000 and 100 000 rimu will have been felled.*

New Zealand. During the 20th century New Zealanders have fought a number of notable conservation battles to try to preserve the remaining podocarp forests.

In 1978 a group led by the 'barefoot botanist' Stephen King perched high in a giant totara to protest against logging in Pureora Forest. Within a week logging was halted and today Pureora Forest is under Department of Conservation control. In 1997 an equally passionate band of protesters took to the treetops in Buller to protest against rimu logging, charging that it was damaging to the environment and especially to native birds such as the kaka and parakeet. The tree cutting in the area is one of the last large-scale native logging operations in the country.

## Did you know?

At Ship Cove in 1773 Captain Cook brewed a beer from a mixture of rimu and manuka leaves. *Resolution* botanist Anders Sparrman described it thus: 'After a small amount of rum or arrack has been added, with some brown sugar, and stirred into this really pleasant, healthy drink, it bubbled and tasted like champagne.' To some extent the brew would have aided the crew's health, as rimu has antiscurvy properties, but its main benefit would have been from the alcohol.

# Rivers

New Zealand's complex geology and changeable climate have combined to create an impressive variety of rivers: the stately Waikato, the slow-moving Whanganui, the mighty Buller, the immense Clutha. Though none are especially long—the Waikato at 425 km is the lengthiest—they are each capable of drama.

More than anything, a river owes its character to the type of rock through which it flows. The soft sandstone/siltstone landscape that the Rangitikei River carves through is markedly dissimilar to the formidably hard schists of the alpine-fed Shotover River gorge, and produces contrasting waterways.

Rivers have played a pivotal role in New Zealand's human history. Maori used the waterways of the Waikato and the Whanganui as arterial routes to and from the hinterland. Early Pakeha learned the hard way the dangers of unpredictable, flood-prone rivers; 1115 people had been recorded as drowning in them by 1870 but the actual figure would have been much higher; this way of departing life became known as 'the New Zealand death'.

Many rivers have been tamed for hydroelectricity schemes. The Waitaki, Waikato, Clutha and dozens of rivers around Mount Ruapehu have been harnessed for power generation, but the untouched waterways are now more valued for their wildlife and recreational values.

The country's high rainfall and youthful geology is reflected in the fact that the Waipaoa River at Poverty Bay disgorges out to sea 10 million tonnes of sediment a year, and even more during times of flood. Only China's Lo and Ching Rivers transport more erosion. The Buller River, only 177 km in length, nevertheless holds the New Zealand flow record for a flood—10 400 cubic metres of water a second.

*Sinuous strands of the Waimakariri River transport rock and shingle from the Southern Alps, dumping it to create the Canterbury Plains. Worldwide, such braided river ecosystems are rare.*
*(Inset) The Aan River, Waitutu, meanders through swamps and a wide, glacial valley.*

*On the alert for prey, a North Island robin perches in a tree. Robins also like to hunt for food on the forest floor where they tremble one foot to coax worms and insects to move before snapping them up.*

# Robins

So curious are robins, or toutouwai, going so far as to take food from people's hands, that they give the appearance of being at imminent risk of capture. The truth is that robins can escape on the wing promptly enough; however, predators are causing a general decline of the species throughout the mainland.

There are two species of robins in New Zealand: the Chatham Island black robin (see page 67) and the more common New Zealand robin (*Petroica australis*), which is divided into North Island, South Island and Stewart Island subspecies. These are all of similar size and appearance, except the South Island male robin, which has a distinctive lemon-yellow breast.

In the North Island the healthiest populations are in central forests such as Pureora and Whirinaki, but the bird has been absent from the lower half of the island for many decades. On Kapiti Island it is numerous, though, and moves have been made to use the population there to re-establish robins elsewhere. A number of birds shifted to Mana Island in 1995 and 1996 have started breeding. The South Island distribution is patchy; robins are common from Arthur's Pass north but less so in the south. On islands such as the Outer Chetwode in the Marlborough Sounds, where the capacity of the island to take more robins is exhausted, the birds occupy territories of about half a hectare. On the mainland they have more space, produce more chicks, but have a much higher mortality rate.

Predators find it reasonably easy to enter a robin's nest, and the robin, whose traditional enemy has been the morepork, has not yet learned to escape the clutches of stoats and rats. Possums are also suspected to be predators or to alter the environment to the robin's detriment. Once possums were eradicated from Kapiti Island in 1985, robin numbers increased rapidly. Life expectancy for a robin on the mainland is about 4 years, compared to 10 on predator-free islands.

Fiercely territorial, male robins drive away both male and female robin intruders until the breeding season. The female builds the nest, but the devoted male brings her food and sings encouragement. If the female senses a predator nearby, she tries to lure it away with a 'broken-wing' distraction display.

Robin chicks are ready to leave the nest about 20 days after they are hatched, but need their parents' continual care for up to 50 days afterwards. Meanwhile the female renests to raise at least two more families in the season.

Robins are mainly insect-eaters, capable of dispatching worms and wetas of up to a third of their own bodyweight.

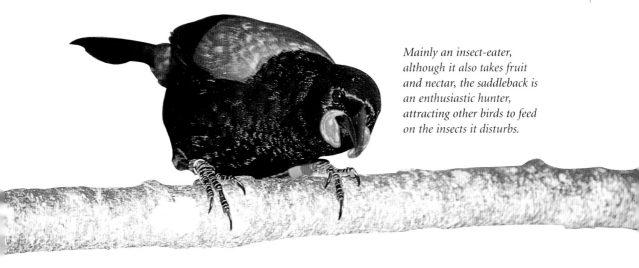

*Mainly an insect-eater, although it also takes fruit and nectar, the saddleback is an enthusiastic hunter, attracting other birds to feed on the insects it disturbs.*

# Saddleback

The saddleback or tieke (*Philesturnus caruncula-tus*) is recognised as being one of the first birds in the world that humans saved from extinction by actively intervening to rescue it. By the early 20th century saddlebacks had disappeared from the mainland, surviving only on Hen Island off Northland and Big South Cape and two islets off Stewart Island. Recognising the perilous state of the species, in 1963 conservation managers decided to relocate some of the 500-strong Hen Island population to Whatupuke Island. Since then the North Island saddleback has been successfully transferred to nine islands, including Little Barrier, Kapiti, Tiritiri Matangi and Mokoia in Lake Rotorua. The population now is a relatively healthy 5000.

Like the kokako and the now-extinct huia, the saddleback is a wattlebird (wattles are the two fleshy lobes under the beak). The saddleback is a New Zealand species that has seen more history than most; its ancestors are thought to have blown across the Tasman Sea more than 50 million years ago. Today it and the kokako are the sole survivors of a unique bird order, the Calla-eidae. There are two subspecies, the North Island and the South Island, set apart by their distinctive plumage. The band of yellow above the chestnut-coloured back of the North Island adult is missing in the South Island subspecies.

Saddlebacks are poor fliers, which led to their downfall when predators arrived in New Zealand. Preferring to bound from branch to branch, or to run across the forest floor, the birds are no match for cats and rats. Furthermore, they are very inquisitive and show no fear of predators.

Proof that Norway rats and saddlebacks cannot coexist was provided on Kapiti Island. There saddlebacks were furnished with special nesting boxes nailed to trees as an incentive for the birds to nest higher off the ground, yet in spite of this saddleback numbers did not show a significant increase until the rats were eradicated from the island in 1996.

Naturally the birds nest in a tree hole or tree fern crown close to the ground, where they lay two eggs between October and January. They

## Did you know?

In Maori legend Maui, having fought with the Sun, asked the saddleback to bring him fresh water, but the bird refused. The angry demigod seized the saddleback with his still-fiery hand and flung it away, leaving scorch marks across its back which became the chestnut 'saddle' that clearly distinguishes the bird, as shown below.

normally have one brood, but in favourable conditions this can be extended to four.

In the south, on Big South Cape Island the saddleback was regarded with affection and reverence by the muttonbirders who arrived every March to harvest the sooty shearwater. So tame was the saddleback that it would enter houses or sleep in clothing left lying around, and it was never harmed by people.

Similarly, the Hen Island saddlebacks must have been left unharmed by Maori who lived there for hundreds of years. The birds also had the advantage of not being bothered by cats or rats.

Early European settlers knew of another bird that looked similar to the South Island saddleback, except it was a uniform coffee-brown colour without the reddish mark across the back. They dubbed it the 'jackbird'; not until many years later was it confirmed that the jackbird was a saddleback in its first-year plumage, before it developed the adult markings and large wattles. North Island juveniles have no such identity crisis, being replicas of their parents soon after they leave the nest at 20 days old.

Ominously, in the early 1960s ship rats accidentally came ashore on Big South Cape; their numbers increased until suddenly in 1964 there was a population explosion, threatening the saddleback and other species. The Wildlife Service was advised and a rescue plan swung into operation, based on the ground-breaking work that had been done on Hen Island.

Again the saddleback proved to be an adaptable species, and today the southern variety is successfully relocated on nine islands off Stewart Island, Breaksea Island in Fiordland and Motuara Island in the Marlborough Sounds. Although its population is less than 1000, the Department of Conservation recovery plan aims to build numbers up to 4000. Unlike some other island sanctuaries, Motuara Island is open to the public, so at least there people can see the unusual bird.

A vigorous feeder, the saddleback is adept at prising insects such as weta out of tree holes with its strong beak. Its energetic efforts are to the benefit of fantails and whiteheads which waste no time in snapping up the insects disturbed in the saddleback's wake. Ironically, in safeguarding saddlebacks by transferring them to islands, other species have been put at risk—tree and giant weta populations on Mercury and Little Barrier islands are examples.

# Salmon

Salmon were first introduced in New Zealand in 1868, but it took until 1921 to properly establish a population, the first in the southern hemisphere. Native to cool waters of the northern hemisphere, salmon adults migrate up the rivers where they were born, in order to spawn and die. Juveniles float out to sea where they remain for 2–5 years before returning to their 'home' river.

Three species have become established: the chinook or quinnat (*Oncorhynchus tshawytscha*), the Atlantic (*Salmo salar*) and the sockeye (*Oncorhynchus nerka*). Of the three, the chinook is the most common, established in four major producing South Island rivers: the Waimakariri, Rakaia, Rangitata and Waitaki. Salmon from these rivers have shown a number of differences, such as age at maturity, date of spawning and weight. Scientists from the National Institute of Water and Atmospheric Research are studying

*After 90 years of establishment in New Zealand, it is possible that genetically distinct salmon populations have evolved in major salmon rivers.*

the salmon to find out to what extent their differences are due to genetic rather than environmental factors.

If it becomes evident that particular rivers are favoured by particular salmon, in the future fisheries managers may release juveniles only into those rivers where their parents lived.

In the past it was believed that big floods were detrimental to the millions of salmon fry which make their way down-river in spring. Young salmon need to be about 3 months old before they can cope with the abrupt transition from fresh to salt water. In their native North America, this has not been a problem. New Zealand chinook salmon are derived from stock from the Sacramento River which spills out into San Francisco Bay. There the fry have days, if not weeks, to adjust to increasing salinity. However, a study of chinook salmon on the Rakaia River has shown that big floods can be good news for the fish, because for some time after a flood, fresh water extends for many kilometres along the coast—in effect mimicking the salmon's native environment by allowing a temporary estuary to form offshore.

Unusually for salmon, the Atlantic species is confined to Lakes Te Anau and Manapouri, and, unlike Pacific salmon, not all the adults die after spawning. Just why it failed to develop as a sea-run population is a mystery. Sockeye salmon are limited to the upper Waitaki River system and Lakes Ohau, Benmore and Waitaki. In the case of both species, dams have now made them truly land-locked.

# Sandfly

'A sort of little craneflies . . . became remarkably troublesome during the bad weather. They were numerous in the skirts of the woods, not half so large as gnats or musketoes, and our sailors called them sandflies,' observed scientist George Forster following the visit of the *Resolution* to Dusky Sound, Fiordland, in 1773.

Maori already knew the pesky biting insect as namu, believing that the goddess of Death liberated the sandfly, flea and mosquito in Fiordland because she feared humans would want to live in the beautiful area forever. She reasoned that the biting insects would remind people of their frailty and mortality. In describing these insects as

*Without a fresh supply of blood to feed off, a female sandfly will not lay her eggs.*

sandflies, Cook's men committed a scientific error: they do not belong to the same family as sandflies elsewhere in the world, but instead to the Simuliidae family which are referred to as blackflies. Nevertheless, the name 'sandfly' is now commonly given to these insects.

In New Zealand there are 17 species of Simuliidae. Two species—one in the North Island, the other in the South Island (mostly on the West Coast and in the Marlborough Sounds)—irritate humans the most. Sandflies enjoy living where there is plenty of running water and high humidity; the West Coast in particular has both and therefore suffers huge numbers of the insect pest.

Only the female sandfly bites, needing a meal of blood to produce her clutch of eggs which she lays on a rock at or just below the water surface. Males are a mystery as very few adults have ever been caught—all the sandflies that people see are females. Over a 6- to 7-week cycle, the eggs hatch to become larvae, which then pupate. After 12 days as a pupa the adult fly emerges.

Sandflies do not bite humans only. Seals, bats and birds, especially the Fiordland crested penguin, are a favoured source of blood. Horses, cattle, sheep, goats and dogs are also common targets. When a sandfly bites it does not take blood directly from blood vessels but creates a small pool of blood from which it feeds. The itchiness caused is created by the anticoagulants it injects into the wound to keep the blood flowing.

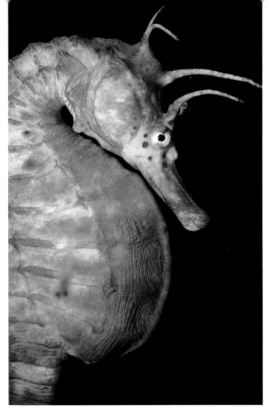

*The distended belly of of a 'pregnant' male seahorse. Growing young seahorses feed off a nourishing fluid which is contained in the lining of the brood pouch.*

# Seahorse

Curling its tail around a seaweed, the oddly shaped seahorse (*Hippocampus abdominalis*) remains upright most of the time, except when it wants to move any distance. Then it tilts forward, straightens its tail and propels itself by undulating its dorsal fins and oscillating its pectoral fins. Seahorses eat minute crustaceans which they suck up through their pipette-like snouts.

The seahorse is the best-known example of 'male pregnancy' among animals. Following a brief period of courtship, during which the male tail-wrestles rival males and dances with his mate, the female deposits her eggs into the male's brood pouch, where he fertilises them and where they hatch. About 30 days after fertilisation he flexes his body, expelling the young into the sea. Every few weeks between October and April his brood pouch receives eggs from his mate.

Related to the seahorse are the short-snouted pipefish (*Syngnathus norae*), the long-snouted pipefish (*Stimatophora longirostris*) and the spiny sea dragon (*Solegnathus spinosissimus*). Unlike the seahorse these fish swim horizontally, but in other respects—including the role of the male in brooding the young—they are similar.

# Sea lion

The New Zealand sea lion (*Phocarcarctos hookeri*), known also as Hooker's sea lion, is the world's rarest species of sea lion, listed by the World Conservation Union as 'vulnerable threatened'. Estimates of their population have varied from 8500 to as many as 15 400. There is no time when the entire population can be counted; the most reliable method is to count pups and then estimate total numbers.

During the 1990s the question of sea lion population size has been a controversial one because of the fact that squid trawlers have caught and drowned significant numbers of sea lions in their nets. On the one hand the fishing industry has argued that the population is greater than estimated, and that the deaths have not had a great impact; on the other, conservation groups maintain that even a small number of kills threatens the future survival of the sea lions.

New Zealand's only endemic pinniped (wing-footed marine mammal), the sea lion is one of three southern-hemisphere and two northern-hemisphere sea lions. It belongs to a group called the otariids, or eared seals. Males are larger and darker coloured than females, which have distinctive creamy-coloured coats.

Before humans settled in New Zealand, sea lions occurred all around the coast, and evidence indicates that Maori ate them. Archaeologists have uncovered sea lion bones dating as far back as the 14th century in 47 middens, from Houhora in the far north to Taranaki, Cape Palliser and the Chatham Islands.

Today, however, sea lions are largely confined to the Auckland Islands, Campbell Island and the Snares in the cool subantarctic. Here they breed on sandy coasts or move up to 1 km inland to forested areas.

## Sea lion society

During winter, males haul out around the South Island coastline, up to Oamaru in the east and the top of Fiordland in the west. Around October or November each year adult males head for the sandy beaches of the small islands close to Auckland Island—Enderby, Dundas and the Figure of Eight islands. Here, in occasional fierce fights with other males, they carve out and defend territories.

Congregating in December on the sand, females give birth to the pups they conceived the year before. About a week afterwards they mate again. One male may service up to 25 females which gather in loose 'harems'. Unlike other marine mammals such as elephant seals, male sea lions do not 'block' a female if it attempts to move away to mate with another male. In order to ensure that the pups are born at the warmest time the following year, the fertilised ovum undergoes delayed implantation.

## A population in peril

The life of a pup is a hazardous one: within a year at least 35 percent of the juveniles are dead from drowning, starvation or disease, or eaten by sharks, killer whales or leopard seals. On Enderby Island, rabbit burrows were an additional hazard to pups which became trapped in them and died. By the mid-1990s the rabbits, and with them the threat to the sea lions, had been removed.

In the early 19th century sealers hunted sea lions to near extinction, even though, in comparison with elephant seals or fur seals, sea lions were not highly valued for their oil or skins. For nearly a century whalers, Maori and the occasional sealing gang killed sea lions, and they were used as a source of food by castaways from numerous shipwrecks at the Auckland Islands. When the schooner *Grafton* was wrecked on the Auckland Islands in 1864, its crew ate sea lions throughout the 20 months they were marooned. The captain, Thomas Musgrave, wrote most of his journals using the blood of the sea lions for ink.

Today the greatest threat to the sea lion is death in squid-trawling nets. In a classic environment–economics clash, trawlers ranging the ocean around the Auckland Islands for squid in an industry worth $160 million a year have killed at least 600 sea lions between 1988 and 1996— despite the fact that sea lions are a fully protected species. The boats trawl for the squid between

*A nursery of sea lions settle down for an afternoon nap on Enderby Island, one of the Auckland Islands. The pups' chestnut-brown colouring contrasts with the creamy tints of the mothers.*

# Seals

*Underwater, sea lions are rated as even more playful than dolphins. In their natural element they delight in performing acrobatics for the camera.*

January and April, the very months when females swim up to 60 km to look for food for their pups.

In 1994 the New Zealand Government introduced a 'kill quota'. This meant that the fishery would be closed as soon as 63 sea lions, or 32 females, were killed—whichever happened first. In both 1996 and 1997 the squid boats had killed more than the quota well before the end of the fishing season.

The loss of mature females is more critical than that of males; most of the sea lions killed are pregnant females which are feeding at sea before returning to their suckling pups on land. This means that up to three animals are lost when a female is caught. Although trawlers are banned from fishing within 12 nautical miles of the Auckland Islands, conservation groups are demanding the establishment of a marine mammal sanctuary extending 100 km beyond the islands.

---

### Did you know?

New Zealand sea lions are remarkable divers, descending deeper than 400 metres into the sea in search of squid, especially during the vital pup-feeding months from January to April. They also eat fish, octopus, krill and crabs. Some have a taste for more substantial prey, eating penguins, seabirds and the pups of fur seals and elephant seals.

---

New Zealand may lack large native land mammals, but the coastline and surrounding waters abound with marine mammals. Besides whales and dolphins, there are nine native species of seals in the New Zealand region: the New Zealand fur seal, subantarctic fur seal, Antarctic fur seal, New Zealand sea lion (see page 298), the southern elephant seal, leopard seal, Weddell seal, crabeater seal and Ross seal.

Most of these live on subantarctic islands or in the Antarctic; the New Zealand fur seal is the only seal in good numbers around the mainland (mainly South Island), although sea lions occasionally breed in southern parts.

Collectively these seals are known as the pinnipeds (wing-footed) because they have webbed flippers instead of paws or feet. Their bodies are streamlined and covered with short, dense hair; valves keep water out of their ears and nostrils when they dive. Superbly adapted for life in freezing temperatures, pinnipeds are protected from the cold by blubber, although fur seals are insulated mostly by dense underfur. It was this luxuriant fur, so valuable to sealers, that almost led to the fur seal's extinction.

The New Zealand seals are divided into two families. The first consists of fur seals and sea lions known as 'eared' seals. They have hind flippers which they can use as legs to move on land, and small ear flaps. The remaining five seals are described as 'true' seals and are the most aquatic. On land their hind flippers are useless, so the animals wriggle or clumsily hump along. They have no ear flaps.

## New Zealand fur seal

Lolling on the rocks, fur seals (*Arctocephalus forsteri*) are a relatively common sight around South Island coasts and some southern areas of the North Island. Driven to the brink of extinction during the 19th century, they are gradually making a comeback.

In the mid-1970s breeding colonies existed only in the deep south or on the West Coast. By 1985 pups were being raised at Kaikoura, on Banks Peninsula and in the Nelson area. In the early 1990s, for the first time in a century, seals started to breed in the North Island—at the southern extremity of Cape Palliser and the

*Fur seal pups are born in early December. Adult males leave the breeding grounds soon after, but the females suckle their pups for about 9 months.*

Sugarloaf Islands near New Plymouth. They also occur on the south coast of Australia and at the Chathams, and the subantarctic islands of Macquarie, Campbell, Auckland, Bounty, Snares and Antipodes.

The best current estimate puts the New Zealand population at about 100 000. This is based on a census carried out in the 1970s (counting 50 000) and known increases at some breeding colonies since then. For instance, numbers at the Bounty Islands have jumped from about 10 000 to 21 000 since 1968, and in the Nelson–Marlborough region the number of pups produced has increased at a mean annual rate of 23 percent since 1970.

By the time fur seal cows arrive at their breeding grounds in late spring, the bull seals are already there and have staked out their territories. Gaining and holding a territory can be a bloody affair, and losers sometimes have to run a gauntlet of other bulls when they transgress their patch

> ## Did you know?
>
> Seals are expert swimmers, combining strength and speed. Californian sea lions have been clocked at 40 km/h in a short spurt, and leopard seals can leap onto an ice floe 2 metres above the water—which means they require an exit speed of 22 km/h.

of rocky real estate. During the 6–10 weeks that the bulls defend a territory they do not eat or drink, so the exercise becomes a test of stamina and temperament.

The resurgence in fur seal numbers has not been welcomed by everybody. Off the West Coast the seals are attracted by the rich pickings of hoki which are hauled up by huge trawlers. Diving into the nets after the hoki, at least 500 seals are drowned each year. The fishing industry opposes a closure of the fishery if seal deaths rise to an unacceptable level (such as occurs with the more vulnerable sea lions).

Sir Tipene O'Regan, spokesperson for the Ngai Tahu, has also raised the possibility of renewing the traditional seal harvest. In pre-European New Zealand, seals were a major food source. The evidence is, however, that once Maori arrived, seals retreated from the North Island and accessible South Island areas.

## Subantarctic fur seal

Although the subantarctic fur seal (*Arctocephalus tropicalis*) does not breed in the New Zealand region, it comes ashore on subantarctic islands. To reach these islands, it is possible it swims from Amsterdam and St Paul islands in the Indian Ocean, a distance of 9000 km. It is distinguished from the New Zealand fur seal by a facial mask and luxuriant white whiskers.

## Antarctic fur seal

Antarctic fur seals (*Arctocephalus gazella*) have recently started breeding on Macquarie Island. From 1810 to about 1820, as many as 193 000 fur seals (of all three species) were harvested on the island, resulting in their complete extermination there, and only recently have numbers gradually started building up as seals return from other areas. Antarctic fur seals also breed at South Georgia, Heard and Kerguelen islands in the South Atlantic Ocean.

*Humphrey, an elderly male elephant seal, was a popular visitor to the Coromandel and Bay of Plenty for 5 years. On one coastal farm he attempted to convert a herd of dairy cows into a harem.*

## Southern elephant seal

The largest of the seals, elephant seals (*Mirounga leonina*) are distributed around the Southern Ocean, although the South Pacific Ocean stocks centred on Macquarie Island, Campbell Island and Antipodes Island do not mix with those in the South Atlantic or South Indian Oceans.

Earning their name from the trunk-like proboscis growing from the nose of mature males, elephant seals are cumbersome on land and not especially agile in the water. Male and female pups are the same size at birth, but males grow much larger than females—up to 4 tonnes compared with only 500–800 kg, making them the seals with the greatest size difference between the sexes. Elephant seal flippers are useless to propel them on land; instead the great beasts contract their bodies like caterpillars to move around.

Battles between bulls for females are intense; bulls are either beachmasters, challengers or assistant beachmasters. By the end of the breeding season a beachmaster may have inseminated 100 females, but he pays a high price for his achievements. A male takes up to 14 years to reach full sexual maturity, then may dominate for three or four seasons, but the constant fighting takes its toll and life expectancy is about 18 years.

Elephant seals can dive to 1500 metres, holding their breath for 2 hours. Each year they travel 2000 km from their breeding island in twice-yearly migratory journeys chasing schools of squid and fish, often feeding at the edge of the Antarctic continental shelf.

Worryingly, numbers of elephant seals are showing a marked decrease. On Macquarie Island they have fallen 50 percent to 100 000 since the 1950s, and on Campbell Island the drop was 97 percent between 1947 and 1986. It appears Antipodes Island may have overtaken Campbell as the main New Zealand breeding area. The reasons for the decrease are most likely to be a combination of ecological factors: a rise in ocean surface temperature which has forced their main food to migrate further south, and an upsurge in predation by orcas on the seals are both frontrunners as causes.

## Leopard seal

Solitary animals, leopard seals (*Hydrurga leptonyx*) are scattered across the Antarctic region, occasionally coming ashore on New Zealand's subantarctic islands and even on the mainland.

*Leopard seals have razor-sharp teeth, designed to sieve krill, and powerful jaws with which to seize larger prey including penguins and other seals. Fast movers, they are adept at capturing their victims in underwater chases.*

*A large, curious Weddell seal gazes benignly at the photographer. These seals can stay submerged for up to 73 minutes.*

*Crabeater seals mount ice floes only to give birth and have a rest; the remainder of the time they spend in the water, even in winter.*

Leopard seal numbers worldwide are estimated at about 260 000. Elongated and sleek, these seals grow up to 4 metres in length and 450 kg in weight. Females are on average 10 percent larger than males.

Like the fur seals, they take warm-blooded prey; penguins and other seals are components of their diet, although krill and fish are staples. The stomach of one leopard seal that was examined contained an adult duck-billed platypus; another seal was observed to catch and eat six penguins in little over an hour.

The reputation these seals have for unprovoked attacks on people is possibly undeserved. There are a number of cases of them suddenly lunging through the ice to snap at people's feet, and in one instance a person was chased 100 metres. However, from under the ice the seal probably mistook the people for penguins.

## Weddell seal

Most southerly living of the seals is the Weddell (*Leptonychotes weddelli*) which occurs along the ice close to the Antarctic continent and is estimated to number around 1 million. Less streamlined than leopard seals, they measure almost 3 metres and weigh 450 kg. Weddell seals sometimes wander north to subantarctic islands, and rarely, New Zealand. Their pups, insulated with a thick coat of blubber, are born on the ice.

Until 1986 New Zealanders killed about 40 Weddell seals a year at Scott Base to feed to their huskies, but the practice was stopped after public outcry and scientific opposition.

## Crabeater seal

This Antarctic pack-ice seal (*Lobodon carcinophagus*) has the most specialised diet of the seals, feeding almost exclusively on krill. Early Antarctic explorers and sealers used the term crab for krill—hence the term crabeater for the seal. The most abundant seal in the world, its population is increasing, with recent estimates ranging from 30 to 40 million. Crabeaters are seen only occasionally in New Zealand waters.

Like all seals, crabeaters are skilful underwater hunters. Scientists believe they owe their agility in the dark waters under the ice to their whiskers, which have about 1200 nerve endings attached to each. It is theorised that sound vibrations travel down the whiskers, enabling the seals to 'see' in the dark.

## Ross seal

Little is known about the Ross seal (*Ommatophoca rossi*) because it lives on inaccessible pack-ice well away from shore. Few sightings have been made of the smallest of the southern seals (maximum weight 186 kg), although it has been estimated that the population numbers around 200 000.

A graceful animal, the Ross seal is silvery-grey on the back and silvery-white underneath. Although the species was initially regarded as solitary, later research has indicated that one lone seal on a float may signal the presence of several under water. One observer has described the sounds they make as reminiscent of bagpipes. Their chief food is squid and krill.

# Seaweeds

From the subtropical Kermadecs to the subantarctic islands, a rich array of seaweeds grows around New Zealand coasts—more than 1000 species. The scientific name for these 'forests of the sea' is algae. The large algae seen around the coastline are the most conspicuous sea plants; floating around in the open oceans there are also microscopic algae which are the vital first step in the marine food chain. These phytoplankton are fed upon by plankton, followed by fish, and so on up to marine mammals.

The large seaweeds have been divided into three broad groupings: green, brown or red seaweeds, which differ not only in their colouring but also in the way they reproduce. These categories can be misleading, however, as red seaweeds often look green, and sometimes the colour changes with age and the season. Red seaweeds are the most numerous and in New Zealand are the ones that are commercially harvested, for example karengo (*Porphyra columbina*), agar weed (*Pterocladia lucida*) and *Gracilaria*.

Karengo, a traditional Maori food, is gathered around Kaikoura for sale to Maori on the North Island east coast especially. Agar is used in food and industry.

Seaweeds come in all shapes and sizes. Some, like the large kelps (see page 179), have long leathery thongs; subtropical seaweeds are small and gossamer thin; others are fleshy, 'crustose' plants which keep close to a rock's surface.

About 10 percent of seaweeds are eaten directly by fish and shellfish. The remainder are decomposed by bacteria and fungi and eventually are consumed by filter-feeders such as oysters and mussels.

To grow, seaweeds need light. In Kermadec waters sunlight reaches down 70 metres below the ocean surface, but in the temperate waters of mainland New Zealand, seaweeds do not grow much below 25 metres. This is because temperate waters have more plankton and dissolved oxygen than waters nearer the equator and this reduces visibility. Seaweeds differ in size according to water temperature. At the Kermadecs they are small but in southern New Zealand the kelps grow to a massive size.

*Leafy carrageen (*Gigartina circumcincta*) is a delicate red seaweed growing at the extreme low water zone. Members of this genus are widely harvested overseas for carrageen or Irish moss.*

Seaweeds multiply in four ways. Most produce spores which grow into new plants, or reproduce sexually by fusing male and female germ cells. Rarely, they can simply divide to form new individuals, or they fragment, and if conditions are favourable continue to grow on their own.

One of the most common brown seaweeds is Neptune's necklace (*Hormosira banksii*), so named for its resemblance to a string of beads. Each of these beads is a bladder filled with water, which guards against the plant drying out when the tide drops. Depending on the habitat, the beads vary considerably in size. In sheltered mangrove swamps and inlets they can be 20 mm in diameter, but elsewhere grow to only half that size.

An obvious green seaweed is the edible sea lettuce (*Ulva lactuca*), which thrives on mudflats close to sewage outfalls.

Hitching a ride aboard the hulls of ships, some seaweeds travel the world and set up home in New Zealand. The most recent arrival is *Undaria pinnatifida*, known as wakame in Japan where it is a popular edible seaweed. Since it was first noticed in Wellington harbour in the late 1980s, *Undaria* has spread rapidly and is now in all shipping harbours from Wellington to Dunedin. Scientists are closely monitoring the plant to see whether it is competing with native species.

*Closely related to Japanese nori, karengo (Porphyra species) is a traditional Maori vegetable. During World War II large quantities were dried and sent to the Maori Battalion for use as a chewing-gum.*

> ### Did you know?
>
> Shags are instantly recognisable because of their habit of hanging their wings out to dry. Unlike those of ducks, their wings are permeable, since waterlogged feathers help them to dive deeper for their food. But once shags regain the surface, they find it difficult to take off and have to perch with their wings outstretched until they are dry. Having easily waterlogged feathers also means they cool down quickly; in cold water the shags can swim no longer than about 30 minutes before hypothermia sets in.

# Shags

Of the world's 33 species of shags, 12 breed in the New Zealand region and eight are endemic. In New Zealand the term shag (from the tuft-like crests on their heads) is used for all species of the long-necked, long-billed diving birds. In other countries the name cormorant (from the French *cor marin*, meaning sea crow) is used for the black, pied, little black and little shag, all members of the *Phalacrocorax* genus.

New Zealand shags are of three types, each with different-coloured feet and each occupying distinct ecosystems. The black-footed shags of the *Phalacrocorax* genus are freshwater and coastal birds with their largest populations in the North Island; pink-footed shags of the *Leucocarbo* genus are marine species which live on rocky coasts or southern islands; and the yellow-footed members of the *Stictocarbo* genus are also marine birds.

The black shag (*Phalacrocorax carbo*), pied shag (*P. varius*), little black shag (*P. sulcirostris*) and little shag (*P. melanoleucos*) all breed in the Australia–South Pacific region as well as in New Zealand. A common northern-hemisphere bird, the black shag's fishing skills have been exploited for centuries by the Japanese and Chinese. The shags are tied to boats by one leg and have a string or soft leather collar around the neck, tight enough to prevent them swallowing any of the fish they catch. In modern Japan shag fishing is a

*This little shag is drying its wings after a fishing expedition. In inland waters little shags eat smelt, bullies and goldfish; around the coast their diet includes flounder and sole.*

tourist attraction, but Chinese fishermen from the Li River of Guangxi province still gather fish for a living in such a way.

For years the four species of the *Phalacrocorax* genus were shot by New Zealand fishermen because it was believed they ate commercial fish and trout, but studies have shown they are no threat to fish stocks, and in fact eat many young eels which prey on trout. Sometimes the tables are turned on the shags; naturalist Robert Wilson reports an incident in the Horowhenua during the 1940s when he saw a juvenile shag fall from a nest into a lake where eels were cruising around. 'It struggled to climb up again but was seized by the leg and dragged under. There was a great commotion where the eels were milling round, and in about a couple of minutes the shag was torn to pieces and eaten.'

The six species of *Leucocarbo* shags are all relatively rare. Least common is the king shag (*L. carunculatus*), which numbers around 500 and breeds on the small islands of the outer Marlborough Sounds. Other species are the Stewart Island shag (*L. chalconotus*), Chatham Island shag (*L. onslowi*), Bounty Island shag (*L. ranfurlyi*), Auckland Island shag (*L. colensoi*) and Campbell Island shag (*L. campbelli*).

The two species of *Stictocarbo* shags differ from other shags in their brilliant prenuptial plumage, which is worn and faded by the time they lay their eggs. The spotted shag (*S. punctatus*) breeds in the North Island and the South Island down to the Catlins. A subspecies, called the blue shag, occurs in Westland and Stewart Island. The Pitt Island shag (*S. featherstoni*), numbering about 500 pairs, lives on Chatham and Pitt islands in small and widely scattered colonies.

Shag parents continue to feed their young, on a mainly fish diet, for more than 20 weeks after hatching, by which time the demanding juveniles are almost fully grown.

*A close relative of the modern white pointer, an extinct 9-metre shark from 25 million years ago attacks a whale in this reconstruction. (Lower) The shark's tooth, found in North Otago, is depicted actual size.*

# Sharks

Fearsome predators, sharks are the largest fish in the sea, but differ from other fish in that they have skeletons of cartilage rather than bone. Evolving along a separate evolutionary line from other fish, they trace their beginnings to a shark-like ancestor which lived 380 million years ago. Starting from 345 million years ago they dominated the oceans and have maintained their diversity ever since.

Around the world there are about 400 species of sharks; 39 of these swim in New Zealand waters but only 15 are coastal species, the remainder cruising the deep ocean. Some such as white pointers and makos are warm-blooded, others like the blue are cold-blooded. As top predators in the marine food chain, sharks play a valuable role in taking weaker and diseased prey, therefore ensuring that fish populations keep healthy and genetically fit.

Aiding the shark in its hunt for food are extremely sensitive senses of hearing and smell. From a distance of 1.6 km a shark can hear low-frequency sounds, such as those of a struggling fish, through a line of detectors running along each side of the body, called the 'lateral line' system. Then at a distance of 400 metres it is able to smell weak concentrations of blood in the water. The shark's sense of smell is so well developed that it can detect one part blood in 50 million parts of water—akin to humans being able to detect a spoonful of sugar in a swimming pool.

Sharks had long been thought to have poor eyesight, but the opposite is true. They can see well in very dim light, and when heading rapidly towards the surface are able to adapt swiftly to the brighter environment. When closing in for an attack, some sharks, such as the blue, swim blind, a protective membrane closing over the eye. A sense that detects electrical activity, such as the contracting muscles of a beating heart, takes over as the shark homes in for the kill. This may explain why sharks sometimes attack boats; they are attracted by the weak electrical currents produced by metal fittings.

Male sharks make sure of paternity by using a dual-purpose sexual organ. One tube squirts a powerful jet of sea water into the female to flush out sperm from previous matings, while a second tube introduces its own sperm. Sharks are also programmed to be competitive from an early age, with the live-born young frequently eating each other while still inside the mother.

Of all the sharks, the white pointer (white shark or great white *Carcharodon carcharias*) has the deadliest reputation and is believed to have been responsible for most of the attacks on humans around New Zealand. Otago is the centre of most attacks; scientists believe the white pointers follow a warm ocean current from the south Tasman Sea, around Stewart Island and up the Otago coast, where it cools when it meets the boundary of the subtropical convergence around Canterbury. Growing as long as 8 metres, but averaging 2–4 metres, white pointers have large

## Did you know?

Maori have traditionally regarded sharks as a favourite food. Dried sharks' ova were a particular delicacy. Early European sailors about to arrive in New Zealand caught sharks and dried them, in order to offer morsels to Maori women as presents. A number of coastal tribes carried out large-scale shark-fishing expeditions. In the 1850s on Rangaunu Harbour, 7000 schooling sharks were taken during two annual hunts by the Te Rarawa tribe.

## The terrors of the deep?

Much has been made of the threat that sharks pose to people. Since records started in 1837, 13 people have been killed in New Zealand waters, including a spate of attacks off Otago beaches in the 1960s.

Most scientists who study sharks believe they do not deliberately attack humans but probably mistake them for seals or other prey. Frequently when sharks attack people they take an initial bite and lose interest.

The truth is that sharks probably face far more danger than they pose in their contact with humans. Taken for sport, accidentally caught in set nets, captured as a by-catch in fisheries and deliberately snared for the shark-fin soup trade, many sharks are being killed at a faster rate than they can reproduce themselves. Compared with other fish, sharks mature late (spiny dogfish females at about 10 years) and produce few eggs or live young.

In the USA and South Africa, white pointers are protected, while off the New South Wales and Queensland coasts the grey nurse and small-tooth sand tiger sharks cannot legally be hunted.

triangular teeth and will eat seals, penguins, turtles and even other sharks.

Tiger sharks (*Galeocerdo cuvieri*), found in northern New Zealand waters, are also feared predators and not fussy about what they eat. Over the years a number of disparate objects have been discovered in tiger shark stomachs: tin cans, a cow's head, a dog, beer bottles, a bag of potatoes and a watch. This shark will attack humans without provocation.

New Zealand's largest fish is the basking shark (*Cetorhinus maximus*), a 12-metre, 8-tonne gentle giant with an enormous mouth which enables it to filter 2000 tonnes of water an hour. Most commonly seen around Cook Strait and the waters off the east coast of the South Island down to Timaru, the basking shark has tiny teeth and eats plankton. Harmless to humans, it is the second largest shark after the tropical-dwelling whale shark. Impressive numbers of basking sharks are still reported off New Zealand coasts. In 1992 the crew of a boat south of Banks Peninsula saw a large school which took an hour to steam past at a speed of 11 knots.

Also harmless to humans is the common school shark (*Galeorhinus australis*) averaging 1–1.5 metres. Highly mobile, one tagged shark swam from the Snares Islands to Taranaki, a distance of 700 nautical miles.

The Maori name for the mako shark (*Isurus oxyrinchus*) is used around the world. Prized as a game fish, it comes down from the tropics to northern New Zealand waters during summer.

Divers who have experimented feeding sharks report that the mako—which normally closes its eyes for protection while attacking prey—keeps its eyes open when hand-fed. This suggests it believes it is not in danger as it takes the bait.

Deep-sea shark livers are highly valued by Asians, who refine them to extract a product called squalene, rich in vitamins. A Kaikoura enterprise sends drums of liver oil to Japan, where it is further processed. These days, however, the oil is not so valuable because substitutes can be produced synthetically.

*The warmth-loving mako shark occurs worldwide but is at its most common in New Zealand waters where its fighting temperament makes it a prized gamefish. Mako on lines have been known to attack boats and even leap aboard. (Inset) Blue sharks are long-distance swimmers; one was recorded travelling 4000 km.*

*A flesh-footed shearwater prepares to dive in search of food. A number of shearwaters catch fish either on the surface of the water or several metres down. Squid and crustaceans are usually caught at night.*

# Shearwaters

Shearwaters take their name from their ability to skim across the surface of the water, sometimes even touching it. Belonging to the same family as petrels (see page 259), shearwaters are among the most common of seabirds, nesting from the sub-antarctic through the subtropics to the tropics themselves. The best-known New Zealand shearwater is the sooty or muttonbird (see page 228).

Few people are privileged to witness the life of shearwaters, which for the most part live on islands or congregate in vast colonies at sea. Their nocturnal habits, strange cries and sometimes bizarre nesting locations (high up in mountains or occasionally in trees) make shearwaters among the most mysterious birds. In spring when they arrive in New Zealand to breed they 'spring-clean' their burrows to the accompaniment of hoarse moans. Ornithologist Lance Richdale likened their cries to a hundred cats calling simultaneously or the groans of a man in great pain.

Male shearwaters return to the colony at the start of the breeding season to await the females. The arriving females call from the air, often in the dark, and the males answer from deep in their underground burrows. Even though they may not have seen each other since migrating months earlier, the birds recognise each other's calls from the period when they first formed a pair bond.

During the breeding season, male and female take it in turn to go fishing for their growing chick. Returning some days later, in the gathering dusk they plot the position of their burrow from out at sea, fly over the coast then drop like plums through the forest canopy and onto the ground. A few scurrying steps and they are home.

*The flesh-footed shearwater prefers warm waters but occasionally ventures as far south as Foveaux Strait.*

New Zealand's seven breeding shearwater species are found almost exclusively on islands; the notable exception is Hutton's shearwater (*Puffinus huttoni*) which nests high up in the Seaward Kaikoura Mountains and is the only survivor of a number of seabird species that once bred in mountainous areas. Scientists knew of the existence of the species, but it was not until 1965 that they discovered their colony, 1200–1800 metres above sea level. The fact that the birds breed at such a height has probably been their salvation because stoats, their main predators, cannot find enough food during winter to survive so high in large numbers. In winter the shearwaters gather at feeding grounds around the Australian coast. There are estimated to be 160 000 breeding pairs of Hutton's shearwaters.

Flesh-footed shearwaters (*P. carneipes*) breed on islands in northern New Zealand down to Cook Strait. They join muttonbirds in migrating to the Japanese Pacific waters, but a few head towards North America. Numbers of this shearwater are reasonably large, with more than 20 000 at the colony on Coppermine Island (one of the Hen and Chickens group). On some islands they share burrows with tuatara.

Another species with a similar distribution is the fluttering shearwater (*P. gavia*). However, after breeding it stays around New Zealand and the eastern Australian coast.

The Poor Knights Islands are the only breeding location of Buller's shearwater (*P. bulleri*) which number about 2.5 million. On Aorangi Island, the population showed a phenomenal increase after pigs were removed in 1936—from 100 to 200 000 pairs by 1981.

Smallest of the New Zealand shearwaters is the little shearwater (*P. assimilis*) which weighs only 200 grams (the weight of the other species ranges between 300 and 850 grams). There are seven subspecies of little shearwaters, three of which—the Kermadec, North Island and subantarctic little shearwater—breed in the New Zealand region.

Wedge-tailed shearwaters (*P. pacificus*) are unlikely to be seen on the mainland as they breed on the Kermadec Islands and afterwards migrate to the southeastern North Pacific. Besides having to cope with cats and rats on Raoul Island, the birds are sometimes hit by cyclones. Ornithologist Mike Imber describes the cacophony of calls from a wedge-tailed colony as resembling 'the yowls and snarls of an alley of cats'.

## Did you know?

Tiny Snares Island, only 328 ha in area, has more seabirds than are present around the entire coasts of Britain and Ireland. Most of the birds are muttonbirds or sooty shearwaters, although other species of petrels and shearwaters are on the island as well. Not all the birds are there at one time, however. There are estimated to be almost 3 million breeding pairs of sooty shearwaters. Thus, at one time 3 million are on the nest, while their 3 million mates are fishing to feed the chicks. A further 6 million non-breeders go on fishing expeditions and occasionally return to land. Inevitably, some birds become casualties when they get trapped in branches as they land. As a result of these high bird population numbers, the Snares is criss-crossed with burrows and walking by humans across the island is a hazardous undertaking as the ground is always threatening to collapse.

# Shellfish

New Zealand has one of the richest shell faunas in the world, with about 3000 species and sub-species. Many of these are land snails (see page 315), as are a number of the shellfish such as limpet, mussel, oyster, paua and toheroa (see separate entries).

Shellfish are molluscs, divided into five classes: chitons (eight-pieced shells); univalves (one-pieced); tusk shells (a one-piece shell with a tapering tube); bivalves (two-pieced shell such as oysters and mussels); and cephalopods (usually with no shell). Octopuses and squid are examples of cephalopods. Australia and New Zealand have a greater number of chitons than any other part of the world.

Sea shells resemble bone, with both an animal and mineral portion. The animal portion is made up of a network of fibrous material, while the mineral is composed of lime salts, creating a hard and compact shell.

New Zealand is divided into five shellfish zones. The first covers the North Island down to East Cape; the second the southern part of the North Island and the northern part of the South Island; the third Otago, Stewart Island and the Snares; the fourth the Chatham Islands; and the fifth the subantarctic islands. Each zone has its distinct species, although some are common to all zones.

All shellfish, except bivalves, have an elaborate series of teeth called radula. If the mollusc is a carnivore the teeth tend to be few and powerful, while if it is vegetarian, they are many and small. Some have one or two teeth only, but the introduced garden snail has 15 000 and the umbrella shell more than 750 000.

Gari strangeri *is a mauve-coloured bivalve of northern regions.*

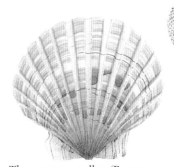

*The common scallop (*Pecten novaezelandiae*) grows larger in southern waters (150 mm) than northern (120 mm). This succulent bivalve mainly inhabits sandy regions.*

*The green chiton (*Chiton glaucus*) hitched a ride on boats from New Zealand to establish in Tasmania.*

*The opal-top shell (*Cantharidus opalus*) is an uncommon univalve of the open coast, which feeds on kelp.*

*In the south the volute shell (*Alcithoe swainsoni*) is often seen on sandy beaches.*

# Silvereye

In New Zealand the silvereye (*Zosterops lateralis*) is also known as the waxeye or white-eye; its Maori name tauhou, meaning stranger, signifies the fact that the silvereye is a recent arrival. Blown over from Australia on a favourable wind, the silvereye was first recorded as breeding at Waikanae, north of Wellington, in 1856, although birds had been seen as far back as 1832. Silvereyes belong to the family of white-eyes, common in Africa, south Asia and the Pacific.

Finding conditions in New Zealand to their liking, in a short space of time silvereyes have become one of the most abundant birds. Their rapid expansion may be attributed to their catholic taste in food, ranging from insects, fruit and nectar, to fat left by people at bird-feeding stations in gardens.

When they first arrived, silvereyes were welcomed because they ate huge quantities of the swarming aphids that infested apple trees, earning the title of 'blight-bird'. Today grape growers are not so enamoured of the small bird, which can cause significant damage to their harvests.

No bird weaves a nest like that of the silvereye. Taking a variety of materials including grass, lichen, moss and sheep's wool, it binds them into a delicate cup which is suspended, hammock-fashion, from twigs and leaves, with spider-web threads acting as guy wires. An average of three eggs is laid in each clutch and pairs lay up to three clutches a season.

*Like all members of the white-eye family, silvereyes characteristically flock together to feed on fruit such as these mahoe berries.*

*On Mangere Island in the Chathams, a brown skua performs a territorial 'heraldic' display, holding its wings upwards to show the white patches underneath.*

# Skuas

Skuas are pirates of the air, stealing food from other birds instead of going to the trouble of catching it themselves. They share this trait, called kleptoparasitism, with a number of birds including gulls and tropical frigatebirds.

Two skua species breed in the New Zealand region: the brown skua (*Catharacta skua*) and the south polar skua (*C. maccormicki*). Both species live about 30 years. The brown skua breeds on the Chatham, Solander, Stewart and surrounding islands, as well as the subantarctic islands. One of the few birds to breed exclusively on the Antarctic continent, around 15 000 south polar skuas are found in the Ross Dependency.

Skuas site their colonies strategically so that they are near other large bird colonies. They harass the other birds to drop their catch, or even force them to regurgitate their last meal, which the skuas then eat. Other birds such as petrels and penguin chicks are an important part of their diet; when skuas are in the neighbourhood, penguin chicks huddle close to their parents because any chick in the open is easy game. Skuas are also very aggressive towards humans, buzzing them and striking at them with their feet.

# Snails

New Zealand is home to a bewildering array of land snails, ranging from hamburger-sized 'giants' to minuscule species that can fit through the eye of a sewing needle. Most of the more than 1000 species are vegetarian, but some of the more spectacular are carnivorous. For a temperate country this large number of species is unusual—the United Kingdom has only 112. A moist but mild climate and a range of habitats from lowland forests to alpine grasslands have given rise to a proliferation of different species.

Pupuharakeke, the flax snail (*Placostylus ambagiosus*), survives in a few remnant populations between Cape Maria van Diemen and Parengarenga Harbour. One of three *Placostylus* snails, pupuharakeke does not eat flax, but leaves of trees such as karaka, kohekohe and rangiora that grow near flax. Pupuharakeke lead a relaxed life—when they are not being eaten by predators—and are estimated to live 10 years or more. They may receive much-needed calcium (to make their shells) by eating the calcium lining from other discarded shells: a researcher who removed old shells from snail habitat was dismayed when he later found that a large proportion of the remaining snails had deformed shells, perhaps as a result of calcium deficiency.

Known to Maori as pupurangi, kauri snails are found on the mainland only north of Auckland, in the area where kauri historically grew. They are also on Great Barrier, Poor Knights and the Hen and Chickens islands. The two species (*Paryphanta busbyi* and *P. b. watti*) are large, carnivorous animals which feed mainly on worms. Their heavy shells, as large as 75 mm across, are firmly attached to their bodies, enabling the snails to climb vertically. They are also quite spry, able to travel several hundred metres across farmland in a night to reach bush.

Ranging from Lake Waikaremoana to Fiordland, but most numerous in the southern North Island and northern South Island, the *Powelliphanta* species are the most spectacular of New Zealand's land snails. Many are highly restricted in their distribution—for example *P. gilliesi brunnea* is now confined to a single coastal forest remnant of less than 1 ha. Originating more than 235 million years ago and surviving in isolation, these ancient snails have evolved into a variety of beautiful forms. Several species are confined to limestone, partly because the calcium they need for their shells and eggs is obtained by eating invertebrates and other snails which themselves are loaded with calcium gained from the limestone environment.

*Powelliphanta* snails dry out easily because, unlike more common snails, they do not have a protective mucous membrane with which to seal themselves. Instead they seek out damp spots under leaf litter, where they eat large native worms. A few, such as *P. traversi traversi* form *koputaroa*, are lowland forest dwellers. In 1986, 10 ha of boggy cow paddock, raupo swamp and kahikatea north of Levin was gazetted as a reserve especially for the rare snail. Other species live in mid-altitude forests, while many occur under tussock above the bushline.

The *Powelliphanta* snails lay 3–10 soya-bean-size eggs each spring, which hatch 6 months later. They take about 5 years to mature and can live up to 20 years.

Medium-sized and drab the *Rhytida* group of snails might be, but they have some of the most bizarre habits of the native snails. *Rhytida* snails eat other snails, biting their heads off before inserting their tails like a corkscrew up into their prey's shells to get at the rest of the meal. The tail secretes digestive fluid which slowly dissolves the prey and is then reabsorbed. Even the calcium from the shell is absorbed, the whole process taking several days.

Another important group of snails is the *Wainuia* group. Some species have been discovered to prey on forest amphipods, similar to sandhoppers found at the beach. Untypically for a snail, they shoot out their extendable mouthparts at speed to grasp their victims with row upon row of sharp, sickle-like teeth. In less than a second they can eat an amphipod whole.

*The exuberantly coloured Oparara land snail* Powelliphanta annectens *is restricted to red beech, rimu, rata and kamahi forest above 150 metres.*

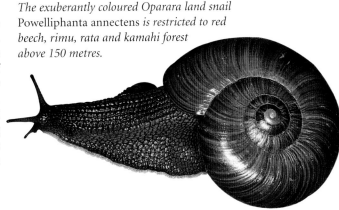

1. *Hochstetter's giant land snail (*Powelliphanta hochstetteri hochstetteri*) from Takaka Hill, one of five subspecies confined to high forested peaks near Nelson and in the Marlborough Sounds.*
2. *The slow-moving flax snail will remain in virtually the same spot for years on end. The scientific name* Placostylus *comes from the resemblance of this snail's spire to a writing stylus.*
3. *Among the largest of the* Powelliphanta *snails is* P. superba superba *from the Heaphy River in Kahurangi National Park. It grows to an impressive 100 mm across.*
4. Thalassohelix ziczag *is a bristly shelled, diminutive (5 mm) species. The outsized, carnivorous snails attract most attention, whereas the lifestyles of the majority of native snails such as this remain as yet largely unknown.*

# Snipes

Related to the migratory godwit and curlew, and the northern-hemisphere woodcock, the snipe was once widespread throughout New Zealand, but the arrival of the Maori dog (kuri) and the rat (kiore) saw it disappear from the mainland before European settlement.

Today two species remain: the New Zealand snipe (*Coenocorypha aucklandica*) and the Chatham Island snipe (*C. pusilla*). Subspecies of the New Zealand snipe live on the Snares, Antipodes, Campbell and Auckland islands.

Many of the world's snipes migrate from the northern to southern hemisphere. However, the two New Zealand species stay bound to the islands where they are born. Fearless and virtually flightless—they will not fly unless forced to—they are especially vulnerable to predators such as rats, cats, dogs and weka.

Considered to be the most primitive of the snipe-like birds, the New Zealand species nevertheless share the manipulative skills of their kind elsewhere. Able to open the tip of its bill while the rest remains closed, the bird can feel for a deeply buried animal, take hold of it and pull it out without having to force the whole bill open against the resistance of the ground.

In the 1920s naturalist H Guthrie-Smith warned of the dangers facing the Stewart Island snipe, which at the time survived on offshore islands: 'Always hangs overhead the sword of Damocles; should rats obtain a footing, farewell to Snipe, Robin, Bush Wren and Saddleback, none of which species are able to adapt themselves to novel conditions.' This gloomy prophecy came true in the early 1960s when rats reached plague proportions on Big South Cape Island, wiping out the snipe in a few years.

The startling night-time call of the snipe gave rise to the Maori legend of the frightening hakawai or hokioi, one of the 11 tapu birds of Rakamaomao (the wind) which dwelt in space and descended to the Earth only at night. Muttonbirders described the bird's call as resembling 'a sound as if a cable chain was lowered into a boat', while others likened it to a jet-stream, or a blind rolling itself up!

*With its long beak the starling-sized snipe probes for worms and insects in open areas.*

# Soils

Just as New Zealand's geology and landscapes are highly complex, so too are its soils. Five main factors are responsible for the wide differences in the almost 100 New Zealand soils: the parent material (the rocks that are the basis of the soil); climate; topography (whether an area is a hill or a plain); biology (the plants and animals which have grown in the soil); and the length of time the soil has been developing.

On all counts New Zealand has tremendous diversity. Rocks range from volcanic, sandstone, limestone, greywacke to schist; the climate is subtropical and moist in the north, dry and summer-hot to the east, cool and wet on the West Coast; 70 percent of the country is hilly; and the forests that once covered 80 percent of the land combined with specialised animals to produce distinctive soils. Soil scientists recognise 12 distinctive soil regions of New Zealand:

- the old, deeply weathered clay-rich soils of Northland, Auckland and the Coromandel
- the deep, friable loamlands of the Waikato and Bay of Plenty
- the volcanic pumicelands of the Central Plateau
- the ringplain surrounding Mount Taranaki and steep, dissected hills of Wanganui
- the marine and alluvial terraces and coastal dunes of the Manawatu
- the dry, eroded hills of the North Island east coast, Hawke's Bay, Wairarapa and central Marlborough
- the rugged hills of Wellington, Nelson and the Marlborough Sounds

- the mountainlands of the South Island
- the highly leached soils of the West Coast
- the dry basins of inland Marlborough, Canterbury and Otago
- the lowlands and rolling downlands of Canterbury and Banks Peninsula
- the fertile Southland plains and the peaty soils of Stewart Island.

With the advent of agriculture and horticulture, particular regions have become noted for their rich soils. These include:

- the Papakauri soils which occur on the slopes of the small basalt scoria cones of the Auckland isthmus, Whangarei, Kaikohe and Kerikeri.
- the Takapau soils found in the Heretaunga, Ruataniwha-Takapua and Wairarapa Plains—these are the soils that provide the majority of New Zealand's apple, grape and stonefruit crops in the Gisborne and Hawke's Bay districts.
- black swelling clays, a small group of fertile soils (less than 10 000 ha in extent) confined largely to Oamaru and Dargaville. They are known as 'tarry soils' and are highly valued for market gardening.

*South of Oamaru lies one of New Zealand's most productive market-garden areas, built upon fertile Waiareka soils.*

## Soil in the making

To see one of the world's finest examples of soil formation and ageing, go no further than the Franz Josef Glacier in Westland. There glacial moraines have been deposited in successive small advances since the last great Ice Age, which gripped the land 20 000 years ago.

On moraines 20 years of age and younger, nitrogen-fixing grasses and shrubs have already taken root; after 150 years rata-kamahi forests are growing in what is now a deep black soil blanketing the moraines. In a further 3000 years tall rimu have colonised the forest, remaining dominant for the next 9000 years.

During this period the soil is at the peak of its fertility, but after 12 000 years the continual leaching of nutrients (because of the high rainfall) has taken its toll. Gradually the soil becomes more acid and the rimu has given way to less nutrient-demanding plants such as silver pine, bog pine and red tussock.

Until the glacier halts its retreat and begins the cycle again, the soils will become progressively less fertile.

*The high terraces of the Cape Foulwind-Charleston area of the West Coast are covered by shallow and stony gley podzols mixed in with alluvium.*

*Electronically charged particles blown on the solar wind are deflected by the Earth's magnetic field, but some enter the upper atmosphere at the poles, causing the phenomenon of the southern lights.*

# Southern lights

Shimmering curtains of light in dark southern skies are the aurora australis, or southern lights, caused when energetic electrically charged particles from the Sun enter the Earth's upper atmosphere and make its rarefied oxygen and nitrogen gases glow—the same gases as in neon lights.

The aurorae are normally seen only from southern New Zealand, southern Australia and Antarctica. In the northern hemisphere they are known as the aurora borealis. During violent auroral displays, people have sometimes reported hearing strange crackling or rustling sounds. One explanation for these is that they are produced at ground level by electrical or magnetic phenomena associated with an aurora.

The highly charged particles are created when solar flares shoot out from the Sun, some as far as 100 000 km into space. The temperature of a solar flare is 10 000°C, much higher than the Sun's usual temperature of 5000°C.

Travelling at 400 km/sec, this solar wind—made up of protons, electrons and alpha-radiation—takes 2–3 days to reach the Earth, 150 million km distant. Sometimes gigantic eruptions occur on the Sun, shooting the particles out at speeds of up to 1000 km/sec.

If it were not for the Earth's magnetic field, which deflects the particles, we would experience intense, harmful radiation. However, some of these particles do get trapped on the night side of the Earth, and can spiral in towards the atmosphere around magnetic fields to both the north and south polar regions. They give up their energy to form aurorae at heights of 100–200 km.

Some years the aurorae are more intense and frequent. This is because the Sun itself becomes more active in cycles of about 11 years. Solar flares are predicted to reach a peak around the year 2000.

*As their name suggests, crab spiders scuttle sideways and flourish their front legs like claws.*

# Spiders

Remarkably sophisticated creatures, spiders are not insects but belong in a group of their own, the arachnids. They differ from insects in having only two body segments, eight legs and either six or eight simple eyes (insects have three body segments, six legs and compound eyes).

One of the distinguishing characteristics of spiders is that they must take their prey live. As a result they have devised elaborate ways of capturing food, most intriguing of which is the web-spinning habit that some have made a specialty; all spiders make silk to enclose and protect a batch of eggs, but only some use it to catch insects and other prey.

Spitting spiders squirt a sticky secretion onto prey before inflicting a lethal bite, while jumping spiders leap impressive distances to make a catch. The hyperactive hunting spider (*Supunna picta*) runs down its prey, often a fly that has alighted for a rest.

When an insect flies into an orbweb the threads vibrate or become taut, telling the spider a victim has been caught. Some spiders wait at the centre of the web while others hide nearby. Orbweb spider-webs contain sticky droplets that trap prey, but cobweb spiders build a tangled web of threads in which prey become entangled. It is the female which builds the webs—the male spends his time looking for a mate.

Naturally aggressive, spiders are attuned to regard anything that moves as prey. They are very sensitive to vibrations; male spiders have to tread warily and put out the correct vibrations when courting larger females which might well eat them. The males have developed various strategies to cope with the danger: hunting spiders leap clear after mating, while others wait until the female moults and her fangs are too soft to be damaging. Some present their mates with a tasty morsel just before mating, as a distraction.

More than 2000 species of spiders live in New Zealand, many of which inhabit forests or other wilderness areas and have not yet been described. Cities and towns are home to many spiders which have arrived here from other countries.

## Spiders great and small

The limestone caves of the Nelson region are home to one of the world's rarest spiders; with a leg spread of 130 mm and a body length of 30 mm, *Spelungula cavernicola* is also the largest native species. Besides being very rare, *Spelungula* intrigues scientists because it is a species that has remained unchanged for hundreds of millions of years and is regarded as a missing link in spider evolution. Most spiders are either primitive, with four lungs, and jaws that move up and down, or 'true', with two lungs, and jaws that operate sideways like pincers. *Spelungula* has characteristics of both species: four lungs, and jaws that move sideways. Its favoured food is the cave weta.

The 200-mm Avondale spider, featured in the 1990 movie *Arachnophobia*, is harmless to humans, although in the film it was portrayed as a killer. In New Zealand the spider is named after the Auckland suburb where it lives and where it arrived in the 1920s from Australia. More accurately the large, crab-like spider is called the huntsman spider (*Delena cancerides*).

An Australian species, the golden orbweb spider (*Nephila edulis*), shares with a number of other spiders an ingenious system of crossing the Tasman. After hatching from the mother's egg sac, spiderlings produce long strands of silk which blow in the wind, making their tiny passengers airborne—a process known as 'ballooning'. Scientists have mounted nets on airplanes and caught the spiders thousands of metres above the ground. They survive the freezing conditions at these lofty altitudes by going into a state of torpor. These spiders have not yet established here.

1. Having stalked its prey like a cat, this jumping spider prepares to settle down to a meal. On vertical walls or ceilings, jumping spiders attach an anchoring string of web before leaping.

2. One of a group called the 'bird dropping' spiders, the two-spined Calaenia spider arrived from Australia in the early 1970s. Here it spins a spindle-shaped egg sac. Infinitely patient, it stays motionless on a leaf or twig until an unwary moth flies into its arms.

3. By dipping its legs into water, the water spider Dolomedes aquaticus can detect the movement of insects, then scuttles across the surface to seize the prey.

### Venomous spiders

Although spiders bite, few of those found in New Zealand are dangerous to humans. After the katipo (see page 174), the most venomous spider is an Australian relative and recent immigrant: the redback (*Latrodectus hasselti*) which has a reputation for hiding under stones or wood—or sometimes under toilet seats. A bite causes immediate pain, swelling and numbness and leads to nausea, diarrhoea and vomiting, but an antivenom has been developed to counteract these effects, which are potentially fatal.

Although not deadly, some other spiders can deliver painful bites which take several weeks to heal. One to avoid is the native tunnelweb (*Porrhothele antipodiana*) which has adjusted well to urbanisation and likes to hide in woodpiles. When its silk tunnel is disturbed, it goes looking for a dark spot to hide—often a trouser leg.

Another Australian, the white-tailed spider (*Lampona cylindrata*), caused alarm in the early 1990s when a Waikanae woman had to be operated on after a bite caused her flesh to rot. While this hunting spider can give a nasty bite, it had most likely infected the woman with a virulent soil bacterium.

*Lampona* has a clever method of capturing cobweb spiders; by using its limbs to mimic the vibrations of struggling prey, it dupes the unsuspecting cobweb spider into coming out of its hiding place, when it is captured and eaten.

---

**Did you know?**

The intertidal marine spider (*Desis marina*) is able to live in kelp holdfasts—the part of the kelp which anchors it to a rock—and has been observed to stay submerged for 19 days. Chitons and limpets hollow out the interior of the holdfasts, creating a maze of tunnels and crevices into which the spider moves and spins a silk nest. The spider must select a cavity which is large enough to hold the necessary amount of air. In addition, this unusual spider has evolved physiologically to exploit its environment. It has a lower respiration rate than other spiders and is very efficient at removing oxygen from the air that is available.

*Using its spatula-like bill, the royal spoonbill sweeps shallow waters to catch small aquatic animals.*

# Spoonbill

Less rare than its Okarito neighbour, the kotuku, is another wader—the royal spoonbill or kotuku ngutupapa (*Platalea regia*). Like the kotuku, the spoonbill is in good numbers in Australia, from where it arrived in the 1860s. However, it did not start breeding at Okarito until 1949.

Since becoming established here it has expanded its breeding sites to include Marlborough, Otago, Southland, Northland and Kapiti Island. During the 1990s the bird's population has increased exponentially, from 242 in 1991 to more than 700 in 1997.

Gregarious birds, they feed and roost in small flocks and can be seen flying in lines or chevrons.

Spoonbills have a delicate sense of touch, gained from special organs on the bill and tongue. These sensitive organs are important when they feed with sideways sweeps of the parted bill through water, snapping it over any small creature they touch. Their ability to find insects, fish or frogs by touch means spoonbills are as likely to feed by night as by day.

The breeding period of September to December at Okarito coincides with the upstream migration of whitebait which forms a significant part of the royal spoonbill's diet. In contrast to the kotuku, which prefers to nest in kowhai or kamahi trees, the spoonbill chooses the stately kahikatea.

# Squid

Related to the humble garden snail, squid are marine molluscs belonging to a group called the cephalopods (octopuses are another member). What sets them apart from other molluscs is the fact that they do not have external shells, although a notable exception is the chambered nautilus. Being small and inactive, most molluscs have inefficient blood systems, but that of the active squid is very efficient, because of the need to supply sufficient oxygen to its muscles and brain.

Superb swimmers, carnivorous squid swim in large schools, feeding on crustaceans and fish caught in the two longest of their 10 sucker-equipped tentacles. They move by drawing water into their mantles and expelling it through a funnel. Usually they travel backwards, but are capable of changing direction by altering the direction of their funnel. Should they be preyed upon, they squirt out a dark, thick cloud of ink which forms a blob the same size and shape as their body. At the same time they turn a pale colour; the attacker aims for the dark blob while the squid swims to safety.

Squid come in different sizes: from the smallest at 12 mm to the giant squid which exist in all oceans. The longest giant squid (*Architeuthis longimanus*) on record was found washed up at Lyall Bay, Wellington, in 1887. It measured 18.9 metres; although its body was a relatively short 2.4 metres in length, its two slender tentacles were each 16.5 metres long. These squid are the stuff of legend and the prey of sperm whales off the Kaikoura coast, where they live at great depths (see Whales, page 361).

New Zealand's squid-fishing industry, returning a minimum of $50 million a year, is based on the two arrow squid species (*Notodarus sloani* and *N. gouldi*). Fishing is centred off the West Coast and in the subantarctics. Since the 1970s squid boats around the Auckland Islands have been implicated in sea lion deaths (see page 299).

*An arrow squid seizes a flying fish. Even in low-light conditions, squid can make out the shape of their quarry clearly because of their ability to use polarised light. Being nocturnal, squid are bioluminescent.*

# Starfish

Nine-tenths water and most of the remainder chalk, starfish do not make an appealing meal. On the other hand, they are one of the chief predators of the inshore region.

In New Zealand there are close to 100 species with variations in colour (ranging from green to brown to orange) and shape (some have long arms, others none at all).

Locating their prey with a keen sense of smell, starfish can make easy work of opening the toughest shell and have an unusual method of feeding. A starfish wraps itself around a mussel or oyster, clinging on with its hundreds of small suckered feet, and prises apart the two halves of the shell. The moment the shell opens, the starfish turns its stomach inside out onto the soft body of the shellfish which it begins to digest.

Not all starfish are predators. The small cushion star (*Patiriella regularis*), which varies in colour from red to brown to grey, grazes upon fine algae and other detritus. It may live 10 years. As a larva, the reef starfish (*Stichaster australis*) depends solely on one seaweed for its food, but once it becomes an adult it switches to barnacles and mussels.

## Did you know?

As well as propagating sexually by producing eggs and sperm, the eleven-armed starfish (*Coscinasterias calamaria*) has a simpler means of reproduction. It divides in two, its new arms taking 6 months to fully grow.

Some starfish have become unwelcome destroyers. In the Kermadec Islands, corals are threatened by the crown of thorns starfish (*Acanthaster planci*), the same starfish that has attacked the corals along Australia's Great Barrier Reef. A recent study showed there were 84 starfish per hectare at the Kermadecs, nearly three times the number considered acceptable.

*Starfish are found from coastal shore to deepwater trench, and thrive even in the icy seas around Antarctica.*

*Male stick insects are smaller than females. This copulating couple may remain in this position for days at a time. (Inset) The black-spined stick insect is found throughout New Zealand. This female has just laid three eggs.*

# Stick insects

Experts at camouflage, stick insects occur most often in tropical and subtropical regions. They have an ancient lineage stretching back more than 200 million years. Of the world's 2500 species, 21 are found in New Zealand, living from the lowland up to 1500 metres high.

The majority of these species are green, the others brown. All are flightless and some grow up to 150 mm long. If disturbed or picked up, stick insects adopt a completely rigid posture and remain motionless up to an hour or longer. Sometimes they 'dance', with the rigid body swaying from side to side and the legs flexing. The significance of this dance is unknown; one guess is that it is an alarm signal.

Some stick insects breed sexually, but in some there are no males known at all, and the insect breeds parthenogenetically (that is, by hatching unfertilised eggs). Entomologist Professor John Salmon bred four subspecies of the *Acanthoxyla* genus and over 6 years discovered no males, but noted that over time the insects appeared to lose vitality, becoming smaller in size and laying fewer eggs. Species which breed either sexually or parthenogenetically hatch males if the eggs are fertilised and females if they are unfertilised.

When mating during autumn, the much smaller male hitches a ride on the female's back, staying there for 2 weeks, even while she lays eggs. Adults generally die once winter arrives. After 2–3 months the eggs hatch and the juveniles undergo at least four moults before maturing.

Voracious feeders, stick insects feed on a variety of plants including manuka, rata, pohutukawa, ramarama, totara, rimu and, in alpine areas, *Dracophyllum* species. When present in abundance they can completely defoliate a plant.

*Trailing a tail longer than its body, the long-tailed stingray cruises the sea floor in a quest for crabs and shellfish.*

# Stingrays

Gliding through the ocean with a rhythmic flapping of their 'wings', rays and skates are among the most graceful looking of marine animals. Stingrays, electric rays, eagle rays, mantas and skates are all related to sharks, with skeletons of cartilage rather than bone. However, they are shaped quite differently to sharks with enlarged pectoral fins which look like part of the body.

Skates are more abundant in cool waters, electric rays in warm temperate regions and stingrays, eagle rays and mantas are more common in the subtropics and tropics. There are 17 species in New Zealand, nine of which are skates.

Skates are edible and often caught by fishers, but are not a popular food in New Zealand. Manta rays are the most innocuous and largest rays, with a wingspan of 3–6 metres.

Lying in the shallows of harbours and estuaries, stingrays are occasionally stood on by unwary swimmers. The outcome can be lethal, as was demonstrated by the death of a swimmer at Thames in 1938 when a disturbed stingray retaliated by stabbing him in the heart. But these incidents are rare, and are accidents; stingrays try to avoid people (although they are sometimes curious), and attack only if threatened.

In New Zealand there are two species of stingray: the short-tailed (*Dasyatis brevicaudatus*) and the long-tailed (*D. thetidis*). Some short-tails have been measured at more than 2 metres in diameter and 230 kg, bearing one or two serrated barbs up to 300 mm long. In summer large numbers gather in shallow waters, possibly to mate or give birth, and are often preyed upon by orcas (see page 240).

The largest electric ray is *Torpedo fairchildi*, widespread in New Zealand coastal waters and averaging 0.5–1 metre long. The two other electric rays are small, blind, deepwater species.

The one eagle ray (*Myliobatis tenuicaudatus*) in New Zealand is common around the North Island and down to Kaikoura. With vice-like teeth, it breaks open shellfish and crabs. A finely barbed spine at the base of the tail is capable of delivering a dangerous sting.

## *Shocking encounters*

**M**ore circular than other rays, and lacking the long tail of the stingrays, the common electric ray should be approached warily. Some large electric rays are capable of delivering a sharp electric jolt of more than 200 volts. Although the most common New Zealand electric ray is not so powerful, it can deliver a shock through the hull of a boat, especially if there is any water lying in it. The gelatinous electric organs of the ray, confined to both sides of the head, are modified muscle tissue which amplify the weak electrical currents set up by normal muscle activity.

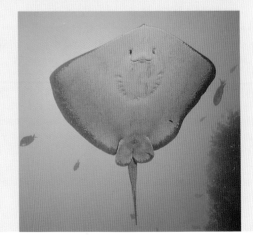

# Stitchbird

Stitchbirds are not renowned for their sewing abilities, unlike the tailorbirds of southern Asia which 'rivet' fresh leaves together for their nests. Rather than signalling any such talent, the name of the stitchbird derives from the explosive note it sounds, often when it is worried.

The rarest of New Zealand's three species of honeyeaters (the others are the bellbird and the tui) the stitchbird or hihi (*Notiomystis cincta*) paralleled the bellbird in that it became extinct in the North Island above Hamilton during the 1860s and 70s, while remaining reasonably common in the lower North Island. However, within a decade it had virtually disappeared, victim of a combination of disease, habitat destruction and predation by ship rats.

Until 1980 the stitchbird persisted only on Little Barrier Island; since then attempts have been made to start populations on five other islands, with marginal success. Once cats were eradicated on Little Barrier in 1980, the population quadrupled to around the 2000 it stands at today; there are fewer than 200 on other islands.

For a honeyeater, the stitchbird is a rare bird in several ways: it nests in tree holes, one of only two of the world's honeyeaters that does so; and on Kapiti Island, but not Little Barrier, more than one male and female breed in the same nest. Several different permutations have been discovered: two pairs of males and females in the same nest, and three nests defended by two males, for example. This behaviour may be explained by a shortage of nest holes and a lack of food plants on Kapiti.

Stitchbirds lay up to five pure white eggs between September and March, in a nest lined with tree-fern scales and feathers. The same nest may be used year after year. However, the average number of chicks fledged is only two; scientists have no clear explanation for this low rate.

The stitchbird diet is dominated by nectar, which it is able to carry back to the nest to feed the young. Other foods include fruit and sometimes insects.

Male stitchbirds are larger and more colourful than the females. The bright yellow feathers of the male often provided colour highlights in Maori cloaks and, rarely, whole cloaks were made of stitchbird feathers.

**Did you know?**

Perhaps the most unusual feature of the stitchbird is its occasional habit of mating face to face, the only bird in the world known to copulate in this fashion. Such unusual mating has been seen only in captive birds and in wild birds on Kapiti Island. In one instance a group of five males were observed chasing a female until one male forced her to the ground and copulated with her. The female would always emit a distress call and try to fly away or kick the male. Researchers believe stitchbirds have developed unusually prominent cloacae in order to make it easy to mate face to face. The male cloaca juts out much further than the cloacae of other birds.

*Stitchbirds are the smallest of New Zealand's three honeyeaters and generally play second fiddle to the tui and bellbird when competing for food.*

*With a swift bite to the back of the neck, a stoat makes short work of a royal spoonbill chick in a nest high up in a tree.*

# Stoat

Are stoats (*Mustela erminea*) victims of a bad press or is there genuine reason to fear their impact on the New Zealand environment? From the time of their introduction in 1884 (in order to control rabbits), ornithologists such as Sir Walter Buller harboured serious misgivings about how stoats would affect native birds. Some also worried about the impact they might have on introduced gamebirds.

After long study of stoats in New Zealand, noted expert on mustelids (the family composed of ferrets, stoats and weasels) Dr Carolyn King cautioned against blaming stoats for harming native bird populations. Writing at a time (1985) when large tracts of native forests were still being clear-felled, she rightly pointed out that habitat destruction was a more serious problem. Since then research on a number of threatened and vulnerable birds has clarified the role of stoats:

• They are responsible for the decline of birds such as parakeets, yellowheads, black stilts, kereru, robins and kaka.
• They are predators on kiwi in a number of areas and Hutton's shearwater in the Kaikoura Mountains.
• They kill large numbers of shorebirds such as the New Zealand dotterel.

All known breeding kaka females monitored by Landcare Research near Nelson Lakes National Park up to 1997 were almost certainly killed by stoats. Parakeets, yellowheads and kaka are at threat from stoats partly because they nest in tree holes which are easy for the mustelids to enter, and partly because of the phenomenon of beech forest 'mast' years. At periodic intervals beech trees produce huge quantities of seed, resulting in a population explosion of mice which feast on the seed. In turn stoat numbers leap because of the extra mice, and the stoats also prey on birds.

Birds and eggs are in fact the chief item in the diet of stoats in New Zealand, making up 25 percent of all foods, followed by weta, mice, insects, rabbits, possums and rats. However, possums, rabbits and rats account for more than half the weight eaten. On hunting expeditions, the stoat takes no prisoners. This behaviour is a response to its northern-hemisphere environment, where food supplies are unreliable and the stoat caches excess kills for times of scarcity. Thus, confronted with a group of trapped prey, a stoat will kill every animal before beginning to feed.

Stoats are relatively small animals (the average male weighs 325 grams), but are prepared to take on animals much larger than themselves. In one instance, a stoat was seen hanging from the neck of a Fiordland crested penguin weighing 4 kg! With small prey, stoats deliver a precise killing bite to the neck, severing the spinal cord. They attempt to repeat the performance with larger animals such as rabbits, whose neck muscles are better developed, but as often as not the victims die of fright.

Each year scientists are improving their methods of trapping mustelids, which are among the most difficult animals to capture. A new technique being tested is the poisoning of eggs with the chemical 1080.

Stoats have colonised New Zealand extremely well. They are present from Northland to Bluff, coastline to high country, in pasture and dense forest and in wet as well as dry regions. A recent study in Fiordland beech forest with radio-tagged stoats showed a young female travelling 65 km in a month, and other stoats regularly moving more than 2 km in only 2–3 hours.

After stoats mate the embryo does not develop immediately in the female. Instead she delays implantation for 9–10 months. If food supplies are scarce, the female is capable of reabsorbing embryos so that she will not give birth that spring. Female stoats are extremely precocious: one 17-day-old kit, blind, deaf, and almost immobile, was mated and a year later produced 13 kits.

*Predation by stoats is the primary cause of the decline of kaka in beech forest.*

# Sunfish

One of the most bizarre fishes in New Zealand waters is the sunfish (*Mola mola*), which has acquired its name from its habit of basking in the sun at the ocean's surface. A relative of the odd-looking leatherjacket and porcupine-fish, the sunfish has two large opposing fins which it uses in a sculling motion, and no discernible tail.

When it comes to size, the sunfish is a world beater. It is rated as the heaviest and broadest bony fish, on average weighing 1 tonne. Although the fish is a heavyweight, it has an extremely light, paper-thin skeleton.

Some authorities claim the heaviest ever sunfish was a monster of 2.2 tonnes captured in New South Wales in 1908. However, according to New Zealand fisheries biologist David Graham, writing in the 1950s, a 3.5-tonne specimen stranded at Gisborne in 1889.

The sunfish holds two other world records: for producing the most eggs and for the greatest size difference between a newborn and an adult. A female was found to carry 300 million eggs, and each newborn sunfish is smaller than a pea. Its open ocean spawning grounds are unknown and larvae have never been discovered.

A sedate swimmer, the sunfish feeds mainly on jellyfish with which it can easily keep pace. Rather than taking jellyfish whole, it bites chunks out of them, and because jellyfish are not very nourishing, the sunfish spends most of its life hunting and feeding.

*Another unintended casualty of the fishing industry, a sunfish trapped in a deadly, near-invisible ocean driftnet is freed by a diver.*

*A trio of hungry swallow chicks clamour to be fed.*

# Swallow

Using their forked tails to hover and dart, welcome swallows (*Hirundo tahitica*) not only catch insects on the wing but also drink in flight, skimming low over water and scooping some up with the open bill as it touches the surface.

Since 1958 when swallows first began breeding near Kaitaia, they have spread rapidly through lowland areas of the country except for Otago and Southland. Self-introduced from Australia, they also occur in the western Pacific and southern Asia.

Swallows nest either in natural sites such as caves or rock outcrops, or they take advantage of human constructions such as bridges or barns to create their nests of mud, strengthened usually with dry grass.

Many swallows are known as martins although there is no significant difference between swallows and martins. The Australian tree martin (*H. nigricans*) and the fairy martin (*H. ariel*) both occasionally wander across the Tasman but neither have established here permanently.

Swallows are very proficient feeders, with wide-based bills that allow the mouth to open into a broad gape to pick up insects. Compared with fast-flying swifts (to which they are sometimes likened), swallows are more than twice as efficient at feeding. Their slower, highly manoeuvrable flight uses up more energy, but as they twist and turn through the air they catch much larger insects.

*Mute swans flying over Lake Ellesmere is a rare sight; at present there are just over 100 wild birds.*

# Swans

The graceful swan (*Cygnus olor*) of *The Ugly Duckling* fame, though introduced in 1866, has never established a strong toe-hold in New Zealand. Today its population stands at only about 100, with most of these in Canterbury where Lake Ellesmere provides the best habitat. Until 1968 there were twice as many mute swans, but the storm which sank the *Wahine* also destroyed the areas where they fed. Ducks Unlimited, a volunteer organisation dedicated to conserving waterfowl, has a programme to introduce the swans into the wild.

Elsewhere in the world the mute swan is reasonably common. Its natural range is northern Eurasia from Great Britain to eastern Russia. At 12 kg, the male mute swan is outweighed only by the emperor (30 kg) and king (13 kg) penguins among birds in the New Zealand region.

The black swan (*C. atratus*) also suffered during the 1968 storm; its numbers fell from 100 000 to fewer than 10 000 by 1978. However, by 1981 it

*Black swan cygnets take up to 140 days to fledge; breeding will not occur until they are 2–4 years old.*

had bounced back to 63 000, including 3000 on the Chatham Islands. Introduced in the 1860s from Australia where they are native to the eastern coast and Tasmania, black swans may also have arrived in New Zealand without human assistance about the same time.

During the duck season about 5000 birds are shot each year in a strictly controlled take. In some areas they have been a nuisance; at Lake Ellesmere before the 1968 storm some birds were culled annually because they ate out pasture.

# Takahe

The takahe (*Porphyrio mantelli*) is one of the bird 'finds' of the 20th century. Once abundant in the North and South islands, by the end of the 19th century it was believed extinct. Only four bird skins, from takahe captured in the Fiordland area up until 1898, existed as evidence of what it looked like.

The best preserved of those mounted specimens, in the Otago Museum, aroused the interest of a medical student, later to become Invercargill doctor Geoffrey Orbell. Over the years Orbell continued to hear rumours from Fiordland of a bird the size of a goose, with blue-green feathers—strengthening his hunch that the takahe might still be alive. Finally, in 1948 the keen tramper and hunter captured a pair of takahe near a lake high in Fiordland's Murchison Mountains. News of the rediscovery was splashed in newspapers around the world; the lake became known as Lake Orbell and the valley as Takahe Valley.

The flightless takahe resembles an oversized pukeko (see page 278), with a similar indigo, peacock-blue and green plumage. Standing about 500 mm tall and weighing 3 kg, it probably arrived from Australia several million years ago, over time losing its powers of flight and, like all flightless birds, increasing in weight. Until recently it was included in a genus of its own,

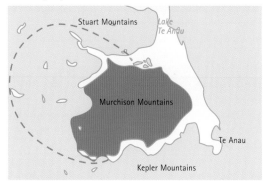

**TAKAHE RANGE**
*Since the discovery of takahe in the South Island Murchison Mountains in 1948, the range of the bird has contracted.*

- - -  Known natural range of takahe since 1948

▇  Area where takahe are currently monitored

*Notornis*, but it is now placed in the *Porphyrio* genus, emphasising its closeness to the pukeko.

At the time Orbell came across the takahe, there were estimated to be 250–300 birds, a number that remained constant until the early 1970s when the population dropped, reaching a low of 120 in 1981. At first scientists thought the culprit might have been stoats but then their attention turned to deer (see page 93) which had appeared in increasing numbers in the Murchisons since the 1950s. It soon became apparent the large mammals were outcompeting the takahe for their favourite foods of tussock grass and herbs (later studies have shown that stoats are also a significant predator).

When deer move into Fiordland's ungrazed alpine areas, they first eat palatable herbs and grasses, but as these are exhausted they turn to tussock grasses (see page 346). The takahe spends up to 90 percent of its waking time extracting the rich juices from these plants; in pulling the tussock tillers out from the base, it actually encourages the plants' growth, whereas deer browsing weakens them. From the mid-1950s intensive deer control was carried out and areas of tussock were sprayed with fertiliser. Tussock grasses are only now beginning to recover.

In 1985 a takahe captive breeding programme was started at Burwood Bush Reserve, just outside of Te Anau. Eggs fresh from the mountains are placed in incubators, and once hatched the chicks are fed by a human hand in a puppet glove resembling the takahe parent. At 6 weeks the juveniles, about half adult size, move to outside pens where they can help themselves to tussock. A few weeks later they are released into the 60-ha red tussock reserve, and at 1 year are left to fend for themselves in the Murchison Mountains.

In an attempt to start a second Fiordland population, some takahe reared at Burwood have been released into the Stuart Mountains, adjoining the Murchisons, but the programme was temporarily halted in 1991 because only one pair out of 58 birds was known to have produced chicks. It appears the Stuarts do not have the habitat suitable for takahe breeding. Effort is therefore concentrated on boosting numbers in the Murchison Mountains, where birds raised at Burwood have mated with wild takahe and reared chicks. The target is a population of 500 to provide a buffer against natural fluctuations. At the same time, around 50 takahe have so far been

*Bearing a close resemblance to the pukeko, the rarer takahe occur naturally in only one area.*

raised on islands such as Tiritiri Matangi, Kapiti, Mana and Maud as an insurance against any disaster befalling the Fiordland birds.

A relatively long-lived bird (up to 20 years), the takahe lays one to three eggs, with male and female sharing parental duties. Although today the Murchison Mountains are their only 'natural' habitat, it appears the birds may have been driven up there after the habitat changes caused by humans and the introduction of predators. On islands with a more favourable climate and better food, they occupy territories of 3–4 ha, compared with 20–30 ha in the alpine tussocks.

## Did you know?

In an attempt to teach artificially reared takahe about the dangers of stoats, chicks have been subjected to 'aversion therapy'. This takes the form of a stuffed stoat beating up a takahe glove-puppet in front of the chicks. A week after seeing the incident, chicks have reacted by hiding when the stuffed stoat reappeared in their cages.

# Tawa

Well shaped and rounded, tawa (*Beilschmiedia tawa*) is a lower-canopy hardwood tree which grows beneath the taller podocarps. A shade lover, it predominates in cutover bush once the taller trees have been removed. Trees deep in the forest have slender trunks compared with those growing in the open. At its highest it reaches 30 metres. Tawa's distribution matches that of southern rata: it is found throughout all of the North Island and down to Westport and the Clarence River.

In far-north forests its relative, taraire (*B. tarairi*)—like tawa, one of the laurel family—is the dominant canopy tree, but tawa takes over that role until it is replaced by kamahi in the South Island. Laurels are largely tropical, examples being the bay tree, avocado, cinnamon and camphor.

At the end of its willow-like, green to honey-gold leaves, small flowers on panicles bear large oval drupes. These turpentine-flavoured berries are relished by kereru; Maori also ate them once they had been soaked, dried and pulped. Cooked in a hangi, they taste like potato.

Tawa trunks and boughs have a smooth, dark-coloured bark. The straight-grained and light timber was used by Maori to make bird spears up to 9 metres long and only 30 mm in diameter. Fashioning them was a long, painstaking task.

Until 1990 significant quantities of tawa were still being chipped and shipped to Japan where it was used in paper manufacture, but the New Zealand Forest Accord in 1991 saw the end of the destructive practice.

*Tawa forms the subcanopy of forests in the North Island and down to north Westland.*

*A white-fronted tern presents its chick with a small fish. These terns usually raise just one chick a year.*

# Terns

Terns are sometimes confused with gulls, but closer inspection reveals a more delicate and aerially elegant group of birds than gulls. Because of the forked tail of most species, which they share with swallows, they are sometimes described as 'sea swallows'. Of 37 species of tern worldwide, 16 occur in New Zealand either as breeders, regular migrants or strays.

The greatest bird migrator of all, the arctic tern (*Sterna paradisaea*) is an occasional visitor to New Zealand shores. Breeding mainly around the shores of the Arctic Ocean, it flies to the other side of the world to spend the remainder of the year in the Antarctic—in a straight line, a distance of 16 000 km. If daily foraging flights are included, many arctic terns may travel more than 50 000 km a year.

Rarest of the New Zealand species is the fairy tern (*S. nereis*) which breeds at only three Northland sites: Waipu Estuary, Mangawhai Heads and Papakanui Spit, South Kaipara Heads. Barely bigger than a bumble bee at birth and weighing only 70 grams as an adult, the fairy tern is New Zealand's smallest tern. In the mid-1980s its population fell to four breeding pairs but the combined efforts of scientists and local communities at the nesting sites have seen numbers creep up to around 30.

The only endemic species is the black-fronted tern (*S. albostriata*) which breeds in braided rivers of the eastern South Island, and in Nelson and north Westland. Described as 'ploughboy' or 'ploughbird' by early European settlers because it picked up grubs and worms from newly turned earth, the black-fronted tern is today a relatively rare species of 5000 birds. In autumn they fish a few kilometres out to sea off the South Island east coast and up to Cook Strait.

White-fronted terns (*S. striata*), the most common New Zealand species, are sometimes called 'kahawai birds' by fishermen for their habit of fishing in association with these fish; anchovies which the kahawai have driven to the surface are the terns' principal prey. These terns also fly over skipjack tuna in a joint fishing exercise, though not in the same concentrated flocks.

*The New Zealand subspecies of the fairy tern number only two or three dozen.*

# Toetoe

Toetoe is a native grass of coastal areas, swamps and open country, sometimes called 'cutty grass' because of the fine, saw-like teeth along the edges of its leaves. There are five species of toetoe: *Cortaderia toetoe*, *C. splendens*, and *C. fulvida* (all restricted to the North Island), *C. richardii* (a South Island-only species), and the Chatham Island rarity *C. tubaria*.

Easy to confuse with the two species of introduced South American pampas grass, toetoe flowers in spring and early summer. By contrast, pampas flowers in autumn and is much larger than toetoe. In northern areas the Peruvian pampas *C. jubata* is a serious pest.

Intermixed with flax, *C. toetoe* grows around the margins of freshwater swamps. *C. splendens* is a northern sand dune or cliff face species.

The Chatham Island toetoe was thought to be a form of the mainland toetoe until 1979 when it was recognised as a species in its own right. Grazing and habitat destruction have reduced it to fewer than 120 plants, and an equally significant threat comes from introduced pampas grass and mainland toetoe, both of which readily hybridise with the Chathams toetoe.

Maori used to fly kites in the form of a human head and wings, made from toetoe stalks and the dried leaves of raupo and hung with strings of feathers. The Arawa tribe made one that measured 4 metres across the wings.

*Creamy feathery stalks of flowering toetoe ripple in the breeze along a river flat.*

*Scientists point to change in the sea currents which bring ashore nutrients as one of several possible causes for the decline of the toheroa.*

# Toheroa

More deeply buried in the sand than other bivalves, the toheroa (*Paphies ventricosa*) has a wide but patchy distribution around the coast. North Island west coast and South Island southern beaches are where this shellfish is most abundantly found. Toheroa are unique to New Zealand, although related species are found in other parts of the world.

As juveniles, toheroa are picked up by the surf and carried up the beach to form a band just below the high-tide mark. Gradually, as they grow to 200 mm in size, they move down the beach to settle at the mid-tide level, burying themselves at depths of between 150 and 300 mm. Toheroa live in dense beds of up to 90 animals a square metre; sometimes whole beds emerge out of the sand just in front of a wave, and in that way migrate up the beach to their preferred habitat. They gain their nutrients from the rich planktonic 'soup' which is washed ashore, especially along the North Island west coast.

Just as trees give away their age by annual growth rings, so do toheroa. During the first year or so they grow relatively quickly, becoming sexually mature by the end of their first year when they measure about 70 mm. From then on growth slows; by 5 years they measure their maximum of 140 mm. Few toheroa on North Island beaches are over 7 years old, but in the South Island they live up to twice that age. Female toheroa are prodigious spawners, releasing 15–20 million eggs in a 3-hour burst.

For decades toheroa have been in short supply, for a combination of reasons: climate change and unpredictable sea currents have played havoc with the phytoplankton blooms along the coast which have traditionally been the source of rich nutrients; people have taken too many toheroa; motor vehicles driven along the sand have disturbed them; and black-backed gulls eat large quantities. A gull can eat about 20 toheroa a day; scientists have noted that when a vehicle drives over a toheroa bed, the shellfish come to the surface where they are quickly taken by gulls. It is assumed that the pressure of the vehicle passing over is taken as a cue for the toheroa to migrate upwards—naturally the cue would be a wave. Once the toheroa are at the surface, they find it difficult to rebury themselves in the hard sand, and are easy pickings for gulls.

In the peak year of 1947, a total of 77 tonnes of toheroa were processed commercially from Ninety Mile and Dargaville beaches, but the canning factories are now closed. The last open season on northern beaches was on Dargaville Beach in 1980.

# Tomtit

Tomtits (*Petroica macrocephala*) are forest and scrub birds belonging to the robin family. This close connection made it possible for the Chatham Island subspecies to foster endangered black robin chicks (see Black robin, page 67).

The Chatham Island tomtit is itself a rare bird. In the 1970s it was removed from Mangere and Little Mangere islands so as not to compete with the black robin. Already it was in low numbers, after being exterminated on the main Chatham Island by predators. It then existed only on South-East and Pitt islands. Having used the tomtit to do the black robin a good turn, conservation worker Don Merton and his team later returned the favour by releasing tomtits onto Mangere Island, where they have re-established a healthy population.

*In the early 1980s the Chatham Island tomtit, itself in low numbers, came to the rescue of the black robin by fostering robin chicks.*

On the mainland the tomtit initially declined when rats, cats and mustelids arrived, but populations are now regarded as having stabilised. Favoured habitat is beech forest and manuka–kanuka scrub. Mature pine forests are also suitable as they are home to large numbers of insects. Aggressively territorial during the breeding season, tomtits often appear promptly to check out the newcomers when people walk into the bush. They join together to mob and drive away moreporks and cuckoos from their territories.

In September the female builds the nest and during the next 4 or 5 months the pair will be busy incubating and raising chicks. They usually raise up to three broods. Both parents feed the chicks, and as soon as the female renests to lay another clutch, the male takes sole charge of the first clutch. After the breeding season is over, the pair remain in the same territory. Renowned for their sharp eyesight, tomtits can spot insects from as far away as 12 metres. Maori recognised this ability; they referred to a keen-sighted person as having 'tomtit's eyes'.

Subspecies of tomtits also exist on the Snares and Auckland islands where they feed in tussock grassland and even on floating kelp. Around penguin, seal and sea lion colonies they feed on the teeming flies.

# Totara

One of the giants of the forest, the totara was esteemed by Maori over all other trees. The equally stately kauri was also held in high regard, but because totara grew as far south as Stewart Island, it had more universal appeal. Great war canoes (waka taua), capable of holding 100 warriors, were hewn from a single totara trunk, and the durable timber was preferred for framing whare and for carving.

Like other podocarps such as kahikatea, totara produce masses of fruit which were gathered by the basketful for eating. Totara were also considered useful for medicine: the inner bark was boiled and the extract kept in a bottle for a week then administered to control fevers.

So significant were totara in Maori life that trees were set aside as heirlooms at the birth of an important boy; arguments over ownership of trees frequently led to clashes. Trees were arranged in a hierarchy, with the giants of the forest called rakau rangitira or chiefly trees. Along with kauri, rimu, kahikatea and rata, totara was placed in this category. The tree's reddish-hued timber also guaranteed it high status, since red was associated with royalty.

Europeans also quickly came to appreciate the qualities of totara. Being resistant to borer and rot, it was used for fence posts, doorsteps, window frames and telephone poles. Its stringy, tinder-dry bark, hanging in thin papery ribbons, was used by both Maori and Pakeha for lighting fires. The bark may be up to 75 mm thick at the base of the trunk.

Found over most of the country, totara grows best in the mixed podocarp forests of the central North Island and the West Coast. There are four species: totara (*Podocarpus totara*) which grows to an average of 30 metres in height, the higher-altitude mountain or thin-barked totara (*P. halli*), the 9-metre-high *P. acutifolius*, found from Marlborough to south Westland, and the alpine shrub *P. nivalis*. *P. totara*'s range is as far south as Foveaux Strait on the east coast and Reefton on the west, to an altitude of 600 metres. To distinguish this totara from the other species, it is sometimes referred to as 'true' totara. Best growing conditions for this giant are fertile, well-drained lowland sites, most of which have now been converted for agriculture or horticulture.

At one time totara was a dominant tree on Banks Peninsula and in Central Otago, but fires lit by Maori hundreds of years ago largely destroyed these arid forests, especially in Otago.

The evidence of the former extent of totara forest is in the tree trunks which continue to be unearthed. So durable is totara that many of the logs remaining from these fires were used hundreds of years later by European settlers for fencing and building.

Although *P. totara* and montane totara differ in size, bark depth and distribution, the two species are known to hybridise. A cultivar, golden totara, is a popular garden plant.

The sharp-needled *P. acutifolius* is a shrub varying in height from 9 metres in lowland, fertile sites, down to only 1 metre in poor soils or at its 600-metre limit. *P. nivalis* or snow totara is a prostrate shrub growing above 1500 metres, mainly on the east coast of the South Island, although it is found in North Island mountainous regions as well. Kea feast on the snow totara berries from March to May.

All podocarps bear male and female flowers on different trees, but the totara differs from other podocarps by producing a green seed set in a fleshy red stalk, rather than the usual black one. Flowers appear in October and November, maturing by March.

Most of the great totara have been felled. The largest remaining is the 39-metre-tall Pouakani totara near Pureora Forest. It has a huge girth of 11.43 metres, and would provide 77 cubic metres of timber if cut. Because of totara's importance to Maori, on occasions they are granted the right to fell large specimens for waka or carving.

*Smallest of the totara family is the alpine shrub* Podocarpus nivalis *which reaches 3 metres.*

*Maori used totara bark for a number of medicinal purposes including treating for skin complaints, piles and fevers.*

*As lake-originating rainbow trout approach sexual maturity, the pinkish stripe along the side becomes a rich crimson red, causing them to be confused with the similarly coloured chinook salmon.*

# Trout

Trout belong to the Salmonidae family, and together with salmon are regarded by anglers as the 'aristocrats' of freshwater fishes. New Zealand's world-famous trout fishery is not native; there are in fact no salmonids that are native to the southern hemisphere.

Brown trout (*Salmo trutta*), present in most river systems from Auckland south, is today the most important recreational fish. It is prized by anglers because it has a reputation for being difficult to catch. Some specimens are very large; a 14-kg brown was found (dead) in Southland's Waiau River in 1981. Imported in the 1860s, New Zealand trout are a mix of varieties from Europe, including sea-run, river and lake fish.

Rainbow trout (*Oncorhynchus mykiss*) have a confused identity. While it has long been believed that they descended from coastal rainbow trout introduced in 1883 from California, today's rainbows may have hybridised with other trout that were liberated earlier. In 1878 some trout of uncertain origin were released into the Karapiro

Stream and the Kaukapakapa River, tributaries of the Waikato River, and the same year 1000 cut-throat salmon were freed into Lake Waikare.

Fisheries scientists have noticed heightened aggression in Lake Tarawera trout, which is typical of redband trout, and other trout have yellow-orange markings beneath the head which are seen in the cut-throat species. To try and solve the question of ancestry, the scientists carried out DNA tests in 1996 on trout captured in the Rotorua, Taupo and Waikato River region, some of which resembled cut-throat trout. However, the tests showed the trout were all rainbows; further studies are to be carried out.

Rainbow trout are renowned for their fighting qualities. One writer described the species as 'the trout on a flying trapeze'. Whereas browns are both river and lake fish, rainbows tend to be lake dwellers only. Their populations are highest in Lakes Rotorua, Rotoiti, Tarawera, Taupo, Coleridge, Wanaka, Te Anau and Manapouri. Their diet is varied and depends on what is present in their habitat. Frogs are popular; a rainbow from Lake Taupo was found to have eight frogs inside it.

# Tuatara

Most celebrated of New Zealand's archaic animals, the tuatara (Maori for spiny back) belongs to the early order of reptiles, the sphenodontids, which appeared about 220 million years ago at the time the dinosaurs were also evolving. It is the last representative of its kind still living. Although it resembles a lizard, it is not one.

Because all its relatives are now fossils, and because the tuatara's reproductive behaviour has been characterised by some as 'primitive', it has been described as a living fossil. However, this is a description that scientists working with the tuatara are keen to play down. They contend that 'living fossil' implies a species that has failed to adapt, is not very complex and is about to become extinct—the reality is that tuatara are well adapted to modern-day environmental conditions in New Zealand, except for coping with the predators which have forced them onto islands.

Until the late 1980s it was considered there was only one tuatara species (*Sphenodon punctatus*), although 19th-century naturalist Sir Walter Buller had earlier discovered a different-looking specimen that he called *S. guntheri*, after the British Museum scientist who named *S. punctatus*. Genetic testing has now established that Gunther's tuatara is in fact a separate species. Until 1995 just 400 survived, on the tiny North Brother Island in Cook Strait, but in that year 68 were transferred to an unnamed island in Pelorus Sound (unnamed for fear the tuatara might be stolen by poachers). A subspecies of *S. punctatus*, with the tentative name of *S. punctatus reischeki*, survives in extremely low numbers on Little Barrier Island.

Best estimates of the total tuatara population are 100 000. Wind-blasted Stephens Island in Cook Strait is home to between 30 000 and 50 000, while the remainder are on 25 islands off Whangarei, in the Hauraki Gulf, off Coromandel, and in the Bay of Plenty. No one knows for sure

*Relatively fast-moving animals such as geckos form only a small part of the tuatara diet. The slow, deliberate hunting strategy of the tuatara allows such animals to escape.*

# — *Gender to order* —

In most animals sex is determined by the genes handed down by the parents, but not so in the tuatara. Scientists have discovered that soil temperature is crucial in deciding the gender of the rare reptiles.

This discovery was made after the young tuatara from one captive-bred clutch were found to be male, whereas juveniles from two other clutches were all female; further study revealed that tuatara offspring from eggs incubated at cool temperatures were always female, but those from eggs incubated at warm temperatures were almost always male.

This has important implications for conservation of the tuatara, which are often raised in captivity and released into the wild.

The phenomenon of temperature-dependent sex determination is known in other reptiles including crocodiles and turtles, but only recently has been proven to occur in tuatara.

when they disappeared from the mainland; some were found in early European times but they may have been introduced from islands. If there were a few survivors they would not have lasted long, as they are easily killed by cats, rats and pigs. A key feature of the islands where tuatara live is the abundant presence of burrowing seabirds such as petrels, prions and shearwaters. Not only do

these birds provide the tuatara with ready-made burrows to live in, they also enrich the soil with their droppings, creating conditions for an explosion of invertebrate life. Weta, beetles, spiders, earthworms and millipedes, all food for tuatara, thrive on the islands. The reptiles also eat the bird chicks and eggs.

Between dusk and midnight on warm evenings tuatara emerge slowly from their burrows to forage and feed, clumsily snatching at anything which moves into their path. On Stephens Island the diet is more than 50 percent insects, mainly beetles, while invertebrates such as worms, snails, slugs, centipedes and spiders make up 20 percent of the diet.

During spring and summer, fairy prion eggs and chicks are important items on the tuatara menu: more than a quarter of eggs and chicks are lost because of tuatara predation. Tuatara eat the eggs and chicks whole, but large chicks are usually too much of a mouthful and escape with severely gnawed limbs. When eating, tuatara use their teeth like a carving knife. Tuatara are also cannibals of juveniles, quite possibly of the ones they have produced themselves. For this reason juveniles are active during the day when the adults are in their burrows, then hide at night.

Burrows are zealously guarded, especially during the breeding season around January and February. Only one tuatara ever occupies a burrow at any one time, and sometimes in crowded situations, as on Stephens Island, burrows are only a metre away from each other.

## A leisurely life

As befits a reptile that lives in a cool temperate climate and has a long life (at least 60 and perhaps over 100 years), the cold-blooded tuatara does everything slowly. This is especially true of breeding. Females take on average 4 years to produce their soft-shelled eggs; they do not lay the eggs until 8–9 months after mating, and the eggs take 11–16 months to hatch.

Males compete with each other for the available females—less than half the females mate each year, but males are able to mate every year. As testoterone levels in the males rise, they inflate their lungs and throat to appear larger than they really are. If territories are invaded they come to blows, a male sometimes locking its jaw around the neck of its opponent as the two scuffle on the ground. Older males often bear the scars of these

*This fairy prion should have reason to be concerned about sharing its burrow with a tuatara. Its eggs and chicks are liable to end up as an important source of protein for the reptile.*

ferocious encounters, including broken jaws and lost tails. Like all reptiles, the tuatara can survive the loss of a tail; the replacement is shorter and differs in colour.

The male tuatara, the only male reptile in the world which does not have a penis, mounts the female and passes sperm from his cloaca to hers. The female digs into soft soil and buries up to 19 eggs, depending on her size (the larger the animal, the more eggs).

For the next few days the female returns nightly to the nesting site to defend the nest from other females. Because of competition for breeding areas, females often dig up other nests, ejecting the eggs before laying their own. Research on the Stephens Island tuatara has thrown up the fascinating finding that eggs hatch more successfully in sheep pasture than in the forest, because of the higher temperatures in open country. This has provided conservation managers with a small dilemma: how much of the island (where a revegetation programme is being carried out) should be kept free of vegetation?

The tuatara's leisurely approach to life is also reflected in the time it takes for a juvenile to mature—anything from 9 to 13 years. They grow for a further 15 or so years, reaching full size (the average for males is 600 grams and 560 mm, for females 350 grams and 450 mm) at between 25 and 35 years.

## Mysterious 'third eye'

The tuatara has a legendary 'third eye' growing on the top of its head, with retina and nerve connection to the brain. The function of this eye is a mystery; one explanation is that it somehow functions as a biological clock. It is connected to the pineal gland which produces the hormone melatonin which controls the cycles of waking, sleeping, mating and hibernating. This biological clock is triggered by changes in natural light which may be registered by the tuatara's third eye.

# Tui

A 19th-century observer facetiously described the tui (*Prosthemadera novaeseelandiae*) as indulging in a peculiar outburst akin to a 'cough, a laugh, and a sneeze'. Accurate enough, perhaps, but the tui also possesses a more tuneful repertoire which makes it one of the most entertaining native birds.

Coming from the northern hemisphere where only male birds sing, early European ornithologists remarked on the fact that both male and female tui sing, a feature shared by the bellbird. The female song is more varied and tuneful than the male's, which uses only one or two notes. Unusually, the female even sings while she is sitting on the nest.

*Largest of the honeyeaters, the tui laps up flax nectar in late spring. During the first weeks of a tui's life, insects are an important food item and it is the male's job to catch them.*

The tui is also a skilful mimic, as 19th-century bird authority Walter Buller noted in a delightful anecdote in *Buller's Book of Birds*. Addressing a group of Maori in the Rangitikei district 'on a matter of considerable political importance', Buller had just finished a speech. Before the chief had the opportunity to reply, a caged tui called out 'tito' (false). 'Friend,' said the chief, 'your arguments are very good; but my mokai is a very wise bird, and he is not yet convinced.'

Tui can imitate the sound of a morepork, blackbird, and even a cat. This ability has convinced some people searching for the vanished South Island kokako that the bird is still alive—at times the forest can be alive with the sound of tui (and bellbirds) mimicking the kokako.

Larger and more assertive than most native birds, the tui has managed to maintain its numbers, and even thrive, in a changed environment. It frequently mobs cuckoos, moreporks, harriers and, more courageously, the New Zealand falcon, which is the country's most skilful hunter and which has been observed killing larger birds than the tui, such as kereru. The tui is essentially a forest bird and a nectar-eater, but now that large areas of native forest have been destroyed, it flies long distances in search of nectar, including into gardens. An Auckland study shows birds fly to feeding stations from a distance of 30 km.

Tui have a strong sense of family, offspring staying close to their parents and later nesting near them. Although 80 percent of their diet is nectar, they also eat insects and seeds. Because the tui has such a wide feeding range, it is an important pollinator and spreader of seeds.

The tui lays three or four eggs in an untidy-looking nest made of twigs, situated in the fork of a tree or on an outer branch of a shrub. The female alone incubates, but the male brings her food during this time and later helps to feed the nestlings once they are hatched. While the female sits on the nest the male spends much of the time nearby, singing.

If its song does not give it away, the tui makes another unmistakable sound: a noisy whirring of its wings caused by a notch in the eighth primary feather (the primaries are the largest flight feathers which propel the bird through the air; the secondaries provide lift). The tufts of white feathers around the tui's neck gave rise to its early name 'the parson bird'.

# Turtles

Sea turtles are uncommon, though not rare, summer visitors to New Zealand waters. Four species have been reported: the Pacific loggerhead (*Caretta caretta*), the leathery turtle (*Dermochelys coriacea*), the green turtle (*Chelonia mydas*) and the hawksbill (*Eretmochelys imbricata*). The largest of these, the leathery, which can reach a whopping 700 kg, has been reported as far south as Foveaux Strait. In 1986 a loggerhead, reputed to be the rarest turtle in New Zealand, was found freshly dead at Mason's Bay on Stewart Island.

A recent report of a turtle visiting Northland over a 15-year period, including during winter, suggests some species can acclimatise to New Zealand's cool sea temperatures.

Sea turtles, originally land dwellers, have successfully adapted to saltwater lives. Like sea otters, seals and marine iguanas, they have kidneys geared to excreting excess salt.

In the Pacific, home to six of the world's seven species, people eat turtles and their eggs; turtles also tangle easily in fishing nets and sometimes mistake plastic bags for one of their favourite foods, jellyfish, with fatal consequences. In an attempt to raise awareness of the threatened status of turtles, 1995 was called the 'year of the turtle'.

*From ribs unearthed in south Canterbury (above), scientists have been able to reconstruct a picture of what a leatherback turtle of 40 million years ago might have looked like. Unlike modern leatherbacks, which have ridged backs, this ancient species had a smooth back. The discovery of the bones of this warmth-loving marine reptile points to the fact that New Zealand must have once had a more tropical climate.*

# Tussocks

Spreading a tawny mantle across vast areas of subalpine and alpine New Zealand, tussock plants endow mountainland vegetation with much of its distinctive character. There are 16 indigenous species of tussock, five of them with subspecies. Tussocks are grasses, but in some ways the metre-high plants resemble forests, protecting small plants and animals beneath their 'skirts'. Some individual tussock plants can be 300 years old.

When Europeans arrived in New Zealand they found tussock in the main North Island ranges and the central North Island; but the most extensive tussockland occurred east of the Southern Alps along a belt of montane country from Marlborough to Southland. Today the extensive grasslands are a shadow of their former selves, not only reduced in extent, but also modified by burning, grazing and weeds. Tussock is the major vegetation component of some 5 million ha (almost 20 percent of New Zealand's land area), while it is a minor part of the vegetation over 3 million ha. Of this, 2.45 million ha are in pastoral lease, a form of tenure held by 360 farmers in the South Island.

What the early settlers did not know was that the immense area of tussocklands they saw was a relatively recent phenomenon. About half the original forest along the eastern South Island was burned by Maori—perhaps to make it easier to catch moa, perhaps for agriculture. It is likely the fires got out of control on tinder-dry, norwester days. Most of the land reverted to tussockland, scrub or fernland. Only in the North Island's red tussock (*Chionochloa rubra*) regions of the Central Plateau is forest gradually reasserting itself.

The modern evolution of tussock grasslands can be traced back to the end of the Ice Age, about 14 000 years ago. For 4000 years grasslands dominated, gradually colonised by bog pine, celery pine, and coprosma shrubs. With climate warming, miro, matai and montane totara asserted themselves, then 7000 years ago beech took over as the dominant cover, while the tussocks retreated to river terraces and flats. Human-induced fire helped re-establish the dominance of tussocks.

Tussocks are well adapted to the rigours of the subalpine environment, able to withstand extremes of climate and temperatures that range from sub-zero up to 40°C. Their ecological usefulness has been recognised: they act as heat conductors, melting and breaking up winter snow,

*Studded with tors of hard schist, Otago's block mountain ranges are dominated by the narrow-leaved snow tussock (*Chionochloa rigida*).*

*Favouring low altitude and damp sites, red tussock plants grow waist high. They are the dominant tussock around the North Island's Central Plateau.*

and they capture moisture from fog, which is then slowly released to the lowlands below.

Tussockland regions can be divided into two groups, based on altitude: snow tussock grasslands (dominated by *Chionochloa* species) which occur in the low alpine zone from the treeline to 500 metres above; and short tussock-snow tussock grasslands (dominated by *Festuca, Rytidosperma, Poa* and *Chionochloa* species) which occur in lower-altitude areas of the South Island formerly covered by forest.

The most widespread species is the mid-ribbed snow tussock (*C. pallens*) which favours younger, better-drained soils. Common throughout the South Island, it also occurs in the North Island axial ranges. The broad-leaved snow tussock (*C. flavescens*) dominates the wetter, western mountains of the South Island, gradually giving way at higher altitudes to the smaller, curled snow tussock (*C. crassiuscula*). Drier South Island mountain areas from the Rakaia Valley to northern and western Southland are the habitat of narrow-leaved snow tussock (*C. rigida*). Carpet grass (*C. australis*) grows in Nelson and Marlborough down to the Lewis Pass.

Short tussock grassland plants are about half a metre high. The main species are hard tussock (*Festuca novae-zelandiae*), silver tussock (*Poa cita*), blue tussock (*P. colensoi*) and blue wheat grass (*Elymus solandri*).

# Tutu

As they did with the karaka, Maori also learned to use the toxic tutu for their own purposes. All parts of the plant except the petals contain tutin, a deadly poison, but properly prepared, the ripe berries provided a refreshing drink.

The key was to ensure none of the poisonous seeds were swallowed; the berries were first squeezed, then the juice was filtered through toetoe flowerheads. Sometimes the resulting liquid was drunk straight; at other times it was added to seaweed (karengo) to make a jelly; and again it was used to flavour bracken fern root or the pith of the mamaku.

Tutu had numerous medicinal uses, including helping to heal bruises and cuts; a preparation from the root called mauru was said to alleviate neuralgia, rheumatism and eyestrain; and a mixture containing juices from the pith was administered for insanity.

As an indication of the plant's toxicity, in Otago in 1870 a circus elephant left to graze in a paddock of tutu died of poisoning soon after. Horses and cattle have frequently succumbed to 'toot' poisoning, although goats are immune to it. Humans can be affected by tutu indirectly. In the 1940s an outbreak of honey poisoning was traced to bees feeding off the honeydew left on branches by passion-vine hoppers which had previously been helping themselves to tutu sap.

Tutu is a plant of river flats or a coloniser of slips. The two species are the tree tutu (*Coriaria arborea*) and the spreading tutu (*C. sarmentosa*). A Chilean relative, *C. ruscifolia*, was used in witchcraft rituals.

*Tutu flowers are replaced by poisonous berries later in the season.*

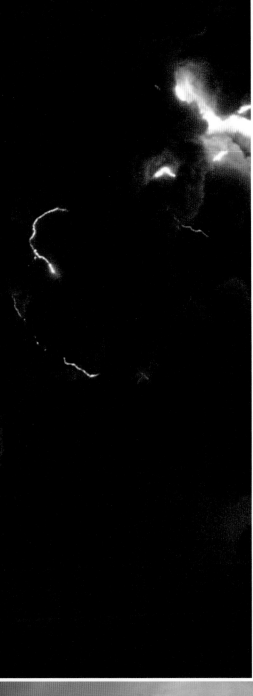

# Volcanoes

Seated astride the Pacific 'Ring of Fire' that loops erratically around the Pacific Ocean, New Zealand is one of the world's major volcanic centres. Our volcanoes are caused by the collision of the Pacific and the Indo–Australian plates, producing magma that rises to the surface from Mount Ruapehu northwards.

Volcanoes have long been a feature of central North Island geology. In AD 181 Chinese and Roman writers reported atmospheric disturbances following an enormous explosion from Lake Taupo, but an even larger one from the same lake occurred more than 300 000 years ago, spreading ash over an area of 30 square kilometres—one of the world's largest eruptions in the last million years

Volcanoes take a number of different forms. In New Zealand the main types are caldera, strato-volcano, scoria cone, lava dome, shield and tuff ring. Lake Taupo is a typical caldera volcano, the most explosive of them all. These volcanoes contain a silica-rich lava called rhyolite, which clogs any vents, sealing in the gases until they finally explode under enormous pressure.

Mount Ruapehu, Mount Ngauruhoe and Mount Taranaki are strato-volcanoes, large cones of andesitic lava with alternating beds of ash and scoria which have built up over thousands of years. Most Auckland volcanoes are scoria cone types, composed of steep sides with a deep central crater. Mount Maunganui, a steep-sided, rounded hill formed of rhyolite lava, is an example of a lava dome volcano, and Lake Pupuke on Auckland's North Shore is a tuff ring volcano—a shallow crater surrounded by a low rim of erupted debris.

*Lightning strikes within a cumulonimbus cloud above the fiery furnace of Mount Ruapehu in 1995. Like other New Zealand cone volcanoes, Ruapehu erupts frequently; in the last 1800 years, there have been 18 blasts of the same magnitude as the 1995–96 series of eruptions. (Inset) Auckland's best-known recent active volcano, Rangitoto, erupted relatively quietly 600–700 years ago to form a gently sloping island.*

*Caterpillars, spiders and flies are the grey warbler's favoured foods. Note the intricate nest.*

# Warblers

No New Zealand forest bird has adapted as well to changes in its environment as the grey warbler or riroriro (*Gerygone igata*) which is common throughout the country and has even settled in urban areas. The songster of the species is generally the male, which produces the soft trill so evocative of the New Zealand bush.

At only 6.5 grams in weight, the grey warbler rivals the rifleman (see page 289) for the honour of being the lightest bird, but the rifleman is shorter. For such a small bird it is relatively long lived; its average life expectancy is 5 years, but some birds are likely to live more than 10 years.

The grey warbler is the only mainland host for the shining cuckoo (see page 91), but the larger parasite has little effect on the abundance of warblers, partly because it arrives from the western Pacific in late October, after the warbler has raised its first clutch, and partly because the cuckoo lays in the nests of only a small percentage of the warbler population.

The hard work of constructing the elaborate nest—the warbler is the only mainland bird to build a roofed nest—is done by the female (see page 232). Starting in late August, she gathers mainly kanuka, gorse and broom leaves (the gorse is useful in deterring predators) for the structure. The male takes an active interest in the busy female's work, constantly following her and singing encouragement.

Like many other native New Zealand birds, grey warblers are relatively unperturbed by human disturbance. When scientist Dr Brian Gill studied them at Kowhai Bush near Kaikoura, one brooding mother allowed him to remove nestlings from under her, while she calmly continued to brood.

By late October the first brood of chicks has usually been raised and it is time for the female to start fashioning a new nest—one that is closely modelled on the first-clutch nest (the nests vary from bird to bird, but most individual birds are consistent in their designs).

According to Maori folklore, grey warblers face their nests with the entrances opposite to the direction of prevailing winds. However, in the Kowhai Bush study, nest-building showed no correlation with wind direction.

New Zealand warblers differ from northern-hemisphere songbirds in their breeding behaviour. In the northern hemisphere, winters at mid-latitudes are harsh, but when spring arrives so does a large flush of food. This encourages the birds to have one large brood quickly. In New Zealand, on the other hand, temperatures are even for much of the year, and the food supply is generally constant, therefore the grey warbler breeds slowly over a long laying season and has two small clutches.

Like the fantail, the warbler is equipped with a fan-like tail, but it does not catch its prey in mid-air. Instead it chases after insects at the tips of branches, hovering in mid-air as it takes them.

Predators of warblers include rats and stoats. Also suspected are cuckoos, magpies and king-fishers. Compared with other mainland birds, however, warblers have a reasonably high rate of breeding success.

The Chatham Island warbler (*G. albofrontata*) is known for its association with the more celebrated Chatham Island black robin (see page 67). Warblers were trialled as foster parents to raise robin chicks, and were able to hatch and care for the robin nestlings, but only until the chicks reached 10 days. Tomtits proved to be more successful substitute parents and were used instead in subsequent fostering.

Chatham Island warblers are larger than the mainland species, and differ in their breeding habits. Instead of two clutches they lay just one—it appears the Chathams warblers time their breeding so that they avoid having to raise shining cuckoo young. By the time cuckoos lay their eggs—usually November—most Chathams warblers are hatched; as a consequence there are not many cuckoos in the Chathams.

The Chathams warbler does not appear to have adapted well to life in the wake of human arrival. Fortunately there are no rats or cats on islands where it remains abundant.

# Wasps

Since the 1880s New Zealand has been invaded by waves of some of the most unwelcome immigrants in its history: wasps. There are four species of these aggressive, bee-size, black and yellow insects: the earliest to arrive was the Australian paper wasp (*Polistes tasmaniensis humilis*), followed by the German wasp (*Vespula germanica*) towards the end of World War II. Common wasps (*V. vulgaris*) became established in the 1970s, and the most recent arrival is the Asian paper wasp (*P. chinensis*), first found near Auckland in 1979.

Since arriving in New Zealand the German and common wasps in particular have multiplied to reach extraordinary numbers in some areas. In the northern hemisphere, worker wasps die off each winter, leaving some fertilised queens to lie dormant and start new colonies in the spring. But New Zealand is 'wasp heaven', with a relatively mild climate compared to the wasps' native

*A German wasp feeds on nectar. The same size as the common wasp, the German wasp has separate black dots on its back whereas in the common wasp the dots are fused with the black rings.*

Europe, and an absence of natural enemies such as badgers. Some colonies are able to survive winter, so that in spring they already have a strong worker force and expand rapidly.

## The wasp plague

Ecologists are deeply concerned about the environmental impact of the wasp plague. At the height of the season in summer and autumn, the biomass of wasps in Nelson and north Westland beech forests is greater than all the native birds, stoats and rodents put together. By robbing nectar-eating birds such as kaka of honeydew (see page 156) and sometimes killing chicks on the nest, wasps are posing a threat to the survival of the birds in these forests.

Native insects, which play a crucial role in the ecology of forests because they recycle nutrients and are an important source of food for native insect-eating birds, are also eaten by wasps. Vulnerable species such as the weta are therefore under threat of extinction. Wasps are able to tackle insects much larger than themselves, such

as weta. They immobilise their prey by stinging, then carve pieces off to carry back to the nest. Even honey bees are not safe. Wasps capture bees at hive entrances, bite their victims in half and carry off the thorax section, which does not bear the bee's sting and is particularly tasty. The weakest hives in a group are picked on, the wasps stealing all their honey until the bees eventually die. Wasps collect sugary, energy-giving food at the beginning of the day, then later change to insects and carrion.

Knowing more about wasps and their life-cycle will help in determining which method of control to use. Scientists have persuaded queens to build nests in indoor boxes where their behaviour has been closely examined. They have discovered that once a nest gets beyond a certain size, the queen will lay about 200 eggs a day. For a biological control to have any impact it would need to have a high egg-laying rate itself or complete its life-cycle more quickly than wasps.

Wasps also attack people. Unlike a bee, a single wasp can sting any number of times. About 10

*The Asian paper wasp's nest is made out of wood chewed and moulded by the insects.*

*The young of the wasp parasite* Pteromalus puparum, *introduced to control white butterfly, also feed on the chrysalis of the red and yellow admiral butterfly.*

percent of those stung become sensitised to the venom; for them, another sting can bring on a potentially deadly reaction. In 1974 a 7-year-old Northland girl became unconscious after a wasp attack and, although she initially recovered in hospital, died 18 days later.

Why are wasps so aggressive? Recent research in the United States has established that they are biologically programmed to respond to an alarm signal from another of their kind. A wasp defending its home or on the attack releases a scent—or pheromone—that brings others swarming to do battle. Someone may unwittingly trigger a wasp to release the same scent by crushing it.

## Wasp control

Efforts to stem the tide of wasps have so far had mixed success. Where attempts have been made to kill them with poison or biological controls, numbers of nests have been reduced. Nevertheless, their range throughout the country is continuing to spread, from the most arid land to the wettest rainforest. Only alpine cold halts them, although recently they have been reported in the upper forest margin of Tongariro National Park and among alpine tussocks of Nelson Lakes National Park. City residents are helping to control wasps over a limited area, but even if all urban nests are destroyed, the wasps will survive in rural areas. Queens can fly 30–70 km when establishing nests, rapidly reinfesting areas.

The main hope for control now lies in biocontrol; in the mid-1980s two of the best prospects, paradoxically, were other parasitoid wasps. Discovered by scientists in Europe, the otherwise harmless little *Sphecophaga vesparum vesparum* (it has no common name) was released throughout New Zealand in 1988. Its close relative, *S. v. burra*, was liberated at two sites in the South Island and one North Island site in 1996.

Somehow these wasps manage to live safely in European wasp nests, possibly camouflaged by a pheromone. They lay their eggs on the larger wasp pupae, which their young eat. The first parasite has become established in at least two sites, Pelorus Bridge in Marlborough and Ashley Forest, north of Christchurch. At Pelorus Bridge, parasitoids were recovered from about 20 percent of nests in 1994, but have not yet measurably affected wasp numbers. Even if it becomes widespread, the parasite is unlikely to reduce wasp density by more than about 10 percent.

Scientists are now turning their attention to microbial pathogens, such as fungi, bacteria and viruses which would specifically target wasps. A Landcare Research/Agresearch team has started preliminary work to investigate whether there are pathogens which attack wasps.

In the meantime, poison remains the most practical way of destroying a wasp nest. One of the most effective modern poisons is a tasty sardine-based chemical which wasps take back to their nests to share around with other occupants.

### Did you know?

In Europe, wasp nests are normally about the size of a football and contain some 10 000 cells. Scientists discovered a nest in April 1963 on a Waimauku farm which was 3.75 metres tall and 1.7 metres wide, containing 3–4 million cells—the world's largest recorded wasp nest.

# Weather

Circling the globe at latitudes just on and below those of New Zealand, westerly winds encounter no obstacles for thousands of kilometres until they reach the New Zealand land mass. These Roaring Forties and Furious Fifties are the predominant influence on New Zealand weather patterns. Occasionally these regular frontal systems are interrupted by cold, winter southerlies, or warm, moist, tropical depressions which move south during summer.

New Zealand's mountainous and hilly terrain also plays an important role in the type of weather experienced, producing great contrasts between the climates of the west and east coasts. Running almost the entire length of the South Island, the Southern Alps block the prevailing westerly airstreams, forcing them north and producing southwesterlies along the west coasts of both islands. At Cook Strait the narrow gap funnels the wind, creating occasional gale-force blasts around the capital.

The one constant of New Zealand weather is its variability, although there is a consistent overall pattern. Typically this begins with a freshening nor'wester, reaching gales in some areas and sometimes accompanied by rain. As the trough moves over the country, the wind switches to the south or southwest, heralding the approach of an anticyclone and settled weather. Generally anticyclones pass over the country at intervals of 3–7 days before the cycle starts over again. A feature of the New Zealand climate is its high winter sunshine hours.

*Clouds shown here over the Rakaia River form the distinctive northwest arch indicating that heavy rain from a westerly air mass has dropped on the West Coast. Now largely devoid of its moisture, the air mass descends onto the east coast as a hot, dry wind. (Inset) This picture, taken by the Japanese GMS 5 weather satellite stationed over the equator, just north of New Guinea, at a height of 36 000 km, is an infrared view, with the highest (coldest) cloud tops white, and the lower (warmer) clouds as shades of grey. The photo shows an extensive cloud band covering New Zealand.*

*Hundreds of years of living near humans has not yet blunted the weka's curiosity.*

# Weka

Engaging and resourceful, the flightless weka (*Gallirallus australis*) is a rail, related to the pukeko, takahe, spotless crake and banded rail. An omnivorous scavenger, its diet consists of berries, insects, birds' eggs and chicks, lizards, mice, rats and worms. Long legs, a heavy body and powerful beak stand it in good stead against many predators—however, cats, dogs, stoats and ferrets are capable of killing it.

Pairs form lifetime bonds; courtship is an elaborate affair, the male lavishing attention on the female by bringing her titbits and building nests for her inspection. Two or three eggs are laid between August and January. The male assists with incubation and rearing the chicks.

There are four subspecies: the North Island, the western (in Nelson, Marlborough and the West Coast), the Stewart Island and the buff (formerly in Canterbury, now abundant on the Chathams where it was introduced). The healthiest population is the western which lives in an area where human pressures are least, but even there the weka's fortunes have declined.

The buff weka only narrowly escaped extinction. In 1905 it was introduced to the Chathams, where it flourishes to this day on the main Chatham Island and Pitt Island, but back in its home range of Canterbury it died out by the late 1920s. Attempts were made in 1962 to re-establish the weka at Arthur's Pass, in the Mackenzie Basin and on Banks Peninsula, but all failed. Although it is protected on the mainland, today the weka can be hunted year-round on the Chathams where it is plentiful.

Of all the wekas, the most intensively studied in recent years has been the North Island weka, because of the efforts to rescue the species from extinction. Once widespread, by the 1920s it had retreated to Northland, Poverty Bay and the King Country. Its final stronghold has been the Gisborne–East Cape region where as late as the

1970s it was still regarded as a pest by market gardeners. Recent surveys have revealed that only a few thousand survive on the mainland. The decline has been swift; from a total population estimated at more than 100 000 in the East Cape–Gisborne region, weka numbers have plummeted to fewer than 2000. The greatest fall, between 1982 and 1984, coincided with a drought, the spread of ferrets, and floods.

With mixed success, conservationists launched a captive breeding programme in 1991 to establish a new and viable mainland population. The difficulties have been not so much with the breeding as with survival of the released birds in the wild. Upwards of 50 were liberated over several years into the Karangahake Gorge near Waihi, but these succumbed to dogs or ferrets.

Fortunately there are populations on the Hauraki Gulf islands of Kawau and Rakitu, and Mokoia Island in the middle of Lake Rotorua. Some of these populations result from the time

## DISTRIBUTION OF NORTH ISLAND WEKA

## *The wily weka*

Over the years people have viewed the weka with a mixture of admiration and loathing. Maori had a saying that when weka broke out of a snare, they would not return because they were fast learners.

When discussing whether the kiwi or the weka should be the country's national emblem, explorer Charlie Douglas, who ate his share of weka, had this to say: 'Why did New Zealand not select the weka? Here is a bird full of good qualities and whose vices lean to virtue's side. Personal valour of a high order. An undying thirst for knowledge—unthinking people give it another name—which causes it to annex everything portable about a hut and carry it into the bush and study it at leisure. An affection for its young, that would face the Prince of Darkness in their defence. And above all an intelligence apart from what we call instinct, far higher than I ever saw in a bird.'

Other commentators have not been so kind, one writing that 'with wekas, thieving is a disease'. More seriously, weka released onto islands have proved a pest to other species.

On Codfish Island, where they did not occur naturally, they preyed on Cook's petrels, reducing them to 100 pairs by 1980. Partly for that reason, and partly to prepare a secure island for kakapo, the weka were removed from Codfish.

Weka have been found to possess a strong homing instinct. Some of the weka which were deported to Stewart Island from Codfish Island managed to swim 3 km back to Codfish, across a difficult stretch of water. Three weeks after some Gisborne birds were released in the Waitakeres, west of Auckland, one of the birds was found at Taneatua more than 300 km south of Auckland and on course for Gisborne.

A long-running debate over whether weka posed a threat to little spotted kiwi on Kapiti Island ended with the verdict in favour of the weka. To test whether the weka were eating kiwi eggs, some kiwi were transferred to another island to start a new population. Within a year the 20-ha gap left was filled by kiwi, proving that weka were, if not helping the kiwi, at least not hindering them.

*Weka are opportunists and versatile feeders, eating both live and dead prey (such as this kereru).*

when 'pest' weka were relocated from the East Cape in the 1970s and 1980s.

Having witnessed the fate of the Karangahake Gorge weka, conservationists have decided to release captive-bred birds on islands. In 1996, 29 were transferred to Pakatoa Island near Auckland and immediately began to breed, and the next year 24 were relocated on 283-ha Whanganui Island, off Coromandel township.

On the East Coast the Department of Conservation is carrying out a weka census, and has started a 5-year 'research by management' project with the largest remaining populations in the Toatoa and Whitikau valleys behind Opotiki. Ferrets, stoats and cats are being trapped in the Toatoa Valley, while no predator control is carried out in the Whitikau. The weka will be monitored to try to gain a better understanding of the nature and level of predation on the birds.

# Weta

Inspiring admiration and fear rather than affection, weta are nevertheless one of New Zealand's most fascinating and significant animals. Even more ancient than tuatara, giant weta are virtually unchanged from their ancestors of 190 million years ago.

Primarily vegetarian, weta belong to the same order as crickets and grasshoppers. In the absence of efficient predators such as rats and cats (although they are preyed upon by lizards, tuatara and moreporks), weta became large and flightless, occupying niches that elsewhere in the world had been claimed by rodents.

Maori know weta as 'devils of the night' because of their nocturnal habit, and 'gods of ugly things' for their appearance. The word weta is the shortened version of the Northland name for the giant weta, wetapunga. The more common tree weta was known as putangatanga, and the cave weta as tokoriro. Weta have evolved into around 100 species, divided into five groups: giant, tree, ground, tusked and cave weta.

## Giant weta

As large as a person's hand, giant weta (*Deinacrida* species) are the most spectacular, but despite their size are quite docile. The biggest exist only on islands, having become extinct on the mainland. Some giant weta that have survived on the mainland include the Kaikoura (*D. parva*), the Nelson alpine (*D. tibiospina*), the scree (*D. connectens*) and the Mahoenui (undescribed).

A giant among giant weta, the 82-mm-long wetapunga (*D. heteracantha*) occurs on Little Barrier Island. Primarily vegetarian, these weta spend their time in treetops. They are the only weta which coexist with kiore, the Polynesian rat—presumably they have survived because they live above the ground and are as large as the rats.

The Mahoenui has had a chequered career. Long considered extinct on the mainland, in 1962 this giant weta was discovered by a school-teacher in a 300-ha gorse patch in the King Country. Although not naturally a gorse dweller, it may have been saved by the spiny shrub keeping rats at bay. Having fenced off the area, Department of Conservation staff are attempting to start a new Mahoenui population on 50-ha Mahurangi Island, off the Coromandel coast where 200 were released. After 4 years the weta are showing signs of breeding. Most common of the giant weta are the scree weta which occur in

> ### Did you know?
>
> A pregnant giant wetapunga weighed a hefty 71 grams, as heavy as a song thrush. Some claim this makes it the heaviest insect in the world, but the *Guinness Book of Animal Records* accepts the African goliath beetle, typically weighing 70–100 grams, as the world's heaviest.

*A female tree weta strikes a defensive pose. Weta do not sting but they may bite if mishandled. The sword-like ovipositor to the rear of the insect is used to lay eggs.*

*The fearsome-looking wetapunga, largest of the giant weta, is harmless but hardly cuddly.*

*Unusual colouring distinguishes the Mount Somers giant weta.*

*Not all cave weta live in caves. This small moss species from Fiordland is our only green weta.*

mountainous areas from Marlborough to Central Otago. Adapted to extremes of temperature, this weta remains under rocks by day, and in the evening ventures out onto the still-warm rocks to feed on plants. It is the most aggressive of the giant weta, intimidating enemies by raising its hind legs high above its head, then kicking down sharply, all the while making a high-pitched rasping sound.

Species of weta presumed to be extinct continue to be discovered. A single specimen of the Mount Somers giant weta was found by a deerstalker in 1957 but it was not until 1994 that a colony was found on a high bluff.

## Tree weta

Widespread throughout New Zealand except in Southland, tree weta have adapted well to the difficulties of modern-day life compared with other weta species.

The three most common species are the Auckland (*Hemideina thoracica*), the Wellington (*H. crassidens*) and the Canterbury (*H. femorata*). Almost as large as the giant weta, tree weta are frequently uncovered in gardens, amongst firewood or hiding inside gumboots—anywhere damp and dark. The tree weta to avoid is the beech forest weta (*H. broughi*) or taipo (devil) from the West Coast which can inflict a painful bite with its large jaws.

Included in the tree weta genus is *H. maori*, but it usually occurs in the mountains above the treeline. One race from the Rock and Pillar Range actually freezes when the temperature drops below zero. Scientists theorise that the weta controls the process by somehow starting to freeze when the temperature is two or three degrees above zero. By doing so the insect protects its cell membranes when the water in its body expands as a result of freezing.

## Ground weta

The ground weta species (*Hemiandrus* and *Zealandosandrus*) resemble tree weta but are smaller and are found mainly in the North Island. These weta occupy small burrows, usually ones originally dug by other insects such as porina moths or cicadas. Like tree weta, they are strongly territorial.

## Tusked weta

One of the most remarkable insect finds of the century occurred in 1970 when lizard expert Tony Whitaker came across a large weta on Middle Mercury Island off the Coromandel coast. The male of this species sports two tusks which it uses to butt other males, or rasps one tusk against another to warn off competitors for territory. Mainly carnivorous, 'Jaws', as the weta became known (it has not yet been described), is one of three tusked weta. Another is a small species from Northland; the third was discovered in 1995 in the Raukumara Range on the east coast of the North Island.

## Cave weta

The final group of species are the cave weta. There are thought to be at least 60 of these long-antennaed, long-legged and non-aggressive weta, which jump out of danger. One species, *Pharmacus montanus*, is popularly called the Mount Cook flea because of the way it leaps about when disturbed. During the day cave weta gather together in large numbers, then at night venture out to feed on plants. Unlike other weta, they neither make sounds with their legs, nor can they hear. Instead they use their long, sensitive antennae to make sense of their surroundings.

# Whales

Located along whale migration paths between rich feeding grounds in the Antarctic and breeding grounds in warmer waters, New Zealand plays host to numerous whale species. Of the world's 80 species of baleen and toothed whales, 37 (including dolphins and porpoises) are seen around the New Zealand coast.

Whales trace their beginnings back at least 60 million years to when hoofed mammals made a gradual change from land to sea to feed in plankton-rich oceans. By 35 million years ago the ancestors of whales appeared in New Zealand waters. Deposits from the Miocene era (5–25 million years ago) have yielded fossils of the sperm whale, the oldest of living whale families.

The two types of whales—baleen and toothed—are differentiated by their feeding methods. Baleen whales have plates in their mouths which sieve small crustaceans or fish,

### WHALES IN NEW ZEALAND WATERS

**Baleen whales**
Minke (*Balaenoptera acutorostrata*)
Bryde's (*B. edeni*)
Sei (*B. borealis*)
Fin (*B. physalus*)
Blue (*B. musculus*)
Humpback (*Megaptera novaeangliae*)
Right (*Balaena glacialis*)
Pygmy right (*Caperea marginata*)

**Toothed whales\***
Melon-headed (*Peponocephala electra*)
False killer (*Pseudorca crassidens*)
Long-finned pilot (*Globicephala malaena*)
Short-finned pilot (*G. macrorhynchus*)
Orca (*Orcinus orca*)
Sperm (*Physeter macrocephalus*)
Pygmy sperm (*Kogia breviceps*)
Dwarf sperm (*K. simus*)
Arnoux's beaked (*Berardius arnouxi*)
Goose-beaked (*Ziphius cavirostris*)
Shepherd's beaked (*Tasmacetus shepherdi*)
Bottlenose (*Hyperoodon planifrons*)
Hector's beaked (*Mesoplodon hectori*)
Scamperdown (*M. grayi*)
Strap-toothed (*M. layardi*)
Andrew's beaked (*M. bowdoini*)

\* Within the sub-order Ordontoceti (toothed whales) is the family Delphinidae which includes dolphins, porpoises and *Orcinus orca*.

whereas toothed whales mostly feed on squid and fish which they find and catch using their sonar.

Whales were prized by Maori who took advantage of the great beasts when they became stranded, for their meat, oil and bone (they made implements out of the latter). A mythical ancestor, Paikea, arrived in New Zealand on the back of a whale, and many families had whales they claimed as guardians. These were often whales they saw when out fishing and which they believed would save them from drowning.

Driven to near extermination over the last several hundred years, some baleen whales are only slowly recovering. New Zealand's early European history is inextricably linked with whaling; up to 200 whaling ships visited ports every year during the first half of the 19th century. Shore stations sprang up and in 1910 the introduction of motor chaser boats and explosive harpoons saw the industry become more efficient at whale processing—in fact it became so accomplished that it caused its own downturn as more and more species declined. On 21 December 1964 the last whale harpooning by a New Zealand boat in New Zealand waters occurred off Kaikoura.

## Right whale

Early settlers in Wellington used to remark on the noisy right whales in the harbour, which kept them awake at night. Scientists studying right whales in the subantarctic islands also remark on their loud, low-frequency moans during the breeding season.

Whalers dubbed this 15-metre, 55-tonne species the 'right' whale because it could be easily reached by rowboat, it swam slowly, floated when dead and yielded copious quantities of oil and baleen (bone). By 1845, after several decades of slaughter, the population of right whales around New Zealand and Australia had collapsed and is only now gradually recovering.

In the mid-1980s French conservationist Jacques Cousteau gloomily referred to 'a hopelessly stagnant relict population [of right whales] centred around Campbell Island'. But only 7 years later a large congregation of right whales was discovered at the nearby Auckland Islands, and reports came in of the same species visiting Southland bays and harbours. The right whale appears to be on its way back. The Auckland Island population, numbering over 100, is possibly the largest single grouping of the southern right whale in the New Zealand region. From July to August the whales gather in Port Ross—the size of Wellington Harbour—to mate and calve. Whales such as the right whale have masses of barnacles which appear to cause them discomfort: they sometimes seek freshwater estuaries where the barnacles fall off.

## Sperm whale

The Moby Dick of whales is the one most familiar to New Zealanders, thanks to the whale-watching ecotourism at Kaikoura which is centred on this largest of the toothed whales. Just kilometres off the Kaikoura coast, the Hikurangi Trough plunges into underwater canyons exceeding 1600 metres in depth, the home of the giant squid that the whales dive for. Herds of adolescent males live all year round at Kaikoura, taking advantage of this underwater bounty.

It was once believed the oil inside the whale's bulbous forehead, which can weigh as much as 4 tonnes, was a reservoir of semen, hence the term sperm whale. In fact the purpose of the great melon shape of the head remains a mystery. Scientists have speculated that it may focus

*Did you know?*

It has been estimated that the world's population of sperm whales (up to 1 million) consume about 100 million tonnes of squid a year. This is quite amazing when compared with the 86 million tonnes of fish and fish products caught by the entire world's fishing fleets in 1994. A sperm whale has to ingest 2.5–3.5 percent of its weight each day.

*Sperm whales can dive to prodigious depths; large bulls can stay underwater for as long as 90 minutes, regularly plunging as deep as 1000 metres, and sometimes to twice that depth.*

echolocation signals, making it easier to locate squid in the murky depths; or that it is used for sparring by males; or that it helps buoyancy control in deep water.

Male sperm whales are much larger than females; the average weight of a male is 40 tonnes, its length 16 metres, compared with the female's 16 tonnes and 11 metres. At 9 kg, the sperm whale's brain is the largest of any creature that has ever lived.

## Pilot whale

The two species of pilot whale, the long-finned and the short-finned, both feed on squid and swim in large groups of several hundred individuals. Also known as blackfish, pilot whales were sometimes driven by Maori into shallow areas where they beached themselves. Pilot whales figure prominently in stranding statistics.

Long-finned pilot whales are much the more common of the two species in New Zealand waters. Since records have been kept, well over 2000 have beached themselves and subsequently died along the coast, sometimes in groups of more than 100 at a time.

## Humpback whale

Of all the baleen whales, humpbacks yield the most oil for their size, and consequently have suffered more than any other baleen whale from hunting. Today there are only a few thousand in the southern hemisphere; they were estimated to once number 120 000. A group of a few hundred migrates past New Zealand on their way from Antarctica to breeding grounds in Pacific Islands such as Tonga.

## Bryde's whale

Bryde's (pronounced 'Broodah's') whales are among the most commonly seen around northern New Zealand. It is the only baleen whale to live year round in warm temperate to tropical seas. Between 12 and 15 metres long, it can weigh up to 20 tonnes.

## Minke whale

Minke (pronounced 'minkie') whales are rare visitors to New Zealand but have a high profile because of the controversy over whether Japan and Norway should have killing rights. Whaling nations, having exhausted the stocks of the large whales, have turned their attention to the smaller species such as the minke, which grow to a maximum of 10 metres. Using the loophole that they are conducting 'whale research', the Japanese captured 440 minkes in the Southern Ocean in 1996. The meat from these sold for $US35 million on the Japanese market.

Different colour forms of minkes live in the northern and southern hemispheres. Some whale scientists have argued one of the southern forms is a subspecies; it has larger flippers than its northern counterpart and lacks a distinctive white patch on the flippers. It is this form that frequents New Zealand waters. These whales feed on plankton and also rely more on fish for their diet than other baleen whales.

Although minkes are the most common baleen whales, any accurate estimate of their population is a fraught undertaking. For example, in the 1980s the Southern Ocean was separated into zones for census purposes; 280 000 minke were counted in one of the zones, but 5 years later Japanese researchers found only 56 000. This discrepancy underlines not only the mobility of the whales, but also how difficult it is to precisely gauge their numbers.

When minke whales are seen in New Zealand waters they are usually migrating, either to Antarctica during summer or northern waters during winter. Males leave earlier than the females. Unusually for baleen whales, minkes strand relatively often on New Zealand shores.

## Blue whale

The largest animal ever to have lived, weighing up to 150 tonnes, the blue whale migrates along both New Zealand coasts from March onwards, on its way from the Antarctic to breeding grounds in temperate or subtropical areas. In the Antarctic it eats up to 4 tonnes of krill a day, then fasts for 4–5 months. Sometimes individuals pass through Cook Strait from the east to the west coast, a fact taken advantage of by Tory Channel whalers in the past.

*Close enough to be brushed by this humpback whale's pectoral fluke, the photographer remained unharmed by the 45-tonne monster.*

*Pilot whales successfully migrate past the sandbank crescent of Farewell Spit, but run into difficulties inside Golden Bay where the shore cannot be easily detected because of the bay's gently shelving slope.*

# Stranded!

**M**ore than 5000 strandings of whales and dolphins have been recorded around the New Zealand coast, possibly a greater number than in any other region in the world. These high figures reflect the fact that the country has a long (18 000 km) coastline covering a range of latitudes, and good populations of the species that tend to mass-strand are found in New Zealand waters.

Strandings often involve a lone whale which is dying, but there are also many instances of mass strandings by certain species such as false killer and pilot whales. The latter are the most frequent stranders in New Zealand.

Numerous theories have been put forward to explain why whales strand. When whales emit sounds, these either bounce off a solid object like the shore, warning the whales of its presence, or an absence of echo indicates the open sea. Whales run into problems where there is a gently sloping shoreline, which the whales cannot detect with their sonar.

Other reasons for stranding could be that a leader is diseased and becomes disoriented and the herd simply follows the leader; predators such as orcas might make a herd panic; or a young whale may strand by accident and the rest of the herd comes to its assistance.

*Different juvenile whitebait swim to different parts of a river to grow into adults. Banded kokopu (centre left) and short-jawed kokopu (top) travel inland, while giant kokopu (bottom) and inanga (centre right) remain near the coast.*

# Whitebait

Whitebait are the juveniles of five species of freshwater fish called galaxiids (see page 119): the giant kokopu (*Galaxias argenteus*), banded kokopu (*G. fasciatus*), short-jawed kokopu (*G. postvectis*), koaro (*G. brevipinnis*) and inanga (*G. maculatus*). At least 90 percent of the whitebait catch consists of juveniles of inanga; the greenish band along the sides resembles a type of green-

stone to which Maori also gave the name inanga. The galaxiid inanga is not an endemic species—it also occurs in Australia, Lord Howe Island, Chile, Argentina, Tierra del Fuego and the Falkland Islands. The kokopu species dwell only in New Zealand, while the koaro is also found in Australia.

Because most inanga live for just a year, spending about 5 months at sea and 6 months in fresh water, there can be large fluctuations in population from year to year, depending on climatic conditions. The West Coast retains the least modified rivers and estuaries in the country, so it is there that most whitebait can be found. The largest commercial operation is on the Cascade River in south Westland. In the North Island whitebait are most common in the Waikato River, rivers between Taranaki and Wellington, and in the Bay of Plenty.

The inanga is unusual in that its eggs develop on land, whereas the other four whitebait species spawn up-river. During the high spring tides of late summer or autumn, large schools of adult inanga begin to migrate downstream until they reach salt water coming upstream. At the peak of the high spring tide, the fish swim together among the flooded bank vegetation. Often half out of the water, females release their eggs which the males fertilise. As the tidal waters recede, thousands of tiny eggs remain stuck to raupo, sedges and rushes.

Inanga have to choose their 'nesting' site carefully. Because fish eggs do not have a waterproof shell, and could therefore easily shrivel and die, they have to develop in an area where there is almost 100 percent humidity. The best sites are above clay soils where the moisture cannot escape; inanga reject sandy or boggy soils.

Depending on the temperature, inanga eggs take between 10 days and a month to develop. Once fully developed, they have to be immersed in water before they hatch—usually during the next spring tide. Even if the eggs are fully developed (because the weather has been warm), hatching is postponed until the water arrives. After hatching, the 7-mm larvae are swept out to

*Inanga, the main whitebait species, spawns and dies before it is a year old, while the giant kokopu may live as long as 20 years.*

sea on the outgoing tide before returning as whitebait 6 months later.

Little is known about what happens to whitebait while they are at sea. They have been found not only in coastal waters, but also up to 200 km from the shore. Drifting among the plankton, the transparent juveniles feed on small crustaceans. They themselves are preyed upon by larger fish, although reports of kahawai and red cod eating them are unauthenticated.

Whitebait do not necessarily return to their 'home' river. They are believed to be attracted to a river by the quality of its water and the strength of its current. Runs usually coincide with the first of the spring floods.

Whitebait catches have diminished for a number of reasons. Most importantly, spawning habitat has been destroyed. Trout have a liking for eating both whitebait and the adult fish, and more and more people fish for the delicacy each year. The Department of Conservation is identifying spawning sites so they can be protected. In some areas which have been fenced off from cattle, the number and density of eggs have increased enormously. When a spawning site was discovered on Christchurch's Avon River in 1989 the city council planted flaxes and rushes close to the water's edge to enhance the habitat, increasing its area seven times.

Whitebait seasons vary according to the region. On the West Coast the season runs from 1 September to 14 November, but elsewhere it begins on 1 August and ends on 30 November. The shorter period on the West Coast is designed to protect the resource, because of the large numbers of people who take whitebait there.

*Inanga gave its name to a fine greenstone of similar colour.*

# Whitehead

The whitehead (*Mohoua albicilla*) is exclusively a North Island species; the South Island has its equivalent, the yellowhead (see page 372). Both are gregarious, insect-eating forest birds, although the whitehead occasionally diversifies its diet with the small fruits of native shrubs such as mahoe or coprosma.

Some 19th-century observers believed the whitehead was a declining species, since it disappeared from a number of areas at that time, possibly as a result of an avian disease. Forest destruction was also a factor in its reduction. Not a strong flier, it loses height over a distance and is reluctant to travel across open ground. Contrary to the gloomy predictions made last century, the whitehead has survived, albeit with a somewhat contracted range.

Today it lives in most forests except north of a line from Hamilton to Te Aroha. Where there is a good covering of native forest in the undergrowth, it has moved into pine forests. The whitehead is abundant on Little Barrier and Kapiti islands; in fact on Little Barrier it is the most common bird. Birds have been successfully introduced onto Tiritiri Matangi Island and Mokoia Island in Lake Rotorua.

Like several other New Zealand birds such as the pukeko, rifleman and yellowhead, the whitehead is a communal breeder. A group of up to six birds, including the breeding pair, will co-operate to feed the new nestlings. In this way these mainly male assistants, the offspring of earlier seasons, help to ensure their genes are passed on.

For a small bird, the whitehead is relatively long lived. Its average life expectancy on Little Barrier is 5 years, but the oldest known bird lived for more than 8 years. Because of this factor, and the high densities of birds on the island, the young delay breeding for several years. However, where densities are lower, 1-year-old whiteheads breed readily.

At 18.5 grams (male) and 14.5 grams (female), the whitehead is much smaller than the long-tailed cuckoo, whose young it frequently raises (see page 91).

*Raising a new whitehead clutch is a family affair, with offspring pitching in to help.*

*The mystery pollinator finally revealed—a short-tailed bat feasts on the nectar of the wood rose.*

# Wood rose

Known variously as the wood rose, flower of Hades and pua-o-te-reinga, the endangered *Dactylanthus taylorii* is one of New Zealand's most peculiar plants. The country's only completely parasitic plant, it has no leaves or roots, but small flowers and a swollen underground stem attached to a host plant. Collectors take the stems to fashion 'wood roses', but at the cost of the plant's death. Most wood roses are found in the central North Island.

Botanists had long puzzled about how the wood rose was pollinated. From the end of February to late May, purplish to grey-brown flowers burst through the soil, with male and female flowers often separated by some distance. At one site where the plant was closely studied, only German and common wasps were noticed feeding on the flowers, yet the large amount of nectar produced by each flower suggested a bigger animal had to be the pollinator. The mystery was solved when video-camera evidence

showed a short-tailed bat (see page 51) visiting a flower 40 times in one night. The wood rose is the only plant in the world flowering at ground level that is known to be pollinated by bats.

At the same time as establishing the plant's main pollinator, scientists also discovered its chief destroyer—the possum, which is attracted to the flowers by their high scent and eats them.

On Little Barrier Island, kiore also find them a tasty meal; on the mainland, ship rats appear to assist pollination because curiously, although they are not interested in eating the wood rose, they visit it regularly and thus spread pollen from plant to plant.

# Worms

Worms are key players in the breaking down of plant material and returning vital nutrients to the soil and ecosystems that rely on them. Together with bacteria, insects and fungi, worms help decompose 90 percent of all plant material; without them nutrients would be locked up.

The worms New Zealanders are most aware of are the 19 species of earthworms that have been introduced since European settlement and are present in gardens and farmland, tilling the soil and feeding directly on plant debris. Their faeces or 'casts' are rich in nutrients.

But in forests and tussocks live a further 173 species of native earthworms which have evolved over millions of years, carving out specialised niches for themselves. Many live in the leaf litter, some high in the forest canopy. These worms are related to southern South American, southern South African, New Caledonian and Australian species, demonstrating the Gondwanaland link once again.

New Zealand has one species of worm threatened with extinction—the primitive ribbon worm *Antiponemertes allisonae* which lives along sandy beaches.

Most impressive of the native earthworms is the huge *Spenceriella gigantea*, which lives in the subsoil of North Auckland and Little Barrier forests, and grows as long as 1.4 metres. It burrows as deep as 3 metres below the surface. Lengthy as this worm is, it comes nowhere near the world's longest recorded worm, a South African species measuring 6.7 metres.

*Near Mount Tutoko in Fiordland a rock wren carries a kakapo feather to its nest. It is unlikely this scene will be repeated (the photo was taken in the 1970s) as kakapo are now presumed extinct in the area.*

# Wrens

The recent history of New Zealand wrens is not a happy one; two have become extinct in the last 105 years and the remaining two—the rifleman (see page 289) and the rock wren—have declined significantly. Fossil records show that a further two became extinct hundreds of years ago, most likely the victims of kiore. Ancestors of New Zealand wrens were among the first birds to colonise the country around 60 million years ago. Without predators to pursue them they gradually became flightless or near flightless, developing very strong legs and long bills.

Rock wrens (*Xenicus gilviventris*) are the only true alpine-dwelling birds. They were once present in the North Island, but now are restricted to South Island mountainous areas at altitudes between 900 and 2500 metres, although in Fiordland they venture down to subalpine scrub. They spend their time among the rocks and low shrubs just above the treeline, eating invertebrates and sometimes fruit.

Weak fliers, rock wrens bob up and down on the spot and repeatedly flick their wings. To help them gain a foothold on rocks they have large feet and long claws on their hind toes.

Much remains to be learned about how rock wrens contend with freezing winters. An early belief that they retreated to lower-altitude areas has been disproved; the fact that they are virtually never sighted during winter has led to speculation that they enter a state of torpor, secreting themselves in rock crevices with the snow blanket providing a degree of insulation from the cold.

The bush wren (*X. longipes*) has not been sighted since the 1950s in the North Island and the 1960s in the South, and is probably extinct. Practically flightless, it fed along the branches of trees rather than on the trunks, as its relative the rifleman does. A subspecies, Stead's bush wren, lived on Big South Cape Island where muttonbirders used to call it the 'thumb bird' because of its small size. When rats invaded the island in the early 1960s, Wildlife Service staff attempted to rescue the ground-dwelling wren and other birds. They transferred six wrens to nearby Kaimohu Island, but these gradually died out, with the last sighted in 1972.

## Cat among the wrens

A lighthouse keeper's cat is to blame for the extinction of the Stephens Island wren (*Traversia lyalli*), which died out in 1894, the year it was discovered. Little is known about the bird because it became extinct before anyone could make detailed observations. Mr Lyall, the lighthouse keeper after whom the bird is named, observed it only twice, reporting that it did not fly but instead scuttled about on the ground like a mouse, among rocks.

The evidence from the 15 dead specimens the cat delivered to the lighthouse keeper suggests the wren was flightless as it had short, rounded wings and soft plumage. If so, at only 100 mm the wren would have been the smallest flightless bird ever. Because the lighthouse keeper saw the wren only in the evenings, it has also been inferred that the tiny bird was nocturnal.

Bleak Stephens Island in Cook Strait is today well known as the home of two rare species: the tuatara and Hamilton's frog. After the 1894 incident with the wren, open warfare was declared on Stephens Island cats. The New Zealand Government placed a bounty of sixpence on each cat's head, increasing it to two shillings and sixpence in 1912. Hunters, attracted by the bounty, killed 700 cats by 1910, but the last was not eradicated until 1925.

# Wrybill

The braided rivers of the South Island's east coast are home to some unusual animals, none more so than the endemic wrybill (*Anarhynchus frontalis*). Like other plovers (see page 272), it is a migrant, but not a long-distance one; every summer after breeding it flies to large tidal harbours in the north such as Kaipara, Manukau and the Firth of Thames. In August it returns south to breed, although some non-breeders remain in the north for the summer.

Breeding on the Rakaia, Rangitata, Waimakariri and upper Waitaki rivers, the wrybill's main nesting grounds, is a risky business. In the past the birds have had to contend with an unreliable food supply, predators such as harriers, and spring floods. One strategy they have adopted to cope is to renest and lay a second clutch if eggs or chicks are lost. Wrybills aggressively defend their nests against intruders with vocal and physical attacks. Camouflaged eggs and the ability of chicks to fend for themselves as soon as they are hatched increase survival.

When a nest is threatened the parents warn the chicks with alarm calls which encourage the chicks to adopt a freeze posture, making them very difficult to locate. Nesting wrybills like to keep a distance from their neighbours of at least several hundred metres and males vigorously drive away intruders in their territory.

Since European settlement, changes in its braided-river environment have not been to the advantage of the wrybill, and it has shown a steady decline during the 20th century to number about 5000 today. The shingle 'islands' which provide the wrybill with everything it needs—good visibility and food surrounded by wide channels of water for protection from predators—have been colonised by weeds such as crack willows, gorse, briar, broom and lupins.

*The wrybill attracts international attention because of its unique characteristics.*

While floods keep the river shingle free of vegetation, they can also spell disaster to a nest. A study during the 1980s found that following major floods, the summer count of wrybills was low compared to years of small floods. However, floods are a natural hazard the wrybill has learned to live with. On some rivers such as the upper Waitaki, the natural flow of water has been dramatically changed by damming, diversion and water extraction.

Project River Recovery, a joint programme of the Department of Conservation and Electricorp New Zealand, aims to restore wrybill and other bird breeding areas by clearing unwanted vegetation from riverbeds.

Bird watchers remark on the striking flying displays of wrybill flocks, when the birds show an uncanny ability to move as one. One of the main advantages of flocking is that birds are better protected from predators in a group than if they were by themselves.

## Did you know?

The wrybill is the only bird in the world with a bill which turns sideways. Turning to the right at an angle of 15–22 degrees, the bill is used like a spoon, enabling the wrybill to gather insect eggs and larvae from under logs and stones. When feeding in estuaries it makes up to 100 turning movements a minute, sieving out tiny animals from the water, but is much more sedate when hunting for larger prey like crabs.

# Yellowhead

'On reaching near the top of the gully, I heard the shrill, ringing notes of a flock of yellowheads . . . They numbered about 200, and were in rich plumage . . . Before the yellowheads had quite disappeared I heard the rich flute-notes of a flock of saddlebacks advancing. Probably no scene in bird life is more attractive or beautiful.'

Today the chances of hearing large flocks of yellowheads or mohua (*Mohoua ochrocephala*), as early ornithologist W W Smith did near Lake Brunner in 1887, are increasingly remote. Once widespread throughout the South Island, the insect-eating yellowhead has declined because of forest destruction and predation by stoats and rats. A relative of the North Island whitehead (see page 368) and the brown creeper, the yellowhead has failed to hold its own in the way those two species have, although its population is estimated at several thousand.

Fiordland is the last remaining region where yellowheads are in good numbers. They favour living in beech forests, especially those dominated by red beech, because they are very fertile areas and produce the most insects. The knot holes in the old large trees in these forests also provide nesting sites.

A number of factors work against the yellowhead. It nests later in the summer, when stoats are at peak numbers, and chicks attract predators because they are very noisy. Its habit of nesting in knot holes means there is no escape for either parent or chicks when a predator strikes. Only females incubate the eggs, so that more females are lost than males.

In spring, pairs select a nest site in old or rotting trees, sometimes as high as 30 metres, lining the nest with moss, grass and feathers. One observer noted a male selecting a site, then working hard to persuade the female of its suitability. The female lays 2–4 eggs and sometimes another female helps in sitting on the eggs. Where food is plentiful the birds may lay two clutches a season. Yellowhead chicks are dependent on their parents for food for 6–9 months, much longer than most other small birds, which usually leave the nest after a month.

Yellowheads are unlike most other insectivorous New Zealand birds in their feeding behaviour. Instead of catching insects on the wing, they perch on a tree trunk using their tail as a support, and vigorously peck at the bark to disturb insects. Fantails like to take advantage of the yellowhead's lively bustle to get themselves a flying meal. Parakeets are also attracted by the yellowhead clamour and are often seen accompanying the smaller birds.

The third New Zealand whistler, the relatively common brown creeper (*M. novaeseelandiae*), lives in the South Island, Stewart Island and some offshore islands. Like the yellowhead, the brown creeper plays host to the long-tailed cuckoo, a bird up to 10 times its size.

As well as inhabiting native forest and scrub, the brown creeper has adapted to pine forests, where it feeds on insects in the high canopy. It builds a cup nest in the canopy of the forest which is less vulnerable to predation than the yellowhead nest. Chicks are fed by the male and the female renests; during a season the brown creeper lays two or three clutches.

# Zooplankton

Zooplankton are sea animals, usually small, which live in the water column. They include one-celled organisms, worms, crustaceans of various sizes including krill, jellyfish (see page 164), and even the larvae of fish. Some zooplankton remain as plankton for their whole lives, others for only the larval part of their lives. The larvae of animals such as barnacles, starfish, worms, paua and cockles also live in the plankton.

What distinguishes zooplankton from larger marine animals is their inability to swim against currents, although they can swim well enough vertically. Some types of zooplankton live permanently in the top 200 metres of the ocean; some are never found shallower than 1000 metres, while others live at intermediate depths, coming near the surface at night. Many of the smaller zooplankton are near the beginning of the food

*The yellowhead, also called the bush canary, is in its greatest numbers in Fiordland. Smaller populations persist in Westland's Landsborough Valley, Arthur's Pass National Park and in other isolated South Island forests.*

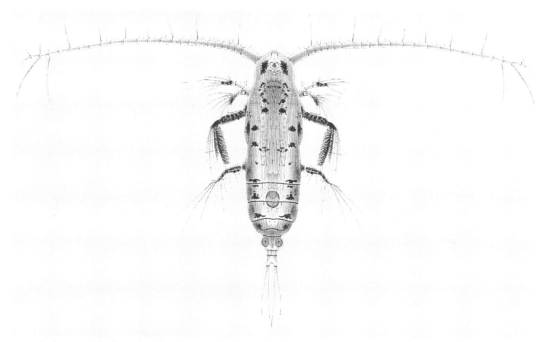

*Zooplankton are the basic building blocks of the marine food chain.* Eucalanus crassus *is a small crustacean (3–9 mm in length) common around northern New Zealand waters.*

chain. They feed on phytoplankton—the small, one-celled plants that have chlorophyll and use the sun's energy to manufacture their food. There are also many carnivorous species which prey on herbivores. Instead of having mouthparts designed to feed on fine particles, carnivores have hooks, spines and other arrangements for grasping their prey.

Some zooplankton species in New Zealand waters become conspicuous to the observer because of their size, their swarming habit, or because they get washed up in storms. In Otago and Marlborough Sounds the late-stage larvae of the crustacean *Munida* (commonly known as krill) can swarm, colouring the sea red and easily stranding on the beach. It is common to see floating strings of transparent 'salps' which are said to have an 'eye' (actually their stomach), or the related colonial form *Pyrosoma*. Portuguese men-of-war can also be washed up because of their inability to swim strongly. When water is disturbed by fish at the surface with seabirds weaving and diving, there will be a swarm of krill just beneath the surface, on which the birds and fish are feeding. Often seen near the shore is the jellyfish *Aurelia aurita* which has purple semicircular marks (its gonads) around the centre of its bell.

Contrary to popular belief, this jellyfish does not sting—it does not need to as it feeds on phytoplankton, which stick to the mucus on the outer part of the bell. Small hairs move the food to the edges of the bell where it is licked off by large mouth extensions.

In New Zealand waters the general makeup of the zooplankton is similar to that in other temperate parts of the world, although the species present reflect this part of the world. In oceanic waters, New Zealand's zooplankton species have subantarctic, Indo–West Pacific, and subtropical distributions. In coastal waters species have either widespread tropical-subtropical distributions, are confined to New Zealand and/or southeast Australia or are endemic to New Zealand.

The coastal copepods *Centropages aucklandicus*, *Acartia ensifera* and *Corycaeus aucklandicus* are endemic to New Zealand, the krill species *Nyctiphanes australis* is confined to New Zealand and southeast Australia. Common in New Zealand and southeast Australian waters, and also found around the southern tip of South America, is the copepod *Calanus australis*. The copepods *Paracalanus indicus* and *Temora turbinata* are found widely in warmer waters around the coasts.

# NEW ZEALAND FACTS

## LENGTH AND WIDTH

New Zealand is 1600 km long, and at its widest point is 450 km from coast to coast. Only 20 km of sea separate the North and South islands at the narrowest part of Cook Strait.

## HEIGHT

Almost 60 percent of New Zealand is higher than 300 metres and 70 percent of the country is hilly or steep land.

## LONGEST PROMONTORY

Farewell Spit extends 25 km from the top of the South Island and partially encloses Golden Bay. The maximum width of the promontory is only 800 metres.

## THE WORD ON WETLANDS

The estimated extent of New Zealand's freshwater wetlands is 100 000 ha, compared with 670 000 ha before European settlement. Five wetlands have been listed under the Ramsar Convention as areas of international importance: the Firth of Thames tidal estuary, Whangamarino Wetland and Kopuatai Peat Dome in the Waikato, Farewell Spit, and Waituna Wetlands near Invercargill.

## RIVERS OF ICE

The longest glaciers in New Zealand, all in the Mount Cook region, are called valley glaciers. The length of the Tasman Glacier (29 km) is almost twice that of the next longest glacier, the Murchison (17 km).

The two West Coast glaciers, the Fox and the Franz Josef, are 15 km and 13 km long, respectively. Of the 140 glaciers in Westland National Park, these two contain two-thirds of the total volume of glacial ice in the park. The other three long glaciers are the Mueller (13 km), the Godley (13 km) and the Hooker (11 km), all close neighbours of the Tasman, and all falling to the east.

## SLIPPING AWAY

Erosion threatens 18.3 million ha of land in New Zealand (out of a total of 27.5 million ha). The regions most prone to erosion are the East Cape, Wanganui, Canterbury and Otago.

## LARGEST PLAIN

New Zealand's largest alluvial plains, the Canterbury Plains (above), spread over 750 000 ha. From their northernmost point at Amberley to their southernmost point near Timaru they stretch for 180 km. At their widest point, from Springfield to the ocean, they cover 70 km.

## LAND AREA

|  | Area ($km^2$) |
| --- | --- |
| North Island | 115 777 |
| South Island | 151 215 |
| Offshore islands | 833 |
| Stewart Island | 1746 |
| Chatham Islands | 963 |
| Total | 270 534 |

## LAND USE

|  | Area (million ha) | % total area |
| --- | --- | --- |
| Forest | 7.5 | 27.4 |
| Pasture, arable land | 13.9 | 50.7 |
| Other land use | 5.6 | 20.4 |
| Minor islands | 0.1 | 0.4 |
| Lakes, rivers | 0.3 | 1.1 |

## OLDEST ROCKS

New Zealand's oldest rocks are crystalline rocks called gneiss (pronounced 'nice') from near Charleston on the West Coast. They are estimated to be about 680 million years old. Fiordland's gneiss, granodiorite, diorite and gabbro are at least 500 million years old.

## OLDEST FOSSILS

The oldest fossils found within New Zealand's rocks are extinct marine mammals related to crabs and woodlice, called trilobites, which are at least 550 million years old. Their outlines can be seen in Trilobite rock, Cobb Valley, Nelson.

## EARTH'S INNER CAULDRONS

New Zealand has a number of geothermal fields with a temperature above 220°C. Geothermal fields with a temperature around this level can be exploited for various industrial processes. The hottest fields (except for the Ngawha in Northland) are in the Taupo volcanic zone. The Rotokawa field has the highest temperature (330°C).

## NATIONAL PARKS

| Park | Size (ha) | Year created |
|------|-----------|--------------|
| Tongariro | 75 598 | 1887 |
| Egmont | 33 543 | 1900 |
| Arthur's Pass | 114 394 | 1929 |
| Abel Tasman | 22 541 | 1942 |
| Fiordland | 1 257 000 | 1952 |
| Mt Cook | 70 728 | 1953 |
| Te Urewera | 212 673 | 1954 |
| Nelson Lakes | 101 753 | 1956 |
| Westland | 117 607 | 1960 |
| Mt Aspiring | 355 543 | 1964 |
| Whanganui | 74 231 | 1986 |
| Paparoa | 30 560 | 1987 |
| Kahurangi | 452 000 | 1996 |

## LAND CONTROLLED BY DOC

More than 8 million ha, a third of New Zealand's land area, are administered by the Department of Conservation. There are 13 national parks covering 2 889 988 million ha, 20 conservation parks covering 1.8 million ha and nearly 4000 reserves (see maps, pages 382–3).

## HIGHEST MOUNTAINS

| | Height (m) |
|------|-----------|
| *South Island* | |
| Cook (right) | 3753 |
| Tasman | 3497 |
| Dampier | 3440 |
| Silberhorn | 3300 |
| Hicks | 3198 |
| Lendenfeldt | 3194 |
| Torres | 3163 |
| Teichelmann | 3160 |
| Sefton | 3157 |
| Malte Brun | 3155 |
| Haast | 3138 |
| Elie de Beaumont | 3117 |
| Douglas | 3085 |
| La Perouse | 3079 |
| Heidinger | 3066 |
| Minarets | 3055 |
| Aspiring | 3033 |
| Glacier Peak | 3007 |
| *North Island* | |
| Ruapehu | 2979 |
| Taranaki | 2518 |
| Ngauruhoe | 2287 |
| Tongariro | 1967 |

# Movements in the Earth

*New Zealand is divided into six tectonic regions, separated by geographical fault lines. The dots on this Institute of Geological and Nuclear Sciences map indicate a greater than Richter magnitude of 5.5.*

*1. Western North Island blocks and basins*
*2. Taupo volcanic zone*
*3. Axial tectonic belt*
*4. Canterbury–Chathams platform*
*5. Canterbury–Otago–Southland ranges and basins*
*6. Nelson–Westland ranges and basins*

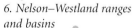

## Mᴇᴀsᴜʀɪɴɢ Eᴀʀᴛʜǫᴜᴀᴋᴇs

Ways of accurately measuring the magnitude of earthquakes were introduced in 1903. To gauge the intensity of shocks before then, scientists study the 'felt effects' as reported by people at the time, and also investigate the effects on landforms. Seismologists use the Richter scale to measure the original force or energy of the quake. This scale is logarithmic—the energy release increases by the power of 10 in relation to the Richter magnitude numbers. Thus the energy released in an earthquake of magnitude 5 is 10 times greater than one of magnitude 4, and a quake of magnitude 6 would be 100 times greater.

## Mᴀᴊᴏʀ Nᴇᴡ Zᴇᴀʟᴀɴᴅ Eᴀʀᴛʜǫᴜᴀᴋᴇs

| Date | Locality | Magnitude (Richter scale) | Deaths caused |
|---|---|---|---|
| 1460 | Wellington | 8 | ? |
| 8 July 1843 | Wanganui | 7.5 | 2 |
| 16 October 1848 | NE Marlborough | 7.1 | 3 |
| 23 January 1855 | SW Wairarapa | 8.1 | 5 |
| 17 November 1901 | Cheviot | 7.0 | 1 |
| 9 August 1905 | Cape Turnagain | 7.5 | – |
| 7 October 1914 | East Cape | 7–7.5 | 1 |
| 16 June 1929 | Buller | 7.8 | 17 |
| 3 February 1931 | Hawke's Bay | 7.9 | 256 |
| 5 March 1934 | Pahiatua | 7.6 | 1 |
| 24 May 1968 | Inangahua | 7.0 | 3 |
| 27 January 1983 | Kermadec Islands | 7.3 | – |
| 2 March 1987 | Edgecumbe | 6.3 | – |

# Water, water everywhere

### LENGTH OF COASTLINE
New Zealand's coastline extends for 18 200 km, including all harbours, estuaries, inlets, sounds and fiords. Almost 80 percent of the coast is exposed to open sea; the remainder borders sheltered waters.

### STRONGEST SEA CURRENT
The tide flows through French Pass, a notorious stretch of water between D'Urville Island and the South Island, at up to 8 knots (14.8 km/h).

### LARGEST FRESHWATER SPRING
Waikoropupu Springs near Takaka, Nelson, popularly known as Pupu Springs, gushes out 2160 litres of water every 24 hours, making it one of the largest freshwater springs in the world.

### HIGHEST WATERFALLS

| | Height (m) |
|---|---|
| Sutherland | 580 |
| Shirley | 365 |
| Stirling | 164 |
| Bowen | 160 |

(Browne Falls in Doubtful Sound descend more than 600 metres, but in a slide rather than a straight plunge.)

### BIGGEST WATERFALL
The waterfall with the greatest volume is Huka Falls (pictured above) near Taupo, where the Waikato River drops 8 metres over a distance of 230 metres and the water is forced into a narrow channel before suddenly falling 11 metres.

### RUNNING WATER
The total area of New Zealand riverbed is an estimated 204 000 ha. The second longest river, the Clutha, drains the largest catchment area—a massive 2.05 million ha, or slightly more than 13 percent of the South Island. A number of rivers have been considered special enough to be protected under Water Conservation Orders. They include the Motu, Rakaia, Manganuioteao, Ahuriri, Grey and Rangitikei rivers.

### RULING THE WAVES
New Zealand has the fourth largest maritime area in the world, with an Exclusive Economic Zone (EEZ) of 483 000 sq km. Only the United States, Indonesia and French Polynesia have larger maritime areas.

### LONGEST FIORDS

| | Length (km) |
|---|---|
| Dusky Sound (above) | 43.9 |
| Doubtful Sound | 40.4 |
| Preservation Inlet | 36 |
| Breaksea | 33 |
| George Sound | 21.2 |

## LARGEST LAKES

| | Area (km²) | Depth (m) |
|---|---|---|
| Taupo (right) | 606 | 159 |
| Te Anau | 344 | 276 |
| Wakatipu | 293 | 378 |
| Wanaka | 193 | 311 |
| Ellesmere | 181 | 2 |
| Pukaki | 169 | 70 |
| Manapouri | 142 | 443 |
| Hawea | 141 | 392 |
| Tekapo | 96 | 189 |
| Rotorua | 80 | 152 |
| Wairarapa | 80 | 3 |

(New Zealand's deepest lake is Lake Hauroko in southern Fiordland, at 462 metres.)

## LONGEST RIVERS

| | Length (km) |
|---|---|
| Waikato (above) | 425 |
| Clutha | 322 |
| Whanganui | 290 |
| Taieri | 288 |
| Rangitikei | 241 |
| Mataura | 240 |
| Waiau (Southland) | 217 |
| Clarence | 209 |
| Waitaki | 209 |
| Oreti | 203 |
| Rangitaiki | 193 |
| Manawatu | 182 |
| Buller | 177 |
| Waihou | 175 |

# Animal record-holders

## WETA WEIGH-IN

Some weta are among the heaviest insects in the world. The heaviest weta recorded was the pregnant wetapunga on Little Barrier Island which weighed in at 71 grams—as much as a song thrush. Other giant weta may not bulk up to quite the same degree, but are nevertheless heavyweights in their own right. The Stephens Island species, at 30 grams, is twice the weight of a mouse. At the other end of the scale is the baby of the giant species, the Nelson alpine weta, at only 7 grams.

## LONGEST-LIVING ANIMALS

| | Age (years) |
|---|---|
| Orange roughy | 150+ |
| Turtle | 100+ |
| Eel | 100+ |
| Tuatara | 70+ |
| Royal albatross | 60+ |
| Buller's mollymawk | 50+ |
| Green gecko | 45+ |
| Kakapo | 40+ |
| New Zealand dotterel | 40+ |
| Wandering albatross | 40+ |
| South polar skua | 30+ |
| Yellow-eyed penguin | 30+ |

## Rarest Birds

| | Population |
|---|---|
| Kakapo (above) | 53 |
| Campbell Island teal | 50–100 |
| Taiko | 50–100 |
| Black stilt | 80 |
| Chatham Island oystercatcher | 100 |
| Kotuku | 100–120 |

## Eggs by the Kilo

| | Weight (g) |
|---|---|
| Emperor penguin | 442 |
| Great spotted kiwi* | 435 |
| Brown kiwi* | 430 |
| Wandering albatross | 425 |
| Royal albatross | 421 |
| Mute swan | 350 |
| Little spotted kiwi* | 300 |
| Black swan | 250 |

* Kiwi hold the world record for egg weight relative to total body weight. A female little spotted kiwi about to lay an egg weighs just 1.3 kg, 25 percent of which is accounted for by its egg.

## Flying Featherweights

| | Weight (g) |
|---|---|
| Rifleman | 6 |
| Grey warbler | 6.5 |
| Fantail | 8 |
| Chatham Island warbler | 8.5 |
| Brown creeper | 11 |
| Tomtit | 11 |
| Redpoll | 12 |
| Silvereye | 13 |
| Welcome swallow | 14 |
| Whitehead | 14.5 |
| Goldfinch | 15 |
| Rock wren | 16 |

## Feathered Heavyweights

| | Weight (kg) |
|---|---|
| *Seabirds* | |
| Emperor penguin (above) | 30 |
| Royal albatross | 9 |
| Wandering albatross | 6.5 |
| Chinstrap penguin | 5.5 |
| Yellow-eyed penguin | 5.4 |
| Adélie penguin | 5 |
| Erect-crested penguin | 4.5 |
| Giant petrel | 4.5 |
| Fiordland crested penguin | 4 |
| Shy mollymawk | 4 |
| Snares crested penguin | 3 |
| Rockhopper penguin | 2.8 |

| *Landbirds* | |
|---|---|
| Mute swan (above) | 12 |
| Feral turkey | 8 |
| Black swan | 6 |
| Canada goose | 5.4 |
| Cape Barren goose | 5 |
| Great spotted kiwi | 3.3 |
| Takahe | 3 |
| Feral goose | 3 |
| Kakapo | 2.5 |
| Royal spoonbill | 1.7 |
| Paradise duck | 1.7 |
| Bittern | 1.4 |

# Watching the weather

## Hᴇᴀᴛ ᴀɴᴅ Cᴏʟᴅ

New Zealand's average temperature has historically waxed and waned. 25 000 years ago, when the country was in the freezing grip of the Ice Age, the average temperature was a chilly 7°C. It then rose relatively quickly to 14°C 10 000 years ago, before dipping slightly to its present average of 12°C.

## Aɪʀ Tᴇᴍᴘᴇʀᴀᴛᴜʀᴇ

|  | Temperature (°C) | Date |
|---|---|---|
| *Highest* |  |  |
| North Island (Ruatoria) | 39.2 | 7 Feb. 1973 |
| South Island (Rangiora and Jordan) | 42.4 | 7 Feb. 1973 |
| *Lowest* |  |  |
| North Island (Chateau Tongariro) | –13.6 | 7 Jul. 1937 |
| South Island (Opihir*) | –21.6 | 3 Jul. 1995 |

*The greatest range in temperature was also measured at Opihir: from –21.6°C to 35°C.

## Sᴇᴀ Tᴇᴍᴘᴇʀᴀᴛᴜʀᴇ

|  | Mean temperature (°C) High | Low |
|---|---|---|
| *Auckland* (30 years' data) | 20.5 (Feb.) | 14 (Aug.) |
| *Wellington* (12 years' data) | 17.5 (Jan.) | 10 (Jul.) |
| *Dunedin* (42 years' data) | 16 (Jan.) | 7 (Jul.) |

## Wɪʟᴅ Wɪɴᴅꜱ

New Zealand's capital is known as 'windy Wellington' (right)—and with good reason. In both 1959 and 1962 the highest winds recorded in the North Island blew at Hawkins Hill in Wellington, on each occasion reaching 248 km/h. Residents of the harbour city are buffeted by gusts exceeding 63 km/h on up to 100 days a year. However, the capital's record was surpassed by the South Island in 1970, when gusts of 250 km/h were recorded at Mount John in Canterbury.

## Rᴀɪɴ ᴀɴᴅ Sʜɪɴᴇ

|  | Average annual sunshine (hours) | Average annual rainfall (mm) |
|---|---|---|
| Auckland | 2070 | 1185 |
| Wellington | 2025 | 1230 |
| Christchurch | 2065 | 655 |
| Dunedin | 1600 | 785 |

The highest and lowest number of hours of annual sunshine were both recorded in the South Island: 2711 hours at Nelson in 1931; and 1227 hours at Otautau in 1983.

## Rᴀɪɴꜰᴀʟʟ

| Period | Amount (mm) | Location | Date |
|---|---|---|---|
| *Highest* |  |  |  |
| 10 mins | 34 | Tauranga | 1948 |
| 1 hour | 107 | Whenuapai | 1966 |
| 12 hours | 473 | Westland | 1964 |
| 24 hours | 682 | Westland | 1964 |
| 48 hours | 844 | Mt Taranaki | 1967 |
| 1 month | 2747 | Westland | 1988 |
| 12 months | 14 108 | Westland | 1983 |
| Calendar yr | 13 219 | Westland | 1983 |
| *Lowest* |  |  |  |
| 3 months | 10 | Clyde | 1966 |
| 6 months | 53 | Alexandra | 1930 |
| 12 months | 167 | Alexandra | 1963–64 |
| Calendar yr | 211 | Alexandra | 1964 |
| *Highest annual average* |  |  |  |
|  | 8100 | Westland |  |

THREE KINGS I.

Cape Reinga

North Cape

# Natural New Zealand

Cape Brett

*Northland CP*

*Poor Knights MR*

● Whangarei

GREAT BARRIER I.

*Cape Rodney–Okariri Pt MR*

LITTLE
BARRIER I.

*KAIPARA
HARBOUR*

COROMANDEL
PENINSULA

*Long Bay–Okura MR*
*Motu Manawa–Pollen I. MR*
AUCKLAND ●

*Whanganui-a-hei MR*

*MANUKAU
HARBOUR*

*Coromandel CP*

MAYOR I.

*Waikato R.*

*L. Waikare*

*Tuhua MR*

WHITE I.

*Kaimai Mamaku CP*

● Tauranga

*BAY OF PLENTY*

● HAMILTON

*Rangitaiki R.*

*Motu R.*

*Pirongia CP*

Haroharo

*Raukumara CP*

*L. Rotorua*

Mt Edgecumbe

Mt Tarawera

*Pureora CP*

*Urewera NP*

HUIARAU RANGE

*L. Taupo*

*Whirinaki CP*

● Gisborne

*L. Waikaremoana*

*Kaimanawa CP*

Sugar Loaf I.

Mt Tongariro
Mt Ngauruhoe
New Plymouth ●
Mt Ruapehu

*Egmont NP*

*Kaweka CP*

*Mohaka R.*

*Whanganui NP*

*Tongariro NP*

Cape Egmont

Mt Taranaki

*HAWKE BAY*

● Napier
Hastings ●
Cape Kidnappers

● Wanganui

*Whanganui R.*

*Ruahine CP*

*Rangitikei R.*

Palmerston North ●

KAPITI I.

*Tararua CP*

*Kapiti I. MR*

● Masterton

*Rimutaka CP*
*L. Wairarapa*

● WELLINGTON

*COOK STRAIT*

*Haurongi CP*

Cape Palliser

| | |
|---|---|
| ■ | National park (NP) |
| ■ | Conservation park (CP) |
| | Dept. of Conservation other land |
| ● | Marine reserve (MR) |
| ● | Other marine protected area |
| △ | Volcano active in last 20 000 years |
| ▲ | Volcano active in last 100 years |
| — | River |

COOK STRAIT

Farewell Spit

*Westhaven (Te Tai Tapu) MR*

*Tonga I. MR*
*Able Tasman NP*

*Long I.—Kokomahua MR*

TASMAN MTS

*TASMAN
BAY*

*Kahurangi NP*

Nelson

*Wairau R.*

*Mt Richmond CP*

Blenheim

Westport

*L. Rotoroa*

*L. Rotoiti*

Cape Foulwind

*Nelson Lakes NP*

Mt Tapuae-o-eunuku

*Paparoa NP*

KAIKOURAS

Greymouth

*Waiau R.*

*Hanmer CP*

Hokitika

*L. Brunner*

*L. Sumner CP*

*Arthurs Pass NP*

*Craigieburn CP*

*Waimakariri R.*

*L. Coleridge*

CHRISTCHURCH

*Westland NP*

BANKS PENINSULA

*Mt Cook NP*
Mt Cook

*L. Ellesmere*

*Banks P. Marine Mammal Sanctuary*

*Rakaia R.*

SOUTHERN ALPS

*L. Tekapo*

CANTERBURY BIGHT

*L. Ohau*

*L. Pukaki*

*Rangitata R.*

Timaru

*Mt Aspiring NP*

*L. Hawea*

*Milford Sound*
*Piopiotahi MR*

Mt Aspiring

*L. Wanaka*

*Waitaki R.*

Oamaru

*L. Wakatipu*

Queenstown

*Doubtful Sound*
*Awaatu Channel MR*

*Fiordland NP*

*L. Te Anau*

OTAGO
PENINSULA

*L. Manapouri*

DUNEDIN

*Dusky Sound*

*L. Hauroko*

*Clutha R.*

*L. Poteriteri*

*Catlins CP*

Invercargill

FOVEAUX STRAIT

CODFISH I.

STEWART I.

KERMADEC I.

CHATHAM I.

SNARES I.

BOUNTY I.

AUCKLAND I.

ANTIPODES I.

CAMPBELL I.

# Natural History on the Internet

Some of the most interesting and up-to-date information about natural history subjects can now be obtained online on the Internet.

Following is a selection of the most useful Internet sites. A feature of the home pages under the <u>Links</u> heading is that they provide easy access to many other sites both in New Zealand and overseas.

## Official sources

### Department of Conservation
www.doc.govt.nz
Press releases, events, native species management, freshwater ecosystems and useful fact sheets with images on individual species, and a variety of official documents.

### Ministry for the Environment
www.mfe.govt.nz
Information on the ministry's workings, including publications and discussion documents, the Resource Management Act and other environmental legislation, sustainable land management, air and atmosphere, water quality, biodiversity, waste management, hazardous wastes.

### Institute of Geological and Nuclear Sciences
www.gns.cri.nz
Bulletins for Ruapehu conditions, and White Island and Ruapehu ashfall predictions.

### National Institute of Water and Atmospheric Research
www.niwa.cri.nz
Research data on atmospheric, marine, freshwater and coastal systems, with sections on oceanographic and fisheries research, climate studies and air quality, coastal oceanography and marine geology, and sea surface temperature maps online.

## Environmental groups

### Coromandel Watchdog
www.bitz.co.nz/watchdog
Irregular newsletter of reports and updates on the group's activities, with press clippings (regularly updated) and selected scientific reports.

### Greenpeace New Zealand
interface.co.nz/greenpeace.html
Strictly functional page with links to Greenpeace International and Greenpeace Australia.

### The Royal Forest and Bird Protection Society
www.nzwwa.com/education/conservation/~ forest-bird/treebird.htm
Background and history, success stories, current campaigns, stories from recent issues of the society's magazine, a full set of the year's press releases, and links elsewhere.

## Links

### Ara Nui
www.lincoln.ac.nz/libr/nz/nzenviro.htm
The Environment and Natural Resource page on Lincoln University Library's informative Ara Nui site, with links relating to New Zealand environment and natural resources, both academic and general—from Antarctica and the Canterbury Environment Diary to the yellow-eyed penguin.

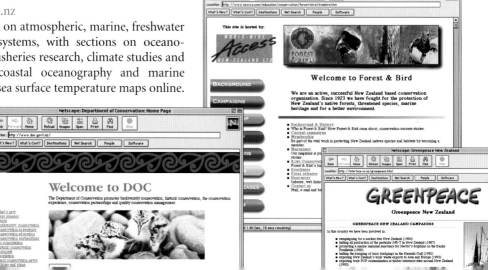

## NEW ZEALAND GOVERNMENT ONLINE
www.govt.nz/

The best starting point for searching all official available sources. If it's official and online, it's here somewhere in this well-organised and easy-to-search site.

## NEW ZEALAND SCIENCE MONTHLY
www.spis.co.nz/nzsm/nzsm.htm

Based on the monthly magazine, with a searchable index of back issues, and a very good list of New Zealand science links.

## RAINBOW LINX
www.gen.com/bigjude/BANNERS/~
Tutorial/Linx.html

Slow-loading but comprehensive set of links to New Zealand environmental defence organisations and New Zealand (and international) environmental interest websites, among others.

## ROYAL SOCIETY OF NEW ZEALAND
www.rsnz.govt.nz/

Bills itself as the Gateway to New Zealand Science 'with news, events, publications, and other documentation that reflects our input into education, policy advice to government, plus wide involvement with NZ science and technology organisations'. Easy to search.

## General

### GEOLOGICAL SOCIETY OF NEW ZEALAND
www.gsnz.org.nz/

Information on New Zealand earth science, including recent PhD theses, reports on Ruapehu and White Island volcanoes and the New Zealand Fossil Record File.

### ISLANDS OF THE HAURAKI GULF
www.bigjude.com/Islands.html

More than 100 pages on the Hauraki Gulf, its culture, geology, geography and ecology. Listen to birdsong—kakapo, takahe, bellbird, saddleback, kiwi and other rare and endangered birds.

### MANAAKI WHENUA–LANDCARE RESEARCH
www.landcare.cri.nz/

Information about land, landscapes, soil, plants and animals and their inter-relationships, with useful fact sheets on, for example, the effects of possums on native vegetation and animals, and poisonous plants in the North and South islands.

### NEW ZEALAND TARGET FISH SPECIES
fishnz.co.nz

Four sections of colour images with informative text about coastal and estuarine fish, deepwater fish, sharks and rays, and billfish and tuna. Aimed at fishermen, but with wider appeal.

### NEW ZEALAND WHALE AND DOLPHIN TRUST
ralenti.co.nz/topics/nzwhale.html

Information on the trust's projects, including those involving Hector's dolphins, bottlenose dolphins, sperm whales, and dusky dolphins at Kaikoura.

### RESEARCH SCHOOL OF EARTH SCIENCES
www.gphs.vuw.ac.nz:80/geophysics/~
geophysics.html

From the Geophysics Department, Victoria University of Wellington. Pages include the 'Latest New Zealand Earthquake Report'.

### THE FABULOUS KAKAPO
www.resort.com/~ruhue/kakapo.html

Everything you ever wanted to know about the kakapo, with good images (and a Japanese version). Run from the USA; an informative and comprehensive web site.

### YELLOW-EYED PENGUIN
www.deepsouth.co.nz/yepnz

The world of the yellow-eyed penguin (hoiho), recent articles relating to the penguin and its environment, reports on the breeding season, a map of the hoiho's distribution in New Zealand, and other news and issues.

# GLOSSARY

**acclimatisation societies**: groups which were set up to introduce species such as deer into New Zealand. Today known as Fish and Game Councils, their role is to administer recreational fishing and hunting

**allopreening**: preening by birds of their mates as part of the courtship ritual

**alluvium**: fine-grained fertile soil found alongside rivers

**Alpine Fault**: the geological faultline occurring along the South Island Main Divide

**ammonite**: extinct marine mollusc

**andesite**: common, dark grey-coloured volcanic rock containing 52-63 percent silica

**angiosperm**: flowering plant. In New Zealand the earliest angiosperms appeared approximately 100 million years ago

**belemnite**: extinct, squid-like creature

**broadleaf**: flowering plant or shrub which has 'broad' leaves in contrast to plants such as beech which are small leaved

**caldera**: a large crater at the summit of a volcano, formed by the collapse of the cone

**cephalopod**: marine mollusc, usually without a shell, e.g. a squid

**chiton**: small marine shellfish with eight overlapping plates

**cirque glacier**: a glacier which occupies high, steep-sided basins

**cloaca**: a body cavity into which the alimentary canal, and genital and urinary ducts open

**conservation park**: an area of land administered by the Department of Conservation, ranked beneath national park in importance

**cultivar**: a cultivated variety of a plant

**cultural harvest**: the taking of native plants and animals by Maori

**diorite**: a darkish-coloured plutonic rock, formed by the cooling of lava beneath the Earth's surface

**diurnal**: active during the day

**divaricating plants**: a group of shrubs with a multiplicity of branches which form a protective mat around the flowers and fruit

**drupe**: a fruit enclosing a stone

**ecosystem**: the basic functional unit in ecology; a natural, stable system produced by the interaction of living organisms and the non-living environment

**endemic**: found in one country only

**epiphyte**: a plant that perches on, or hangs from, a tree

**exotic**: a plant or animal which has been introduced by people or accidentally arrived in New Zealand

**fauna**: all the animals of a country or region

**feral**: animal which turns wild after having been domesticated

**flora**: all the plants of a country or region

**fluke**: the lobe of a whale's tail

**Furious Fifties**: winds occurring at latitudes of 50° and more south. In the New Zealand context, this is the region of the subantarctic islands

**gabbro**: a dark-coloured, coarse-grained plutonic rock

**gley podzol**: type of grey-white soil from which the minerals have been leached

**gneiss**: metamorphic rock formed by great pressure and heat

**gymnosperm**: plant whose seeds are carried in cones (like conifers) rather than in ovaries (like flowering plants). New Zealand representatives are the podocarps, the kauri and cedars.

**Ice Age**: there have been numerous ice ages throughout history. The one usually referred to is the last great Ice Age, which started 2.4 million years ago and ended only 10 000 years ago.

**indigenous**: occurring naturally within a country

**introduced animal or plant**: one which has been deliberately brought into a country

**juvenile**: young animal; a bird in first plumage which replaces birth down

**larva**: immature form of an insect or other animal between the egg and the next stage of development

**lava**: molten rock flowing from a volcano

**lek**: relating to mating behaviour of certain species whereby males gather in one place to attract females. New Zealand bats and the kakapo are lek species

**magma**: liquid rock-forming material generated deep within the Earth, from which igneous rocks are created

**Main Divide**: the chain of mountains in the South Island that separates the east and west coasts

**mainland**: in New Zealand the mainland is considered the North, South and Stewart islands

**malimprinting**: atypical characteristics exhibited by an animal fostered by a different species

**mandible**: the lower jaw

**mast years**: years when forest plants produce an abundance of fruit or seed. Especially refers to beech trees

**melanism**: black coloration of skin or feathers

**migrant**: a bird that travels each year between breeding and non-breeding areas

**moraine**: rocks and other material deposited by a glacier

**mustelids**: a group of predatory mammals (ferrets, stoats and weasels)

**native**: species which are naturally found in (indigenous to) a country

**nocturnal**: active at night

**ornithologist**: person who studies birds

**orogeny**: mountain-building process

**otolith**: granule of calcium carbonate in the ears of vertebrates. By studying otoliths, scientists are able to gauge the age of animals

**panicle**: a compound raceme

**pied**: with markings of two or more colours

**plutonic rock**: igneous rock formed from magma that has cooled deep within the Earth

**podocarp**: a type of conifer producing a sticky seed rather than a cone. New Zealand's larger trees are podocarps, e.g. rimu, kahikatea, miro, matai, totara

**population**: a group of potentially interbreeding individuals

**predator**: an animal that eats other animals, their young or their eggs

**raceme**: method of flowering in which flowers are borne along the main stem.

**radula**: teeth of a mollusc

**rain shadow region**: a region on the lee side of a mountain range which receives much less rain than the other side. The inland east coast of the South Island is the principal rain shadow region in New Zealand

**raptor**: a bird of prey

**ratite**: family of flightless birds, usually large. The moa and the kiwi are New Zealand examples

**rhizome**: thick, underground stem

rhyolitic lava: lava containing more than 69 percent silica

Roaring Forties: westerly winds sweeping across New Zealand between 40° and 50° latitude south

scoria: solidified lava with many cavities

shield volcano: flat-topped volcano; magma oozes from central core and flows in all directions

speciation: formation of a new species

species: a group of animals capable of interbreeding

subspecies: a subdivision of a species

taxonomy: the system of classifying plants and animals to reflect their natural relationships

tectonic: relating to movements in the Earth's crust

treeline: upper limit of altitude at which trees will grow

vagrants: animals, usually birds, which appear in a region because they have wandered off their course when migrating

wading birds: birds with habitats confined to lakes and estuaries, but which also migrate across oceans

water column: water current which runs vertically, in the form of a column. Animals which cannot swim float up and down in this column

**HOW PLANTS AND ANIMALS ARE CLASSIFIED**

Example: brown kiwi

Phylum: chordata (animals with backbones)

Subphylum: vertebrata (vertebrates)

Class: birds

Order: Apterygiformes

Family: Aptergidae

Genus: *Apteryx* (wingless)

Species: *Apteryx australis* (literally, 'wingless [bird] of the south')

# FURTHER READING

Bellamy D, Springett B, Hayden P. *Moa's Ark: the Voyage of New Zealand*. Auckland: Viking, 1988

Bradstock MC. *Between the Tides: New Zealand's Shore and Estuary Life*, rev. ed. Auckland: David Bateman, 1989

Brooker SG, Cambie RC, Cooper RC. *New Zealand Medicinal Plants*. Auckland: Heinemann, 1987

Burstall SW, Sale EV. *Great Trees of New Zealand*. Wellington: Reed, 1984

Cave MP, Lumb JT, Clelland L. *Geothermal Resources of New Zealand*. Wellington: Ministry of Commerce, 1993

Cometti R, Morton J. *Margins of the Sea: Exploring New Zealand's Coastline*. Auckland: Hodder & Stoughton, 1985

Conly G, Conly M. *New Zealand Pohutukawa*. Wellington: Grantham House, 1988

Cox G. *Slumbering Giants: the Volcanoes and Thermal Regions of the Central North Island*. Auckland: Collins, 1989

Crisp P, Daniel L, Tortell P. *Mangroves in New Zealand: Trees in the Tide*. Wellington: GP Books, 1990

Crowe A. *Which Native Tree?* Auckland: Viking, 1992

Crowe A. *Which Native Fern?* Auckland: Viking, 1994

Crowe A. *Which Native Forest Plant?* Auckland: Viking, 1994

Dawson J. *Forest Vines to Snow Tussocks: the Story of New Zealand Plants*. Wellington: Victoria University Press, 1988

Dawson J, Lucas R. *Lifestyles of New Zealand Forest Plants*. Wellington: Victoria University Press, 1993

*Forest & Bird*, quarterly publication of the Royal Forest and Bird protection Society of New Zealand

Given D. *Rare and Endangered Plants of New Zealand*. Wellington: Reed, 1981

Heather BD, Robertson HA. *The Field Guide to the Birds of New Zealand*. Auckland: Viking 1996

Hutching G, Potton C. *Forests, Fiords and Glaciers: New Zealand's World Heritage*. Wellington: Royal Forest and Bird Protection Society, 1987

Johns J, Molloy B. *Native Orchids of New Zealand*. Wellington: Reed, 1983

Malcolm B, Malcolm J. *The Forest Carpet*. Nelson: Craig Potton Publishing, 1988

McCulloch B. *Moas: Lost Giants of New Zealand*. Auckland: HarperCollins, 1992

McDowall RM. *New Zealand Freshwater Fishes*. Auckland: Heinemann Reed, 1990

Miller D. *Common Insects in New Zealand*, rev. ed. Auckland: Reed, 1984

Ministry for the Environment. *The State of New Zealand's Environment 1997*. Wellington: GP Publications, 1997

Morris R, Smith H. *Wild South: Saving New Zealand's Endangered Birds*, rev. ed. Auckland: TVNZ in association with Century Hutchinson, 1995

Morton J, Hughes T, Macdonald I. *To Save a Forest: Whirinaki*. Auckland: David Bateman, 1984

*New Zealand Geographic*, quarterly magazine

Newsome PFJ. *The Vegetative Cover of New Zealand*. Wellington: Ministry of Works and Development, 1987

*Notornis*, quarterly journal published by the Ornithological Society of New Zealand

Orbell M, Moon G. *The Natural World of the Maori*, rev. ed. Auckland: David Bateman, 1996

*Reader's Digest Complete Book of New Zealand Birds*. Auckland: Reed Methuen, 1985

Stevens G, McGlone M, McCulloch B. *Prehistoric New Zealand*. Auckland: Heinemann Reed, 1988

Thompson B, Brathwaite R, Christie A. *Mineral Wealth of New Zealand*. Wellington: Institute of Geological and Nuclear Sciences, 1995

Thornton J. *Field Guide to New Zealand Geology*. Auckland: Reed, 1985

Towns DR, Daugherty CH, Atkinson IAE, eds. *Ecological Restoration of New Zealand Islands*. Wellington: Department of Conservation, 1990

# INDEX

# C O N T R I B U T O R S

Thanks to the following who have given freely of their time checking texts and providing information: John Booth, Adam Broadley, Hamish Campbell, Lionel Carter, Cyril Childs, Trevor Chinn, Malcolm Clark, Greg Comfort, Shannel Courtney, Bob Creese, John Darby, Charles Daugherty, Barry Donovan, Murray Efford, Tony Eldon, Bob Evans, George Gibbs, Brian Gill, Ann Graeme, Olwyn Green, Janet Grieve, Rod Hay, Mike Imber, Allan Innes, Paul Jansen, Don Jellyman, Mike Meads, Don Merton, Ron Moorhouse, Wendy Nelson, Chris Robertson, Peter Saul, Sue Scheele, Philip Simpson, Roly Taylor, Alan Tennyson, Jocelyn Tilley, Jocelyn Thornton, Martin Unwin, Ingrid Visser, Kath Walker, Geoff Walls, Kim Westerskov, Graham White, Tony Whitaker, Murray Williams.

   Librarians have been patient providers of information and photos. Chief among these are staff of the Miramar Public Library, Fern McKenzie of the Department of Conservation library, Key-Light Image Library and Suzanne Knight from the Museum of New Zealand.

The sources of the photographs and illustrations are listed below. Abbreviations: L= left; R= right; T= top; TL= top left; TR= top right; C= centre; B= bottom; BL= bottom left; BR= bottom right; IN= insert; P= photograph; I= illustration.

**Endpapers** Rob Brown/Hedgehog House. **1** Rob Brown/Hedgehog House. **2** Kim Westerskov. **4** Kim Westerskov. **6** Kim Westerskov. **8** Rob Brown/Hedgehog House. **10** Kim Westerskov. **12** The Dominion. **14** Tui De Roy/Hedgehog House. **15** T Shaun Barnett/Hedgehog House, B Brian Chudleigh. **16** Collection of the Museum of New Zealand Te Papa Tongarewa, C 000108. **17** T Alexander Turnbull Library, F-3136-1/2. B Jane Ussher/N.Z Magazines Archive. **18** Alexander Turnbull Library, D-P B-K11/3-CT. **19** B.Enting/Key-Light. **20** Alexander Turnbull Library, G-10822-1/1. **21** Collection of the Museum of New Zealand Te Papa Tongarewa, C15391. **22** Dave Gunsen. **24** Dave Gunsen. **26** P Craig Potton, I Chris Gaskin. **27** I Chris Gaskin. **28** P Craig Potton, I Chris Gaskin. **29** I Chris Gaskin. **30** P Nic Bishop/Key-Light, I Chris Gaskin. **31** I Chris Gaskin. **32** P Craig Potton, I Chris Gaskin. **33** I Chris Gaskin. **34** P Denis Page, I Chris Gaskin. **35** I Chris Gaskin. **36** P Brian Enting/Key-Light, I Chris Gaskin. **37** I Chris Gaskin. **38** P Kim Westerskov, I Chris Gaskin. **39** I Chris Gaskin. **40** Brian Enting/Key-Light. **42** Kim Westerskov. **43** T & B Kim Westerskov. **44** P Kim Westerskov, I Chris Gaskin. **45** Chris Gaskin. **46** L & R Kim Westerskov. **47** Kim Westerskov. **48** Chris Gaskin. **49** Rod Morris. **50** P Craig Potton, I Chris Gaskin. **52** Rob Lucas. **53** Rob Lucas. **54** Rob Lucas. **55** Rod Morris. **56** Brian Chudleigh. **57** L Brian Chudleigh, R Gerard Hutching. **58** Chris Gaskin. **59** Chris Gaskin. **60** Brian Chudleigh. **61** T & B Brian Chudleigh. **62** Brian Chudleigh. **63** Chris Gaskin. **64** T & B Brian Chudleigh. **66** Brian Chudleigh. **67** Don Merton. **68** L Don Merton, R Rob Chappell. **69** Rod Morris. **70** T Rod Morris, B Ron Redfern/Key-Light. **71** Rod Morris. **72** Chris Gaskin. **73** Rod Morris. **74** Brian Chudleigh. **75** L & R Rod Morris. **76** Rod Morris. **77** TL & BL Rod Morris, R Rob Lucas. **78** Philip Simpson. **79** Philip Simpson. **80** T Rob Lucas, B Ross Beever. **81** Derek Hearn/Icon. **82** Rod Morris. **83** P Andy Belcher, I Chris Gaskin. **84** Rob Brown/Hedgehog House. **85** T Brian Chudleigh, TR & BR Rob Lucas. **86** T & B Rob Lucas. **87** T & B Kim Westerskov. **88** L Roger Grace, R Kim